WALNUTS & GOAT CHEESE

WALNUTS & GOAT CHEESE

Léonard Lassalle

MY LOCAL MEDIA COMPANY LTD · ENGLAND

Published in 2015
by My Local Media Company Ltd
Copyright © Léonard Lassalle 2015

ISBN: 978-0-9576475-2-7

The moral right of the authors has been asserted.

All rights reserved.
No part of this publication may be reproduced, stored in a retrieval system, or transmitted, in any form or by any means, without the prior permission in writing of the publisher, nor be otherwise circulated in any form of binding or cover other than that in which it is published and without a similar condition including this condition being imposed upon the subsequent purchaser.

Cover Pastel Picture: Honor Gell
(of Françios-Xavier Lassalle aged 6)
Cover Design: Laurence Lassalle
Book Design: Dahlan Lassalle
(with thanks to Marcus Bolt)
Typeset in Palatino
Produced through www.lulu.com
for My Local Media Company Ltd, England

Contents

Acknowledgments   7

Introduction   9

Prologue   11
Some historical notes on the Gell family and Mother's life pre-1937

Chapter 1   22
The Île du Levant at the dawn of World War II, Life on the island, The war starts and things change

Chapter 2   42
Dieulefit 1942-1944 Maison Marefours/Les Tilleuls, First days at school, An unexpected addition to the family, Trying to adapt, Dangerous games, frustrations bring out violence, Searching for food, The Americans arrive

Chapter 3   90
Dieulefit 1944-1951 Maison Martin, The attraction of insects and animal life, Difficulties with Fonsou's ways, Learning that life has different realities, Fonsou goes to prison, our life changes, First visit to England, Back to France with a new dimension, Finding our Maman's limits, The first contact with religious language, Closing the door of spontaneous expression, Love, music and friendship, Coming to terms with my own fears, Faced with the sexual realities of male/female attraction, Pain separates consciousness

Chapter 4 *189*
Return to the Île du Levant 1948 – 1953, Discovering the complex behaviour of adults, Getting to know my brother, A newcomer, A traumatic realisation brings about an identity change, I changed into a teenager, life unfolded

Chapter 5 *236*
Summerhill School 1951 – 1953, Life without maternal presence, Dealing with my hunter's instinct, Finding a new friend, Schooling at Summerhill, The art room reveals my hidden pains, Awakening of my bodily senses, Sylvette in her own world, English culture becomes part of my world, Lip to lip contact brings a new dimension, The influence of Summerhill changes my behaviour, The unique self-educating school, Meeting with A.S. Neill, Discovering the subtleties of English, Finding more confidence with the girls, End of the first year, The second year at this wonderful school

Chapter 6 *327*
Vallauris 1953 and Student life in Paris 1954-1956, Life in Paris, A stroke of artistic good fortune touches the family, Moving closer to the centre of Paris, First steps towards a relationship, Tasting the flavours of wealth, Over drinking leads me into a strange experience, A taste of the commercial world, The party, Short visit to England

Chapter 7 *410*
Student life in London 1956 - 1958, Discovering cultural differences, Coming into contact with a new awareness, New digs and a girl friend, Attracted to the Fine Arts, Tempted by fame and money, New awareness of the feminine, Darker sides of life, A welcome holiday, Changes in my love life, A new direction, Jean, Changes in the pulses of our individual lives, My dear reader

Epilogue *488*
Discovering a large leather case in the attic

Glossary   *490*

About the author   *491*

Acknowledgements

I thank the editor of the original version, Adrienne Campbell who so attentively encouraged me when I started the book; may she rest in peace as she sadly passed away in UK, before it was completed.

Thanks to Mélinda my wife, our children for their supportive interest and especially our two sons: Laurence and Dahlan who gave their caring attention doing the graphics, photos and layout.

Thanks to Rosanna Hille who took much interest and greatly contributed with her comments and suggestions while she edited this second version.

Finally, thanks to Dorothy Jellinek who did the final editing and proof reading.

Léonard Lassalle
Beaumont du Ventoux – France
April 2015

Introduction

I'd like to explain to the reader the reasons that have motivated me to write Walnuts and Goat Cheese.

From the magic of creation to birth, I was completely united with my source of life. Everything I did while growing up originated from my initial being, as it interacted with the environment. At first my consciousness was wide open to experiment and taste this attractive world; then 'presence' gradually shifted to my heart and mind and formed my ego with its many facets, which numbed my original oneness.

The book has two main themes: my growing up into adulthood in a turbulent and seemingly chaotic world, and secondly, describes the complicated and intricate web of relationships that life weaved around and into me, forming my character.

It is true to say that each child born will certainly develop and be shaped in completely different ways, due to their inherited lineage. Once we are conceived, it is mainly by the 'cells' of our being adapting and adjusting themselves to their constantly changing surroundings that shapes us. The love received or not received, our joys or sufferings and our education and schooling are factors that have great influence on our making.

The book starts at my birth in 1937 and shows how controlled and uncontrolled life circumstances shaped my character and had an impact on the dynamics of my development. It is written from the child's point of view, as I develop into adulthood, without judgements, comments or deductions.

So, from birth to adulthood, Walnuts and Goat Cheese, traces how the boy François, started life on a sparsely populated Island off the Mediterranean coast, coped with what life brought to him through war and peace and managed to grow up in spite of the complexities of existence.

Education played both negative and positive roles, through the schools I attended. You will notice how the two years in Summerhill School in England, drastically changed the direction I was taking and helped me to find the way in my complex self.

The book also gives a taste of the artistic life of the time in Paris and in London. Through the names of the artists present in the text, I invite you to discover who they are, via the internet or other means. I trust this will give you an in depth feel of the artistic atmosphere in the two cities.

And of course I wrote Walnuts and Goat Cheese for my seven children and sixteen grand children who will, I hope one day, enjoy reading about and learning where their parents came from.

If you have enjoyed reading Walnuts and Goat Cheese, there is another book already written, which is a continuation of my life story. It tells how in 1957, my wife Mélinda and I came across a spiritual path that gradually enabled us to reconnect the oneness of our initial consciousness. Its practice trains us to recognise where our passions and impulses come from, so that we can consciously choose what is beneficial for us as individuals, within the context of ourselves, our family, and the wider community. That book is called 'Source of Life'.

Prologue

Some historical notes on the Gell family and Mother's life pre-1937

This prologue will give you a taste of our English family history, which will help you to understand better where I come from. It will give you a frame in which to place the characters that have had an influence on my make-up and personality. I am giving you this background because somehow I know in myself that the life of our forbears, what they went through, what they endured and loved doing, their talents and their characters, has to a large extent formed what we as their descendants are today.

The story of the Gell family goes back a long way, way back into the many layered history of England. Apparently, it started when the country was under the domination of the Roman Empire. A Roman Centurion named Philippus Gellius was posted in the Pennines at Willowford Fort on Hadrian's Wall. This fortified wall, built to prevent the 'barbarian' Scots from invading the north of England, took six years to build and was completed in AD 128. If by chance one day you happen to be walking along Hadrian's Wall, you might come across this large stele where you can see his name clearly engraved.

When his military career ended, this Roman felt the need to start a family and decided to establish himself near Leeds where he married a local girl. Philippus Gellius was a mining engineer and used his skills to start a small mine to extract lead, a precious mineral that the region had in great quantity at that time.

During the dark Middle Ages we have no traces of our ancestors, but they re-appear a few hundred years later in the 12th century, when they show up in the records kept in a small church in

Derbyshire. From then on our family tree begins its long, captivating journey.

The Gells seem to have mainly lived in Derbyshire in the northern part of England. During the late15th century Ralph Gell made a great deal of money in the lucrative business of lead mining and he bought the Hopton family manor house and surrounding land and named it 'Hopton Hall'. This property stayed in the Gell family until quite recently when the last Gell owners, a brother and his sister, decided to sell the property after a dispute over the inheritance. This drastic decision to sell Hopton Hall and its valuable contents unfortunately scattered the family collection, acquired over the centuries that recorded much of our history. I was an antique dealer at the time of the auction in the early 1990's but the prices were so high I was not able to purchase anything except a wrought iron shoe mud-remover! The auction was followed by the sale of the mansion with all its grounds.

From my brief research into the family history, after the lead mining industry collapsed in the early 18th century, the Gells became travellers, writers, musicians, painters, priests and military men. This long historical background of the Gells was the root of an arrogance, which greatly irritated our mother Honor and, as you will discover, she reacted strongly against the family. That is probably why she never talked to us in her mother tongue, or about her family history, the church or religion. It also partly explains why she searched for a more natural way of life and returned to basics on a deserted island in France.

My great-grandfather Canon Francis Gell sent his son Edward to Cambridge to follow in his footsteps and become a clergyman. But Edward found church life too monotonous and needed something to challenge his adventurous character. Keeping to the family tradition of Army and Church, upon seeing a request in a church newspaper for an Army Chaplain for the British Forces in South Africa, he decided to apply for the job and obtained it immediately. The fact that the Second Boer war was raging did not seem to trouble him whatsoever. This powerful experience gave him his first taste of military life. On his return from South Africa, he married my grandmother Gertrude (GG, as we later called her) and was soon assigned as the Clergyman of a small town called Corsham in Hampshire. It was here that our mother Honor was born in 1903.

This grandpa of mine fascinated me when I was a child – all his war stories used to raise my adrenalin to exciting levels. My mother showed me a photograph of him taken during the First World War. When I saw the distinguish soldier dressed in a perfectly tailored military uniform, I was indeed very impressed, especially by his enormous moustache pointing up on either side of his face almost touching his thick bushy eyebrows. Mother explained that he had brought her up with a Bible in one hand and a stick in the other! He did love his first and only daughter, but had difficulty giving her any affection during his life.

Honor and her brothers Ralph, Francis and Tony were brought up by nannies. GG's mainly spent her time following her husband overseas and even when she was at home, the servants looked after the children, cooked the meals and completely ruled the house. For over three years while Edward and GG lived in Cairo, Egypt, the children were educated in French-speaking Switzerland. This is why our mother and uncles spoke such perfect French.

When the 1914 First World War came and Grandpa, in his white collar, went to the front in northern France, his job as a chaplain was to pick up the dead on the battlefield, see that they were properly buried in the Church of England manner and, whenever possible, inform their relatives.

By early 1915, he wrote to his Bishop in Canterbury to say that he wanted to leave the church and go to the front to fight as an ordinary soldier. The Bishop gave his approval and Edward was sent for officer training in Dover. Three months later he was back on the front, this time not as a Chaplain but as an officer of the British Army who soon was promoted for his courage, initiative and ability to lead men. Of course, he had no time to be at home with his children, and this created in them a great deal of resentment. When he did come home on short leave from the front, he spent most of his time with his wife GG.

At that time the family lived in Colchester, Essex and in 1916 our mother's closest brother, Francis, suddenly died of meningitis at the age of 10. His sudden death shook Honor greatly because she adored Francis and in her immense sorrow, she found no comfort or compassion from either her mum or her dad. At this time in upper-class society in England, there was very little communication between the children and their parents, especially about the real and important things in life. All feelings and emotions were not to be expressed or shared. This situation brought the children closer to each other and my mother became a bit of a mum to her beloved younger brothers. She was already discovering her motherly nature.

Honor was very talented in all the arts especially playing the piano and painting, which she preferred although she mentioned once to me that she wanted to be a pianist. But strangely enough, in 1920 her authoritarian father decided she should be a painter and sent her to Paris to study at the Academy Julian. She was 17 years old.

After the war the British Army gave our grandfather the enormous task of doing a death inventory of all British soldiers who died in the 1914-1918 War. This task included seeing that they were properly buried, locating their graves, and ensuring that their relatives were properly informed. While Ralph and Tony went to different boarding schools in England, Edward and GG moved to St Omer to be close to his new job on the now deserted battlefield of northern France. This honourable work took him over five years to complete after which he was personally decorated by the King George the V for this great achievement.

Edward had rented a small flat in Paris to use when he visited the capital and Honor lived there while she studied. Our mum developed her talent rapidly. It was at the Academy Julian that Honor met Emmanuel David, called Mano by his friends and family, who was taking evening drawing classes there. They fell in love and their artistic affinities and interests no doubt brought them close together. Mano studied law and at the time was working as a lawyer's clerk in Gisors. He originally came from a small village in the Vaucluse called Camaret-sur-Aygues where his mother, Mamiche, owned a large family house.

"We were engaged for three years, before we even dared to kiss!" Mother used to like telling us when she talked and laughed about her past. "We didn't do anything sexual, he was so shy... we just held hands and looked at each other fondly!"

Grandfather Edward took a liking to Mano whose intelligence and humour attracted him. Without hesitation he agreed to their marriage and it took place in Gisors in 1925.

Honor was painting full-time now and had several exhibitions including at the Salon d'Automne in Paris. The lively likeness of her portraits and her direct application of paint using her fingers or a palette knife make her well known amongst the bourgeois and artistic society of Paris. Mano loved art, especially painting, and he was also good at it. They enjoyed going out together to paint from nature. However, soon he realised that she was extremely talented and decided to stop painting himself, saying that he could not compete with her genius. He then started an art gallery and discovered his new passion for selling paintings.

In 1926 mother gave birth to my eldest brother Philippe and his arrival re-awoke her great maternal qualities. Between breast-feeds, she carried on painting as they had a servant to help in the house. In truth she found the youthful beauty of her maids so inspiring that they became her models! Soon after, the young family moved to from Gisors to Boulogne-Billancourt on the outskirts of Paris, and this is where their first daughter Maxence was born.

Life in the Paris art world was very social and active in the 1920s. Writers, musicians, actors, philosophers and painters socialized, discussed their work, held late night parties where drinking was the norm and the most adventurous ones took hallucinogenic drugs. Art was going through a period of great changes and inventiveness was the thing, whether in design, fashion, architecture, theatre painting or sculpture. It was during these times that our mother became close friends with artists who later became well known, such as the Delaunays, the Derains, Henry Valensi and many others.

Then a great drama occurred in the young family. Against our mother's wishes, the local doctor insisted on giving Maxence an inoculation against tetanus. She suddenly became very ill with a high fever and, while our mother was breast-feeding her baby died in her arms; she was only three weeks old. Maman had been very reluctant to give her daughter this injection, especially as Philippe had previously become very ill from a similar medical intervention. But not being sure enough in herself and under the pressure of Mano and the doctor, she gave way to the officials representing modern medicine of the time. Honor was of course completely devastated by the death of her daughter. She lost all trust in allopathic medicine to the point that my sister and I were never given any injections or traditional medicine of any kind, and were never taken to see a western doctor.

This tragedy became the trigger for our mother's desire to change her whole life, to completely rediscover who she was and what she really wanted, to decide how she should re-direct her life and educate and bring up her children. In this 1920's era of a new age Paris, a close friend introduced her to two brothers who were naturopathic doctors, Gaston and André Durville. The Durville had their practice in Paris on avenue Foch and their revolutionary ideas greatly attracted our mother. They advocated for healthy food, physical exercise, breathing properly, and to only cure illness through plants and diet. She came to know them well and, while she was pregnant with my sister Sylvette, she followed their advice by doing physical exercises every day, carefully choosing a diet of good foods, relaxation and breathing exercises.

A short time after the Durvilles told her about their decision to buy from the French government the western part of the island Ile du Levant in the Mediterranean 15 kilometers off the Var coast. This intriguing and thrilling news was just what my mother needed to satisfy her desire to a complete change in her life. The land faced the sunset and the view extended from the highest hill, down to the sea along three kilometres of coastline and faced the majestic island of Port-Cros.

At that time the island had been given to the French Navy, which had not yet taken possession of it, leaving it wild and completely untouched. The two doctors created an association called La Société Naturiste, which our mother eagerly joined together with many Parisian patients and friends of the Durvilles. As early as 1929 they organised long health holidays in the summers where they would camp in the tall maritime pine forest near a small harbour called Le Grand Avis, where food and passengers landed from the nearest coastal harbour of Lavandou.

The doctors were good planners and organisers. Their basic idea was that modern city life was generally unhealthy and people needed to de-stress to regain their vital energies from exposure to the sun, swimming in the sea and physical movement classes. Not to mention lots of walking and climbing up and down the many hills. The long walks, together with the pickaxe and the shovel power needed to create roads and clear spaces to build the village, added to the health program. They called the future village Héliopolis and they placed it up high cradled between the island's two tallest hills, slightly protected from the fierce mistral wind. A beehive of activity started at Héliopolis. Roads were built and the land was divided into allotments and quickly sold to the new nature lovers.

On a brief visit to see her ever-travelling parents, Honor enthusiastically shared the good news with GG and Edward and they immediately made the decision to visit the island. As the small fishing boat neared the Grand Avis, the magic beauty of what they were seeing completely enchanted them. Without hesitation my grandparents immediately purchased three hectares of land for her at the bottom of what was called La Perspective, 200 large stone steps descending from the west side of the Fort Napoleon, the doctors' residence that dominated the hill. These steps made from the island stones possessed high mica content and glittered as if they were made of gold.

From their fort the Durvilles oversaw all their newly bought land. The 360° view is really magnificent: to the east are the blue Maures Mountains in the distance, and to the south facing the open sea the horizon loses itself into the sky. Facing the sunset, a string of islands called Les Iles d'Hyères stretched towards the distant harbour of Toulon.

After the birth of Sylvette in November 1934, life in Paris became too turbulent for our Maman. She decided to leave Mano and move indefinitely to the island with her two children. She didn't take much with her and left most of her belongings in the Paris flat with Mano. She took her precious art materials, health and education books, a few belongings and a large tent.

It was on this island that my mother met Marcel Lassalle. Probably at the Grand Avis (the only harbour on the Island at the time), where he must have been loading bags of lime and cement, or shovelling sand into his old, desert coloured Citroën lorry.

His family came originally from Brittany and he had been raised in North Africa. Marcel was the handyman of the island: tall, with dark curly hair, deep jet black eyes and well-defined feature. His body was muscular and supple and he moved with quick precision. He qualified as an electrical engineer and he over the years built many of the houses at Héliopolis and our three residences: La Fourmie, La Cigale and La Coccinelle.

Being the only person with transportation, a black Ford taxi and later the Citroën lorry, Marcel was very busy carrying goods and people from the Grand Avis and to all parts of the village Héliopolis.

He was a very different man from Mano, the artistic, intellectual businessman. Marcel was more interested in health food and physical exercise. My mother told me later that he was fascinated by spiritual matters and astronomy, wrote about his hobbies (clock making and mechanical inventions), enjoyed music, played the mandolin and knew much about the local wildlife. They fell in love and soon lived together, first in our mother's tent pitched under the magnificent maritime pines near the Grand Avis. Then camped at Les Eucaliptus near the well. When he finished building La Cigale, they moved in together with Sylvette and Philippe, who he instantly accepted as his own children.

My brother later told me how much he loved Marcel who was especially kind and caring towards him. It was the same with Sylvette who thought Marcel was her real father for the first 10 years of her life. Philippe was seven years older than his sister and remembered his father Mano. It must have been horribly painful for Honor when, one day in 1936, Mano arrived on the island to take 10 year old Philippe away. True there was no school on the island and it was quite understandable that Mano, who had an orthodox Catholic education, wanted his son to go to school. So he sent Philippe to board in a Jesuit school in Avignon. When his father came down from Paris to visit his mother, Mme David in Camaret, Philippe was able to join them for weekends. These events on the island happened during the five years before I was born in 1937.

My mother found this sudden separation extremely hard and missed her beloved boy terribly and so she thought of conceiving another. It must have been at that time that I prepared myself to enter into the cycle of my earthly existence.

GG and Edward Gell, my mother's parents

Belgium 1918: Col. Edward Gell showing King George V
the graves of the English soldiers

PROLOGUE

Mano and Honor on their wedding day
1925 in Normandy

Camping at Les Eucalyptus,
Honor and Sylvette at six months

Areal view of the west side of the Ile du Levant

Chapter 1

―――――― ঌ⚬ঌ ――――――

The Île du Levant at the dawn of World War II

And so, on December the 7th 1937 I was born into this earthly world in a small private clinic in Nice just behind the Russian Orthodox Church. Marcel Lassalle, who had not yet officially married our mother, went to the Town Hall to register my birth under the names François Xavier, son of Mme Honor David-Gell.

A few days later I was wrapped up in a thick blanket and taken to the island. Some years later my mother told me one evening at snuggle-time, "You were only a few days old when we returned to the island from the Lavandou. The sea was very rough due to a powerful easterly wind and there was a dark, menacing sky. I felt the journey was going to be precarious."

Her soft voice now carried much emotion, "In the middle of the strait the engine of the small fishing boat suddenly burst into flames! Le Père Pégliasco, the captain of the small fishing boat, yelling loudly so as to be heard over the howling winds and huge rolling waves, asked for your blanket to help put out the blazing fire. The Pirate, as we called him because of his rough manners and the black patch on his left eye, ordered me to hand you over to his son Loulou who was sitting in the prow. The old Captain noticed that I was not well and about to vomit! Loulou was just sixteen and he held you in his arms all the way back to the Grand Avis. Once the situation with the fire was under control, we finished the perilous crossing with the oars. It took hours! How relieved we were to find Marcel already at the harbour waiting for us in his yellow lorry!"

L'Ile du Levant, which means 'The Island of the Rising Sun', was at that time a magical place - magic because it was idyllic, like in a good dream, but truly real at least for me as a young child. Its name is probably derived from its geographical location east of a string of islands that stretches east to west off the coast of Provence. In the early 30s the French Navy owned L'Ile du Levant. It was practically uninhabited and undeveloped except for the Napoleonic Fort and the small fishing hut at the Grand Avis. It was wild and beautiful, especially its rugged coastline that stretched 11 km from the rising to the setting sun. At its widest part the island was only 2 km across. Its geological diversity included very high cliffs; colossal black iron boulders at a place called Les Pierres de Fer, literally the Iron Stones; flat rocks at les Pierres Plates; and sharp pointed ones of all sorts of shapes and colours. The shore curves and the coves revealed delightful white or black sandy beaches. There was also a well-hidden, small-pebbled beach Rioufrède, which means cold stream in Provençal. This was my preferred beach because it was sheltered from the mistral wind and faced south to the open sea. I could sit there and enjoy the taste of its colourful, wet, salty pebbles. Its undersea world was equally attractive with rich fauna and marine life. I used to spend as much time in the water as out of it. In the winter when it was too cold to swim, I would throw in my fishing line and wait for a bite while gazing at the horizon in search of something unexpected to catch my interest.

The island was hilly, the highest point being 160 metres, and from the top one had a 360° view, covered in most parts by a dense, high maquis of briar, strawberry trees and many aromatic shrubs and plants. At the time it had large forests of tall maritime pines, and I spent hours under them cracking the cones for their delicious kernels, listening to the whistling wind high up above while enjoying the hot sun on my back. These sacred silent moments enveloped my whole being, all my senses absorbing what nature was generously giving me. At that time, there was still much space in my inner feelings, a space in which I could just be. A place where there was no thinking, no wanting, no wishing but just being. Now, with reflection today as I write, I could say that I was close to my soul, although when I was a child this word did not belong to my vocabulary.

The bird and the insect life were very active on the island. I was living in a young entomologist's paradise, an entomologist who accumulated his knowledge of nature by observation without the use of words, names or references. With an insatiable curiosity, I would do all kinds of experiments with my little insect friends. Ants were a constant source of interest. They were rather big with large, black shining heads and had great strength. They could lift logs several times larger than themselves, trot along as if they carried no weight at all and lay them carefully at the entrance of their busy, volcano-shaped city. They had large roads too with much traffic going either way. I was intrigued by how they always seemed to be in such a hurry, and in their haste still managed to find an instant to stop when meeting one another, waving about their antennae as if to say, 'No time to talk now, we'll talk later!'

I saw them attack a grasshopper once. In a few seconds they had mastered the struggle and taken the comparatively enormous unconscious fellow onto the side of their crater, carefully cutting and separating the legs, the head and parts of the body so that they could shelve them in their underground stores. This showed me a way to enlarge my field of experiments and soon I was giving them live wasps, cicadas, worms and even scorpions!

Spiders fascinated me too. One type was huge and, with its dark charcoal-grey body with a creamy mark, reminded me of a human skull. One of these spiders became my very good friend and I called her Aunty Arthur. She had stretched her web in the front of our terrace, from high up in the tall cypress tree straight across our view and into a large aloe cactus that was in blossom. Her hiding place was high up at the top of the tree and I would only have to delicately tap the silk thread that formed the armature of her territory to get her to rush down at great speed to see what she had caught in her web.

Butterflies, horseflies, wasps, hornets, green flies, scorpions and many other creatures became her regular meals. It was only several years later, when my sister, mother and I immigrated to the mainland and I went to school, that I learned about the word 'cruel'. I was only following the natural path shown to me by the animal world. I was fascinated by the behaviour of Aunty Arthur and how, with her long hairy legs, she quickly managed to wrap up the protesting prey into a sticky, silky bundle. She was so quick that even scorpions and hornets were not a danger to her. Wrapped up like mummies, she would take her future meals up into her storage space in the high corner of her web and hang them there, as one does with saucissons, until she fancied one for dinner.

Snakes were also my friends. There were no venomous vipers on the island, but all kinds of grass snakes. Some were very big, like the grey one who lived in the crack of the dry stonewall that was part of our lower terrace. This friendly specimen had a musical ear and always came out when I whistled. My mother told me that they liked to drink milk, so I used to take it some in the lid of a jam jar. I was fascinated by the way it was able to move slowly without any legs, just by wriggling and curving his long, powerful, shiny body. He could even climb trees to get up and pinch the eggs in the nests of the numerous little birds that lived in the maquis. My entomological education was a full-time job and I was so busy that I did not have a moment to get bored.

My sister Sylvette, who is three years older than me, had a girl-friend about her own age called Didi. With her round body and pretty, pale blue-eyed face surrounded by a mass of golden curls, Didi attracted me with her giggly nature. She and my sister laughed a lot and I always wondered what they were laughing about. I must have been about three and a half when, on a day that my sister wasn't around, Didi took me excitedly by the hand and led me into the depth of the maquis. I was wondering where she was taking me and felt excited while at the same time a little nervous, as I never had been alone with Didi before. My heart was beating loudly by the time we reached a little clearing at the foot of a large, grey rock covered in orange lichen and shaped like a menhir.

There we were completely sheltered from the whistling mistral. Sitting in the sun with her back to the rock she giggled and asked me if I had ever seen a fanny before? I shook my head slowly with much embarrassment, blushing up to my ears. Looking at the ground, not knowing how to take this unexpected question, I sat down with my feet tucked under my body. In a joyful chuckle, she ordered, "Look here, look!" and threw her knees fully apart, suddenly revealing what looked to me like glittering rubies. As I slowly focused on her jewels I was startled, transfixed and my heart was now thumping so loudly I was sure she must have heard it.

What she displaying so generously did intrigue and fascinate me. My world seemed to come to a stop as I silently absorbed this amazing scene. With another burst of laughter, Didi took my left hand gently and directed it to her colourful treasure… then made me feel it. What a strange thing it was… it reminded me of the sea anemone, but it was warmer and shiny and smelled quite differently too. I was so deeply taken by this situation that it made my whole body feel unusually strange, almost numb. In silence, my being became fully aware of the parts of the female I did not know about; I had discovered 'female' in its integrity and would never forget it.

While immersed in our mutual worlds of discovery, we suddenly heard an adult's light laugh coming from above the rock and I just had time to see my mother's fair hair as she vanished behind the menhir. She was looking for us because it was lunchtime. When she finally found us, she had the delicacy not to interfere, but to disappear and let us continue our investigation in peace. Of course, her sudden appearance cooled us right down and we stood looking at each other in silence with timid smiles on our faces. We went back home in deep private reflection, in our own individual worlds. We both still felt the effects of this new experience and were now hypersensitive to these special parts of our bodies and their strong, direct link to our emotions. Didi never showed me her attractive rubies again, but after these instructive moments, I knew a little more about how girls were made and that made me feel much more conscious of the opposite sex.

Life on the island

Marcel and Honor were popular on the island, my father for being always available to give a hand, and mother for her kindness and good humour. She painted nudes, portraits of locals and seascapes, and met many interesting people visiting the Ile du Levant in the holidays. Mother began to be interested in alternative education. She decided she wasn't going to give her children the same kind of education as she had received, and began to read the latest books on the subject: Pestalozzi, Steiner, Montessori, and she also read A. S. Neill, the Scottish educator.

Just before the war started, she met an Austrian Jewish lady called Lena Münz, who had been with A. S. Neill when he started his first school in Germany. When the Nazis came to power, he moved the school to Wales. Honor devoured all she could read about A.S. Neill and promptly started to apply his ideas to her own children. Reading his books helped her to understand a great deal about herself with regards to her relationship to her parents, and how damaging had been the education she had received from the repressive English and Swiss private schools.

During this time Honor met two ladies, Simone Monnier and Marguerite Soubeyran, who were spending a few days at Héliopolis on vacation. They talked about their mutual interest in education and, as the war was budding, about their political ideas. They were both devoted communists and told her about their private school called Beauvallon in the Drôme, near a small village named Dieulefit.

They generously offered to take her children into their school free of charge in case a war broke out again and things became too difficult to stay on the island. This kind offer reassured our mother enormously and she stored it carefully in the back of her mind.

By 1938 Marcel had parted from his 1926 Ford taxi and replaced it with a small Sahara coloured Citroën lorry. I have wonderful memories of trips down to the harbour at the Grand Avis to meet the boat and wait while the lorry was being loaded. We played on the shallow beach or stayed on the quay, looking through the slats of wood into the clear water below where a multitude of mullet fish waited for a bit of bread or biscuit to fall. When time was up Marcel called us and we ran to him. I was too small to climb up the high step to get into the cab, so he joyfully lifted me up into the air, letting me fly for an instant before catching me and settling me on the shiny, brown, imitation leather canvas seat. I was always in the middle between Sylvette and Papa. On the return journey, half asleep/half awake, I completely abandoned myself to floating between my inner and outer worlds. My head on his right knee, I peeped through half-closed eyes at the upside down pine trees marching by, set against the pink sky lit by the setting sun.

My sharp sense of smell picked up Marcel's sweaty and spicy body odour, mixed with the hot motorcar oil leaking from the exhaust. The engine made a whiny, high-pitched, singing noise that went up or down according to the gear we were in. For reassurance I sometimes turned my head to look up at Papa's square chin, often bristling with beard, his well-designed mouth and his fine nostrils. I couldn't see much further as it all disappeared towards the top of his black curly hair. My body rolled as if in a cradle, and when the lorry met a deep rut or hole the jolt would suddenly bring me back to my senses. They would tell me that it was safe to let go again and to sink back into this wonderful world where I felt loved and protected. Usually by the time we got home, I was fast asleep and woke up in Marcel's arms as we entered the house for supper.

Once a week when the weather was fine we walked down to a

place called l'Ayguade. If the wind was favourable we could sometimes hear the sound of a conch-shell brought up by the sea breeze announcing Loulou's small fishing boat arriving from the mainland. It delivered the odd passenger, the post, food and different materials needed by the inhabitants of the island. Sylvette and I loved running down to l'Ayguade with Mum. She was so nice to be with, so kind, so attentive and with such a light spirit. She took each of us by the hand, my sister on one side and me on the other, and we danced and skipped down to the sea in good time before the boat arrived, which in summer gave us enough time for a swim. Loulou's boat was often in a hurry to go back to the distant coast just in case the mistral or some other strong wind started blowing harder, making his return to the mainland precarious.

While Mum talked with her friends on the jetty, which could take some time, Sylvette and I disappeared to the right of the tiny harbour and played on the pebbly beach where the rocks met the sea. The beach always hid interesting things, like fascinating piles of wood rounded and shaped by the sea; to our fertile imagination they looked like a thousand and one different animals and even people. Once my sister recognised a horse in a hairy piece of cane root. Sometime we discovered a dead seagull, or a frosted glass bottle, or parts of nets attached to large, round, dark green glass floats that were part of the fishing equipment in those days.

I often left Sylvette at her nature sculptor games, while I went looking for crabs in the deep cracks of the rocks, where they hid for protection behind their larger claw.

If I got a bit of fish from the fishermen, I tied it with a slipknot to a piece of string at the end of a stick and let it dangle in the front of the hungry crab. Immediately his strange mouth would start frothing, and with one of his telescope eyes on me, the other watched over the lump of fish. His mind was probably thinking about a plan to catch the bait without being caught! Moving slightly sideways, opening his claw in the direction of the irresistible bait and forgetting the strong grip he had on his hole, he extended it slowly into the waiting loop. I would pull gently upward until the string became taut and then I grabbed his shell with my thumb and index finger and lifted him out of his hideout. If my sister was not too far away, I adored teasing her by pretending to put the angry crab on her or in her hair. I have to admit that I was a terrible tease, and never missed an occasion to get the better of my sister by doing some awful trick. It was fun to throw the spiky creature back into the sea and watch it swim in its awkward way back to the shallow cracks of the shore.

Once while watching one of these side walkers, I saw a cigarette end floating by, deposited by a little wave just in the front of the hole of a large black crab. With great hesitancy, he finally came out to inspect what the sea brought him. He stretched out his big claw, delicately picked up the wet fag and proceeded in slow motion to pull out one thread of tobacco at a time, feeding it into his complicated hairy mouth with two jagged shutters in front. It must have tasted quite strong because he started to froth profusely, maybe from the excitement of his tasty new discovery. It must have been good because he finished the old fag - even the paper ended up in his strange-shaped mouth.

Mother called us back for the long climb home, but she stripped off all her clothes first and took a quick dip by diving beautifully from a rock with her legs perfectly twinned. When she came up her long thin body stretched out, her face still down in the water, gently moving her legs up and down from the hips and floated like this as long as she could hold her breath. She then turned over on her back and in complete relaxation slowly swam back to the rocks. We usually did not take towels, so still wet after the swim we'd start the long climb home.

To help our Maman, we each carried something. In the summer I liked to carry the crates of fruit, especially peaches, because I knew that somewhere on the way up that steep hill when we needed to rest, I'd be the first to choose one. We then sat and ate our fruit, looking at the beautiful seascape spread out below us. When at last we arrived home hot, salty and sweaty from the climb, we deposited the goods in the kitchen and bathed under the outdoor pump. One of us activated the pump and another crouched under the soft water flow to wash away the salty sea and sweat from our backs. Usually my sister went first, then me, and finally it would be our mother's turn. Afterwards she wrapped a towel around her waist and went into the small kitchen to prepare our lunch. There was no water on the part of the island where La Cigale had been built, so rainwater was collected from the roofs into a large cistern. This was the only water we had, and it seemed to be sufficient for our needs throughout the year.

One day as we walked up the steep hill back home from the sea, we were talking and asking questions about where babies came from. Later when we were at the under-the-pump shower and dried off, our mum pointed to her vagina and said, "You both came out of here…" "But that is the pipi hole mummy!" my sister remarked. "No, not there! But through here my darling." Mum now pointed to the correct place, saying this with a hint of laughter in her voice.

You must remember, dear reader, that for at least six months of the year, we did not wear any clothes and if we did, they were only the minimum. Our mother was a natural and free person, especially regarding anything to do with the basic aspects of life. There was no embarrassment whatsoever and there was no exhibitionism. She was simply matter-of-fact. We quietly registered these origins of life explanations as they came to us without feeling that they were particularly funny or not to be spoken about openly. She talked about these things in the same way she would explain how a flower is fertilised.

Sylvette was my big sister and I was impressed by her assuredness. To the little brother I was, it was a great privilege when she gave me her attention. This usually happened when she was bored and didn't have her friends to play with. She would say for instance, "Let's go into the maquis and make the bird traps jump!" We were at the beginning of the World War II and with no boats coming from the mainland; food became scarce on the island. A lonely man called

Maurice scraped out a meagre living by catching birds in powerful metal traps and selling them to the remaining inhabitants of Héliopolis. Saddened by the awful death of these little birds, my sister took me by the hand deep into the maquis to hunt for the hidden bird-torturing machines. When we did find one, sometime quite far away from our home, we had great fun throwing pebbles at the shutter-release and watching the traps jump high up into the air, emitting a loud crack.

One day, on our way home from one of these birds-saving patrols, we heard the menacing, raucous voice of a man as we approached our house. It was Maurice shouting, "These fucking children of yours are letting my traps off! Tell them that if I catch them at it, I will pull their ears off!" On hearing these menacing and crude words, we disappeared deeper into our hiding place and waited a long time before we dared to come out. Later on, Mum explained that this was his only income apart from fishing and that it was better in the future to leave him and his traps alone.

Mum was a wonderful cook. She was an artist, not only as a painter, but also in whatever she decided to do or make. She told me that when she came to the island she did not know much about cooking. It was Marcel who had taught her Mediterranean cooking, using all kinds of herbs found in the maquis. We used to look for seagull eggs and catch fish. Mum managed to find a few bags of the basics, such as flour, wheat or other cereals, dried peas, or chickpeas and what ever luckily came our way. My passion for fishing drew me to an old fisherman who gave me one of his fishing secrets, "… use a special worm as bait, not the maggots we find in our outdoor toilet, or the earthworms we might find in rich soil, instead use the orange-legged worms that are actually more like centipedes. They live in their intricate houses at the base of the brown seaweed that holds fast to the rocks as it rises and falls with the movement of the waves." Then the old fisherman kindly showed me how to firmly hold the lower part of the seaweed, and pull it energetically away from the rock. "Make sure you don't fall in the water while pulling!"

he added with a burst of laughter that revealed his numerous golden teeth.

When I pulled with all my force on the stem of the brown seaweed, I was intrigued to see that its slimy roots came away with lumps of brittle calcium with many corridors. They were full of life, busy with orangey-yellow creepy crawlers that protested by wriggling angrily when I held them in my fingers as they tried to escape. I caught the first one and put it on the end of my hook and quickly threw it into the sea with my long, cane fishing rod. The first time I used that worm I was amazed by what happened! As soon as the lead weight at the end of my line touched the seabed, I felt frantic bites… and started to pull out a whole array of colourful fish. I was excited and imagined my mother's amazement when she saw how many fish I had caught. I was now running up the long hill back home and thinking that they could either be fried or boiled into a soup. The old fisherman revealing his fishing secret, woke up a hidden fisherman's instinct in me, much to the delight of my mother.

The island had a few rodents, including some healthy-looking fat red-brown rats. One day I saw one of these rats entering our cellar through a door that had been left slightly open. I had heard from a villager once, that they were good to eat, so I ran up the stairs into the house and found my mother talking with friends. "Quick, quick, come, I've seen a big rat go into the cellar," I shouted excitedly. Without losing a minute, we stretched a piece of fishing net across the doorway. I was asked to go to the back of the untidy cellar and shout and make a lot of rattling noises. The handsome fellow carried by the fear for his life, dived through the doorway and into the net. My mother's friend was quick to grab it by the skin of its neck and the rat disappeared from my sight until supper. When it reappeared on the dining table steaming in a brown sauce, it smelt deliciously appetising. We ate it with potatoes and it tasted similar to rabbit, but tenderer and with more slender bones.

The War starts and things change

For the little boy François, or Sounet as my mother and papa affectionately called me, life was straightforward, uncomplicated and lived in the instant with little reference to any painful memories or future anticipations. For our mother it could not have been so smooth. Difficult times started to be felt from the autumn of 1939 when France and England declared war on Germany after the invasion of Poland. Food started to get scarce and confusion spread amongst the population. Marcel, who was not a young man any longer, was called up to join the French reserve force and every so often would have to go to the military camps on the coast for training.

Mum never believed that men would be crazy enough to start another world war. She had suffered greatly in the 1914 - 1918 war where her father Edward had been so involved. She was not at all prepared for what was to come and thought that Marcel would always be with her and the children. From 1939 up to 1942 the island gradually lost most of its inhabitants including many of my mother's close friends. Marcel's mother, who lived in a house near the Heliopolis, also left to go somewhere on the coast near Hyeres, we never saw her again. War was now raging in Europe, especially in the North. There was no more news from Paris or England and slowly we found ourselves totally isolated, as if forgotten by the outside world. There was no money, except the little savings that Marcel had put aside, on which we survived.

In the early summer of 1942, Marshal Pétain, President at the time, gave most of France away to the Nazis by separating the country in two. Two-thirds of France became The Occupied Zone including the North and West down the Atlantic coast to the town of Vichy. This part of France came under Nazi laws. The remaining third, the Central and South Eastern part was ruled from Vichy by Marshal Petain's government, which was actually pro-German and controlled the press. Then, under the pressure of Germany, the Vichy government agreed to recruit a work force of over 650,000 French technicians to work in German factories, as their own men were needed to fight on Russian front. From all over France they were gathered near Paris where Nazis specialists selected each man according to his qualifications. They were called STO for 'Service Travail Obligatoire' and Marcel had to leave suddenly as one of them, our mother explained, and we never saw our loving papa again.

Because of the war, the situation on the island became unbearable. The Italian army had now invaded the Côte d'Azur from the East and their troops, together with the German army were stationed in the Rhône Valley. They took all the available food and raw materials, used all the transport and started arresting people who travelled.

After Marcel left as STO, life on the island became too hard and in late October 1942, moved by hunger, Honor decided to leave for the village of Dieulefit in the Drôme. She was acting on the invitation of Simone and Marguerite Soubeyrand, the educators who, a few years before, had invited her to their school if ever there was a war. When she heard that a boat was leaving for the mainland early one morning, she hurriedly gathered some clothes and a few valuables in a suitcase. Being winter this part of the Island was in the shade, and it was cold and the light dim at this early hour. The first rays of the sun rising behind our hill stroked the island of Port-Cros opposite, emerging like a dream out of the vapory sky and sea. The easterly wind did not disturb the sea on this side of the island but it told us that the crossing would be choppy and wet.

Stepping onto the narrow gangplank of Mr Pégliasco's small fishing craft was slightly precarious. He offered his huge and rough hand to our Mum who took it as she stepped onto the boat. We were the only passengers and we departed immediately.

Mother was wearing a finely woven, pale grey houndstooth suit. I had never seen her dressed this way before. I cuddled under our small tartan blanket, my head against her thigh and looked up at her. She looked somehow different from that angle and I saw that she was far away in herself, gazing absently at the island gradually getting smaller as we sailed away. Sylvette was sitting with her straight back at the prow, her legs tucked together under her, also looking at our island… distancing places of memories. I suddenly felt how much I loved her.

Night had fallen when we arrived at Toulon and found a hotel on the square by the railway station. It was the first time my sister and I had slept in a hotel, and we were excited by the idea. When we opened the bedroom door, the first noticeable thing was a strange, musty smell in the stuffy dark room. When I asked my mother later what it was, she told me that it must be the usual smell of hotel rooms. The pink and red flowered wallpaper carried the marks of many squashed mosquitoes; there was a black metal double bed to the left and a window beyond, which looked over the square. The traffic noise from the busy square reverberated into the room as if we were in the belly of a drum. We were quite exhausted from the long day and, having had practically no food that day, we nestled against either side of our Mum under the grey sheets and soon fell asleep. This first night away from home was unpleasant to say the least, because early in the night we started scratching and scratching at what felt like little animals rushing about on our bodies. Maman was the first to jump out of bed, frantically shaking herself while switching on the bleak central light. We asked her what was the matter since we could not see anything in the bed, so Mum asked us to get up, and we lifted the mattress. To our horror we saw the cause of all our itches and bites; colonies of large rust coloured insects the size of drawing pins trying frantically to hide under each other. "They are called bedbugs!" she said with disgust in her voice. We shook out the top sheet and blankets, moved to the opposite corner of the room and tried to sleep on the hard floorboards.

We were up early the next morning and, after a quick breakfast went into the Toulon railway station. Mother tried to find out if there was a train to Marseille or to our destination, Montélimar. We waited all day - each passing train was full and people fought to get on them. I had never experienced anxiety before, and now it descended on me, accentuated by the feeling of having no security at all and of being

CHAPTER 1

in fear of losing sight of my mother or my sister. For reassurance my hand gripped my mother's very tightly.

Finally by the evening a train came and the door of the carriage stopped just where we were sitting. After a few people stepped down, Sylvette dived forward and in a flash was up the high steps and onto the landing. She put out a hand and helped me up, then the heavy suitcase, and then, finally, our mother. Mum beamed a smile of relief. After all the waiting, we were able at last to continue our journey and this was so comforting. As the long train released its brakes with a creaky sound and whistled, we saw that we were on a train that was completely packed. The corridors were so full of suitcases and people, there was no way we could have gone further in either direction. The other carriages were also full up to the gunnels. The only place left was in the dirty, smelly toilet that had neither seat nor cover. Climbing over sleepy bodies, bags and suitcases, we settled into this temporary make-do home. I remember hearing for the first time through the thin half-open flap of the toilet hole, the monotonous rhythmic noise of the heavy metal wheels, hitting the space between the rails. Our stomachs had been empty since the light breakfast in Toulon, yet I managed to let go of the smells, of the noises, of my mother and sister to fall into a deep sleep.

I woke up with a jump, hearing sounds I had never heard before coming through the open door of our carriage - men's voices talking in a strange language. Maman told me the voices came from a group of German soldiers standing on the platform. It was still dark and cold when we stopped at the Marseille train station. We stayed there for a long time, and when we finally moved on we were going backwards! I was intrigued by this sudden change of direction and asked my mother why. She was obviously too tired to talk much, but mumbled that Marseille was like a cul-de-sac; we had to go out backwards and later on we would go forward again.

I took refuge in my dream world again and came back only when my mother gently called to say it was time to get off this train. It was daylight, the train was stopped in a long tunnel station, a cold mistral

37

blew and my still sleepy body was shivering with cold. We were in Avignon and the station was full of bags, suitcases and people, some in grey army uniforms. The invading army had requisitioned our train, so we would have to wait for another. There was plenty to look at… everything was new to me; what I saw, what I heard, what I smelt and especially these fascinating steaming bellowing railway engines! The engines resembled huge dragons and stimulated all my curiosity; white steam came out of its sweating body, and a bad egg smell came from the black chimney smoke invading the platform. The unexpected face of a man appeared in the high square window of the engine, looked down and gave me a white toothy grin; his cheeks, forehead and mouth were completely blackened by the coal dust. The noise was tremendous and I had nothing to compare it with, except when the sea pulled away from the beach rolling back its many pebbles, but this engine noise was much louder and carried voices.

Mum found space on a seat next to an old lady and from there we could see the activities taking place on the station platforms. Some trains did not stop and sped through the station blowing their whistles and creating a tremendous draught. Some carried large cylinders on wheels, while others carried army equipment, tanks and cannons, jeeps and lorries. "Where, are they going, Maman?" I asked. "Up north, my darling." Then came an exceptionally long train, each wagon a flat railcar with cannons, jeeps, tanks or simply full of men in uniforms holding their guns. One of them stopped just in the front of us and after a while the soldiers proceeded to have their lunch. I had almost forgotten about food but when I saw the men pulling baguettes out of their bags, splitting them open with sharp knives and covering the inside with a strange creamy paste, I wondered what it was. "Maman, what is it that they're putting on their bread?" "It's called butter, my darling." "Maman, what is butter?" "It's made with the fat that floats on top of the cow's milk."

On hearing this my curiosity sharpened and I walked to the carriage to get a closer look at what they were eating. By now they were drinking wine, cutting up sausages and ham and shoving it into their long baguettes. Throwing my head back, I gazed up, my mouth wide open from the hunger... and to my amazement, I felt as through I was also eating. One big soldier pointed his long sandwich towards my open mouth and said something in his strange language, which immediately triggered an explosion of laughter from the other men. I didn't like the feeling in that moment and I went back to where we were sitting. "Maman, tell me, what's so funny, why are the men laughing?" "I really don't know my love," she replied absently. I continued, for there was so much I wanted to know...

"Maman? What are those funny long yellow things they are eating now? And the round orange ones?" "They are called bananas and oranges." "Where do they come from Maman?" "They come from Africa, François."

We waited all that day in Avignon station, and then finally, we were able to board a train that took us to Montélimar.

île du Levant

The Grand Avis in 1937

WALNUTS & GOAT CHEESE

Maman, Sylvette and François at l'Ayguade

François, Didi and Sylvette 1939

Marcel in his quarry with his yellow lorry

CHAPTER 1

First steps with papa and Sylvette 1938

Chapter 2

Dieulefit 1942-1944 Maison Marefours - Les Tilleuls

Night had already fallen when we arrived in Montélimar. It was cold as we climbed down from the high carriage steps. There were no French people on the long platform, just a small group of German soldiers wrapped up in their long winter coats. They were standing close to the exit, stamping their feet on the ground to keep them warm and did not seem to see us as we walked by.

We were hungry. Maman had told us that we could probably find some food in Montélimar. She looked into her purse and found just enough coins to buy us a baguette and a lump of cheese. As soon as she came back, we sat down to eat on the wooden bench in the waiting room of the small station, and waited for an unknown person sent by the Beauvallon School to pick us up.

Dieulefit is situated about 30 km east of Montélimar at an altitude of 600 metres, and is surrounded by mountains. There was no regular transportation, no buses or local trains, although there had been a railway line from Montélimar to Dieulefit, that was now out of service. The effect of the war closed down all the secondary transport. The intruding army controlled everything with much identity checking of travellers, because there were orders that no one should travel without a special pass.

CHAPTER 2

Deeply in herself, our mother hid the truth about her origins in order to protect us from the fear of being arrested, and she had never even talked to us in her mother tongue. If it had been known that she was English we would have been sent to camps in Germany. No étranger was allowed to travel in France at that time. Our journey, as I reflect on it now, was indeed a very high risk, but our mother took it, for she had no alternative. Somehow, the little fair-headed family had not so far drawn any attention to itself; it was as if we had become invisible to the enemy.

I fell asleep on my mother's knees, when she woke me up gently saying it was time to move. Before us stood an elderly man in a ragged gabardine raincoat, a sad face with a long, purple, dripping nose and pale-blue watery eyes. He took our suitcase, walked silently out into the yard and stopped by an old horse and carriage. I had never seen a horse or a carriage before, and was fascinated by the tall thin animal. Steam was coming out of his sensitive nostrils and, as I stood near him feeling his body heat, he turned his head and looked at me and brought his ears forward. What I found strange was his weird headdress: flat square leather pads covered his eyes and, on feeling my presence, he turned his head right round to look at me because his blinkers stopped him from looking sideways. His coat was reddish brown with an attractive white lozenge patch on his forehead. I instantly liked him and wanted to stay there just to look at the beauty he revealed, but it was time to go.

The old coach-driver lifted me up onto the horse cart seat that was protected by a black, shiny canvas canopy with folding sides. As we made ourselves comfortable, mother wrapped us up in a khaki coloured blanket that smelled of horse.

"Maman, why has the horse got flaps on his eyes?"

"It is so that he does not get distracted by things happening around him; he only sees the road ahead."

The old man suddenly uttered a raucous sound, "Yuppie! Yuppie!" and unlocked the handbrake to free the two large, wooden wheels. The old horse leaned, pulled ahead and the cart moved forward, we were off!

WALNUTS & GOAT CHEESE

I curled up against my mother with only my nose and eyes peeping over the blanket. I felt secure and, as a snail coming out of his shell with eyes and horns erect, almost wearing a smile, I was ready to absorb the fascinating new world unfolding in front of us. From the carriage driver side I saw the funny movement of the horse's wide buttocks and its two long ears dancing in an opposite rhythms to the clip-clop of the horseshoes hitting the stony road. I could hear the fairy-tale ringing of bronze bells that must have been hanging somewhere on his leather harness. By now the horse had found his trotting rhythm, and the air felt pure but sharp. Snow came down in light flakes, so I searched with my cold hands under the blanket to find my mother's warm and reassuring hands, and I gathered my body closer to hers. The three of us were silent, each in our own world. The cart was well out of the town by now, and although the snow came down more densely, I could just distinguish high hills on the other side of the road. It felt colder as the night absorbed the light, and I fell into a deep sleep.

I woke up the next morning in a strange child's bed. I recognize my mother's suitcase, not yet unpacked, at the end of her double bed, and saw that she was already up. There was much light reflecting from the ceiling into the bedroom and this drew me out of bed to the window to view my new environment, which was covered in thin snow. I had seen snow on the island the winter before, but it was only end of October and the glittering snow was like a welcome in the morning sun. Below the bedroom window was a large courtyard fringed by tall lime trees, beyond a field, then, further in the distance, a farm and high hills behind.

We were staying at 'Maison Marefours', also called 'Les Tilleuls' (the lime trees), a long 19th century stone building facing south, on two floors divided into 4 small flats. From the large courtyard, we entered our flat through French doors that led down into a square living/dining room covered with yellow and white cement tiles. On the left opposite, was a small passage that led to a dark kitchen. On the left of this passage was a door that was closed, and to the right an unlit cupboard where we later kept salt and vinegar in large stoneware jars. We had to go outside and back in to find a stone staircase to reach a corridor that led to our bedrooms and toilets, with a tiny window from which we could see fields and mountains. The whole place echoed and the oak floors creaked loudly.

Other people lived at Les Tilleuls, mostly Jews and foreigners. In peacetime the small town of Dieulefit housed 3000 inhabitants, but during the war its number rose to 5000, and this increase came from the people who were hiding from the Nazis. The town was only accessible by three roads each through a gorge, which made the town easy to defend. A Maquisard hidden behind a rock or a tree could easily throw a hand grenade onto the road below. A lorry full of unfortunate German soldiers was blown up on one of these roads and no one survived. After this incident, the district military authorities decided that it was not worth risking their soldiers to occupy our village. From the summer of 1942 on, the town never saw the invading army again.

Coming from the island into this new turbulent world was for me the beginning of new experiences that started to affect my emotional balance. Most of my tears on the island were linked to light physical pains, such as sea urchin spines in my foot, tummy pains, stubbing my big toe on a root, or scratching my knee on a rock, and, although I started to miss my Papa greatly, at that time I did not cry much for his absence. I had not yet really encountered emotional suffering; but it wasn't too long before life showed me its darker sides.

One early Monday morning, Maman dressed us up in our best clothes, took each one of us by the hand and said in a joyful way, "Today, we are going to school!" It was cold and very windy, so with scarves and bonnets well set in place, we started our walk round the back of the house, in the direction of the hills where the Beauvallon School nestled. Soon we came to a fragile wooden bridge with wide slats through which we could see the river flow below. Each plank made a different sound under our shoes. Tall trees, many of them poplars, lined the road that rose up steeply with high banks on either side. The wind was not blowing so hard there and it was much easier to breathe; if I opened my mouth when the North wind blew, it stifled me.

The landscape opened up; to the right, fields fenced and barbed wire descended towards an enormous sand hill in the shape of a horseshoe, crested by pine trees and heather. An oval hole like an ox's eye beside a long, narrow section reminded me of a nose. It was a kind of beautiful monster with funny curly hair on top. Later I learned that it was called la Sablière (the sand hill).

The road curved left towards a mansion that belonged to a doctor Soubeyran, but just before that, we turned sharp right into a beautiful alley of apple trees which took us to the school's farm. It was a fascinating place. I immediately recognised my friend, the brown horse that had brought us from Montélimar; he lived there with the chickens, geese, turkeys, pigs, and many cows.

Past the farm the rocky road started to climb again before turning left into a large chestnut tree forest. The ground was still covered with nuts popping out of their prickly shells. Then we came out of a small wood called la Bute, with high sandy banks covered by oak and acacia trees that rose on each side of the road. Suddenly, our mother exclaimed, "Look over there, that's the school, the two white large buildings... you see?"

First days at school

I immediately felt an emotional ball of fire within my chest, my knees became wobbly and it was a job to walk the last 50 metres. The thumping of my heart made the children's voices hardly audible and my hand gripped my mother's tightly. I felt slightly sick. As we came closer, the children surrounded us and stared. We were the newcomers that they had been told about. The truth was that we were going to be the only day children of the Beauvallon School. I looked down at the ground, not able to face all the stares. To my relief a bell rang and all the children rushed away in the direction of the main entrance and organised themselves into two distinctive lines. Then, in an orderly manner, with the youngest first, they walked into the main building.

Gripping mother's hand even more tightly, we walked up the few steps leading into the main school to meet the house lady. Atty was extremely tall with short, black, greasy haircut to the shape of her head, and it reminded me of a German soldier's helmet. Large glasses rested on her long, thin nose and I noticed a few thick dark hairs over her non-existent thin lips. After a few words with Maman, she asked us to follow her down the corridor and she walked so fast that we had to run to keep up with her. Atty showed us the 3 classrooms, the large dining room and the kitchen to the right, finishing the tour with the double toilet-rooms.

By now the children had found their seats in their respective classes, the noise and the chatter was gone and I felt more at peace. Atty started to climb the stairs to her office two by two, but halfway up she stopped, turned around and said not so reassuringly to my mother 3 steps below, "Don't worry, your kids will get used to it. Make sure that they are on time tomorrow - gym starts at eight o'clock!" Behind her military appearance, I felt there was a kindness, buried somewhere inside her.

The mixed school had been started in the 1920s by two ladies we familiarly called Tante Marguerite, the headmistress and Simone, her loyal assistant 20 years younger, who seemed less fierce. The two buildings were set in the most beautiful countryside, facing full south with their backs against Montmirail Mountain. There were tall trees on one side of the sandy sports ground, oaks, pines and white poplars, which in the spring covered the ground in a white fluffy snow called 'kapok'. By 1943 Beauvallon had become a shelter for Jewish and other children coming mostly from Paris. Our Headmistress was a convinced communist who ran the school with great authority and discipline. She walked with bare feet in the snow, which impressed me very much. I scrutinised with interest her wide purple-pink feet with large, black crevasses round the heels, and toes invaded by large

47

white thick toenails. She told us the reason she did this was to share the pain of the poor, shoeless Russians queuing up for food in the snow in Moscow.

I was relieved and so happy when we started on our way back home that first morning. We had come just to learn the way to the school, and to meet Atty who was going to keep an eye on us.

Next door to us at les Marefours was an old Irish lady we called 'la Glean.' She was very keen on our mother, probably because she could speak English with her. The first time I heard them talking together in this unusual tongue, I realised my mother was not French. She had never spoken English in front of us before and, feeling excluded, I objected because I couldn't understand what she was saying. This was a strange feeling for us, as if la Glean had taken over our mother temporarily. Sylvette and I took a dislike to her, and her insistence on giving us wet, sticky kisses with her overly painted, lipless mouth. As she approached us we experienced her potent smells, the corners of her mouth frothy with brownish liquid; and her oily hands covered with bits of bread pudding gave us shudders. Streaks of greasy long hair made an upside down V over her sad face. We avoided physical contact with her and when she appeared uninvited in our dining room, I quickly disappeared into my hiding place under the many legs of our extendable dining table, leaving Sylvette to deal with la Glean.

On the other side of our apartment lived a Jewish mother called Clara, and her daughter Florence who was in her early teens. At unexpected moments, André Malraux, the husband and father, would arrive looking tired, and stay for a few days. To my young eyes, he was always elegantly dressed compared to the other men at les Tilleuls. He was a nice man who was attentive to us, and discussed arts and politics at length with our mum. We soon learned that he was an important member of the resistance movement, and years later became, in Charles de Gaulle's government, Minister for Cultural Affaires. Other people lived in our building, but we didn't come into contact with them, except for a painter to who lived on the other side of the Malraux's flat. We came to know him as Voltz and Sylvette used to chat together, and he often talked about painting with our Mum.

On the east side of the building was a washhouse where running water constantly filled two washbasins. One day Sylvette and I had an embarrassing giggle when we saw that an old lady dressed in a long black skirt stopped scrubbing her clothes on the sloping stone, and turned around slightly spreading her legs, and looked up to the sky in a vague dreamy state. We checked but there was nothing special in the sky, so we looked down at her feet and saw a little, hot, steaming river running down from the hump of earth she was standing on. She didn't seem to notice our presence, being too absorbed in her pleasant feelings, nor heard our laughter overridden by the loud musical sounds of the waterfall nearby.

The morning after our visit to Beauvallon it was very hard for me to get ready for school. Sylvette was feeling positive, looking pretty with her little fair plaits tied with red ribbons resting on her cherry cardigan. She was all ready to go and I couldn't help but admire her courage. After a too quick breakfast she took my hand with great assuredness, which comforted me a little, and we were off by ourselves onto the gravel road that would carry my lagging feet for many years to come. I found it difficult to walk fast, feeling no enthusiasm for where we were going. My dear sister would pull me along and say, "Oh, la-la! Come on hurry up! You're so slow!"

We finally arrived at the farm. I ran up to the stable double doors, the top was always open, climbed onto the ridge of the lower door frame and rested my chin on my hands gripping the upper rail. The contrast of this warm air with the strong smell of the animals with the pure cold air from outside was overwhelmingly rich and pleasant. As we got used to the poor light inside the stables, we saw the fat farm boy, sitting on a low stool milking a cow. The rhythmic metallic music made by the jets of milk hitting the sides of the bucket delighted me. The sound became deeper and more subdued when the milk hit the warm frothy bubbles. His hands were going at a frantic rhythm when he turned his head towards us, and, with a grin that revealed a few missing teeth, ordered in a strong Spanish accent, "Open your mouth!" A powerful tepid jet of milk first hit my left eye, then ran down my cheeks. The farm-boy adjusted his aim and this time the jet went into my wide-open mouth, making a different sound as my mouth filled up with the delicious liquid. I soon learnt how to swallow while keeping my mouth open to stop the milk dribbling out. I was very happy and comforted to see that Sylvette enjoyed it as much as I did. Wiping our faces on the back of our sleeves, we trotted on joyfully up the winding road and finally arrived at the sports ground. We heard the school bell calling the children; a teacher arrived and we were so relieved to be on time.

When it was cold, the sports teacher took us cross-country running for half an hour in the hills surrounding the school. We had already walked a good 3 km from home, but I still enjoyed this run for we never went the same way twice. I liked discovering new places jogging while hearing my rhythmic breathing as my feet hit the frosted ground, my nostrils wide open, always searching for new rising smells that came from the trampled earth. After gym all the children were taken round the back for assembly in a large meeting room. First we stood in a row outside in silence. At the sound of the teacher's whistle, we entered and were asked to sit on the cold concrete floor in a lotus position, keeping our hands on our knees. The reading began, usually some famous Russian communist writer describing how the brave comrades built the great dam on the Volga, or how the courageous comrades were fighting at the front for the Battle of Stalingrad. The lecture would be followed by classical music, mostly by Russian composers, but also by Bach and other classical musicians. I enjoyed the musical part, and gazed around the room in a semi dream, floating in my space, in my own dimension, living the full pleasure of not being interfered with by the adults, who seemed to spend a lot of their time taking us out of our dreams. Precisely at nine o'clock the bell rang to tell us to form two neat rows, first the little ones like me, followed by the bigger ones, like my sister, and we walked to the classrooms.

CHAPTER 2

On that first day I felt happy and positive, looking forward to sitting next to a boy companion and ready to take part. I never saw such small chairs and tables, which were facing south towards the blackboard on the wall between two windows. I stood by the entrance, waiting to be shown where to go. The children seemed to know where to sit and were quick to find their usual places, but slowly I became self-conscious standing there, while all the others were now sitting comfortably. The lady teacher was tall and plump. I noticed right away her big hips and, further up, an impressive bosom that wobbled from side to side as she walked. I soon found out that her powerful stature, as well as her quick-tempered snappy character, was quite the opposite of my mother's gentle way. Nelly's dark hair with large curls fell on her wide round shoulders, her tortoiseshell glasses kept slipping forward down her nose as she talked or shouted and then were instantly pushed back into place by a sudden flick of her right index finger. Nelly looked at me and pointing that same finger to the small table by the entrance and waved it up and down to show I should sit there. It was such a relief to be at the back where none of the other children could stare at me. I felt quite protected there. The positive, well-intentioned boy that I was felt quite ready to like her; my feelings were very open, ready to absorb all the wonderful things she was to teach me. I gave her a big smile. I took out of my school bag a pencil, a rubber and a brand new notebook covered in horizontal and vertical lines, creating squares that were asking to be coloured in to create patterns, as I had done so many times at home. Suddenly I heard Nelly's voice telling me to write my name on the top right corner of the new notebook. This was my dreaded moment, as I did not know what to do. I had never written anything before, and a pencil in my hand meant drawing not writing. So I started to scribble as if I were writing where she had asked. I managed to go through that first day studiously mimicking writing without being noticed. The teacher was busy on the opposite side of the room, facing her blackboard, shaking her body with the movement of her hand writing with the chalk, leaving behind a trail of white words that I could not read. The day seemed interminable and I felt such a relief when I heard the bell announcing that it was time to leave. Nelly asked us to leave our notebooks on the corner of her desk.

I was so glad to find my sister's hand in the hallway and then to walk home with her. Maman was in the kitchen preparing supper and greeted us with a large smile, so pleased that we finally arrived home. She asked us how it had been: Sylvette could already read and write so she was able to follow what the teacher said. She liked her teacher, she did interesting things, found a friend and generally her day had been positive, except for her lunch that she did not like. I agreed with her about the lunch and took the opportunity to change the subject of the classroom, describing in details what we ate. How I sat right next to a teacher serving from the middle of the long refectory table, how the fish smelt of ammonia and how I gave it discreetly to the cat waiting under my chair. I liked being a comic and felt good when people laughed, so I enjoyed selecting the funny parts of the day, amplifying them with mimicking sounds, body posture, face grimacing and specially imitating accents and voices. The more laughter there was, the longer the story went; my sister and mother enjoyed and appreciated my amusing reports and I found it a good way to divert attention away from the darker realities of my life.

Straight after supper I went to bed exhausted. This day was the first time I had not been allowed to choose what to do next in my small six years of existence; the first time I mixed with so many children; the first time I ate food not prepared by our Maman. Every night she came to our bed to kiss us and I know on that night I asked for more kisses than usual before she left the room. I felt deeply confused and disturbed and it took me a long time to find sleep.

After that first day at school, Nelly realised I could not read nor write. She decided to move me to her table, next to the blackboard with the whole classroom behind me... I could not hide my incompetence any more. I felt as if I was on stage with my back to the audience. I faced the wall with a radiator and a bookshelf above it, acutely aware that I was being looked at, and giggled at especially because of my large ears. I was teased about them because they were big and stuck out on either side of my head. When I became embarrassed, they would go bright red and I felt as if my heart was thumping inside them! Fortunately, from my seat I could look to the left and see the front-yard with the prickly row of pyracantha bushes, with their small red/orange berries that I loved eating, beyond was a silver birch by the swimming pool...

Once Nelly organised the children with something to do, to free her time, she sat close to me and proceeded to teach me to read from a book named Toto and Lilli. Each page had a picture drawn in black with orange and white colouring. Nelly's index finger, which I spent much time studying, always pointed at the word with great fervour, sometimes pressing her nail into the paper to underline a word and, as I stumbled trying to find the corresponding sounds, I felt her body heat rise up until she'd burst out calling me a 'stupid boy.' Behind me I felt all the children watching, and the more upset she became, the less I could see the words because tears flooded my eyes.

Pushed by her impatience, she grabbed my left ear and twisted it forward, stopping only when the word came out correctly, and twisting it further when the word was wrong. She would never twist it back to relieve me a little from the pain. Finally, I read from the corner of my eye, for I turned my head sideways in the direction of the twist to find relief. These were moments of public torture and humiliation. Nelly didn't know about the existence of dyslexia, and simply believed that her brutal methods were the only way to teach me to read, but in truth it had the absolutely opposite effect. Did she find in me something irresistible to touch, as she obviously seemed to take a delight at it? She often came too close to me when explaining something specific, so I felt one of her big breasts rubbing or pressing against my ear or shoulder. During the freezing cold winters months, when I entered the warm classroom, her sadistic act of welcome was to place her large hands on my purple and hypersensitive ears and rub them energetically backward and forward at high speed until the pain forced me to fall down on my knees to escape the torture.

It took me a long time to accept the school; there were too many incidents when I was humiliated and misunderstood. I was so terribly teased about my prominent ears, that before I went to bed my mother tried patiently to keep my ears back, first by using sticky tape to force them against my occipital bone. Then later by putting a ladies' hairnet tightly over my ears, just like the ones women wear when coming out of the hairdresser. But all our efforts were to no avail, for every morning when the oppressing gadgets were removed, my ears sprang back to their original position as if to say, "Hello, good morning!" After some weeks Maman abandoned the task and said softly with conviction, "You know, I actually like you much better as you are, it enhances your character, and do you know that in India it is recognized as a sign of wisdom?"

There was no father figure in the school I could associated with, talk to, or be recognized by. The teachers and the cleaners at the school were all women, with the exception of a hot-tempered, wirily Alsatian man who was the cook. His head was too large, his sunken piercing eyes were pale blue and he waved about his long sharp knives to frighten the children. I was a slow eater and was often left crying at the end of the long dining-room table because I hadn't finished my plate. Therefore I missed my sweet as a further punishment, and this was painful, especially when the pudding was cherries or peaches.

Gradually I learned all the ways and tricks to protect myself. I learned to disconnect from the turbulent outside world of school, to harden myself outwardly and not to show my feelings to adults or children.

During the first few weeks of school, trying to go to sleep at night, I found it difficult to reach the space of wellbeing, which had been so accessible to me before. I re-lived the difficult parts of each day; I went into a dark place in myself, feeling as if I was disappearing into a black hole, tossing and turning many times, sucking frantically on my fingers trying to find comfort so I could just let go. Finally, I found refuge when I projected myself back in time, walking barefoot towards the Cigale, feeling peaceful and light and finding my Papa standing by his yellow lorry with a big smile, waiting for me. Lifting me in his arms, with mine round his neck, my body right next to his, my nostrils, picking up his scent mixed with the fragrance of the rosemary bushes under the hot sun… invariably these comforting emotions led me to sleep.

I started to miss Papa very much. He had not been with us for a long time now and I wondered: was it because of the war that we had no news from him? Where was he? Why didn't he contact us? When we asked our mother she shrugged her shoulders and in an uncertain voice said, "I don't know, maybe he is not able to." It must have been difficult for her without the man she loved. Not only emotionally but also financially and physically, as there were many heavy tasks to do to keep our little family going. I never heard her complain about anything, not even the lack of money or food. She went on positively doing what she could to ensure our survival. Strangely enough when there was so little money around, she started smoking seriously. In wartime there were coupons for basic foods and cigarettes and without these precious coupons one could not get flour, sugar, bread or tobacco.

Sometime in the early winter of 1943, our mother called us around her – she was holding a blue piece of paper. It was called a 'télégramme' and on it was stuck strips of white paper with black typewriting. I felt it was not good news because our Mum looked drained by some indescribable pain. She slowly read aloud, "Marcel Lassalle has died, accidentally electrocuted in Germany while he was repairing a high-tension line."

At that moment I didn't understand what the telegram was really saying, but my sister instantly burst into tears and exclaimed, "I will not see Papa any more!" Maman was trying to console her, hugging her against her chest. I walked off in a complete blank, not feeling, not imagining, not thinking, and walked silently in the direction of the river to listen to the soothing sounds of its waterfall.

Maman found me there sometime later and put her arm gently around my shoulders and brought me back to the house. Sylvette was still distressed, her face puffed by tears. I stood there feeling serious and not wanting to upset her more by doing something that might be out of place. I had not seen my sister cry like this before. The death of our father started to really disturb me when at school one day, a boy told me proudly that his father was a pilot, and next holiday they would go to the seaside together. When he asked me about my father, I fell silent. I did not know what to say, my throat seized up and I could not remove the lump in it. He then repeated his question with more intensity and I managed to whisper, "My Papa is dead." I became aware of how often my classmates referred to their dads, boasting about what they did with them, where they had been and so on. Each time a boy talked about his father's exploits, I would feel pain inside. As they talked, I felt as if I had lost a part of myself, as if my masculine identity had somehow vanished.

In those days boys never boasted about their mother's exploits, except sometimes about their cooking; it was the father figure they needed to proudly display. Irritation and anger sprouted in my feelings. Some of the boys noticed my weak points and enjoyed pressing on them, teasing me about the fact that I had no father. I became easily upset and hot-tempered and reacted by asking them to stop teasing me, but this request only stoked the fire even more. I invariably ended up chasing them and when I caught one of them and got him to the ground, I asked him to stop teasing and started hitting him violently with my fists. I hated seeing myself do this, for anger tasted nasty in my mouth, but lashing out seemed to relieve something in me. This fighting became my pressure valve release, that the unfortunate teaser endured. The more resistance, the longer the fight would be. I then got up, my legs and body shaking all over, feeling hot and embarrassed by my reaction and walked off... feeling very alone. When I was out of sight, I looked for damage to my clothes and for bruises on my hands and face. The age or size of my opponent never seemed to matter. I just went for the one who I felt was unjust to me by intentionally pressing that hypersensitive spot in my disturbed feelings.

We had not been so long at the school when one day after the assembly, for some unknown reason, we were asked to stay in the large room. Maybe it was a cloudburst that kept us in. The children gathered together in small groups of friends and I was chatting with my mates when I saw from the corner of my eye the tall, Egyptian boy harassing my sister. He was at least two years older than her; she was protesting and didn't seem to enjoy his approaches. So I rushed up and put myself between them, asked him to stop and firmly pushed him away. That didn't work, for he brushed me aside and carried on with his macho nagging. A long handled broom was resting against the wall and I grabbed it with my right hand and positioned it as if I was holding a javelin. With the brush end behind me and in a menacing voice I ordered, "Leave my sister alone!" Sylvette moved aside and frowned at me with disapproval, while he laughed arrogantly. In the split second that followed, the broom flew across the room at high speed and the round end of the handle crushed straight into the bully's open mouth. The laughing stopped and there was a long silence while his hand searched for the damage. His upper lip was bleeding and already swelling; he pulled out a small white triangular piece of tooth. My accurate shot hit his large right incisor. He started crying when he realised the corner of his front tooth was gone. Then he shouted with fury, "My father is King Farouk's brother - he will come in his helicopter to take you away and put you in prison for that!" I didn't know who King Farouk was at the time and I didn't believe what he was saying. I walked away feeling heavy and guilty about having broken his front tooth. Sylvette asked me as we walked home why I did this to the Egyptian. "I don't like it when the boys annoy you, and I will always protect you!" She then told me that the teasing was not so bad after all, and I should not have thrown the broom.

An unexpected addition to the family

One sun-shining Saturday morning in the spring of 1943, our mother took each one of us by the hand and said positively, "Come on, we're going to look for a man!"

"But who Maman... and where?" Sylvette asked surprised. "I don't know really... we're going to the pottery studio, you know, the one near la Croix?" Mum did not usually take us for walks. When we went out with her it was for shopping or another specific purpose.

When we arrive at the studio, we searched for the entrance and finally found one under an old tiled and beamed canopy. Two wide, wooden doors welcomed us and led us into a large, dark workshop. We stood there for some time at the entrance, getting accustomed to the darkness. I was struck by the smells of wet clay and rotting, damp hemp sacking. I finally distinguished the dusty, uneven, earthen floor leading to a spider-webbed window, from which a ray of sunlight lit the corner of the room. My attention was suddenly directed to a pair of powerful legs covered in ginger hairs glittering in the beam of light, with their feet tucked into a ragged pair of espadrilles. Maman, still holding firmly onto our hands, went straight towards the ginger legs and stopped a metre away. Slowly I looked up to discover a pair of clay-covered shorts held up by their tightness. A grey, sleeveless vest was roughly tucked into them and a profusion of orange bushy hairs stuck out of the low neckline. Hairs also covered two muscular arms rhythmically shaking the short-fingered hands holding a sponge over an oval mould. It was set on a tall tripod turntable where the mysterious man stood. His unshaven face turned towards our mother, his smiling mouth opened slightly revealing two chromed teeth. His laughing pale blue eyes looked inquisitively into my mother's as she said gently, "Could you possibly help us?" He looked up and down at her and said simply, "Yes, sure."

It was the first time I was in a pottery studio and my child's inquisitiveness was already looking at all the fascinating tools and objects in this large workshop. Mother was still talking with the man, but I wasn't hearing their conversation. I investigated the place, disconnected from her hand and their reality. In the evening of that same day he arrived at les Tilleuls, riding an old discoloured bicycle.

It was our routine on Sunday mornings to creep into our mother's bed and snuggle against her before we went down for breakfast. When we got into her double bed the next day, we instantly noticed the powerful smell of a man and Sylvette said, "Where is Papa then?" Both of us rejoiced at the thought of having him back into our lives, but she answered with a faint smile on her face, "No, my darlings, you know that he will not return, so why do you ask that question?" My sister in a puzzled, fuzzy voice answered, "Because we can smell him in the bed!" During breakfast, she told us his name was Alphonse, but he preferred to be called Fonsou. He worked at the pottery studio where we had seen him, and he offered to help us financially as much as he could. She added that we would see him more often now, and he might come and live with us. There was a long silence then she added, "Don't worry, my darlings, all will be fine, you'll see."

And so it was that Fonsou came into our lives. We saw him more and more often until one day he stayed with us permanently. A few months later we learned that he was the father of five children, and his family lived in a dark ground floor flat in old Dieulefit. From that time on the atmosphere in our small home changed completely. Fonsou was in the Maquis, the anti-fascist underground movement active in our part of the world. At night our small sitting/dining room became a meeting place for eight to twelve maquisards, who came in as if they were in their own homes, hung up their machine guns, bullet belts and other warlike things on our coat hooks and sat down for a basic meal that our Maman had prepared, which consisted of a vegetable soup, bread, walnuts, goat cheese and fruit or chestnuts when in season. Yes, Maman became part of the maquis as she repaired and washed their dirty clothes, and sewed on armbands with the blue, white and red Croix de Lorraine, symbolizing free France. She cooked, laid the table, served, cleared and washed up. We never saw Fonsou nor any of the Maquisards ever help her in the kitchen.

At times they brought food with them and would talk outside if it wasn't too cold, and came in when Maman called them for the meals. They all called her Honor and she certainly became popular. She was always helping wherever she could, sometimes writing letters for them in her impeccable French. She was asked to translate war messages written in English, because the maquis was in contact with Churchill's war organisation. After their lively meals, they pushed their chairs back, lit cigarettes and often one of them took me on his knees, hugging me tightly. I remember not quite knowing how much I should let go in those embraces. They told jokes but I could not quite grasp them; some sounded rather rude. And, in the smoky atmosphere, they laughed loudly and asked Fonsou to sing. He let himself be asked many times before he timidly stood up and, looking into the distance with his upper lip quivering slightly, his emotions filled his big chest and he started singing. Sometime, his eyes filled with tears, and, as the moving words burst forth his nostrils swelled. Many of the songs are still with me now. His voice was soft, rounded, clear and in tune, similar to the famous Corsican singer 'Tino Rossi'. He certainly was very appreciated around our table. The songs that moved him most were 'Petit Papa Noël' and one called 'Maman'. Fonsou adored his mother who had 11 children and brought them up all by herself. He was a fan of Edith Piaf and sang many of her songs. When my eyes became heavy and I was numbed by all these impressions, my mother lifted me from some Maquisard's lap and took me to bed. It felt as if I left the unconscious weight of my body on the man's knees, as there was no more gravity in my world.

From time to time people stayed for the night. I remember once an attractive lady in her 20s called Maude arrived at our home without a bag or suitcase. Our mother explained that she was going through a very difficult time and she needed to rest. I liked her - she was pretty with large blue grey eyes and long, brown curly hair, and she smiled gently as she looked at me with affection. Mother said to us lowering her voice, "Maude picked up an illness called scabies; it's like a little worm that nestles under the surface of the skin. I will have to scrub her with a scrubbing brush and Savon de Marseille (a traditional Provencal soap made with olive oil & potassium) in the bath-tub." Maman looked at me as if begging for compassion, her voice hardly audible, "I hope you won't mind if she sleeps in your bed for tonight. There is nowhere else for her to rest and she is so, so tired."

I usually slept on my side in a foetal position. I felt warmer that way especially when Maman gave me a glass hot water bottle (which was a corked wine bottle), which I tucked between my folded legs. That night, cuddling my hot bottle, I fell asleep quickly.

Feeling for my warm bottle for reassurance during the night, instead my hand found a warm, silky round shape. To separate dream from reality, my intrigued hand delicately and slowly followed the extended form and suddenly came to a slow downward curve. My hand paused for a moment while the information was transmitted to my sleepy brain, and I considered its origin. "Feels like a hip," I thought. When I realised this was Maude's warm body, my hand furtively drew back to its original position against my chest. My folded knee was tightly imprisoned between the silky legs. It was a strange feeling and I didn't know what to do. I felt very warm and cosy and did not want to disturb this pleasant but unusual situation. As my senses began to wake up, my nose discovered new comforting scents – a mixture of Marseille soap with the smell of rose-honeyed sweat. I was now fully conscious and felt on my forehead and cheek, as if coming from a regular motion of waves on the beach, soft swells of warm damp air caressing my face. Maude had indeed come into my bed. I was actually her hot water bottle. Maude completely encircled me, and held me against her body as if I was her teddy bear. I held my breath so as not to disturb this new experience and let my awareness absorb it quietly. Instinctively I knew that being in her arms had a kind of reassuring and healing effect on Maude. Although I felt like scratching my back, I resisted and waited for sleep to take me away. When I woke up, the next morning, I was alone in my bed. Maude, re-nourished by sleep, was gone on her perilous journeys and I never saw her again. The experience of her short visit is still deeply stored in my feelings. Later Mother told us that Maude was working as a liaison messenger for the Maquisards and that the SS eventually arrested her, we never saw her again.

There was always something new happening, especially at weekends and at night.

On several occasions Fonsou or some of his friends arrived at Les Marefours in a stolen German car, always with their headlights and taillights intentionally smashed so as not to become an easy target in the dark. If they were caught the punishment was severe: immediate death! The SS used to carry out reprisals by taking innocent citizens of any age and sex and shooting them in the village square.

A friend of mine called Claudibus was in his early teens when he lived a war drama. He was the son of a poor Provençale family who lived in the small town of Valréas, and the school took him on to work in the kitchens with the Alsatian cook, which paid for his lodging and education. He was an extremely shy boy. His fair hair was brushed aside just above his eyes, almost meeting his dark eyebrows, protecting his fragile, sunken, pale blue eyes. I felt compassion for him; we would go for walks and sometimes I invited him home for a Sunday meal. One day there was a big change in his behaviour when I greeted him. His eyes did not look at me as they used to but escaped furtively to the ground. His mouth was tight as if he had no lips and no words came. He did manage to give me a tortuous suffering smile, then turned away. I was intrigued by this sudden change in my friend, and, when I got back home, I mentioned it to my mother. She heard from her maquis connections that two days before, on the village square of Valréas, 36 people were shot in reprisals for the 'murder' of a German soldier. Most hostages were children, women and old people and Claudibus' whole family had suddenly vanished.

A few days later I learned that my friend's older brother, who was 16, was also part of the group of hostages. He acted as if he was dead by falling when the firing squad fired. He was dragged with the other bodies into a heap, thrown into an open lorry and taken to a large pit outside the town. It was May with a nearly full moon lighting the sky, and waiting till the early hours of the morning, he escaped from the macabre pile. Unnoticed and covered in blood, he struggled out of the pit and walked 25 km into the mountains to Dieulefit where he found his younger brother Claudibus. My feeling of care for him grew enormously but nothing was ever mentioned between us about the drama. His brother did not stay at the school but was taken to a distant uncle. Claudibus started to isolate himself from the other children and began to eat too much, gaining much weight.

Once a term there was a ritual at Beauvallon called the 'health check-up'. For this ritual the girls were separated from the boys. We were taken into the washrooms, asked to take off all of our clothes and stand in a line, with the youngest in the front. Next to the entrance was a small table with a notebook of columns listing our names. Tante Marguerite sat on a stool like a man, with her legs wide apart. Simone called our names, and one at a time we were measured and weighed on a fascinating, old-fashioned scale. It had a big brass cylinder that slid up and down on a square rod engraved with elaborate numbers. When we stepped up onto the platform it wobbled a little, and the rod rose or fell at one end. Simone grabbed the cylinder and slid it up or down until the long metal rod found its level. Then she twiddled a flat gadget underneath to secure it. After these manipulations, she shouted the height and weight of each person to the attentive headmistress, who wrote them down in the notebook. Then Tante Marguerite solemnly grabbed us firmly by the arm and brought us to a standstill facing her, by locking us into position with her enormous legs to dissuade escape. I could not help glancing at the powerful legs dressed in woolly pink-brown long johns that got lost somewhere under the darkness her grey tweed skirt. She proceeded to feel us with her freezing fingers, starting up under our ears and jaws, to our armpits and further down to our groins. My body went tense as she proceeded, apprehending what was coming. Then with extreme concentration, frowning a little and turning her head slightly to one side, her eyes closed and her cold fingers came up suddenly to inspect our little bag. She held it in between her right thumb and fingers as if looking for something that the purse was hiding, even pushing up a little if she could not find what she was looking for. She would then say loudly and write in her notebook, "none down", or "left one down", or "right one down" and sometimes, with a kind of relief in her voice, "both down!" These sessions took the whole morning and I remember the peculiar unpleasant odour when we were all naked together. While waiting for our turn, we silently examined each other's different body shapes and parts. Some boys found it very difficult to be completely naked and used to keep their hands firmly in the front of their private parts. Claudibus, after the loss of his family, found these moments horribly difficult, because, not only he had become very fat, but also his penis had shrunk to a tiny thing that could hardly be seen. It just peeped out of the dimple created by its fat surroundings. Of course, there was always a team of cruel boys who teased him about it, increasing his embarrassment.

Trying to adapt

Beauvallon School was built on the southern sandy slope of the Montmirail Mountain with a courtyard along the lower front of the main building. Arches led to different storerooms: coal store, boiler room, washroom and a place where mattresses were cleaned and repaired. It contained a fascinating machine to sit on, similar to a saddle, where one held a handle connected to a curved plank with sharp nails on the underside. The plank rocked to and fro to lighten up and untangle the compressed horsehair and wool in old mattresses, creating a cloud of dust.

All the classrooms and the dining room on the first floor gave onto a long terrace. Every day from one to two o'clock after lunch, without exception, whether freezing or very hot, windy or not, we were given one military blanket and had to lie down on our backs or on our tummies. Lying on our sides was strictly forbidden. The hour session was called 'La Cure', literally, the Cure. With my overactive nature, at first I found it very difficult staying still for an hour – it seemed impossible. The prefects supervised us by sitting in the middle of the terrace under the porch at the entrance of the geography and history classroom. It was so tempting to lie on one side or the other so as to chat with whoever was there but such an act was fiercely reprimanded. Sleeping was not allowed either, and while reading was, I was not yet capable of taking its refuge. So the only thing to do was to go into my inner, daydream world. I soon discovered that at this time I was not hassled by adults. I allowed myself to float back to the island that I loved so much: to be by the sea, fishing on the rocks under the hot sun, feeling the waves gently teasing my feet, in Rioufrède sucking the salty pebbles or being with my father in his yellow lorry. These moments would graciously allow me to smell, to hear, to feel as if I was there.

I liked it when the mistral wind blew, lying on my back looking up into the sky and getting lost in its deep blue immensity. Sometimes when I went too far into it I felt vertigo, as if I could fall into its vastness and lose the gravity holding me to the earth. Or let myself be distracted by the sudden arrival of bright white clouds rushing at high speed high above the roofline of the school, giving me the impression that we were moving on a very fast train. It got to a point where the whole terrace seemed to spin; to stabilize myself I quickly just looked at the wall and all came to a standstill again.

When it was warmer I searched for an eagle or buzzard high up in the sky, or for the pale grey lizard that came down the wall upside down to take a closer look at me. When lying on my tummy, I studied the opposing traffic of the intertwining trails of small ants. They were only preoccupied with themselves, carrying the goods they found to a crack at the junction of the coloured tiles and the vertical school wall. Once they had deposited their loads, they frantically rushed the other way on the lookout for something interesting to take back to their hidden cities. At two o'clock precisely, the strident sound of the prefect's chrome whistle always made me jump out of my skin forcing me back into the hard realities of school.

Dangerous games, frustrations bring out violence

One and a half kilometres south of Beauvallon School was a magic space called 'La Sablière' where we loved to play. It was a large 50-60 metres high hard sand hill, shaped like a horseshoe; its top covered by heather and wind-blown pine trees; the south side was very wide and gradually descended to the chestnut forest below. The other side rapidly became narrower until its ridge was no wider than a foot. At the top-end of this perilous ridge, nature had carved a huge oval hole that we called the oxen's eye. Two of us could sit inside it and comfortably admire the view all the way to the school and the mountains beyond. A few of the daring lads tested their skills and bravery walking down along the narrow crest, with arms stretched out to keep in balance, teasing the precipice. It was thrilling, fun and generated much adrenalin. When it became too narrow to secure one's footing, we carefully turned around towards the inside of the Crescent and bending our knees until our bums touched our heels, we jumped down two or three metres out of danger onto a high pile of fine sand.

I was agile and enjoyed explaining my techniques to the others, especially how to tackle a point of no return on the steep slope, and where we had to run non-stop to get to a point where it was safe to stop. If we hesitated and stopped running, we would invariably start sliding down faster and faster and finally fall into the precipice. One day we convinced a hesitant shy boy, Uri Goldenberg, to follow the daredevil's track of the narrow ridge. We egged him on, "Come on! Don't be frightened, just run… but don't stop till you get to the flat spot!"

Plucking up his courage he stood up on his trembling legs and shot off without looking where he was actually going. He took his run a little too low, became frightened and did the fatal thing: he crouched down on his feet trying desperately to find something to hold onto. Uri was now irrevocably sliding down toward the precipice and was shaking all over with fear. A sharp stone protruding out of the hard sand temporarily stopped his slide.

Holding onto a branch of heather, I stretched out my hand as far as possible to help him but, imperceptibly at first, he started to skid again. He was now screaming as we saw him pick up speed and disappear into the abyss; we heard the thump of his body hit the ground and then complete silence. We hurried down the dangerous crest, jumped onto the fine sand, ran through the Acacia forest as fast as we could, along the little stream along the north side of the Sablière, up the slope to the top where our companion was crying softly, holding his broken left arm. We were so relieved that he was alive and hadn't landed on a rock!

On another occasion it was my turn to experience a difficult situation. We were having great fun on the top of the sand mountain playing gendarmes and robbers. Dividing ourselves into two camps, I always made sure that I was one of the robbers. I liked being the first to find a hiding place, carefully choosing a spot from where I would see the gendarmes without being seen. Lying flat in the tall heather was a good hiding place, and I delighted in touching its softness; while I waited, the sun warmed my back and I listened to the wind. I enjoyed these moments so much that I wanted to stay like this forever. Once, I had not been found and returned to the camp, taking care not to be seen to free the prisoners. But my companions were already putting on their shoes. I felt annoyed that they had not bothered to let me know they had stopped playing, and were getting ready to go back to Beauvallon. We usually kept our shoes tucked away under a low pine tree, but this time I could not find mine. I asked Petit-Jacques, one of the Parisian twins, where my shoes were and my question amused him. Then looking at his brother Gaby, who could not keep a straight face, I realised that the twins were responsible for their disappearance. "Please, Gaby, where are my socks and shoes?" I was trying to keep a cool voice. He shrugged his shoulders and turning to Petit-Jacques. I asked with some irritation, "Where have you put them?" He giggled and said, "Don't ask me!" He now appeared gravely serious. The other children were grouped together ready to go back, anticipating what was going to happen next, as they all knew my explosive character. They were aware that the Parisian twins were my friends and were good at fighting, especially as they always stuck together. The tensions built up; now there were no more smiles.

"P'tit-Jacques! Where are they?" With a sharp tremor in my voice, I turned to Gaby repeating the question, this time louder. I did not want to fight the twins. "Where did you guys hide them? Give them back to me!"

Very slowly Petit-Jacques bent down and pulled one of my socks and a shoe from under a heather bush. He stretched his arm as if offering me a flower and, just as I was about to take it, he suddenly threw it to his brother Gaby, but it fell on the sand. I went to pick it up, but Gaby got there first and threw it back it his brother. I understood that due to my quick temper, I was being made fun of by the others and I felt trapped and desperate. For an instant a quiet feeling descended and a space opened within me from where I understood what was happening. But already my ego had developed into a proud cockerel and, giving me no time for reflection, it took over the situation.

Petit-Jacques was now standing in front of me with the shoe and could not resist throwing it to the others who formed a circle around us. I suddenly saw red and flew at him head down; we fought on the sand, rolling one way, rolling the other. He was quick and difficult to hold and finally he sat on the top of me pinning me down. His pale grey eyes were cold, his nose and cheeks were white with sand dust and his breathing fast. I was now working out a way to get out of his grip, and took him by surprise when I suddenly threw my long legs up from behind, caught his neck in a scissors hold and twisted myself round until he was on the ground jammed between my knees and my thighs. He was wriggling furiously, trying to free his neck from my grip, but I held on tight. I was thinking whether it was time yet to let him go. Unexpectedly, Gaby came from behind and jumped onto me to save his brother. The spectators cheered, sand was flying, some went in my eyes prickling them terribly, fists were flying in all directions some landed on my ear and cheek-bone, others on my mouth and I wondered how it would all finish? I was finally immobilised with both boys on the top of my arms and chest, all of us breathing as if we had run a marathon, covered in dust, blood and sweat. One of the younger spectators said anxiously, "Come on, let's get back to the school, it's getting late!"

Hesitation, then stillness came, the grips lightened, the breathing became softer, and the twins slowly rose. Feeling sore and bruised, I rose up and tucked my unbuttoned shirt into my shorts, found my missing shoes and socks from under the heather, sat down and proceeded to clean the sand off my feet and toes. When I had finished I looked around and saw they had all left. Tired, I quickly inspected one by one, the bruises on my head and body. My knee had been badly scraped in the fight and the blood had coagulated with the sand forming a painful dark crust. The sun was close to disappearing behind the mountains and the air cooled as I briskly walked home.

It was dark by the time I arrived home, and as I descended the steps into the dining room, my mother joyfully announced. "He is here, at last he is here!" I came into her arms and she hugged me for a long time, then pushing me gently away, holding my shoulders with both hands, she looked me up and down and exclaimed, "Darling, where on earth have you been? What's happened to you?" Taking my hand she led me into the warm kitchen, and I smelled the delicious supper keeping warm on the stove. Sylvette was doing her homework sitting erect at the end of the table. I briefly told them that we had been playing nicely at the Sablière, gendarmes and robbers, and that the Parisian twins had hidden my shoes, teased me and I got very angry and that it ended in a big fight. Sylvette could not resist saying, "You're stupid. You always get into fights!"

There was nothing to say; my sister always spoke her mind. Maman put hot water into a blue enamelled dish; my pyjamas were already nicely hanging off the stove. She took a dark bottle from the medicine shelf and poured a few drops of the brown liquid into the steaming water. "What's that Maman?" "It's called calendula mother tincture, it will sting a little, but disinfect and help your knee to heal quickly." Holding my leg across her knee, she took a wad of cotton wool, dipped it in the warm solution and with the other hand held the dish under my damaged knee and washed it gently, carefully removing all the dry blood and sand. Her movements were gentle and caring, nursing was in her nature and I always enjoyed watching her while she attended to my sores. She asked me to take off my sand covered clothes, while she refilled the dish with the hot water from the singing kettle that lived permanently on the wood stove. Feeling the water with her elbow to make sure that it wasn't too hot, she asked me to hop in. The warm water was delicious on my feet that were still sore from the fight, and she washed my whole body lightly using a square lump of Marseille soap.

I liked these moments, standing in the warm water being washed by Maman, facing the cast-iron wood stove, with its door open so that I could see the flames, but without losing contact with the sensuous awareness of her delicate soapy hand cleaning my bruised body. Then using a dented, wooden handled aluminium saucepan, she poured the lukewarm water from my head down, accompanying it carefully with her left hand to make sure that the soap was rinsed from all the nooks and corners. My skinny body then began to shiver, and she wrapped me up in the warm towel, lifted me onto her knees and hugged me with one arm, while turning her attention to Sylvette and her homework.

Maman had learned about natural medicine and healthy diet from the Durville Brothers when she lived in Paris. When we complained of a sore throat, she made us open our mouths wide, while she scrutinised the inside. I would look at her face to see if I could detect from her expressions how infected my tonsils were. She told me whether they were just red, swollen on the right or the left, with white spots or whether they were grey or all white. Gargling was the answer to that, and before going to bed a wet handkerchief was applied around the neck, with a thick woolly scarf secured with a safety pin. The compress generally did the trick.

With good health, Sylvette was rarely ill and hated to miss a day of school. When I felt not well, she'd say I was just putting it on to stay at home. From her strong healthy point of view she could not possibly understand how it was for me. With my emotional nature, my liver made too much bile and my bubbling energy often harmed my delicate frame.

When not feeling well I came down to breakfast a bit later, but dressed, to show my good intention. Then through breakfast I clearly showed something wasn't right, by leaning over my plate and eating very slowly. Maman would then say in a soft convincing voice, "Sounet, stay at home. You're not well, go back to bed and I'll come and see you." That felt wonderful, I already felt much better and my spirit would lighten. Sylvette didn't like this at all, and she gave me a reproaching look before leaving for school.

While on my back in bed, I waited for my Maman-doctor. All my attention was now on listening… finally I felt reassured on hearing the sound of her feet sliding up the stone steps. Once by my bed, she sat on the edge and started to ask the round of questions. If tummy pains, she put her soft and slightly scratchy hand flat on it and rubbed slowly clockwise. That felt really good and when she massaged in large circles I usually fell asleep. If I had a headache or felt sick, she tucked her fingers under the right side of my rib cage and pressed up, looking at my face to see if there was any sign of pain. If so, she said, "Ah! It's your liver again. It is making too much bile, poor darling. Artichokes and boiled leek water will be your remedy." When we developed a high fever she felt our forehead then, "Turn round and show me your bum." She shook the glass thermometer violently to get the mercury right down, and shoved it delicately up our bum and left it there a few minutes, which seemed like hours. She pulled it out carefully and announced the temperature. If it was high she did what her father had taught her: a large towel dipped in hot water and wrung out and, while still steaming, wrapped round the body surface from under the ribcage down to the pubic bone. Then I was wrapped in a thick woollen blanket, tightly secured with a safety pin. She leaned over and kissed me tenderly on my forehead while I slid into a comfortable sleep. By the morning the fever was usually gone. At the end of the war when we moved to a house a little closer to the town, she discovered Dieulefit had a homoeopathic doctor she could trust. She took a real interest in this medicine, which at the time was considered revolutionary, and soon used it for the family on every occasion.

Fear and courage were states of being I experienced within myself almost everyday for the nine years that I went to Beauvallon School. Once we had crossed the wooden bridge and walked up the steep hill a few hundred metres, we came to a fork in the road. Turning left led to the courtyard of a large mansion belonging to Doctor Soubeyran. Turning right led to a long alley of apple trees ending in the farmyard. My throat started to go dry as we reached this feared fork, my heart thumped, and my knees trembled and I felt weak at the anticipation of seeing the creature. Nine times out of ten the aggressive beast was there on guard waiting for us. The beast was a dark Alsatian dog with vicious eyes and frothy white teeth. Once he spotted us, as if kicked up his backside by some invisible giant, he shot forward in our direction growling and looking like a black hairy ball with a menacing white grin. By that time Sylvette, who was usually ahead of me, was safely out of reach. The dog chose me as his prey leaving me no choice but to run after my sister down the apple alley as fast as my legs could take me. I knew that if I reached the seventh apple tree the raging animal would stop dead. It was the end of his territory and he sat down as if he won the battle and watched us getting further away from him. Unfortunately, I did not always have the time to reach freedom, and to avoid the bite I turned round and faced the aggressor, protecting myself with my leather satchel. This made him stop dead in his track, barking, frothing and showing me his sharp canines. Now closer, I picked up his strong dog scent of sweat and bad breath. To save myself from being mauled, I found that spinning fast like a mad top, holding out the satchel and at the same time slowly moving towards the seventh tree, was my only way to safety. While spinning like this my heavy satchel would hit his frothy black muzzle enraging him even further.

To avoid the monster, we sometimes turned left soon after the bridge and climbed up through a damp forest of oaks, chestnuts and poplars to the flat field at the back of the Soubeyran house. That way was longer and more tiring because of the steep climb, so we took it less often. The problem with this route was the geese. There were 12 of them, and, as soon as they saw us, they went into a V formation ready for battle, stretching out their wings and pulling their necks forward as far as they could. Opening and closing their ridged orange beaks, showing us their sharp violet-grey tongues, they made a screechy sound punctuated by hissing warnings. The dog was frightening - yes, but somehow easier to handle than the geese. It was their clever strategy that was so intimidating, with the dominant male aggressively in the front. The way to deal with them was for us to charge through the lines, speed and courage was the thing, then quickly turning around and walking backwards while slapping the cheeks of the furious goose. One side then the other at a fast rhythm until, like with the dog, the birds stopped their pursuit at a certain spot. We were out of their territory, feeling relieved.

One-day coming up to the Soubeyran corner we saw ahead of us the farm boy who was walking to work. We heard the dog's growl and saw it run towards him as wild as ever. Coolly, the Spaniard bent down to pick up a stone and took the action as if to throw it at the animal. The Alsatian stopped dead, turned round and with his tail between his legs doubled back home. This was a wonderful piece of education, and we now knew how to protect ourselves from this nasty beast.

Sylvette taught me how to ride a small lilac coloured bike that Fonsou put together for me. Riding a bicycle was like finding a new kind of freedom. I spent much of my time riding it when not at school. One day I decided to go school on the bike. The bike had no gears so after passing the bridge I had to push it up the hill. Using the stone trick, I managed to keep the dog off, and once at the fork, got back on the bike safely. But, in the evening on the way home from school, the nasty creature was waiting in hiding. As I passed the fork in the road, I heard to my horror that the dog was after me. I accelerated, but he was getting closer all the time, my legs could not possibly go faster and the white fangs finally caught up with me. He came up on my left, menacingly trying to catch my heel. We were now going down the steepest part of the hill where the poplar trees lined the road; my heart was pumping, my watery eyes blurred my view. I felt a hard knock on my calf and my whole bike was violently pulled to the left. I counteracted by leaning to the right still peddling crazily. But the dog was pulling on my trouser leg with all his weight to stop me. Finally I heard a tearing sound then a sudden sense of freedom. By some miracle, I managed to stay on my bike and did not look back, concentrating all my energy on getting home. With tears running along my cheeks into the hollow of my ears and my hands numbed with the cold, I turned my head to check that my satchel was still securely tied on the luggage rack. Trembling all over, I jumped off my bike, leaned it against the wall under the window of the house and looked at the damage. My brown woollen trousers were torn and the dog's teeth had just bruised and scratched the surface of my skin. Once in the warm kitchen, standing with my back to the fire, holding the long brass rail to warm my hands, I told my mother what had happened. She right away looked at the damage, reassured me that she could mend my trousers and attended to the back of my leg, cleaning it with the magic calendula lotion. I never went to school on my bicycle again.

The farmer le père Busac had a farm at the foot of the Montmirail, east of Beauvallon and sometimes we hitched a lift from the school farm to the sandbanks on his ox cart. It was periwinkle blue with large wooden wheels encircled with iron that were much taller than me. The cart had three sides around a worn out plank floor. The old man lived by himself on his partly ruined farm. His sad-looking face carried a droopy pepper-coloured moustache that completely hid his mouth; his brown corduroy trousers were too long for him. When we asked him for a lift he pushed back his cap revealing a sweaty white forehead, wiped it with a dirty handkerchief and, without stopping the slow oxen said, "In you get!"

I found it amusing that his moustache lifted when he smiled to reveal a mouth full of gold teeth. Thrilled by the ride, we would hop on and sit at the back.

It was a sunny autumn day on the way back from school, when we climbed onto the cart, Sylvette sitting at the back with her leg dangling. Holding on with one hand I enjoyed letting my body sway with the rhythm of the two oxen. After sometime we heard, "Oh! Oh!" And the oxen cart stopped dead. Le père Busac rested his long hazelnut staff against the cart, ran to the edge of the forest, turned his back to us and pushing his greasy cap back on his head proceeded to pee. We were in the middle of the chestnut forest. The leaves were turning from pale green to yellow and the air dense with the smell of the oxen mixed with the musky smell of rotting leaves and spiny hulls on the ground. I was happy to see the school far away. Suddenly, a powerful jerk made the whole cart tremble and without any warning, the oxen shot forward at great speed, probably bitten by some insect. I stood up bending my knees to counter-balance the bumps, gripping on to the sides with both hands, and looked ahead with my hair waving in the wind. I was enjoying this thrilling moment feeling like a Roman centurion going into battle… when I heard a long agonizing yell. I turned round to see that my sister was no longer in the cart but standing by the side of the road crying. Le père Busac picked up his long hazelnut staff and was running behind the cart, angrily calling for them to stop in oxen language. I could hear them now breathing heavily, getting tired from their sprint and they finally slowed down to a stop. I jumped off the cart and ran up the path, crossing le Père Busac going the other way, and found my sister complaining that her bottom hurt. I asked her to show me and she lifted her skirt, pulling her pants down just enough to show me where the pain was. Effectively, her bum was blue with bruises and covered with hundreds of chestnut prickles. I pulled out the thorns I could, but it was difficult, because I used to bite my nails and couldn't hold the end of the tiny prickles. She became impatient with my hesitant attention, pulled down her skirt and started to walk home fast. I felt inadequate. I loved my sister so much I wanted to help her, and I knew how painful these prickles were, having walked on them barefooted several times. Isolated by her pain, Sylvette was shooting along to get home. I was running behind trying to keep up with her pace, wishing I could show her how much I too suffered from the situation, wanting to show her my compassion. But nothing doing: the accident had separated us. I realised that our worlds were now far apart and that I could do nothing about it. When we got home, Maman acted right away to relieve Sylvette from her agony, by removing the prickles one by one. I stood there in admiration until all the visible prickles were removed, then Maman took a big cotton wad dipped in an arnica solution with warm water and applied it to the bruised cheeks. After this experience, my sister refused to go on the ox cart again.

War was raging on in France. The occupying enemy decided to shell the area with a cannon from 20km away. We first heard a boom, followed by the shell making a whistling sound as it flew through the air, and then a deafening explosion when it hit the ground, provoking clouds of dust and fire. In the long silence that followed, everyone wondered where it fell. Fortunately it never fell on anyone's property and no one was ever hurt. Once one of the shells whistled over our house and landed beyond the road. After this explosion I rushed excitedly up the stairs to the small toilet and standing on the wooden seat, looked through the little window in the direction of the dust cloud. My blood froze on hearing a high-pitched scream. Then again more razor-sharp sounds, echoing down the corridors of Maison Marefours. I rushed down to the kitchen, "What was that screaming Maman?"

She explained that it was Florence, André Malraux's daughter, who had been chased by the Nazis, caught and put into camps where she suffered greatly. Hearing the bombshells woke up in her the pains she had endured. This pulled me out of my own self, and brought to my awareness that something pretty big and horrible was happening outside our privileged valley. I became more and more conscious of what was going on; our side was fighting the other side, with many people dying and suffering.

We children waged our own wars with the village boys who came in groups of 12 to 15 to attack us on the school grounds. Both sides had splendid homemade wooden swords and shields. Often dressed as pirates, we clashed at a place we called the 'sand banks'. The invasion invariably came from the village lads, who send a scout with a provoking message, "If you have any balls, come and prove it. Tomorrow at 4pm, usual place!"

On an autumn D-day flat out in the bracken of the oak forest, like leopards stalking their prey, we waited for the alarm signal sent by our chief. I liked the profound silence before the battle and I thought of my father wondering if he had been in battle, was he frightened, did he remember me? Suddenly, our chief sent a strident yell, "Attack!"

This surprised me as much as it must have our enemy not yet in formation, so the unexpected alert created a disorder in their ranks. We stood in line in our preferred spot at the top of our sand bank where they started to climb up the step banks.

We rushed down towards them with raised swords making a noise like American Indians at war from the black and white movies. Then came the inevitable contact and much concentration was needed. It was important not to look at the others, but to deal with one enemy at a time. When one of us got badly hurt the only safeguard was to run away to avoid more bruises. When we had too many casualties and could not hold the fort, we retreated. Regrouping in the forest, we compared our bruises, cut and knocks, and proudly exchanged our personal exploits. Strangely enough, like the adults in their wars, the girls did not participate.

Amongst the adults, the activities at night heightened. Fonsou was not often with us during this period, and disappeared for weeks at a time. When he came back he was dirty, red-eyed, tired and hungry. He told us about the battle stories in the Vercors where the maquisards were trying to oust a large group of German soldiers defending a fort at the top of a steep mountain called 'la Mauriènne'. To capture this strategic position over the landscape with many roads below, it took the maquisards several months and many of them lost their lives.

On a stormy night before bedtime I found Maman in the kitchen scrubbing a pair of military trousers, "Maman, why is there poo-poo inside these combat trousers and why are you washing them? Whose are they?" She stopped scrubbing, turned round towards me and replied calmly, "They belong to one of the Maquisard, my darling and he got scared when the Germans were firing at them from the fort on top of the Maurienne Mountain. They are trying to take it over from the Nazis!" I understood then that war was not an amusement.

Once in the middle of the night in May 1944 I was woken by the sound of an airplane circling low over our house. The night was crystal clear, the moon was full, and I saw a large bomber flying over with its big belly, double tail and the moonlight reflected on its aluminum body. Then as if giving birth from between its tails came a long string of white parachutes. The plane quickly disappeared carrying away its deep reverberating sound. I was left hypnotically watching these magic jellyfish silently and slowly gliding down sideways and then disappearing somewhere in the darkness of our wooded valley. The next day I learnt it was an English light bomber sent on Churchill's order to bring ammunitions, arms and food to help us to combat the tenacious aggressor. The English government knew about the privileged situation of Dieulefit and that it was a relatively safe place to send the greatly needed war materials to the maquis forces.

Some time later in the summer of 1944, the immense sky vibrated with a deep purr that penetrated everything even my ribcage. I looked up into the milky blue sky covered in tiny grey spots and saw hundreds of aeroplanes flying at a very high altitude. Maman and Sylvette came out of the house also pulled by the disturbing sound. Without taking my eyes off the sky I asked with my insatiable thirst to understand, "What's going on in the sky Maman? Why so many planes?" "They must be the allies going to bomb the German cities." Her answer was unemotional.

At times we heard a loud crash from somewhere in the neighbourhood as airplanes dropped the empty fuel reserve-tanks they carried under their wings. Immediately a great hunt started because people knew that there was kerosene left in them. Playing with my friend at the foot of the Sablière one day we came across one that had landed next to the stream. It was oblong, pale grey, cigar shaped and several metres long. A very strong smell of petrol came out of the open top and this heightened our excitement. It was still one third full! Feeling proud of our discovery we ran back to Maison Marefours to bring the good news, but when we returned with our adult friends, there were already locals frantically scooping the precious liquid into their jerry cans.

Searching for food

I was becoming conscious that war was a reality, as everyone was short of something and had to adapt their lives accordingly. When food became really short in the village, mother took her bicycle with a large wooden hamper tied on its rack, and took us to a farm 12 km away to find food, or to the mill near the Lance to turn our wheat into bread flour. We started at the crack of dawn, mother pushing her old bike and we walking on either side of her. When I felt tired she lifted me onto the saddle and when I felt the pushing was becoming too hard for her, I asked her to lift me down.

Finally we arrived at the isolated farm among large chestnut trees near the Miélandre Mountain. There were no men around since they were working in the fields with the horses and the oxen. A shaky old dog barked to announce our arrival. The inner poultry courtyard of the farm was very muddy with many footprints of farm animals. I was very careful where I put my bare feet so as not to step in the smelly white and khaki chicken droppings. Pursued by the leg-sniffing, growling old dog, we knocked at the ancient chestnut door. After quite some time it opened leaving a small gap. A wrinkled granny peered through at us and our Maman asked if she had any food for sale. The reply was invariably, "I don't know. I don't think so, but I'll see what we can do…" and then she closed the door. After a long wait, she returned to say in a low husky voice, as if we might be overheard, "I have found a few things, come in."

While they negotiated the price, I followed my curiosity and entered uninvited the universe of the dark kitchen. The floor was covered in huge stone slabs, a well-worn walnut kitchen table stood in front of an open fireplace glowing with red embers, and a delicious smell came from the big black cauldron that hung over the fire. I looked in… floating amongst the bubbles were lumps of bacon with potatoes, leeks, carrots and white haricot beans. The concoction looked appetising. I wondered why couldn't we have any of that lovely soup – it was always lunchtime by the time we got there? But we were never offered anything to eat. Maman's bicycle was now fully loaded, and this time to my great excitement, we took with us a black and white kid. It had long knobbly legs with yellow patches on the knee and when it walked, it seemed to go sideways. Its beautiful little face expressed happiness and interest, keen to discover the world of its new friends. We tied a rope loosely around its neck and I had the privilege of leading it part of the way home. Maman was really struggling on this bumpy road with such a heavy load, so now and then Sylvette and I helped her push the bike from behind. I got tired from the long walk and she put me back on the saddle when we were going down hill. I held onto her the best I could, as I kept falling asleep. My head was loaded with numbness, rolling from side to side and waking me up just enough to straighten up again.

It was usually dark when we arrived home, and this time we had an exciting little guest with us. I took the rope off and it jumped down the steps skidding onto the slippery dining-room floor. Fonsou was already back from work and remarked that it would make a few nice meals. I thought he was joking and I didn't like what he had just said. I held the baby goat's neck tightly, feeling the coolness of its wet muzzle on my cheek. The kid had some difficulty walking for its legs kept sliding apart on the slippery tiled floor, and it would bray in a trembling voice, as if to say, "Where is my mummy?" I wanted to take it to bed with me, but was told that it was not possible tonight.

I came down early the next morning. "Maman, where's our kid?" She took time to give me an answer. I could sense a strange atmosphere and the smell in the kitchen was unusual, and she finally said softly, "We bought it for food my darling, it will last us for a month or more at least. It is now stored in salt in the cupboard." I wanted to see for myself, as it didn't seem possible that the life of my little friend had been taken away just for food. My mother showed me the lumps of meat stacked up in salt in the big grey stoneware jars and I could not relate them to the kid. Sylvette did not want to see any of it! I felt that my perky, jumpy four-legged friend was still alive in me, as I had been so impregnated with its lively presence. The next day I saw its white and black fur stretched out on a large board drying outside in the yard.

Fonsou came from a farming background and knew many basic survival skills. For instance, he knew how to kill animals with long and sharp knives, how to take off the skins and stretch them in order to sell them to the skin and rug man. He knew how to talk to and handle a horse, how to harness it ready for the plough. He knew about growing vegetables, lavender, making cheese and wine. In truth, he considered himself a workman and he didn't like farm life. In her positive ways Mum encouraged him to do what he wanted. Whether he was whistling, or singing his emotional songs, or his eating habits at the table, (he held his wood handled Opinel pocket-knife while he ate), the way he raised his voice in conversation or shouted rude words at my mother, I could not associate myself with him. His lack of patience was the opposite of our mum. He instantly got angry when things didn't go his way and became furious when he hit his fingers using a hammer. I did not see a father figure in him and he did not replace my father Marcel. I only had a tiny place in my heart for Fonsou.

In the autumn the local farmer delivered a large pile of logs outside our dining room with his horse cart. Maman happened to be away that morning and I was helping Fonsou to carry the logs in. After a while, feeling tired, I found it much easier to crouch on the ground instead of bending down to load my arms. To my surprise, he got angry with me and told me off in his loud voice, "Your just a lazy bugger! You'll see, I'll teach you how to carry logs!" That was too much for me to hear; I threw the logs back on the pile and ran into the dining room to hide under the big square table. His anger increased and he chased me, shouting. From my hideout I saw his newly stolen, black leather German army boots coming violently at me until finally one of them hit me in the ribs. I was now terrified to come out from under the table and when my mother came back from shopping she found me there, my cheeks covered in tears. She took me in her arms and hugged me and enquired gently. "What on earth has been happening darling?"

"He kicked me, because I did not carry the logs like HE wanted me to! I want my Papa, Maman." She sat me on her knees, holding me and swayed gently… taking me into a peaceful space with great tenderness, which slowly dissipated my pains.

The Americans arrive

'La Croix' was the name of a crossroads where a spectacular incident occurred at dawn, creating a big stir amongst the population of Dieulefit. In the summer of 1944 the Allied forces coming from North Africa, were forcing their way north pushing the resistant German army home. One American battalion with all their heavy war machinery secretly chose to come into our Valley from the southeast, using the narrow road. Before reaching the village, at 'La Croix', the road went over a high narrow stone bridge spanning a deep and brambly ravine. The lead tank hit the bridge parapet and fell right down into the ravine and fortunately no one was hurt. It took three days to get a special army crane to come and pull it out! The 2 km convoy came to a standstill, and our whole neighbourhood became their encampment. The wheat and the rye in the fields were almost ripe, yet our flamboyant liberators did not seem to realize when establishing their camp that they were tramping all over the farmers crop! Officers were shouting orders in English and the soldiers and their equipment rapidly displayed themselves all over the delicate harvest. Tanks, huge lorries, jeeps, canons and every thing that makes an army, settled wherever space was available.

A translator was needed and our mum was immediately fetched to help. We went with her to La Croix, excited about the prospect of seeing the friendly army we had been hearing so much about. When we arrived a group of American officers stood around a jeep in the wheat field and a few locals were standing a small distance away, including representatives of the Dieulefit town hall. Our Maman had made herself very pretty, with a red cardigan over a white shirt and her tight pale grey skirt. With her shiny fair hair she stood out in the crowd and she set to work right away. I had heard her speak English to Glean, and I noticed a different accent coming from the Americans. Sylvette was interested to listen and stayed by Maman. The attraction of the heavy machinery, tanks, lorries, and enormous canons I could see from the corner of my eyes became irresistible and I bubbled with excitement. All my senses were wide open and I let myself dance away in the direction of the broken bridge.

The ordinary troops were not allowed off their massive lorries because they were still standing on the top of them waving and smiling at the many local onlookers. Some came with baskets of fruit and tomatoes, which they threw to the soldiers who immediately devoured them. In exchange the soldiers sent down packets of chewing gum and cigarettes. I was not interested to catch any of these for I didn't know what they were. I was more intrigued by the undercarriage of the lorry I was standing by and I examined it carefully. Behind the driver's cabin were many khaki coloured pickaxes and folding shovels and the wheels were huge, with lumpy and bumpy tyres that were much, much taller than me. I saw the White Star inside a white circle printed on the door of the cabin. My mother told me that was how you could differentiate the American from the German army vehicles, which carried a black and white swastika cross. My mechanical mind discovered how the tank's caterpillar worked, driven by strong metal spiky wheels slotted into the caterpillar ribbon. All the tar on the roads had been broken up into long ridges like bars of chocolate from this. The cannons impressed me; some of them were covered with netting, "Do they go fishing?" I asked myself. Some were camouflaged, I didn't understand why, and I stored many questions to ask Maman later.

I finally got to the bridge without being seen by the guards on the other side preventing people going through to where the tank had tipped over. From my position, I could see the broken parapet, but not the tank too far below. Feeling a little frustrated I started to walk back to my family at La Croix when Sylvette appeared, "I've been looking for you. Quick, Maman is going off with the Americans and we are having lunch with our friend Jacques who lives just there at la Croix!" We arrived just in time to see our mother go off in a jeep to the village with the American officers. We climbed up the few steps to the house of our mother's communist friends. During the meal I listened to their conversation, not quite understanding what was being said. I understood enough to become aware that there were not just two sides in this big world, the good and the bad. There were also Russians who were called communists and Americans who were called capitalist and that they didn't get on at all. I was surprised that my mother's friends, who came from northeast France, were so anti-American when in fact they were just helping us to get the Germans out! I began to realise that the world of the adults was very confused and complicated, not as clear and simple as implied with their individual set of convictions. The tone of their voices revealed what they were feeling and this did not always correspond to what they were saying. They could not keep quiet when they talked about politics, but became emotional and ended up talking very loudly and all at the same time.

The noisy arguments made me switch into my own world, and I rested from the adults by peacefully looking through the window of their dining room. Down below were some interesting activities going on in the wheat field, to the left of the dusty road leading to the school. A huge cannon had been dragged there, flattening all the wheat. The soldiers were scattered about in the fields, eating their brown beans in tomatoes sauce straight out from the cans. I suddenly noticed my mother's red cardigan near the cannon – she was talking with a group of officers. I became excited and told my sister, since the adults in the dining room were busy talking and drinking, could we join our mother in the field below?

The cannon barrel was pointing directly at the smallest of our school buildings, some 4 kilometres away. Our Maman was interpreting for an American colonel who was trying to converse with Tante Marguerite, our school headmistress. I could see that she was in a bad state, her deep brown eyes were filled with fire, and the upper part of her wrinkled mouths was trembling as she talked extremely fast in a cold snappy voice. Our mother was trying to keep up the translation and looked worried herself. Almost shouting now, Tante Marguerite walked up to the end of the long steel cannon and tried to push its nozzle away from the school. The officer said coolly in a monotone voice, "We have good reasons to believe that the Germans will attack Dieulefit either in the night or at dawn! They will use the North Road, between the two mountains and go straight into the school for shelter, that is the reason our canon is aimed at this building." On hearing this Tante Marguerite went purple in the face and violently protested, shouting rude words while trying to shift the enormous cylinder, screaming desperately that the school was full of children. The high level officer then gave an order, "Tonight, we want every individual in the village and neighbourhood to move OUT of their homes, take food and blankets and sleep in the mountains, the hills or the woods. We do not want the civilians to get mixed up in the battle, do we?" Tante Marguerite finally won her case. The cannon was turned away from the school and now faced the space between the two mountains.

We left the Americans to prepare for battle and walked home with Maman to get things ready for the night camp. What an exciting day that was… and now more was coming! The little boy that I was did not see any problem, had no fear, and felt this was all a big game the adults were playing. So we rapidly got ready, each carrying our own blanket, mother with food and drinks in a basket and, with a few precious belongings, we set off for the night. Fonsou wasn't around; he must have been in the Vercors at that time, where 3500 Maquisards were engaged in a big battle to gain a fort held by the Germans.

I was full of questions about the tanks, the lorries, the Americans, and why the soldiers had flattened all the farmers' wheat? What was chewing gum? Was it true that if you swallowed it would stick your guts together? Were American cigarettes nice? Why did they devour the fresh food we gave them? Patiently, Maman answered my questions while we walked. I was full of curiosity, as if that amazing amount of new material and equipment had filled me to the brim; my mind needed to sort it all out, to put it in order, to shelve it somewhere. As my questions were answered, another wave came to fill the space, there was no respite, my brain could not rest until all the questions that tormented me, had been answered.

We arrived at the school farm, went past a big green field on the right where the cows were browsing and took a small path that led down to the brook. We crossed it and went up into the bracken and the chestnut forests, with the Sablière rising a short distance away on our right. The chestnut trees were impressively majestic. Their large, rugged elephant-grey trunks had a slight twist to them making them look as if they were screwed into the ground. I knew them well because after the summer, in the chestnut season, I filled bags with chestnuts for us and, in exchange for a few coins, acorns to feed the farm pigs.

We decided to settle behind the Sablière, among the bracken under a large century old chestnut tree, where there was a naturally hollowed out space, just big enough for the three of us. Sylvette and I gathered lots of bracken and piled it into the depression; we had great fun making this our new home. It was getting late and Maman took out our light supper, peaches, goat cheese and bread. While we were eating in our hole we heard other people settling in for the night some distance away. Their voices were more of a whisper, mixed together with the bristling sound of the leaves in the trees, moved by a light evening breeze. After being hugged and kissed by our mum, tired, I let go of everything that had happened that day, and felt the weight of my body wrapped up in the blanket on the bracken bed. I was now back in my own world. Through the trees above I could see the deep black sky with its twinkling stars. There was no moon that night; the Milky Way seemed to be alight against the deep sky. High above I could see the black shapes of the chestnut tree leaves moving slightly with the breeze, revealing at times a shining star. The voices vanished. I buried myself further into the hole, closed my eyes and was delightfully absorbed into my own darkness.

The bird song woke me up early with the sun rising from behind the mountains and Maman getting ready to go. I sprang up and disappeared into the bracken. My body was stiff from the night outside and I enjoyed extending it fully while making patterns in the sand with my pee. When I returned to the camp, Sylvette was asking Maman why it was all so quiet. She answered that she didn't know, and that we should go back home to find out. Apparently the Germans army had no intention of attacking Dieulefit that night and to everyone's great relief, the American Colonel had received false information. There was no battle.

The US forces spent the day pulling the tank out of the ravine. At dawn the following morning they left, as suddenly as they had arrived, to continue their road north in pursuit of the escaping enemy. In the flattened fields they left behind empty packets of cigarettes and chewing gum, and many empty khaki coloured tin cans. Tank caterpillar marks roughened all the roads they used, and the damaged ramp of the bridge was left unrepaired. Our Maman enjoyed their visit and from that day on she was known as l'Anglaise, the translator of the US officers. Being a foreigner didn't seem to matter any more since the short visit of the Americans had left a feeling of excitement and joy among the population. The word "liberation" was being heard in the adult conversations, and the atmosphere was so much lighter, almost euphoric.

WALNUTS & GOAT CHEESE

North east view of Dieulefit

The main buildings of the Beauvallon School

CHAPTER 2

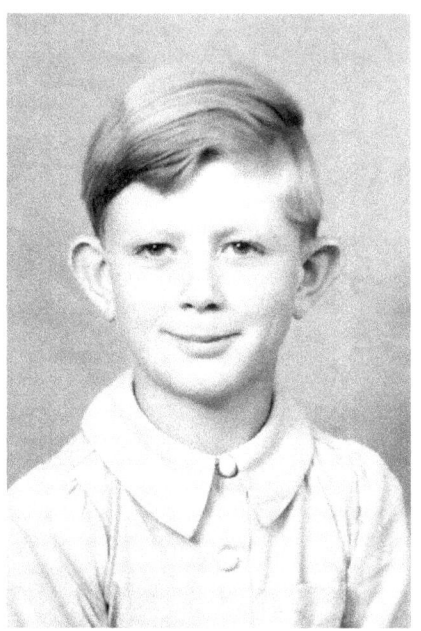
François early 1943

Maman by the wash house, Winter 1943

Fonsou (bottom left) with Maquisard friends and their wives, Summer 1943

Chapter 3

Dieulefit 1944-1951 - Maison Martin

Time had come for us to move out of our dark, semi-underground flat at les Marefours since the proprietors needed to renovate. Our mother explained that this had only been a temporary place for us anyhow, and she heard that a Mr Martin was building a house on the plateau of 'Les Rouvières', 35 minutes walk west of les Marefours. "… and he agrees to let it to us very cheaply! Isn't that wonderful? I will take you there tomorrow." We named the house 'Maison Martin'. It was set on the rising sun hillside of the plateau, just low enough to be a little sheltered from the winter north wind the locals called la bise.

It was quite a climb to get to the small house, but once there, the 180° view was breath taking. It was built of local stones roughly bound together with cement and not fully completed when we moved in. The doors were not yet installed; the windows were in but there were no shutters; the dusty floors were made of solid rough concrete. The winter had been hard and it was still cold – the house felt damp and draughty. There were only of a few rather basic rooms, and a tiny hallway with an angled staircase leading to two bedrooms with windows facing south. Sylvette, who was quick off the mark, chose the first one over the hallway, so mine became the one over the kitchen. Immediately to the left of the entrance to the house, up a small step, was a kitchen the size of my bedroom with a large double window facing south, a concrete sink, and counters set into the wall and surrounded with brown, glazed tiles. There was no tap, simply a water jug that was filled from a pump 60 metres down the path. Opposite the entrance was a door leading to a draughty lean-to with no ceiling, only a corrugated asbestos roof and this was the largest room of the house. Maman and Fonsou would sleep there with the only window looking over the nice view of the Miélandre Mountain. There was no bathroom and the toilets were outside around the back of the house.

Fonsou returned from the Vercors and with his enormous strength helped us move with a Percheron farm horse and cart that he borrowed from a friend. I liked that gentle pale grey, elephant-size horse and noticing my affection for the animal, Fonsou lifted me onto its wide back. The dominating view from up there was superb but the horse's back was so large that my legs were split apart, so after the pain became unbearable I asked to come down. We didn't have many belongings so the wooden cart could hold it all: a large double and two single beds, our sheets and blankets, the heavy black cast iron cooking stove with the brass hand rail, our clothes in the leather suitcase that had belonged to our English grandfather Edward, and a few other kitchen bits and pieces.

The move in itself was exciting, but the house wasn't so comfortable without running water, a bathroom or indoor toilets. For the first year we used wooden fruit boxes instead of tables, chairs and cupboards and shelving made with bricks and old building planks. Fortunately we were well trained to live simply from the Ile du Levant and here by ourselves we felt tranquil in the middle of nature with a most beautiful view. I looked forward to discovering all parts of the land that surrounded our house and rapidly forgot all about les Marefours.

From the main road into the village, our path, actually a dry riverbed, started by Mr Dufour's old farmyard. Past the barn in a small field lived a perky black goat that was chained to an old iron stake; its enigmatic, pale yellow eyes always seemed to be watching me. Its sharp horns curved backwards, partly hiding the independently moving, long ears. When it rained the water rushed in between glossy flint stones on the path. Once in the ravine, which was so completely protected from the wind, we could not hear anything but our own steps. As we climbed, the path became steeper and our breathing more raucous. Suddenly the path opened out revealing an almond tree to the right and, as we rose further, fields that stepped up to the high plateaux. A few hundred metres more and we reached the narrow path leading to the house. Walking up this ravine was the shortest way home.

The attraction of insects and animal life

Our outside loos were a magnificent place to observe nature and to reflect on its processes and metamorphoses. The toilets were built on a steep slope at the back of the house and made of a wooden, rectangular box nailed together. It had a sloping, rusty corrugated iron roof and it stood over an unattractive, dark pit that reminded me of the one I was used to on the island. I would crouch comfortably on the wide shelf, my feet well apart and look down through the circular hole into the pit, which gave me all kinds of information about the intricate processes of nature. With my insatiable curiosity and fascination for any insect behaviour, what went on under the toilet plank greatly attracted this young entomologist. This natural classroom, without the presence of a demanding teacher breathing down my neck and without fear of doing something wrong, gave me a platform to observe life's natural unfolding process throughout the seasons. I could assimilate freely at my own speed within my own space, the information my brain was so keen to absorb and understand. During these moments of intense concentration, my whole being was one with itself in complete peace, only immersed in the moment.

Different types of maggots and black beetles lived in the pit. The variety of grubs was captivating, long thin ones, short ones, fat white ones, some changing magically into elegantly colourful flies: green bottles, charcoal grey ones with brown spots, little skinny yellow-orange ones. Each expressed its character through its movements, whether dancing, running along, cleaning themselves with their front legs as if they were rubbing their hands together in satisfaction, or by their different ways of walking or flying. The way they flew was interesting to me as well because each created their own music by the fast vibrations of their transparent wings. Similar to myself in the colder season, they landed where the sunrays hit a sheltered surface, inadvertently exposing their magnificent colours and diversity of patterns. In the heat of the summers though, they preferred to stay cool in the shade.

During the mating season, I watched with interest the charcoal grey and brown flies that didn't seem to care when or where they did their coupling games. The bigger female seemed to wait for the smaller male who, attracted by the feminine scent, landed on her back, did what males do to females, and then she would simply fly off into the air ignoring completely the presence of the poor fellow. He was simply taken up by her powerful wings, and, not wanting to let go of this comfortable position, held firmly on to her back. They reminded me of a bomber, too heavily loaded to fly in a straight line, staggering through space like a drunkard. It took the puzzled male some time to react, and fly off in the other direction! As soon as she was freed, the female landed and frantically cleaned her backside with her many hind legs, then she cleaning her head with her front legs by turning it one way then the other. Finally she rearranging her wings into place, and it seemed to me that cleanliness and appearances were obviously important to her. On the inside of the doorframe, a yellow hemp string threaded with squares of old newspaper hung from a nail. Even when the door was partly closed with the help of a thick bent wire, there were many gaps between the planks, some of them wide enough to admire a long slice of the view.

When the bise blew, the place was not so comfortable. The cold wind rushed under the planks to freeze my bare backside. On a non-windy day, I left the rickety door fully open and enjoyed the panoramic view.

Far below in a narrow valley was a farm from which I could hear animal sounds echoing up the steep hill and a dog barking. I wondered - was it his vision or excellent hearing or sense of smell that always told him that I was on the loo? Even if I made absolutely no noise getting there he would detect my presence. I had great fun imitating the different sounds of the animals, including a cocky cockerel that immediately responded to tell me that I was on its territory and to remind me that He was the Boss.

On the left looking into the distance stood three conical shaped mountains that disappeared into the east. Our school was just visible at the base of the first hillside called the Montmirail. Part of this natural backdrop was the majestic mountain named le Miélandre, with its long back covered by a thick blanket of snow in the winter months. Standing in the middle was the Sablière, which I could caress in just one short affectionate scoop. Looking south to the right, another elegant mountain called la Lance stretched itself up into the sky. Gradually we settled in and found our rhythm. The school was now further to walk, 4 to 5 km away depending on whether we took shortcuts across the fields. We were now closer to Dieulefit but there was that steep path to deal with on the way back from shopping.

Fonsou borrowed the same horse to plough the land. On the upper fields he planted lavender, which didn't need watering. On the lower field near the pump, we planted vegetables and melons. Unfortunately the few fruit trees we planted were too young to give us fruit, but a large fig tree and walnut and almond trees grew in the wild around the house. We obtained meat by raising chickens and rabbits. Fonsou built three rough rabbit hutches against the east side of the house with tall wooden legs to support them. Their doors were covered with chicken wire and hinged with bits of leather made from an old belt. Every time I went to the toilet, the nearest male rabbit firmly hit the floor of the wooden cage with his hind legs to warn the others of my presence. To feed them was simple, all they needed was a bowl of water and some fresh grass every day. I soon learned what type of grass they preferred, dandelion, and carrots' greens; the orange part was kept for us, of course. Wild fennel was another green they relished; they were similar to us, preferring the tastiest bits. On my way back from school, during the last hundred metres, the rabbits' needs became my priority and I took pleasure cutting up generous bunches of grass for their supper.

The situation was quite different with our chickens. They decided that the safest place to sleep at night away from the fox was right up in the tall almond tree at the back of the house. As for their eggs, each hen had her own hiding place in the tall grass or under the shrubs. Fortunately for us, they just could not help announcing proudly that one more egg had been laid, so I started my search from where I heard the call.

During the weekends Maman often asked me, "Please Sounet, be a darling, go and find me some eggs." It was a bit like a rehearsing for the Easter Games when my task was to find the hidden nests. When I came to know each hen's hiding place, the round was quickly done, but sometimes I discovered a new one with 12 or even 20 eggs in it. That usually meant that most of them were either bad to eat or filled with waiting-to-be-born chicks.

We acquired a powerful, handsome red-feathered Cockrell with a dark green and black tail. He soon became the chief of the surroundings, ruling over the hens with great authority and caring attention. Before lunchtime when we fed them, he always let his ladies eat first. Sometimes he would disappear for a day or two and come back looking poorly with feathers missing, his crest darkened by lumps of clotted blood, probably damage done by the Cockrell from the farm down below. I was proud of our Cockrell; he seemed to have no fear of the cats or the stray dogs that came to visit. Although our fowls were free to roam they were quite tamed, often coming right up and pecked my foot gently to beg for food. At times I had to chase them out of the house for if we let them, they would be on our table taking over the kitchen. Once a year like proud mums, they brought to us their new broods. It was a shared family pleasure to watch the chicks rushing around: arguing, tweaking with excitement when they found something good to eat, or when they felt a danger, suddenly rushing all at once under their mum's wings.

Difficulties with Fonsou's ways…

Fonsou moved in with us full time. Our house was now closer to his family in town, which he visited regularly on Saturday mornings. His passion was football, once he played on the town team, and on Sunday afternoons he sometime took me to watch a match on the football pitch of Dieulefit. I then walked home by myself while he stayed in town with his friends. He usually came back late on Saturday evenings smelling strong of Pastis, his face red and his watery eyes looking vaguely happy. Sylvette and I found these moments very difficult and did not want him to touch us or be near him when he was in this tipsy state. Sometimes, he shouted loudly criticising us for not doing what he demanded and this always ended in an argument with mum who never failed to take our side, which he greatly resented.

One day as we entered the kitchen, Sylvette and I were shocked to hear him shout at our Maman, "If François did a crap on this fucking kitchen table, you would say absolutely nothing! Wouldn't you?" She replied quietly, "Oh no! Sounet would never do such a thing! And if he did, well, I would just clean it up, that's all!" Her response infuriated him, so now he was shouting at the top of his voice, "Your filthy brats are badly brought up! One day, I am telling you, when you'll ask them for help, they will spit in your face!" And she replied softly, "Of course not! They would never do such a thing, would you my darlings?" We kept quiet; we both hated to hear them argue. Fonsou had been very strictly brought up as a Catholic and had often been smacked or beaten by his parents. Our mother's approach to bringing up her own children was miles apart from his ways. She never agreed with him on the subject of education, but never tried to convince him that her way was better, neither did she criticise the way he was.

Some time in early 1945 just before the war ended, Fonsou turned up one evening with a large, brand new Telefunken radio. He had been in Montelimar railway station and discovered one wagon stacked with luxurious radios. While the watchman was at the end of his round, he stole one and brought it home. This changed the atmosphere of Maison Martin, for we never had a radio before. It was placed facing the room on the small kitchen dining table against the wall. Fonsou always sat in the warmest place with his back to the cooking stove, while I sat opposite with Sylvette on my right next to our Mum. The presence of the Telefunken took over the room when Fonsou was home. He leaned over the table, and with the murmur of a smile, hardly breathing, and his eyes half closed, delicately turned the large knob with his thick clumsy fingers searching for the appropriate station. Once he successfully found it, he drew back his chair, took a big breath and listened attentively with his hands across his belly. No one dared to talk when the radio was on except me when I was burning with a question. "Shush! Can't you see that I am trying to listen?" He whispered with a forced gentleness.

At times we managed to get the London BBC News programme, which Maman would translate for us. It was the only way to hear the truth about what was going on in Europe, as the French radios carried much German propaganda, including the most amazing lies about the English, the Americans and the Russians.

When the war ended, the rhythm of life changed with it. Fonsou adored listening to Edith Piaf and Tino Rossi, boxing matches like the one with Marcel Cerdan against Jack La Motta, and of course football matches; I did enjoy listening to sports with him. Listening to the news at breakfast, lunch and supper became a regular ceremony.

One day in Dieulefit shopping with our mother, we saw a few young women wearing scarves when they normally did not. This had greatly intrigued me and on the way home I queried, "Maman, why are some young ladies wearing scarves now?" After some time she stopped pushing the heavily loaded bike and replied, "It is because they are accused of sleeping with the German soldiers. The people of the town shaved their heads publicly to make them feel ashamed, and now everyone can humiliate them further by pointing fingers at them." I could not understand why the adults were so horrible to each other. Now that the war was finished, they seemed to fight and argue with each other more than ever before! The majority of the people in the town were now what they called "communists." Fonsou was one of them and regularly went to meetings. Stalin was seen as their saviour and was greatly admired, in fact 'worshipped' would not be a too stronger word. Now that the nasty War was over, the press expressed itself more freely and communist newspapers flooded the newsstands.

Fonsou never talked nicely about our cats, but chased them and shouted at them while trying to hit them with his table napkin. He did not comment on beauty: for instance how incredibly attractive the large green lizard was when he came up on our doorstep to listen to the music from the Telefunken, with its mouth open, turning its head sideways to hear better, perfectly still. Or point out the inspiring sky at sunset, nor did he ever talk quietly with mum, or ask her how was she feeling? Where had she been? What had she been doing that day? Sometime, she tried to engage him in conversation about education, about our feelings, or how he was feeling about this or that. But that usually led to an argument, he'd say that she was getting at him and started raising his voice. Mother's gentle quietness, always trying to do her best to make things easier for everybody, irritated Fonsou. He exclaimed loudly before going off in a huff, "Anyhow, you're always right! Aren't you? What's the use of talking then?"

In his own way, he did show us some affection at times, for instance he would let me wrestle with him. I enjoyed this very much, wriggling out of his strong grip, laughing, giggling, and then going back at it for more. I had endless energy and he would end up saying,

"Stop, stop, that's enough for now!"

I liked to participate when he worked in the garden. On one special occasion he allowed me to hold the plough while the friendly Percheron pulled. I felt the immense power of the horse forcing the clean and shining metal blade through the heavy dark earth, revealing many bad tempered earthworms, which I carefully avoided stepping on. But it was much too heavy work for me; I hung on with all my weight so the plough dug deep and did not just skim the top of the soil. To break up the lumps of earth, he replaced the plough with a harrow to make the field smooth and ready for the lavender plants.

In the early summer we all helped him cut the lavender with scissors, which was back breaking but rewarding with its rich intoxicating scent. The bees, not wanting to stop drinking its sweet nectar, passionately gripped onto the flowers until the last moment when the cut bunch was thrown onto the large open sackcloth. At times, many butterflies of varied colours and shapes came to visit us; I blew gently on their delicate structures to entice them to go elsewhere. That was the nicest part of the job. After a few hours I invariably developed blisters around my thumb and felt tearful from the pain and longed for the working day to finish.

Our Maman chose Fonsou as her man and she cared for him, did everything in the house with love – cooked, washed and ironed his shirts, cleaned the house, did the shopping without ever showing any resentment or complaining. Our love for our mother was such that we did not want her to suffer, so we didn't share with her our real feelings about her partner. We kept them to ourselves, but when we were alone during the long walks to school, Sylvette and I exchanged our grief created by his behaviour. Maman very rarely shared her sufferings with us, when we saw sadness and worry in her eyes, we insisted on knowing the reasons why, but she would shrug her shoulders and say, "oh, its nothing really."

Learning that life has different realities

One Saturday evening Fonsou took my favourite dark grey rabbit out of the cage to prepare it for the Sunday lunch. I saw this animal grow up and I knew all about him, for instance that he preferred dandelions, to vetch and other grasses. He had an impatient nature too; when I opened the door to feed him, he invariably stood up and with his little yellow pipi coloured front paws armed with sharp claws, and pushed against the wire netting of the door. As I undid its lock, his weight push it open and I had to push him back by using a bunch of freshly cut grass from which he quickly pulled out the dandelions while looking at me with mischief.

I watched Fonsou killing animals and soon learned how to separate myself from them when it was necessary without getting emotional about it. Taking the rabbit by its back legs, the heavy body hung, and the large ears dropped forward, revealing a delicate white fur around the base of the skull. With a sudden powerful blow, the side of Fonsou's hand came down on to the delicate spot, taking suddenly the life out of my companion; at that instant he became fur and food.

Absorbed in the pursuit of his task, Fonsou sat on the nearby chair, took the lifeless body across his knee and asked me to pass him the scissors and a bowl, which he put on the floor between his feet. He then proceeded to cut the tip of one ear. Thick drops of dark blood splashed into the white enamelled bowl, creating a whole realm of deep poppy red droplets, which turned an aubergine brown colour as it thickened. A dense odour came from the almost full bowl kept for Maman to make a wonderful sauce with thyme, red wine, garlic and the minced liver. The rabbit was now lying inert on the oilcloth of the kitchen table, all four legs splayed out revealing its wide soft tummy. Fonsou sharpened the large Opinel knife and asked me to place the enamel basin under the end of the table.

Holding the back legs of the animal firmly with his left hand, he gave a sudden shove with the pointed blade right at the base of its stomach, and drew the blade slowly up to the rib cage. The rabbit's body was still warm and steam came out of the neatly open gap; I saw its complicated insides and a very specific smell spread out, not pleasant, not unpleasant, a new smell to which I could not bring any comparison. There was always a sacred silence in the house during these procedures, taking the life of an animal was a serious matter and each movement became a ritual. It was done with care, never in a hurry, methodically with great concentration. I watched, captivated, taking every detail in, only asking questions when I could not hold my curiosity any longer.

"Fonsou? What's that you're pulling out?" A dark, red-brown, shiny shape intrigued me,

"It's the liver for the sauce... now I must find and take out the gallbladder. It's a small green bag, and I must do it very carefully for if it bursts, it will make all the meat uneatable - its very bitter. Look! Here it is!" He now pointed with the end of the blade to a tiny bag hidden in one of the folds of the liver, hardly 2 cm long - a spinach green liquid held in a transparent pocket. With his blood-covered fingers, he delicately freed it with the knife and threw it into the enamel dish below. The liver was carefully detached and laid on a white plate. Now he firmly pulled out the guts that dangled like ribbons into the enamel pan until the blade freed them. Fonsou made sure to not burst the bladder while removing them; then he took out the heart, the lungs and kidneys. Finally, the whole ribcage cavity was empty, revealing the spine flanked by the strong back muscles.

The blood was washed off his hands in a bucket of water. Then he cut just above the furry paws and down the inside of the legs up to the initial cut, and used his powerful index finger to free the skin from the bones and muscles. Fonsou then asked me to hold the two back furry feet steady. He pulled the skin from the legs slowly away from me, separating gradually the rabbit's fur coat from its delicate pink muscles. This last action made a strange sound, like popping bubbles. With the Opinel, he cut around the mouth, ears and eyes, freeing the skin totally. Later, the skin hung outside to dry in the sun, and later was sold to the rabbit skin man in Dieulefit.

I related closely to live animals and I often felt them within me, whether it was a bird, a rabbit, a fox, a chicken, a cat or even a snake. Their wholeness, their dignity and their spontaneity I admired. Each one living only for what it was destined for gave me a reassuring feeling, as if they complimented my nature and were a part of me. I secretly kept the white tail of my animal friend in my trouser pocket, and while at the table eating Sunday lunch, I thought how wonderful it would be if Maman could sew the tail onto the back of my trousers for school Monday morning. In the evening Fonsou was not back from town, so I pulled out the delicate tail and asked my mother:

"Please Maman, could you sew it onto the back of my trousers?" She looked perplexed and replied, "Really? Do you mean on your school trousers?" "Yes Maman, I want to be like a rabbit!" I was serious and determined. "Oh well, if you are really sure that's what you want!" I felt she was willing but not really so keen; she asked again, "Are you sure my darling? "Yes, I am!" "Go and fetch your trousers then, they are clean sitting at the end of your bed, I'll get the sewing box." This time she had more reassurance in her voice. The tail was sewn on, I could not resist putting the school trousers on but the problem was that I couldn't see it. I hopped around the kitchen like my animal friend would have done and I felt wonderful. I was half in the human world, half in the rabbit world and felt very excited at the thought of sharing this with my friends at school.

When Sylvette came into the kitchen neither of us said anything about it, since we knew what her reaction would be. We were talking about our homework - had we done it for tomorrow? I forgot all about my tail but walking across the kitchen to fetch my satchel I heard her voice! "What on earth have you got stuck on the back of your trousers?"

"It's the rabbit's tail." I replied surprised she had not recognized it. She examined it,

"But Maman, you've sewn it onto his school trousers!" She was horrified.

CHAPTER 3

"Yes, that's what he wanted. It looks okay, doesn't it?" Maman said, hoping for her approval, "I think that it looks really stupid!" She shrugged her shoulders and went back into her homework.

It was cold on that memorable Monday morning, we went to school wrapped up in our coats, which covered my tail. Sylvette did not mention it again. Maybe she forgot and since she seemed to disapprove, I wasn't going to talk about it either. We arrived and hung our coats in the main hallway before going out for the daily morning gym. As I came into the courtyard, one boy saw the rabbit tail… "Hey you guys, look at what François has at the back of his trousers!" The boys gathered around me, I turned rapidly round as they came from behind to try to catch it. Suddenly I felt completely stupid, trying to protect my tail as I hit blindly behind me. When one of the boys managed to catch it and held on firmly, other boys joined in the pulling. It was an agonising situation. I thought at one time that my trousers were going to come off! But luckily my mother's sewing gave in to the boys who cheered loudly and ran off displaying their trophy. Unfortunately this left a small tear at the back of my trousers. I had lost my beloved tail together with my dignity. But I learned from the experience that some of my worlds are better kept to myself.

In the early spring of 1946 our mother's close friend Lena came to look after us while Maman was taken urgently to the hospital in Montélimar. The hernia she had developed through carrying too heavy loads became dangerously large and needed an immediate intervention. The following Sunday in the cool early-morning air we set off with Fonsou on our bicycles to visit our Maman, a distance of about 30 km. The wheels of my bicycle were small compared to the others and I had to use much energy to keep up with the bigger bikes. At last we arrived at the hospital and found Maman in her bed smiling, delighted to see us. We kissed and I climbed onto the bed to be next to her while Sylvette stood beside it; we both wanted so much to tell her how difficult life was without her. But it wasn't possible to express all these feelings with Fonsou present, so we smiled and told her about the cats and the animals and asked her when she would be coming back. Fonsou was standing there smiling still holding the picnic basket, Maman asked him a few questions about the house, his work, if Lena was managing and then turned her attention back to us, "Have you eaten?" We shook our heads. "Come on then, bring the basket here on the bed, let's see what you've got in there!" Time went by quickly and then it was already time to go considering the long ride home. We said goodbye with extensive hugs but it was difficult to leave her there.

"Come on, my darlings, you don't want to cycle back in the dark, you better go now." She encouraged us, but I knew from the tone of her voice that it was hard for her too.

The way back was tough; my legs were so tired and Sylvette's face showed that she was finding it hard too. Exhausted, we arrived, put our bikes in the farmer's courtyard, and slowly and silently started the final walk up the stony path. Night had fallen when we finally arrived home and Lena comforted us with a steaming hot soup.

Maman liked to talk in English with her best friend, Lena Münz, who often came to Dieulefit. I discovered a new aspect of our mother, her culture and English origin. Lena stayed at the old Busac's farm on the flanks of the Montmirail. She was an Austrian Jew, whose husband, Walter, had escaped from a concentration camp. He once discreetly showed us his white forearm with an indigo tattooed identity number. They had been in hiding and now that the war was over, moved back to their flat at Porte de Versailles on the outskirts of Paris. Lena came down by train by herself to de-stress from the city life, and she and Maman spoke English nonstop all day from the moment they met. Sylvette and I found this difficult for we did not know one word of this strange language. Maman told us how she felt about England, her education and difficult relationship with her parents; she rebelled against the authority of her father. Because of the war our mother never spoke a word of English to us.

With Lena she talked about what really interested her, about education, especially on the subject of Summerhill School where Lena had been herself. They talked about music and the arts, about fashion, about men, about their feelings, about their pasts, the books they had read. Maman was starved for these subjects since she left the Island, and it was good to see her so talkative although we did not know what they were talking about. They laughed a lot and I started to discover a different Mum. I could hear in the tone of her voice, her excitement in the joy of being able to communicate without having resistance and arguments. I liked Lena, because her presence made our mother happy.

Fonsou goes to prison, our life changes

Coming back from school one day we saw that our mother was very anxious. She told us that the Gendarmes had been and arrested Fonsou and taken him to a prison in Valence, some 100km north.

"But why Maman? What has he done?" She hesitated and then murmured slowly, "He tells me that it is because he is a communist."

Sylvette and I found that reply strange. "But you are a communist! Will you go to prison too, Maman?" I was concerned.

"No my darling! I will not go to prison, and anyhow I've already resigned from the communist party." Sylvette joined in the conversation. "I know… He's done something wrong, hasn't he? Something bad?" Obviously our mother had a problem giving us a truthful answer and replied in a cloudy voice, "No, not really…" "How long will he stay in prison?" My mind was suddenly flooded with questions. "I don't know exactly, maybe a year or more? I will have to go up and visit him to bring him cigarettes and food." She then changed the subject and said in a more joyous and comforting voice, "Come on! Let's have some supper now." "Who will look after us when you go to visit him in the prison, Maman?" I persisted. "Probably Lena… and how was it at school today, tell me now?" she replied, while she put the heavy soup saucepan on the table, keen to change the subject and adding a question to divert our curiosity.

Sylvette and I noticed the enormous difference in the house

without the presence of Fonsou. Maman was now entirely with us in the evenings and at weekends, but she struggled more to make ends meet for he did share with our family a small portion of his monthly pay.

She took on more work at the pottery studio behind the Reboule's farm. Decorating pots was her forte, sometimes helping with other jobs like keeping an eye on the large wood-fired kiln. It was a huge construction built inside a gigantic barn, with a square chimney straight up through the sloping beams and tiled roof, almost the size of the kiln itself. When lit the kiln gave the impression that the roof was on fire, with so much black smoke pouring out of the many holes between the staggered bricks. The space inside was so high that the potter needed a ladder to pack it up to the top. On its sides were the air intake holes, from which flames belched out reminding me of the tongues of a large dragon. Sometime on these monthly kiln-firing nights, usually a Friday evening when it was our Maman's turn to help, she took us with her to the kiln room while she fed the fire with long pinewood logs. Blankets, a pack of cards and a picnic basket with baguette, walnuts and goat cheese always accompanied us to ease the long hours.

I liked the dense smell of burning pine resin, together with the intense heat and the bright orange light coming from the open mouth of the fire. It made all the surfaces facing it a wonderful bright red/orange colour, obliterating the grades of tones leaving only the lit parts and the deep black shadows. At a reasonable distance from the heat in a sheltered corner we laid one of the old blankets on the dusty floor to make our camp. Having eaten, we would play a few card games, but I did not last long in this cosy atmosphere and soon fell asleep. Beside nourishing the demanding fire with the long pine logs, when the heat reached its peak, Maman put on her sunglasses and looked through a small hole into the white blaze to see if the temperature test cones had melted; they told us when to stop feeding the ogre. Usually between midnight and one o'clock was time to re-join our beds. I was gently woken up and we were out into the dark cold night climbing our way home.

Maman started sewing lessons in the town with an elderly lady, whom Sylvette and I liked. Our Mum became very clever at it and started to make clothes for us. She bought reddish-brown wool tweed and made me a pair of golf trousers plus a jacket to go with them! I had never seen golf trousers before and felt a bit strange in the suit, especially when I went out. From the way people looked at me, it seemed no one else had seen trousers like these before. Maman and Sylvette spent much time looking at patterns and enjoyed making skirts and blouses together. The sewing machine was a small black Singer covered in fancy gold decorations that had belonged to grandmother GG. A manual handle fixed on a wheel activated its intricate mechanism. The delicate handling of the cloth was done by the left-hand, while the right made the machine go. Sometimes in the difficult parts, Maman would ask us to give her a hand and turn the wheel for her.

She took on work from the lady in the town and soon our kitchen became her workshop. Later more and different work came, making Walt Disney toys such as Donald Duck, Pluto, Mickey Mouse, and others out of colourful, shiny oilcloth. They were stuffed tightly with kapok, which flew round the room and tickled our nostrils. She was paid per piece, so the more she made, the more she earned. Once the orders were completed, she packed them into large cardboard boxes and took them to the post office.

One day I was in my bedroom, when I heard a short scream. Sylvette also heard it and we both shot down to the kitchen to find our Maman with her left index finger sewn onto the leg of a grinning Pluto, both still attached to the machine. She was brave, and asked Sylvette in a calm voice to put some calendula mother tincture in a bowl with warm water. I helped Maman to get her finger out by turning the wheel forward and releasing the pressure of the sewing machine foot, while she freed her index finger from Pluto by cutting the white cotton. We were all trembling; I felt faint and had to sit down. Maman patiently removed the thread piercing her fingernail. Sylvette had prepared the bandage with the magic potion for her finger to soak in. Then she dipped a piece of gauze into the brown liquid and wrapped it round her finger, finishing with the bandage tied into a neat bow. "Voilà Maman, it must hurt terribly?" "Hum… yes a little, but it will soon heal, do not worry my darlings." She answered faintly. I felt completely dizzy, all the blood vanished from my head and the room spun around me, so I lay down on the floor and passed out.

Maman took up knitting again, making scarves, jerseys and cardigans for us, with designs from the pattern books she discovered at the wool shop. She found time to paint too, some landscapes, but mostly portrait of Sylvette or myself in oils and pastels. We liked it when she painted. I enjoyed watching her and sometime borrowed her paints to try the difficult medium on some special oil-proof paper she had from when we lived on the island. When I sat for her and she looked at me with concentration, I couldn't help smiling, and she would say in good humour, "Wait a minute, I'm just doing your mouth, come on, stay still! You're terrible - can't you sit still a second?" This would make my smile even broader, and we would end up laughing together.

Teasing my sister when she posed was a great delight for me. She always sat with such seriousness, her back straight not moving one bit. I could not resist clowning around and try to make her laugh. Sylvette would end up by telling me off, "Stop it! Leave us alone, go away, or I will come and get you!"

On a Saturday morning, early in 1946, mother said that we were going to Dieulefit to shop and have our photographs taken. She gave us clean clothes and took time doing Sylvette's plaits. All looking immaculate, we went down to the village. The photographer's shop was in "Rue du Bourg", a busy narrow shopping street that went through the village. I could not resist stopping by its window displaying photographs of babies, well-groomed children and newly wedded couples. My mother touched my arm calling me into the shop.

CHAPTER 3

Behind the desk was a large velvet curtain, and the photographer pulled it back energetically to reveal a small lobby, he invited us in. On the opposite wall was a black cloth and in the middle was a swivel seat stool. I was the first to be invited to sit surrounded on either side by huge spotlights; I could feel the heat on my cheeks from their powerful bulbs. Opposite my seat was a square-box camera on an adjustable tripod with a black cloth resting over it. The man disappeared under the cloth and, splaying his legs wide apart, adjusted the lens with his right-hand. His left hand held a long flex and, as I was trying to work out what it was, he suddenly said, "Smile!" At precisely that instant, the two spotlights flashed, blinding me so that I couldn't see what he had done. He repeated this action three times and then it was my sister's turn and Maman was last.

The post office started to function again; during the war it had more or less stopped, so now it was possible to communicate with Paris and England. Maman received a letter from GG who invited us to come and stay with them in England near Disley. A week later mother went to fetch the photographs and returned with lots of papers to fill. She explained we were going to obtain passports so we could travel from one country to another. Some time later while I was feeding the rabbits, I heard Sylvette bouncing round the corner of the house, sounding full of joy and excitedly singing, "I've got a daddy, I have got a daddy…I am now called Sylvette David and you're called François Lassalle!" She opened a little pale-brown book showing me the page with her photograph and next to it was written clearly Sylvia Jocelyn David. She had been called Sylvette shortly after her birth.

The shock was tremendous and, in that instant, I'd lost my identity. My world exploded, a thick dense fog invaded my insides and I became speechless and numbed. I felt I mislaid myself, and I was not there any more, and the connection to my feelings had been severed, leaving me floating in an unknown space. My eyes were dry; no tears came with the disturbing news. It was as if I had gone back into a foetus form and had been catapulted far into space. I withdrew into silence. Now, I could hear faintly my sister's voice talking to me but I had no wish, no desire, to understand what she was saying, she had run back to the house carrying her new reality away with her. The fog started to dissipate a little and a new image of myself slowly began to appear, with much self-pity in it, and a sudden loneliness. I felt completely abandoned. When we came to Dieulefit my world was Maman, Papa (in spirit) and Sylvette they formed my home and security. Our papa Marcel had died and I knew Fonsou could never be a replacement. Out of the blue, life had decided to reshape my relationship with Sylvette who became my half sister with an existing father she could identify with, a real one, alive! That was disturbing and unfair and strengthened my inner bond with my father Marcel Lassalle who became even more my beloved papa.

A shiver went down my back. How long I had been standing by the rabbit hatch? I didn't know. It was getting dark and I was feeling the cold. I looked at the rabbits. They had almost finished what I had given them and were chewing the last bunch of cut grass on the floor of their cage. The strong smell of their urine, mixed with the fresh grass, their round bubbly eyes looking at me while they ate, their whiskers going up and down frantically with the speed of their chewing, made a crunching sound and this brought me back to a welcome, comforting and earthly reality. When I heard my mother calling that it was suppertime, I walked back slowly round the house into the kitchen. It took me a while to adapt to the bright light in the warm kitchen, the table was laid and the delicate smell of Maman's cooking filled my nostrils and sharpened my appetite. Sylvette was still looking through her passport, "Maman? Where is my passport?" I said, looking round the kitchen to see if I could see it anywhere. "You're on mine, look here!"

She stretched across the table and handed me over her little pale brown book. Effectively, there I was, my photo was clipped next to my pretty Mum's, I felt reassured. Obviously, Maman and Sylvette had talked about her new dad but I was full of questions and I wanted to find a way to include him in my own perspective. His name was Emmanuel David, mother called him Mano, and he was an art dealer who lived in Paris. She told us a little about her life story with him and we also found out that we had an older brother called Philippe and another sister called Maxence who died when she was only 20 days old.

When I heard about an older brother called Philippe, a vast loving space for him appeared inside me. I couldn't place any image in it, but knew he would be kind, tall and he would play with me. An inner cloud unexpectedly threw a shadow on my excitement as a nagging voice inside me said, "But he will only be your half brother, like your half sister. They have a different dad, don't they?" That was an unpleasant truth, I knew that it would stay with me always and I pushed it far away, deciding that I would just call them my brother and my sister as I felt them to be.

Letters started to come through the post, including some from Mano, and Sylvette was always excited when they arrived. Holding us close to her, Maman would read them aloud, always answering the flow of questions that they would create. Mano wrote once a month, his letters were always decorated with funny drawings of little dogs dancing and usually contained a postal order for 300 old French Francs which Maman cashed at the post office in Dieulefit. This money quickly became our lifeline and when it arrived, Maman would say, "Come on, let's go to the post office and shop in the village!"

We'd come back home, the bicycle loaded with food and fish for the cats, with magazines, comics, notebooks and drawing paper. Our cats were waiting for us sitting on the edge of the concrete lavoir. As soon as we came in sight, they ran towards us with their trembling tails straight up in the air mewing for food, and then stopped our convoy by getting in the way of our legs and bicycles. At the pump Maman rested the bike and looked into the basket for fresh sardines, hold them up in the air by their tails, one by one, while the frantic cats leapt up with their claws out. Our two feline friends were 'Tigrette' who was Sylvette's, an elegant thin tiger stripped and mine,

'Camouflée', with half her face black, the other white. This made her appear to look through only one eye, her long hair marked like the camouflage of the American tanks. They slept in our respective bedrooms and were very much part of the family. Early one morning I woke up still half in a dream, feeling wet in my bed. "Oh no, oh dear, I've peed in my bed!" Tentatively, I felt my pyjamas with my hand… surprisingly they were dry. "That's funny, I must have dreamt it." When stretching out my body, like I often did in the morning, my feet came to a cold wet place again. In a flash I threw back my bedding to discover at the bottom of my bed Camouflée purring, looking at me with half closed eyes full of tenderness, stretching herself round to reveal six long baby kittens busy having their first day's breakfast.

First visit to England

The day came when we left for our first visit to England. We took the bus to Montélimar to catch a night train to the Gare de Lyon in Paris. From there we would have to change trains and cross part of the big city to another station called Gare St. Lazard. From there we would travel to Dieppe, catch a ferry to Newhaven, then travel by train to Victoria Station in London. We soon discovered that travelling with our Maman was always a kind of suspense - this time we had left Dieulefit with only a few coins in her purse. Was it the correct train and carriage? Were we on the right seat number? These questions stayed with us until we reached our final destination.

Not without difficulty we managed to climb on to the high train, a man helped us with our heavy suitcase and kindly found our three seats in the correct compartment. We were alone and I started bouncing up and down on the domed slippery seats. I was feeling so light and happy, although we had a short scuffle when I realised that my sister had taken the seat by the window. To bring back peace, Mum gave me hers and I sat next to her opposite my sister, my back facing the direction the train was going. We opened the picnic basket out

CHAPTER 3

with our chicken's boiled eggs, goat cheese, tomato dipped in salt and a baguette bought in Montélimar. There wasn't much to look at through the dirty window in the night; the rhythmic sound of the metal wheels quickly cradled me into a light sleep, my head on Maman's knees.

With a loud squeal the train had stopped in some station, there were noises of doors sliding open, voices calling. The light was switched on in our compartment and five people moved in, talking loudly as if we were not there, shifting their suitcases into the nets above. I felt them as intruders of our space. Finally, the light was switched off, the train was moving again and I snuggled back into sleep. A bad egg smell kept coming in waves into our compartment, as I heard the sound of the engine slicing through the air. In the semi-darkness, my nose detected other odours not from our family, particularly one that my nose was trying to detect - where did it come from? And I found the answer... it came from the fat man who was fast asleep with his mouth wide open, his legs stretched out in our direction. His shoeless feet carried a pair of dirty socks. The stench became unbearable until I finally turn round the other way, my head near the window resting on my mum's coat. At six o'clock in the morning Maman shook me gently saying, "Wake up now, we have arrived in Paris."

The Gare de Lyon station was gigantic and the air was colder than in the South. Looking up, I saw pigeons flying onto the platform and walking around looking for crumbs, not at all disturbed by the many people who were rushing along each caught by their own thoughts. The smell of the coffee and sandwiches being sold from stalls woke up my appetite. Making sure not to get lost, I held onto Maman's skirt, we followed her to a taxi that took us straight through Paris to the Gare St. Lazard. She had just enough in her purse to pay for it, explaining, as we were walking into the station, that we would not be able to have breakfast. We took some time to find our train and settled into our new compartment. Now it was daytime and we could see through the windows, but unfortunately we had to sit on the corridor side. I noticed that the couple by the large window spoke English to each other in soft voices and I recognize something familiar in the feeling they projected. Was it because they were from England like my mother? I smiled to them and they smiled back. When they were talking it sounded gentle, softer to the ears and not like the sounds I had been used to in Provence.

I felt awake and my curiosity lead me into the corridor to a large window with a chromed bar across it which I held with both hands and gazed out, my forehead on the glass. I had never seen a landscape like what I saw in front of me. It was bleak, I could not see any mountains anywhere, the colours were not bright but all in grey pastel tones. The fields rushing by were vast, the farms looked different, with sloped slate roofs and enormous barns. I was feeling happy, glancing occasionally back through the indoor window to check that my sister and mother were still in the compartment, reassured by their presence, I would go back confidently to my semi-dreams. Mostly men were in the corridors, some smoking, looking out without looking, as if far away in their thoughts and their universe. Amongst them were quite a few young military men, who could not have gone to war. It was over so probably they were going back home to see their mum, I thought.

I was going to see my grandparents for the first time, my mum's Mum and Dad. She had spoken to us a little about her father, that he had been a clergyman that he'd participated in many wars and battles and was now a colonel. Sometime before I was born, when he was in his 60s on holiday on the island, he attempted to cross from l'Aygade to Port Cros, a distance of some 1500 metres. When he had almost reached the rocks of Port Cros, he fell unconscious and drifted on his back taken by the strong currents. Sometime later, fishermen lifting their nets saw grandpa floating out towards the open sea. He was apparently on his back with just his moustache and nose sticking out of the water. Totally unconscious but breathing, he was pulled up onto the boat, wrapped in a blanket and taken back to the Grand Avis. Once there, he was laid on to the sand and the old Pégliasco, who lived in a hut on the beach, with his great peppery moustache, his strong breath of garlic and wine, had given the colonel the kiss of life. This action had an immediate result, making him sit up and say, "What on earth do you think you're doing!" After this event, on his return to England, Grandpa developed polio; both legs became paralysed and he was now in a wheelchair.

The train slowed down, we were coming into Dieppe, an old grey fishing town. I saw boats and was surprised to see them so far into the town. They were all shapes and sizes, much bigger than the ones I knew, some made of metal with cabins and masts. It all was completely new and fascinated me. The dirty houses around the harbour were tall and narrow with dark blue slate roof and the streets were paved. The train was now going along slowly until it finally stopped beside the biggest boat I had ever seen! She was so tall that from the train window, I had to bend my head backwards to see the top of it. It was white, with two huge red and black chimney's, several levels and the sides were full of little round windows. Maman's voice called me across the corridor, "Sounet darling, put your coat on, we have arrived!"

As we descended the train onto the platform, the first thing that hit me was the strong odour of the sea mixed with a smell of tar and fish and the cacophonic cries of seagulls flying over the fishing boats. Gigantic cranes were loading our ferryboat. The passengers started walking towards a decrepit wooden building faded pale blue and we followed the crowd. While waiting in the queue, I asked, "Maman, where are we going? Why are there so many seagulls?" "We're going through the customs before going up onto the boat. There are many seagulls, because it's a fishing harbour, and they come for food."

An icy and distant custom officer came up to us and directed us to put our suitcases and baskets onto the worn low counter that separated us from him. Did we have anything to declare? Maman answered negatively, then he asked, "Wine? Cigarettes? Records? Animals? Money?" She laughed, amused by the questions, "Oh no, we have none of these things, we have absolutely no money. We're going to see my mum and dad that I have not seen since before the war!" Sylvette and I always felt embarrassed when our Maman talked to people we did not know more than what we thought was necessary, especially concerning private family matters. His mouth smiled, melting the ice and with the piece of chalk in his right hand, he scribbles on our suitcase and bags. Then, as if we did not exist any more, he turned to the next travellers.

We followed the crowd to the quayside in the front of the gangplank leading up into the boat. Sailors waited for us at the top and helped us to jump into the boat with our belongings. We climbed through a small door and went down a staircase that took us to an enormous lounge, where we soon found a bench by a dirty window covered with dust and sea-salt. My nose, always being the first to detect the atmosphere of a new place, noticed an unexpected smell of sweet tobacco, beer and pork sandwiches. Once we settled, I told Maman that I was hungry but Sylvette immediately snapped back, "We have no money, so no food, so don't talk about it!" Maman added calmly, "We'll have to wait until we get to England. My brother Tony will have some money when he meets us at Victoria Station. Do not worry my darlings, it won't be long now." I was feeling tired, I nestled up against her and went into a deep sleep.

In 1946, the journey from Dieppe to Newhaven took four to six hours depending on the state of the sea. I woke up some hours later, when we were already far out at sea, and I wanted to go out on the deck. I looked at my sister in case she'd come with me, but she was neatly curled up on the bench seat, fast asleep. She looked happy where she was, her face at peace. With my mother's agreement and the recommendations to hold on tightly and to be careful not to slip, I went by myself. As soon as I started walking I noticed the boat was rocking slowly one-way, slowly the other, as well as up and down. It was difficult to walk straight and it took me some time to get to the staircase. Through the windows I could see that the Nile green sea was very rough, with frosty white on the large waves. I buttoned up my coat, pushed down my knitted hat and wrapped my scarf round my neck. Climbing the stairs was difficult, and when I reached the top, I saw some people looking terribly ill, white faced and droopy eyes. I admitted to myself that I did not feel so great either. It appeared that the sea was much rougher now, and I made for the little door leading to a part of the deck where there seemed to be less wind. The air was sharp and wet; the cries of the seagulls were swallowed up by the howling wind. The waves were violently hitting the boat that trembled as its engine's resisted the push, making the boat shudder.

The sky wasn't at peace either. Dark and light clouds passed by rapidly allowing at times the blue sky to appear. I snuggled into a sheltered corner out of the wind where I could hold on securely and have a good view of the open sea. This was a heavenly place resting my back against the side of a cabin, holding the safety rail behind my back, I felt part of the boat, the uneasy feeling that I had felt downstairs was now gone, all my senses were nourished and satisfied. The sun came out again, and I felt its gentle warmth on my closed eyelids, I wanted time to stand still, that moment to stay forever.

Suddenly without warning, a cold spray of seawater and foam soaked me and drew me out of my short-lived paradise; I was wet but happy. Coming towards me on the deck was a couple holding on tight to each other and laughing, the wind moulding their clothes against their bodies, wet through like mine. I took the opportunity when they opened the small door to climb back into the ship. Sylvette was awake chatting with mum, and as I came to them, they saw me beaming, my face and ears bright red from the wind and sea. In my usual manner I made them laugh with my clowning and shared what I had seen and experienced.

We entered Newhaven harbour, the sea had quietened and the ferry gave a tremor before coming to a standstill along the dock. The passengers were picking up their suitcases and rushing up from the lower decks. It was still daytime, the wind had stopped, the tide was very low, and the gangplank led us directly onto the wharf. My eyes were looking everywhere, absorbing the many new impressions, everything was different, nobody spoke French, the smell from their cigarettes was similar to the smell of our 'pain d'épices'; but the seagulls made the same cries.

In no time we were in front of the English custom officers, differently dressed from the French with wider and flatter caps, their dark blue uniform did not have a wide red line down the side like ours, and some of the custom offices had impressive moustaches. They spoke English to Maman, she showed them our two passports and they stamped them, and smiled nicely as they made a white chalk mark on our luggage like the French customs had done in Dieppe. Coming out of the customs, we found ourselves in a railway station with a long canopy held up by metal posts. The train was waiting for us and it looked smaller than the French ones, especially the engine, being level with a platform, one didn't have to climb up into it. The carriages were made of highly varnished wood with small velvet seats. I was intrigued by the strange system of opening the windows: you unhooked a wide leather belt from a brass knob, held on to it tightly and let it disappear slowly inside the thickness of the door until it reached the desired level, then you fixed the belt to the knob. This was also the only way to open the door of the carriage, as there was no handle or lock on the inside! The scent was very different from the French trains, which were dominated by the odours of Gauloises tobacco mixed with wine, cheese and garlic. In England, beside the pain d'épices scent from the cigarettes, was the smell of fried fat and disinfectant. The ladies wore funny complicated hats and so did some of the men. I saw one man walking by all dressed in black, with a black rimmed melon-shaped hat on his head and holding a long black umbrella. "He is from the city," whispered Maman seeing my amusement.

Maman and Sylvette found our seats, and a large, peppery, fair-haired man was talking to our mother while he was placing our suitcase on to the luggage rack. He turned round and looked at me, and smiled broadly through his short grey beard. He wore glasses, and a tweed cap and jacket. I sat opposite him with Sylvette on my

CHAPTER 3

right and Maman facing. More people came in, the train moved off smoothly and the landscape started to unroll as it accelerated. I could see round green hills with white cliffs, and fields, all much smaller than in France, with trees and hedges around them and cows and sheep. There were rows and rows of identical houses with long narrow gardens. Instead of tiles on their roof, they has dark grey slates like I had seen in Dieppe; they all seemed to be made of red bricks, but some were painted white.

I looked at the man engaged in a deep conversation with our mother. His brown suede shoes were worn in places, creating darker shiny patches, and the sole of his shoe was slightly squashed out because he was heavyset. His short socks were mustard yellow with orange diamond patterns; I had not seen such fancy ones before. And while I was studying them, Maman spoke French to us, saying in a low voice, "This very nice man is offering us a meal on the train! Isn't that great? Come on, let's go!"

That was great indeed, we all got up and followed the nice man through the narrow corridor to the restaurant car. It was a long carriage with seats and tables to take four; the tables had small lamps with orange fabric lampshades, giving a warm yellowish light. Sylvette and I sat down excitedly next to each other, and Maman, still speaking English with the new friend, sat opposite me. We had never eaten in a restaurant before, yet alone on a train! There were lace tablecloths, fancy silver-plated cutlery, two glasses each and in the middle of the table were two narrow square shaped bottles, one with Heinz Tomato Ketchup written on it and on the other, Daddy's Sauce. A man with black trousers and a white jacket, with ginger hair neatly parted in the middle and flattened by some unknown oils, came presenting our new friend with the menus. Mother had not had bacon in many years, immediately decided to have that, and, curious to see what it was, we chose the same. It took ages to arrive and we were by now so hungry.

Surely the man in the white jacket did not know how hungry we were... I glanced outside the window but I couldn't see much in the

119

night except that we went through many towns. At last the ginger haired man arrived with heavy plates loaded with fried bacon, a fried sausage, fried tomatoes, a fried toast with a heap of reddish beans on top and lots of thickly cut chips! The white bread was strange and cut into thin triangles that stuck together when I bit into them. To her delight, Maman and the man had a glass of red wine; we were served terribly sweet lemonade. This was the first time I had a fizzy drink, which I found difficult to swallow as it made me burp. Our meal wasn't finished yet, for then came what they called 'steamed pudding'. This cake was presented steaming hot in a deep plate covered with a thick yellow liquid, which I recognized as corn flour. It was also very sugary, stuck to my teeth and didn't taste much of anything. I felt really full and satisfied and so very different from before the meal. Maman and her friend had a cup of coffee, smoked an English cigarette and were still talking when the train slowed down as we arrived at London Victoria Station. Before we left the train, the man gave Maman his card, shook her hand politely saying "au revoir" and while he came off the train, we thanked him profusely in French as he disappeared into the dense crowd.

Victoria Railway Station was as big and as noisy as the ones in Paris and the people also seemed to be in a hurry. I didn't see any pigeons and thought to myself, "maybe they have gone to bed, it is night-time after all." Our mum stretched out on her toes as she whistled the family tune and looked out for her younger brother Tony. Our Granddad had taught his children to whistle a tune he had heard from an African bird in South Africa and had adopted it as a family alert system. It was most efficient, as our uncle soon appeared out of the crowd!

All my feelings were wide open to my mum's brother, and as I saw him approach, waves of love immediately started to flow towards him. He had a tall thin body and a small head perched on top, a big moustache and bushy eyebrows. He took off his soft grey felt hat and gave a long affectionate hug to our mother, embracing her tightly and lifting her off the ground. Tony obviously loved her very much and was overjoyed to see his elder sister again. In one scoop, he picked up my sister and me in his powerful arms. That uplifting feeling I recognized instantly and I felt a real papa in him. My face was now closer to his and I could study him in detail. His bushy eyebrows captivated me - they reminded me of some old dog I had seen - and I wondered how he could see through all the bristles? His ears had ginger hairs coming out of them and big dangling earlobes. He kissed my sister first, and said something to her I did not hear. His sparse hair was light ginger and cut short; he smelt nice. He turned his head and looked into my eyes for what seemed a long time. His pale pinkie-blue eyes were smiling and tender like my mother's and when I looked into them, I felt appeased by their great kindness.

Maman had told me that he was a policeman, and I longed for him to tell me about it; did he wear an English policeman hat? Did he have a gun? Had he caught any robbers? His moustache touched my cheek and brought me back from my reveries. He kissed me with affection and asked me in French if I'd had a good journey. His voice was deep and resonated through me, and I was very pleased he spoke French so well and so I could ask him the many questions that I had. As he took our suitcases, I looked at his strong hands, with long the fingers knobbly at the joints, and well-groomed nails. There was something soft and gentle about them.

We drove to Carshalton in his small Ford, where he lived with his wife and two children. Betty was waiting for us in their tiny semi-detached house, with supper on the table. I was excited to meet our cousins Antonia and Peter. Although we could not communicate with words, Peter and I got on quickly with each other, using our hands and facial expressions. He showed me round the house; to my amazement in their sitting room, on the wall above the fireplace, was the view that I loved the most and painted by my mother before the war. It was a sunset scene of Port Cros, the sun hidden behind a dark cloud lighting all the islands beyond and fading into the horizon; the silvery grey and pale gold-orange sea was in foreground where a part of our island was painted deep indigo. Discovering this painting was like recharging my batteries and I felt whole. A strange form of heating was below the painting; a tiled gas fireplace with small flames fiercely climbing up pierced tubular ladders. The sitting room was small with only place for two large comfortable flowery patterned armchairs and a settee. There were other paintings by Maman in the house, a portrait of Betty when she was younger, and a very large one of Tony in his late teens, wearing a straw hat, sitting on a Normandy beach, with his arms around his knees.

Peter and I were called in for supper. I was curious to see what they cooked and sat at the table but I was not hungry after the big meal on the train. There was the same cut white bread covered by a thin layer of dark yellow, salty butter. White plates were brought in with a pale greyish soup called 'cream of mushroom'. On the centre of the table was a dish with small hard tomatoes, long white and green onions, and some plain salad leaves. Next to it was a small bottle, they called it 'Heinz mayonnaise' and apparently one was meant to pour its pale yellow fluid onto the lettuce leaves. The dining room was tiny and was adjacent to an even smaller kitchen. In the corner, I noticed a strange kind of stove in which they put little dark grey lumps, Maman told me later that it was called 'coke'; the stove had pipes coming out of it and I soon realised it was part of their central heating system.

After supper we were all back in the sitting room, Maman, chatting in English to Betty, Sylvette communicating with Antonia, and I sat next to Tony on a small leather poof. I asked him, "Can you show me your gun?" He laughed, "But I haven't got a gun!" I thought, how could that be if he really is a policeman? "You mean the English police don't have arms?" "Yes they do, but we keep them at the police station." He explained and continued amused. "If I need a gun, I have to go back to the police station, sign a book and one is given to me for a specific mission." "Do you mean the policemen we see in the streets do not carry guns?" "Yes, that's correct, they don't."

This conversation gave me a completely new perspective on the role of the police, which made sense to me. In France, people feared the police or the gendarmes with their huge pistols hanging on their hips; it gave them an impression of arrogance and power. But here, having no gun made an enormous difference, it made the policeman more accessible. "Can I see your policeman uniform please?" "Yes, of course, come with me." His legs were very, very, long and, when he was sitting on the low sofa they came up to near his ears. Under the narrow staircase of the entrance hall, was a small door which uncle Tony opened… it was packed with things, screwdrivers, pincers, a cylindrical black torch, a fire extinguisher, narrow shelves with lots of little glass jars containing all kinds of nails and brass screws. Hanging from a nail on the right, was a long black truncheon. He laughed when asked him if I could hold it; it was very shiny, heavy and extremely hard. I thought, 'it must hurt terribly when it lands on your head!' He pulled out the policeman's dark suit and hooked its coat hanger on the handle of the door, and showed me the helmet with its chinstrap of black leather. It was shaped like a round-top mountain with a chromed star in the front with rays coming out. The helmet was so hard that I thought, this is what one has to wear in case a truncheon hits one. How funny!

Throughout the house were soundless fitted carpets, which were nice to lay, sit or walk on. There were so many things to look at, especially in the bathroom. I had never seen one before so I asked Maman if I could have a bath, since we were all filthy from the long journey. My first hot water bath was a wonderful experience, before I had been washed in the zinc tub in the kitchen by the fire. Here, I had warm water right up to my neck and I could even go completely under it holding my nose and breath, like I did in the sea. Maman soaped and scrubbed me all over and I suddenly felt very tired, ready for bed.

It was at Betty's that Sylvette and I had our first English breakfast; it was copious, just like a full meal. I discovered crunchy cornflakes with fresh milk and sugar sprinkled on top, soft-boiled eggs, English toast with the salty butter and marmalade together with many cups of tea. My aunt had offered me fried bacon, but after the previous day's experience on the train, I turned it down.

Cousin Antonia was roughly my sister's age and her red hair was plaited into one long, thick plait falling in the middle of her back. She was keen to try her French on us, pointing at things and saying "sel?" Or "oh!" I would correct her and say, "non, eau!" She was obviously a very well behaved girl, who knew all the correct manners and must have studied well at school. Peter was younger than me and showed me his railway tracks and all his toys before breakfast. I must admit I was very impressed by the number of toys my cousins had. Peter's railway carriages and engine were miniatures of the English train we'd be in on the previous day. He had lots of small motorcars and children's books. Maman had not had enough money to buy us such things, and coming to England showed me the big difference between countries that have been invaded by a foreign army and those that had never been invaded. Well, the last time for England was apparently in 1066 by the French Normans, Maman told me once.

Tony came in asking if we were ready to leave for the station. We sat in his little two-door, sea green Ford with high narrow wheels, chrome bumpers and headlamps rims and comfortable light brown leather seats. Maman sat in front in one of the bucket seats, so she could chat with her brother. Our aunt and cousins stood on the pavement and waved us goodbye. We were going off to catch a train to see our other uncle at a village called Disley, near Altringham, not too far from where GG and Grandpa lived. I hadn't been in a car like this before and I was taking in everything. The painted metal dashboard had a bunch of keys dangling from it. There was a round dial showing the speed, Tony told me that the numbers were in miles, not in kilometres, and that the English did not use centimetres and kilometres, but the longer inches and miles. I asked him why measures were different in the two countries, and he explained about Napoleon and the French Revolution. My uncle knew lots of things and I loved listening to his voice softened by his moustache. Outside, looking through a small window, I could see rows and rows of brick houses, all looking as if they came out of a mould. The lorries were smaller, somehow cleaner, with lots of writing all over them and many of them didn't have any tops, but were just flat platforms with things tied on to them. I asked Tony why they drove on the left side of the road in England, he did not know, but said. "You know why the trains in France run on the left side?" I had no idea… "It's because English engineers started the train system in France." That was interesting information I would tell my friends about it back in Dieulefit.

When we reached King's Cross-station Tony parked and helped us with our suitcases while making sure we found the correct platform, carriage and seat.

Uncle Ralph was at the Altringham station, immaculately dressed in a short grey flannel coat, his hands in a pair of fine light leather gloves, were holding a pale grey felt hat. He was delighted to see his sister, gave her a reserved but long embrace. He turned to Sylvette beaming, looking at her for a long time before kissing her. Then, he bent down slightly towards me, holding my face in his gloves, I smelt their delicate sweet scent and he kissed me rapidly on one cheek. Then called a Porter to take our luggage and said, "Come! I'll take you first to Edward and GG's at Bowdon Hydro. They are expecting us for lunch, you will stay in a house nearby." We walked to his car, a celadon grey Austin 10 with chrome bumpers carrying a number plate: FNE 663. The porter loaded our luggage neatly into the boot while Ralph found the few coins to give him for his service. Our mum and uncle spoke English all the way - they had a lot to say to each other. Sylvette looked out of the window at the Cheshire Hills while I inspected the car. It was very different from the old French Peugeot van that belonged to our school. The dashboard was of fine burr walnut; the inside of the doors also had strips of the precious wood. The comfortable seats where covered in soft shiny leather, behind the front seats were nets to hold maps & newspapers.

The sound of gravel under the tires brought me out of my car inspection, I looked out to see green grass and beds of colourful roses.

We parked by an Edwardian redbrick mansion, apparently a rest home, standing in the middle of beautifully laid out gardens. Our grandparents lived there in a large apartment that they rented. Our Grandmother GG came to greet us; she was round with thin legs in white stockings, her feet in tiny marine colour shoes and she was dressed in a blue suit with a blue hat and a white blouse. A black velvet ribbon was tied round her neck. She looked so pleased to see us and immediately spoke to us before she talked to her own children. She had a strong English accent when she spoke French; her eyes were pale blue, her hair silver grey. When she came close to kiss me, I smelt lily of the valley. Her hands were petite, with her little finger sticking out independently, her nails very neatly shaped and shiny with transparent varnish. In French, she complimented Maman on how beautiful her children were as she gave us a quick kiss on both cheeks, then it was our Maman's turn to be hugged, and then Ralph's.

Uncle stayed for lunch in the vast dining room overlooking the rose garden. There were lots of other old people there, whispering to each other and all discreetly watching our arrival. Grandpa was already sitting at the dining table waiting for us, obviously hungry and wanting his meal. He was sitting in a chromed wheelchair with large double wheels, I couldn't see his legs, they were under a Tartan grey and brown blanket, but he was just at the right height for me to kiss him. He looked so much like Uncle Tony, but with even bigger eyebrows! His white moustache tickled my cheek as Tony's had; he was smiling but when his deep blue eyes met mine, I felt his authority and their piercing intensity forced me to look down. He was very pleased to see Sylvette and held her hand, gently caressing it and he looked at her for a long time. Maman, bending down over the wheelchair, hugged her father for what seemed like ages; his lovely old hand that fought so many battles gently rubbing her back. Obviously, there was much emotion flowing between them, for when she straightened up I could see tears in their eyes.

The tables were laid with even more things than I had seen on the train. Lots of silver and glasses, salt and pepper pots, a cut glass water jug, the usual red, white and brown sauce bottles were there, the white bread cut in triangles, the bright yellow butter was rolled up in little barrels displayed on a small silver plate with a funny short handle knife. A pretty young lady stood timidly by the table. She was dressed in black and wore a very small round white-laced apron and in her hair was a strange stiff visor made of lace that pointed up to the ceiling. She was standing next to me so I looked at her feet trapped in black semi-high-heeled shoes decorated with a black ribbon tied in a bow. Resting her body weight on the outside of each foot, made the heels and soles almost face each other, forcing her body weight on her ankles. I knew that she was feeling nervous because the fingers of her hands resting over her apron, twiddled nervously. Now all my attention was swallowed up by her feminine presence, I smelt her body odour...

I suddenly heard my mother's voice, "François, would you like some beef, boiled potatoes and sprouts?" My attention was brought back to the world of eating manners; Maman was serving. The brown meat was cut into very thin slices, covered by dark brown gravy, the sprouts and potatoes were plainly boiled. Grandpa, GG and Ralph were asking all kinds of questions of our mum; so much had happened in the past seven years. I looked around to find the serving girl, but she had disappeared. I thought she'd come back with the pudding and waited for that moment. Finally she reappeared with the pudding and looking in my direction, gave me a beaming smile, which made me completely melt into myself feeling discreetly a shy pleasure.

Uncle went back to Disley in the grey Austin soon after lunch that day, I stayed outside to play in the gardens, while Sylvette and Maman were talking together on the bench; the sun was shining and the high sky was a pale misty blue. After a while, GG called to ask me to go up and see Edward. I climbed the grand wooden carpeted staircase up to their flat, knocked at the door and heard grandpa's trembling voice say, "Come in." I was feeling a bit nervous to be alone with him, as his intense presence impressed me. He waved for me to sit right next to his chromed wheelchair; he was wearing a scarf round his neck and smelt of pipe tobacco. I noticed that he was wearing knitted gloves with the fingertips missing. As he held my hand affectionately, I could feel his dry, cold and thin finger tips in my warm palm, and looking into my eyes fervently, he said.

"So you want to hear about my war stories, do you?" I replied timidly, not knowing what else to say, "Yes." So, in a good French, he started to tell me some parts of his amazing war adventures. He had been in the Boer's War in South Africa where he was a military chaplain, where his work took him right to the front to fetch the dead soldiers and bring them back to bury them, this was done while bullets were flying all around him, he was hit in the leg by one of them.

He was now getting right into exploits, we were in the 1914/18 war, where he decided to stop being an army chaplain, as he had enough of picking up bodies to put into graves. He went to military schools for three months in Dover and came out as captain. With his men they were sent right up to the front lines to fight in the trenches facing the enemy.

He told me how, in his shelter once, he had shared his meagre sandwich with a mouse caught with him when the shells were flying above their heads. Also how once, he and his men were caught in a fierce shooting exchange with the Germans and as they came out of a wood into a village, he had noticed one of his men agonising by a farm building, his leg half torn off. While he was telling me the story, Grandpa was looking straight at me, I could feel that he was in a sense, reliving the experience, his eyes were now bloodshot and disturbing, burning with a violent fire, I felt uneasy, cold and trembling slightly inside. He continued… and while he was attempting, with a tourniquet, to stop the escaping blood of his companion's leg, he felt the sharp point of a bayonet pressing on the upper part of his chest. Looking up, he saw a large German soldier about to kill him, when their eyes met, Grandpa burst into uncontrolled laughter. He told me he thought it funny to die while caring to his companion.

That laugh saved him! The German soldier, surprised by the unusual situation of a man who starts laughing when he is about to die, burst into laughter himself. The pressure of the bayonet on the chest lightened, and at gunpoint, he allowed grandpa to finish his tourniquet and took them both prisoners. Re-living these battles had tired my Granddad; he looked at me, his eyes now tender, and giving me a gentle smile said, "I need to rest, you can go now…"

We saw our grandparents for a week, I came to like GG very much she had a good sense of humour, and she was surprised that I did not know anything about Jesus or God. She told me she went to church regularly and she always carried a little blue prayer book with her. I was interested to see how neatly her teeth were arranged when she smiled and how well they fitted their bright pink gums. They looked so perfect I wanted to touch them but did not dare. She walked with short little steps, and carried with her always a small black leather bag. She cared for Granddad all the time for he could not move easily without her help, and I understood that his handicap made him short tempered and not easy to live with.

We stayed in a large Victorian house, which belonged to some friends of GGs. One day the ladies of the house asked us for tea. The large sitting room had high ceilings and bay windows and we sat in enormous flowery armchairs. A dainty tea service with sweet smelling biscuits on a porcelain plate arrived on a fancy trolley. We sat round the low table and tea was poured into delicately painted cups so thin that I could see the light through them. I noticed that the elderly ladies were not resting their backs on the settee or armchairs but were sitting straight up enjoying chatting and savouring their tea; at times they laughed but with much restraint. I was now looking at Maman, and, to my amazement, she poured her tea from the cup, into the saucer and proceeded to drink from it while making sucking noises! I turned to GG and saw her hands manifesting her embarrassment, as the fingers were twisting into each other like intertwining snakes. Finding the atmosphere suddenly icy, Maman burst out laughing and exclaimed, "It's to cool the tea down, it is a very good trick! I recommend it!" I had seen our mother do this at home sometimes when her drink was too hot, but here I knew she had done it to provoke, she wanted to show these old ladies that there were other ways of living; she was keen to show them that she was free. I would not have been surprised if she had taken her clothes off and danced around the armchairs, just to shake them up.

Knowing that her action had drastically changed the atmosphere of the tea party, she tried to change the conversation as if nothing had happened. She pointed at the bouquet standing on the tea table and expressed exuberantly, "How awfully beautiful is this bouquet of flowers! Are these roses from your garden?" During the continuing silence, one of the ladies vaguely nodded, but GG put an end to the embarrassment and turning to Sylvette and said, "I am afraid we have to go now, Sage will be needing me at Bowdon Hydro." On the way back to the rest home, I could hear GG in a low reprimanding voice complaining to mother about her behaviour; Sylvette had been very embarrassed too and told her so. "Yes! I agree... I've never been so embarrassed!"

To appease the reproaches Maman said, "No, is that so... really? Well I promise that I will never do this again in public!"

The days went by in a flash and soon Ralph was back to fetch us. It was strange to say goodbye to our grandparents; I had a strange feeling that I would not see granddad again and as we waved goodbye, I felt an enormous swelling of emotions in my heart. We drove for a long time through rows and rows of semi-detached houses, and factories and the lampposts in the endless streets gave off a strange orange light. Finally, we arrived in Disley and when we came out of the car I heard coming from the huge trees, a noisy cacophony of sound as hundreds of crows seemed to announce our arrival.

Ralph's house was welcoming and bigger than Tony's. Aunt Kay came to greet us holding a cigarette and smiling. It was the first time I had met her and our other three cousins, Brian, Philip and Tim. They were looking at us grinning. I noticed that my cousins kept on looking at my sister who I knew was pretty and always attracted the attention. I didn't mind; I actually felt rather proud to be her brother. When Kay gave me a kiss, holding her cigarette away, I felt her high cheekbones against my cheek - she smelt of tobacco and whisky. Her dark brown eyes were smiling all the time, and she excused herself, as she had to prepare supper, Maman followed her.

Tim was round and very young, maybe two or three years old; Philip was about my age, good-looking, fair-haired and thin, he seemed to be highly sensitive and refined and I liked him instantly; Brian the oldest, was a little podgy, with blue eyes and red hair, a light skin with many freckles. After a long devouring look at Sylvette, he disappeared to his bedroom where he was apparently doing homework. Philip's bedroom walls were covered with posters of cars and trains, he proceeded to show me all his intriguing toys. They were different from Peter's, for instance, the trains had smoke coming out their chimneys, lights in the front, and they seem to go faster too. The railway tracks, the railway station, the crossroads were all in perfect miniature. Philip showed me his drawings; like me he liked to draw, and he told me his mother Kay illustrated educational children's books. The ones he showed me looked like much more fun than the 'Toto' and 'Lilli' that I had to read in Beauvallon.

It was time to go down for supper, the table was laid and the smell coming from the kitchen was appetising. There was wine on the table, French bread (a kind of rolled baguette) and the stew Kay had cooked reminded me a little of my mother's cooking. I couldn't understand what they were all talking about, but obviously mother was telling them about the war period in France. Now and then, I recognized a word and instantly felt part of the conversation, but then, I'd get lost again into myself and observed my aunt or my uncle and cousins at the way they were eating, talking, laughing, drinking. They also owned two enormous cats, which compared to Tigrette and Camouflée, were very placid and apparently were neither male nor female, as they could not have babies. We only stayed two days with Uncle Ralph's family, and we did not see much of him. He left early in the mornings to go to the big Ashton Brothers cotton factory where he was the director and came back late at night, but he did find the time to put us back on the train to London.

Once on board at Newhaven we noticed that the sea was quieter than when we'd arrived. The ship announced its departure by sounding its loud whistle, and slowly we moved out of the harbour. From the top deck we looked at Newhaven disappearing into the horizon together with the seven sisters, the famous white cliffs of Dover. The weather was perfect, the seagulls hovering over us sent out their usual cries. We stayed on the deck all the way to France, sitting on a long bench in the sun, each in our thoughts. I found again that peaceful place deep inside and I was happy to be going back to Maison Martin with Sylvette and Maman. Our journey home was easier this time, more comfortable and to some extent, I carried now, deep in my heart, a larger family. Having cousins, uncles and aunts, a granny and a granddad, gave me a more stable base and brought me a sense of security. Having such an English family was actually quite nice but made us different from the totally French.

Back to France with a new dimension

As we left Montelimar, and drove up into the mountains, my heart felt more and more bubbly and joyful at the prospect of being in our own world again, up on our hill, with the cats and other mammals and birds. Maman had arranged for a car to drop us at the bottom of our path, since we had done a little shopping previously. The walk home with our heavy luggage was slow; we had to rest many times on the way… Finally, we saw the house at the end of the small lane. The cats were there to greet us, purring loudly.

In our absence, Lena had stayed in the house to care for the animals, and they all looked in good health. I quickly went into my bedroom just to say hello—nothing had changed. Sylvette was already unpacking, looking at the new things she had brought back from England. Downstairs in the kitchen, Maman was feeding wood to the kitchen stove, the large suitcase was on the table, fully open and she was taking out the English goodies - packets of tea and biscuits, Marmite, golden syrup and placed them into the cupboard.

I did my rounds of the outside of the house, first going to see my friends the rabbits; they needed some grass and I feed them. The view east was still as magnificent and I stood there, drinking it in as if it was a necessary beverage. Then I popped round to the loos and while doing a pee, thought how different they were from the English toilets, with their roles of white soft paper, their oval polished seats and their white enamelled base.

Nothing had changed, it was evening and the chickens were already on the branches of the almond tree, talking to each other in their warm, gurgling language. There was a pile of oak logs in front of the house, so I fetched the axe and started splitting them. It is an exercise I still like doing, it makes me feel good in my body and relaxes my mind. Once standing on an old block, the log showed me the weakest place to hit. Neither Sylvette, or Maman could handle the axe properly; it seemed to be a thing that men like doing. While I was cutting the wood, mother came out of the kitchen and, with her wrist resting on her hips, looked at me with admiration and asked, "When you have finished, be a darling and do me a favour; go down to the pump to fetch me a bucket of water."

Fonsou was still in prison and at the age of 8, I became the man of the house, enjoying every occasion to test my strength. I knew that Maman had an unresolved hernia problem, and that she was anxious about it, so I did all I could to avoid her doing physical work. Sylvette was very strong, and she helped carrying the heavy shopping baskets. Our short visit to England had initiated a change in me, which was hard to define. I had become more aware of my mother's fragility and feelings; meeting her family showed me how different she was from them, how much more free she was, how much lighter and I understood how much she loved France.

The Easter holidays were over and I went back to school a different boy, filled with new experiences, broader in my feelings and more confident. The trip to England had given Sylvette and me a new perspective and awareness of our roots. We both became conscious of an invisible line attached to our far away English family and it sparked many questions about our ancestors. Maman would always answer them, telling us about her brothers, her mum and dad being away so often, and their 3 years in Switzerland where they learnt French. She told us about her grandfathers, especially her dad's father, who had been a sailor from the age of 13 and sailed away from Greenwich on her Majesty's Navy sailing ships to attack Aden and then to fight in China. It was five years before he'd returned to London. He was an artist and did beautiful watercolours of where he had been, which she showed us some in a thick drawing book. They were beautiful, indeed, so fine and delicate and were a true picture-diary of where her Majesty's ships had been, including the bay of Shanghai being shelled by the British fleet with its multitude of cannons. She told us also the intriguing story of how, her great uncle with his long cutlass had cut off the plait of a Chinese man he'd caught stealing ammunitions from the tender boat that he was guarding while his squadron was in Shanghai on a mission. "I think GG still has it somewhere at the bottom of a drawer!" Maman said bursting out into laughter.

Mother often read to us in the evenings, sitting on the sofa in the hallway. I recall one story by Victor Hugo, called 'Sans Famille.' A very sad and moving story, yet captivating, and once she'd started reading, our curiosity kept us up late into the night. In some parts, the story became so sad, that Maman would start crying, and the words became inaudible, usually by that time Sylvette and I were sobbing as well. When we all cried, she would suddenly laugh and we would all join her while wiping the tears from our wet faces.

One a cold windy night, sitting close together reading, goose pimples erupted all over my body when I saw an unshaven man staring at us through the window. He looked rough and pop-eyed eyed. With my elbow, I indicated to Maman that something was wrong, she and Sylvette looked up; I felt a tremor going through their spines, followed by a wave of emotions loaded with fear that brought tears to our eyes. Maman's arms were around us protectively as she squeezed us closer to her. Then the face vanished as suddenly as it had appeared. I rushed to the front door to turn the key in the lock and we stayed there without moving, silently, attentive to the slightest sound. After some time Maman said in a whisper, "I think that he has gone." Sylvette queried, "Who is he Maman? Do you know him?" "No, I've never seen this man before!" The face did not reappear again, but it left us with a strange feeling of insecurity that lasted for sometime.

So as to arrive at school for gym at 8 o'clock, we had to get up at six and by then Maman was already in the kitchen lighting the fire and preparing breakfast. After a quick wash in the kitchen sink, I sat on the chair watching mum grill slices of bread on the top of the cast iron stove. We ate the grilled slices with goat's cheese and homemade jam or honey and drank tea with milk, or a malty milk chocolate drink.

One morning we set off to school as usual, the snow had started to fall…and by half way to school the snow was up under our knees. I stopped and said to Sylvette, "We better go back home now, otherwise will never get back this evening the way the snow is falling!" Our mother was delighted by our return, "How clever of you to have come back!"

The snow fell all day, it was warm and cosy in the kitchen, the house had become like a cocoon and fortunately we had a good stock of logs stored in the hallway. Dieulefit, stands at an altitude of 600 metres, the winter can last two months and sometimes up to three before the spring shows any of its first green shoot. Putting my nose out of the front door, before going up to bed, I saw that the snow was already up to well over my knees and it was still falling, I felt thankful to be in our house and not stuck up at the Beauvallon school.

When I woke up the next morning there was so much light coming in through my window that I hurried to the frosty panes to look out. The snow had stopped falling, the outside was so white that it was difficult to distinguish any forms and to my amazement, I saw that the snow was right up under my window sill. I had never seen so much of it before! I hurried to my sister's bedroom, excitedly telling her of the night's heavy fall. Then, we rushed down to the kitchen were Maman was already lighting the fire, the light was poor and the electricity was cut off. From inside the kitchen, the windowpanes were a dull luminous light grey-blue colour. Curious, I went to the front door, bare feet and still in my pyjamas, and pulled and pulled until finally the door opened. Bits of starry snow floated down into the hallway and I felt their wetness on my feet. There, in front of me, stood a wall of snow, all the way up to the frame of the door and beyond. There we were, blocked in our house kidnapped by the elements; it was an unusual situation. After breakfast, I dressed for the snow, put on my ski boots, found the shovel, opened the door carefully, and started with my youthful energy to deal with the white wall. I rapidly realised that this was impossible, I had created a kind of small cave by pushing it away and squashing it down, but there was no where to dispose of the extra snow. Sylvette came to see and said with her usual authority, "You're crazy, what are you doing? It's impossible, come back in!" Reluctantly I followed her command. Every so often, Maman would ask me to fetch some more snow to fill the large two-handled zinc washbasin, which she'd put onto the stove to melt for our water supply.

The following day I manage to open my bedroom window and saw a beautiful frosty morning. The snow glittered as the low rays of the early sun caught the trillions of tiny crystals, the sky was deep blue and it had been so cold in the night that the top of the snow had hardened. In no time I was fully dressed and got out through the window to experiment and see if it the frozen crust would support my weight. Making my self as light as I could, hardly breathing, step by step I moved away from the windowsill. I noticed that the wind had created massive snowdrifts against the house while in other places the snow was only a few feet deep. After breakfast, I decided to shovel out a path to free the entrance door, starting from my first floor window. By 11 o'clock I'd made a one square metre, 2-foot depression in the drift and I felt tired and too hot to continue. I decided to do one last shovel load before having a break. As my shovel went into the softening snow, the surface I was standing on suddenly gave way and I found myself on the ground in front of the entrance door. I did not hurt myself, the snow had supported my fall, creating hardly any sound except a soft rumble, I found myself resting in a comfortable snow armchair! Looking up saw the large hole, the blue sky grinning at me. Feeling peaceful, quiet and very happy with my achievements, I stayed there surrounded by a profound silence.

While taking my sopping wet clothes off to dry, I told Sylvette and Maman of my exploits leading to the sudden fall and made them laugh. They came to the front door with me to see the result of my hard work, Maman complimented me, as she always did, on how marvellous was the result, what a clever boy I was, now we could opened the front door safely. Sylvette, on the other hand, caring for her younger brother, said protectively, "You could have hurt yourself very badly, you should be more careful!" This observation and advice took a little off the glory of my achievement and Maman added, "Yes, Sylvette is right, you could have fallen in a hole further away from the house and it would have been difficult to find you and to get you out! It is better that you don't walk on the top of the snow when it is frosty and so deep. We have some food left in the cupboard to last a few more days, we will wait for the snow to melt by itself." I had not realised this danger and I accepted their wise remarks.

Discovering our Maman's limits

We were trapped in the house for two weeks, until finally were forced out by our empty stomachs. I managed to clear away the snow from our front door up to where the path started and armed with two large shopping baskets we optimistically set off to the village. We found to our delight that the frozen ground appeared in many places, where the wind had swept it clean; but to avoid the riverbed, we went the longer way through the fields. What a strange feeling it was to discover that, after two weeks of forced hibernation, people were walking about, riding bicycles, driving motorcars, going about their business as if it had never snowed. I reflected, while we walked to the shops, that the rest of the world had obviously forgotten our little family up there on the hill, I realised that it would not have mattered to them if we'd never reappeared again! "Was the world not one? Or were there as many worlds as there were individuals living on it? Yes, that's it, only 'myself ' is aware of my world." I deducted, feeling satisfied with the answer.

My papa came to my thoughts and I wished he still lived with us to share everything and to help Maman. I could see that some parts of our life were difficult, even painful for her.

We did more shopping than usual and picked up our post, but the thought of having to walk all the way home made us feel tired. Maman had a brilliant idea - she took us to the popular café on the square opposite the church. We pushed the large heavy glass door and were hit by a dense atmosphere and loud voices. The noise took me by surprise after the weeks spent in the silence of our isolation. I found it very difficult to breathe the smoky air that smelled of Pastis, red wine, coffee, and above all Gauloises tobacco. The room was hot and stuffy and I breathed just shallow enough not to faint from the lack of oxygen. Everybody seemed to be smoking, everyone talking louder than the other to be heard. Card and drafts players took most tables, but Maman managed to find one in the corner by the steamed windows. When the garçon came Sylvette and I ordered hot chocolate, our mum her usual coffee. I enjoyed sitting down and just look around. I noticed a few scruffy dogs, sniffing the dirty floor that was covered with sawdust and cigarette ends and pushing their way through the many legs of the card players in search for a place to lay down. To me, cafés were places where the men met, where they smoked, talked about hunting, politics, drank Pastis and white wine. I recognized in quite a few of them the semi-unconscious condition that Fonsou came back in on most Saturday evenings: watery eyes, much giggling and somewhat argumentative.

CHAPTER 3

Wanting to be home and not looking forward to the long walk back, I day-dreamed that we could fly over the church, over the hills and trees and the fields, feeling the cold air on our ears, looking at the beautiful snowy landscapes below, and landing in front of our house with all our shopping! That was a wonderful dream... Maman took me out of it by saying gently, "Come on, my darlings, we have a long way home, let's go now." She paid for the drinks; we picked up our heavy baskets and came out into the vivifying fresh air. We walked and walked silently, every so often stopping to change hands, Maman insisting on carrying the two heaviest baskets. We finally came to the corner where we had to leave the main road and start the climb up to the house. It was too difficult for our Maman to climb up back into the fields, first because of the high stonewall, secondly because it had barbed wire fences. So we started to go up the steep stony riverbed. Soon we had snow well over our knees, and it became too difficult to go forward, so we managed to climb on the right bank of the ravine, grabbing any twig we could find to pull ourselves up to the top where there was a snowless narrow edge. Sylvette and I took our mother's baskets that she handed over to us from below; taking one each, we both hurried along the narrow edge to a place where we could see our house.

We turned round to look for our Maman but we could not see her... she'd disappeared! Then we heard her muted voice calling for help. She had slipped off the narrow edge onto the frozen surface over the riverbed that had not held her weight. We discovered her in the bottom of a hole she'd created in the 2-metre snowdrift. She was angry. We thought the situation terribly funny and laughed looking down at her. She was trapped and it was difficult to find a way to help her out. Finally Sylvette held the fencepost with one hand, and mine in the other as I walked on the frozen surface, stretching out as much as I could to grab Maman's hand, we managed to hold each other. Slowly, with much huffing, giggling and puffing, we managed to free our mother who was not at all amused, out of the hole. Running back quickly to pick up the bags, before our Maman could carry them, we started walking home. Then we heard our Maman shouting to us, "Wait for me! Let me carry the bags, they are too heavy for you, put them down! You are naughty children!" But we walked on. "Listen to me, stop! Listen to your mother!"

We could hear desperation in her voice; it was not usual for her to be like this, so we decided to stop and sit down by the bags to wait for her. She was definitely very upset and she came right up to us and gave us each a light slap on our cheeks, adding trying to finalise her action, "Voilà!"

There was no physical pain, for when her hand came to touch our cheeks, it had slowed down considerably, but we were in deep consternation! She had just hit us! That awful gesture! Never before had something like this happen between us, never before had she been aggressive towards us or punished us in any way. Sylvette and I broke down in tears feeling completely distraught. Touched by our reaction, she sat down between us, put her arms around us and we all cried together… "Why did you hit us Maman?" Sylvette said reproaching between two sobs, "I don't know, I am tired and I don't want you to carry these heavy weights." She answered, and continued, "Usually parents slap their children when they do something wrong, but here, I slapped you when you were actually so kindly helping me! What a silly Maman, I am… will you forgive me my darlings?" Without waiting for an answer, she gave us both an enormous hug and kiss, then laughed at the stupidity of the situation, we joined in, but not quite as freely as her.

Rising to our feet we shook the snow off our bums, and proceeded home still feeling shaken. She let us carry the heavy bags the rest of the way.

I realised then that Maman was fallible, was not as strong as she gave us the impression to be. What had just happened showed me her fragility; it made an imprint on the virgin space that I had given her deep inside my feelings and brought me to a new reality. I became conscious of my mother's vulnerability, and it made me want to protect her, to help her more wherever I could to lighten the burdens that life was putting on her. This event had the effect of bringing us even closer together and strengthening the bond between us.

The first contact with religious language

The first time I became aware of religion was when I wanted to invite a friend home for Sunday lunch, and he explained why he could not accept the invitation, "I'm going to church in Dieulefit this Sunday." Surprised, I queried, "To church, what for?"

I did not understand why he was going to this mysterious building on the main square, especially on a Sunday. I had only seen its facade, but never gone inside. "It's to please my mother; we are Catholics you know." He answered dryly, slightly embarrassed by my questions. "What do you do in there?" My curiosity was increasing. "Nothing special, we stand, we sit, the priest tells us about Jesus and God and all that stuff." His eyes were by now looking into the distance, where some boys were playing football; he obviously did not want to go on with this conversation. Jesus, God, church, these words rang a vague bell in my mind and I remembered my grandmother GG mentioning them on our visit to England, but at that time, they had not struck my curiosity. Now I wanted to hear more about the existence of a world that seemed to exist out there, but of which I knew nothing. "Who is Jesus? Who is God?" I asked him eagerly. "Jesus walked on the Sea of Galilee…" He answered mechanically and giving me a quick evasive glance, got up and ran off towards the football players. I was left completely unsatisfied by his answers and was already looking forward going home to ask Maman about God and Jesus and the Sea of Galilee.

On the way back home, I asked Sylvette, "What are Catholics?" She answered mechanically, "They go to the church on the square, every Sunday and there are some other people who are called 'Protestants', they go to the Temple, the building on the small square at the other end of the town." "And what do they do there?" "I don't quite know, some of my school friends go there. But I am not interested; I looked in the small opening of the door of the Temple once, the place was dark, cold and very sinister, brrr… spooky!" She answered with a shiver in her voice. We continued the rest of the way home in silence, I tucked my numerous questions into the back of my mind and went on walking, floating in my space, not thinking, just listening to my breathing and the sounds made by my steps as they hit the hard ground.

At supper, I asked. "Maman, what is God?" There was a short silence. Obviously Maman was taken aback by this unexpected question coming from her son. "I don't know really, I am not sure what is meant when people use the word God? Why do you ask that question?" The tone of her voice expressed a slight irritation. I told her about my friend who was going to church that Sunday, and that he wouldn't be coming to lunch. "Never mind darling, we'll invite him for another Sunday." She replied confidently.

"Maman? Tell me, who is Jesus?" There was another short pause… her pale grey-blue eyes, looking deeply into mine with intrigue, wondering who had put these words into my head, "He was a man born almost 2000 years ago, far away in a land called Palestine and he was a Jew, by the way." "Was he a Catholic Maman?" "No, the Catholics came much later." "Was God, a Catholic? Maman." She and Sylvette burst into laughter. "No, my darling, at least, I don't think so!" she added with a touch of irony. I was feeling rather puzzled, and tried to put these pieces of information together. "Why is it so funny?" I said, not letting anything go by. "It's because God is not really a person, my love… well, as far as I can gather?" I was back to square one. By now, Sylvette fell into a fit of laughter; when she laughed, she would stretch her head backwards and rapidly tap her right hand against her thigh. I liked it when she laughed, and I felt happy that my questions brought so much lightness and amusement to them both. "Have you ever walked on the sea, Maman?" Sylvette was now laughing so much, that tears came rolling out of her eyes, Maman tried to be more serious, "No, if I go on the sea, I sink immediately, that is if I don't swim of course." That sounds logical, I thought, then

I continued, "My friend told me that Jesus walked on the Sea of Galilee. Is that true?" "I don't know if it is true, but some people seem to believe it."

Then Sylvette joined in, "I think these are just tales, I don't believe them, just because they come out of the Bible, I think they are a lot of rubbish!" This word Bible was yet another unknown added to the others that I learned that day, clouding my mind with more abstractions. "What is the Bible?" As my sister seemed to know about this word, I addressed myself to both of them. "It is a very old book telling the history of the Jews, written long before Jesus was born, it contains also a part about him, called the New Testament." "Wasn't grandpapa, before he went into the army, a man who worked in a church with a Bible then?" I had the bit between my teeth now and I could not stop the questions. "Yes, he was and that is called a clergyman, but he was not a Catholic, he belonged to the Anglican Church, that is the equivalent of the French Protestants." The tone in her voice reassured me, she continued, "The difference between the Catholics priests and the Protestants clergyman, is that the Protestants marry and have children when the Catholics do not!" This did not seem at all fair, "Why can't the Catholics priests have children?" "I don't know, you better ask one next time you meet one." She was obviously getting tired of my questioning, "Come on, I must wash up now, it's getting late." She got up, went to the stove, opened the top rings with the poker, wriggled the ashes down, put on another log and started to clear the table, Sylvette helping, I was still in my thoughts, puzzled, especially by the walking on the sea part.

Before I could believe something, I wanted to have proof, so as to understand, to make it real for myself or at least see it with my own eyes. Why did my school friend tell me such an irrational stories? Did he really believe in them? Yes, he must have, otherwise he would not have told me those stories in the first place. To keep my integrity, I decided to leave these stories where they were - as something that did not belong to my world.

Closing the door of spontaneous expression

When I finished my homework on Sunday mornings, I usually went outside the house, there was so much to do there, the rabbits, the chickens, the insects, play with my bow and arrows, chop the logs, fetch water or simply go wandering into nature. At times, when I was on my own, I'd often spontaneously sing and dance to myself, letting my body and my feelings express themselves freely without resistance, do funny things, and make strange noises. I allowed this to manifest only when I was sure that no one was around. I felt good when my body and my voice expressed themselves harmoniously without restriction, without self-consciousness or awkwardness. During these moments I did not think, thinking wasn't part of it, I was just being. Being by myself surrounded by my presence made me feel at ease in myself, peaceful and happy. Sometime I would laugh, because what came out was funny, or run suddenly, or jump or leap, as if something inside me needed to express jumping. When this happened I became very wide, feeling one with everything around, as if there was no more boundaries. It was like I'd left the ground, without my personality or my ego. François the shy self-conscious boy had flown off freely into a different dimension.

One hot Sunday morning near the wild fig tree, I was singing and dancing freely, completely taken in my free consciousness. When suddenly, I heard refrained giggles followed by an explosion of laughter. I had just been discovered in my most intimate moment of self-expression. My whole being froze to a standstill. Sylvette and her girlfriend were there, spying, watching, laughing and mockingly pointing their fingers at me. I felt absolutely self-conscious and stared at the ground speechless. My sister, obviously feeling embarrassed by what her young brother was doing, exclaimed,

"Have you gone completely crazy? What do you think you're doing?" Being pulled brutally from my magic space was a violent shock; I trembled all over and could not answer. I certainly did not know why I did spontaneous singing and dancing; it simply felt natural and good. I was so embarrassed that I blushed and my ears started throbbing. My sister's friend said, "Oh look, he's gone all red, he is blushing!" She pointed her finger at me again and laughed condescendingly*.

<small>* I never again let that natural flow run freely during my childhood. It was only some 10 years later that I reconnected to it, but that is another story to be found in "Source of Life"</small>

Love, music and friendship

It was shortly after this event, that my mother gave me a small mouth organ for my birthday. I was instantly taken by this instrument and would wander off into the nearby hills where I would not be heard. I had a good memory for tunes and sounds, as I did for visual things and would play tunes that I heard on the radio, or at the ball on the village square, when Maman and Fonsou went dancing. They both danced well together, and I watched them, leaning against the stage of the musicians listening to the music of the accordion. We had music classes once a week at school and sang many of the French traditional songs. Also we were taught how to make and play recorders out of bamboo and cork. I enjoyed working with my hands, and I found that there was something magic in making accurate sound out of a simple piece of bamboo. During these music classes, we were together with the older ones, and so I was able to discreetly watch the beautiful older girl that I secretly loved.

She was called Rosaline. Her thick and shiny dark brown curls fell on her round shoulders; the ochre freckles on her short straight nose and her deep blue eyes surrounded by dense black eyelashes, reminded me of the colours of the sea around the island. Her generous lips were round and well defined, and shone as if they were wet. Her appealing beauty disturbed me. She was a serious girl and it was difficult to make her laugh, but when she finally did, it was like a volcano erupting, revealing her perfect, glittering white teeth. I would feel at these rare moments, rewarded for my clowning performances. She possessed the body of a young woman, her narrow waist and perturbing firm bosoms made her whole figure so feminine. I knew that her breasts were firm, because once to my great delight, when she was behind me in the queue for lunch, someone pushed from the back and as she lost her balance, they had rubbed gently against my shoulder blades. An exiting shiver went all downs my spine, blood flushed my ears and face and I did not dare to turn round. Like an imprint done on clay, that unique feeling stayed with me for years. Rosaline was about my sister's age, I was so shy that I found it difficult to address her, it was only when I was clowning with the other boys, to get her attention that she some times took notice of me and our eyes would meet for an instant, just enough to show me that although she liked me, I was still a very young boy.

I had a tendency to make friendship with children older than myself and there was one I particularly liked called Jacques. He came from a Protestant family, his mother was from Alsace, and they lived in a small village high up in the Massif Central, called Le Chambon sur Lignon. His father had died in the war, and his uncle Eric had married his mother. Jacques was not a particularly good student, but he was brilliant at sports especially swimming or skiing. The Beauvallon swimming pool was a fair size and in the hot season we had great fun playing all kind of games, including one for the bravest one. It was to jump from the tall oak tree that stood at one corner over the deep end and when the adults were not around, my friend showed off by standing precariously on its protruding main branch and dived in an immaculate splash. The school organised races, and Jacques always won. His crawl was perfect, in fact, just by doing a foot movement, without the use of his arms, I'd have a job to keep up with him, his large feet acted like a propeller! Sylvette was the fastest at the breaststroke. She liked me to stand on the wall watching her neat dive. "Were my legs straighter this time?" she would ask as soon as she came to the surface. "Yes, that's better, but there is still a little bent in the right knee!" I'd acknowledge enthusiastically. She amused me when she swam, her body laying flat just under the water, her arms and legs made impressive long, regular strokes, her long neck and head erect at a perfect right angle gliding over the water with regular rhythmic intervals, like a very dignified swan.

As my friendship with Jacques grew, we spent our spare time together and he often came home for Sundays. One weekend we went off on our bicycles with a frying pan, a reel of nylon thread, fishing hooks and weights, a little salt and oil, a baguette and some fruit, not forgetting a box of matches. We knew all the local small rivers and decided to sett off to the one we particularly liked called Le Lez, South East from our house at the foot of the Lance Mountain. Hot and sweaty from the long bike ride, we stopped by the river where we found a nice fishing spot. We took off our clothes and shoes, except for our bathing costumes and rushed into the river to swim and cool our bodies down. There was much life in this river, including trout, crayfish and snakes of different bright colours, yellow ones, pale blue ones, green ones, grey ones and black ones. I would watch these grass snakes with their tails ringed round the low branches and roots, letting their long bodies float in the current; sometime, they intermingled with each other into intriguing knots. There was the odd Viper too, but we were careful to leave them alone. Many coloured dragonflies and butterflies came to the river edge to quench their thirst. Water spiders were busy, gliding on the water surface as if they were ice-skating, while I was observing aquatic life, hordes of minute fishes came around my feet and toes and feasted on them, nibbling the dead skin.

In some places were large pools, deep enough to swim, while in others the frothy water cascaded from one rock to the other. Jacques considered me the fishing expert with my experience learned on the island. With my Opinel I'd cut a long flexible green cane that grew by the riverside to make a fishing rod and quickly caught enough small fish to fill the frying pan. Jacques lit the fire; studying carefully the direction of the wind, he arranged large stones he'd collected to obtain a good draught and enough flatness to steady the frying pan. Soon the air was filled with smoky clouds that smelt of burned dry river-wood and fried fish. Once ready, we sprinkled the catch with salt and proceeded to eat it with our baguette while planning the rest of our day. We decided to sleep at the foot of the Lance, so we started our climb early the next morning. By the late afternoon we left the river, picked up the bikes and rode up the narrow lanes that led to a farm hidden in a small valley just at the foot of the giant mountain. The ride was further than we anticipated and by the time we got there it was dark. A beam of light coming from the farmer's kitchen window guided us and soon we heard a barking dog coming towards us in the semidarkness. Fortunately it was a friendly hairy sheepdog, which wasn't often the case with farm dogs, and we were happy to stroke it and make friends.

The farm was small, with a high open barn to the left; through the window we saw an old couple eating their supper. We knocked timidly at the door and waited. As it opened suspiciously, an appetising smell of leek and potato soup invaded our nostrils. The old lady at the door stared at us briefly and, with a reserved smile, invited us in. She was dressed in a long grey skirt, over a grey blouse and her shoulders were covered with a thick knitted pale mauve woollen shawl, crossed under her generous bosom and tied round her back. Her shrivelled face was kind. An untidy bun sat on top of her head and her knotted hands were wrinkled and told us that she worked the land.

The old man had not stopped eating his soup when we entered; he just looked up blankly in our direction. Jacques asked, using his most gentle voice, "Good evening… would it be all right, if we slept tonight in the hay in your barn? Tomorrow, we want to climb up to the top of the Lance." The old lady turned towards her husband with a long questioning look. "Well, if they don't start a fire, I don't see why not." He said in a low husky voice. The kind lady turned round and asked invitingly, "Have you eaten, my lads?" "Well, not really, but please do not bother for us, we'll be all right." I wished that he hadn't said this last bit about being all right, as my stomach was making gurgles sounds, but she knew we were hungry and invited us to join in their meal.

CHAPTER 3

 The log fire glowed in the chimney, a large black cauldron hung over it with the soup ladle in it. Over the chimney mantle, I could distinguish a Peugeot coffee grinder, just like the one we had at home, and a metal candleholder. The old table was the main feature of the room and by its wear and patina it had obviously been there for many generations. The poor light came from a single bulb with a flat white enamelled shade, circled with a pale brown piece of lace. The farmer sat at the end of the table, opposite, sat his wife, with her back warmed by the fire, and I thought they probably had always sat in these places. Jacques took the seat close to the door at the other end of the table; he had taken on the conversation, which I happily left to him, leaving me free to observe their kitchen. The old farmer head carried a few grey hair that grew down to his black frowning eyebrows, his skin was extremely white, with long wrinkles across the forehead. I wondered if he ever removed his cap when outside. Uncle Tony had a moustache that went up at either ends, but the farmer's was hanging down heavily on either side of his mouth, just over his jawline and leaving his upper lip completely hidden by the thick dark bristles that curled round and under. They seemed to act like a harrow filtering bits of food from his spoon. The soup was exquisite so when the farmer's wife offered another round, we accepted. She served us also their homemade goat cheese with farm bread. It was a big round loaf and the brown crust had bits of charcoal stuck underneath it, but it was stale. My mother explained to me once, "The country people believed that it is bad for their health to eat fresh bread." After the bread and cheese, the old man pushed his chair backwards, took either end of his serviette in each hand, stretching them apart and making the cloth taunt, started from one end and dragged his mouth across it cleaning his moustache in one long swoop. Then he said, as if he wanted us suddenly out of the house, "Well, I'll show you where to go, have you a torch?" Jacques pulled one out of his pocket; we thanked him, kissed the loving old lady, and followed the farmer out of the house.
 It was pitch black outside, I looked up to see a clear sky full of stars;

it was cool, but the frogs were already croaking, joining in with the crickets. He took us into the barn to a rustic wooden ladder and said briefly, "Up there, you will find the hay, go right at the back, its safer, goodnight!" And he disappeared into the darkness. The place smelt of dried flowers, mint and grass and we quickly found places to make our individual nests. I then gathered hay over my body and found to my irritation that there was the odd thistle in it! I mentioned it to Jacques, and we started laughing shifting into a giggling mood - everything became funny. We talked for a while, inspired by the soft undisturbed atmosphere that filled the barn, and Jacques told me about his father dying when he was younger and how his father's brother, who had no children himself, took on the family of four, married his mother and gave her another child. Jacques was the eldest, he felt very responsible for his three sisters and younger brother. Lowering his voice, he told me that he actually had a difficult relationship with his true father, who was extremely authoritative, always telling him to be a good example to his sisters. He found Eric easy to live with; his new dad took interest in him and done many things with him. He had no problem adopting him as his father. Jacques also told me about his home, the castle by the canal and how he would like to take me there for the Easter holidays. We would paddle his canoe, fish and swim in the places he knew where we could catch fish by hand...

I shared with him the difficulties I had living with Fonsou and that he could not replace the empty place in my heart that my papa had left. I talked about the island, the freedom one felt and how happy I had been there.

We were woken up by sound of the cockerel. We had both slept well and took some time to stretch and pull out all the bits of grass and prickles imbedded in our clothes and hair. We had a quick wash in the stone fountain that stood in the courtyard; the water was cold, but awakening. We dried ourselves with the first rays of the rising sun leaning against the wall of the house. The farmer's wife came out of the kitchen and called us in for breakfast. The fire was already alive, and she had set the table with two large bowls filled with hot milk, a pot of honey with a knife in it and four slices of bread. She said invitingly, "It is our honey, eat it! And see how good it is." Indeed, it was delicious, the milk from their cow was rich, the stiff white honey smelled of lavender, and once spread on the bread we dipped our slices in the warm milk. It was a wonderful breakfast. The farmer was already attending to his daily routine with the animals, so we thanked his wife profusely and told her how well we had slept, and how much we had appreciated her hot milk with the bread and honey. We placed our bicycles in their barn, took the few apples and biscuits we had left and went off by foot up the narrow valley, following the small stream right into the forest.

The forest was dense with huge boulders covered here and there in dark green moss and the little path was getting steeper as we rapidly went on. The vegetation now changed, they were more oaks and light filtered into the forest. Large rocks framed the little stream that was now cascading. We walked silently each in his world, when suddenly we both stopped and listened. Voices were coming from down below, across the stream, and at times we could hear the sound of a whistle. We silently crept up behind a massive rock, making sure that we would not be seen, then saw in a clearing, an encampment of Boy Scouts! The sound of the whistle came from an adult who obviously kept discipline; he also was dressed like the Boy Scouts. A group of boys were trying to light a fire, probably to warm up their breakfast, but they were not succeeding and were having an argument on how to light it. Jacques and I smiled to each other, we knew why the fire wasn't catching, in no way were we going to show them, we were too keen on our freedom. We felt like red Indians, and after observing them for sometime, we discreetly set off again up the mountain. We lost the stream, as we climbed now using bushes and shrubs to pull ourselves up. On our right, was a 4 metre wide scree of grey stones running steeply down, they came from further up gathering at the foot of the rocky cliffs. It was difficult to cross, as if one stepped onto it, the stones rolled you away down with them.

While Jacques and I were thinking about how to cross the obstacle, on our left we heard a rumbling noise. Suddenly, a huge black boar shot out of the dense bushes, followed by a herd of mothers and their young, they ran at great speed straight across the stone river without stopping, and started a small avalanche. We stayed there for a while as we were fascinated by the unexpected spectacle, though we both felt a little shaky.

I took the opportunity to turn round and look at the view, it was impressive: looking down into the valley made us feel like a hawk flying over the farm where we had slept in, it looked really tiny. Immediately to the left, was another hill that hid part of Dieulefit, and then we saw the Sablière, Beauvallon School and the hills beyond. To the right, from an angle I had not seen before, was the Miélandre, it did not look as majestic as it did from Maison Martin; from here, it looked more like a dromedary seen from the back with its grassy top still patched with snow. Having learnt from the boars how to cross the scree, we gathered momentum and ran up and across wildly. As soon as the stones gave away under our feet, we were already on the next ones but further up.

We had been climbing for a few hours, yet I still could not see the top of the mountain, but it did not feel so far now. On reflection, we decided that it was too difficult to climb straight up, as we would have to tackle the cliffs that formed the summit on that side of the mountain, so we decided to walk west on a boar path that rose less steeply. We'd pick up the crest of the mountain further down. There were fewer trees now giving way to rocks, grass and tiny shrubs. The air was much colder; all the shady parts of the ground were still frozen with snow. The last climb seemed interminable but with a few more efforts of scrambling more rocks, a fine flexible dry grass appeared and we found ourselves on the back of the Lance. We ran to a large round boulder to get shelter from the cold north wind and sat in the tall grass. Resting my elbows on my knees with my hands over my eyebrows to shade my eyes from the brilliant sunshine, I scrutinized the view.

It was a breath-taking sight. Sitting, our backs against the large boulder, we both silently gazed at the striking panorama. An immense misty grey blue valley spread way down below us, southeast to west. Like a silver ribbon, stretching through the landscape, we saw the Rhône river glittering down into the mists of the far away sea. From our height, it all appeared as if in two dimensions, the hills, the forests, the farms and villages were as on a map, their flatness displaying an assortment of pastel colours fading in perspective to the horizon. To the right, the Mountain stretched slowly down several kilometres to join the hills below, now and then a rock, or a resilient pine tree turned into a bonsai by the elements, stood like Easter Island statues. Looking left a slow grassy and rocky slope led to the skyline. The height of the sky was emphasised by long strips of fluffy and streaky cotton clouds giving it a curved appearance.

We were both feeling tired from the long climb but decided to go for the summit. We left our small rucksacks under a very old bent mountain pine. It was not higher than 1 m 50, its tiny, dense needles made a kind of thick shield against the wind, which obviously blew most of the time from up the valley. Its twisty pearl grey trunk and branches started from the ground and went round making a kind of tepee, leaving a small opening facing north. Once inside its protective cover, the wind stopped and we decided to have our meagre meal. Jacques lit a cigarette, he always carried a lighter and a packet of Gauloises with him; always smoking away from adults and when there was a peaceful moment.

It took us longer than we thought to reach the top. We stood speechless facing northeast; the wind was so sharp that our eyes watered and distorted our vision. A sea of snow-capped mountains waved away as far as the eye could see. From where we stood, laid below a dramatic accidental landscape, with high cliffs, and deep ravines, gigantic boulders rested on each other precariously; I thought, probably no one has ever been in there… That thought attracted me, to be the first to discover an unknown place, a new cave, a new spring or an unusual rock. However tempting it was to climb down and investigate the mysterious landscape, we decided that if we did so, we would never have time to find our way out before dark. We glanced at the sun and it was getting low on the horizon, realising this gave us an uneasy feeling. Leaving the summit, we started running down towards our camp. When we reached it, the sun was sending its last rays of light into the now golden sky and we realised that we would never be able to reach the farm before dark. It was now too dangerous to climb down the steep mountain and we decided to make camp in our vegetation tepee.

While Jacques was preparing the fire, I went out to look for wood, it was not too difficult to find, and I came back with a good pile. With my Opinel, I cut bunches of long dry grass, which I displayed round the inside of the tepee to make it more comfortable as it was going to be our tiny improvised bedroom. My companion made the fire just by the entrance, and when I turned round I found it already giving heat into our refuge. We both went out again to collect more branches so that we would be able to feed the fire well into the night.

We shared the few crumbs of biscuits left, the last apple and the little water that was left in the bottle. On our empty stomachs we exchanged on how great it would have been, if I had taken my bow and arrows, or even better… if Jacques had with him his 22 rifle! We could have then caught a rabbit or a bird and roasted them on our fire! I went out some distance for a pee; the wind had lessen but I noticed how cold it was on my bare legs, luckily I had a long and thick woollen jersey; I looked up into the dark sky, it was filled with stars and they looked as if alive, sparkling in all directions. I felt peaceful and wide in my feelings and would have stayed gazing had the cold not made me rush back into our improvised shelter.

My friend was already curled up, he had built the fire up so that it would last into the night and gave a short grunt as I came in. I curled up into a ball myself, knees tucked under my chin, the stretchy pullover over them, one of the rucksacks against my back with my two hands under my cheek as a pillow. With my body heat I managed to create a microsystem of relative comfort, enough to be

CHAPTER 3

able to close my eyes and doze off into my inner world.

Floating in a semi-conscious state, appeared my mother's lovely face, I felt her anxious and her wondering where we were, where we would be sleeping? I talked to her from inside, "We are okay, Maman, I'm just going off to sleep, don't worry." My awareness went back to her, and I felt as if she had heard me and was reassured as if she had seen, in her mind, her boy and his friend sleeping in the hay in some barn somewhere near the Lance. My thoughts went to her and Sylvette in Maison Martin, sleeping safely and warm in their beds, flows of love went to them flooding me on the way. It was a funny feeling to see, as if I was outside myself, both of us on the top of the Lance at 4500 feet, sleeping under an old bent mountain pine, next to the camp fire, and over there under the same starry night, Maman and my sister sleeping in their beds. It amused me, and while feeling them inside my heart, I fell asleep.

I don't know how long I slept, the fire was now right down, and it seemed that dawn was rising. I was cold, feeling stiff and wanted to stretch, but didn't dare to move in case I lost my precious body heat, my attention went to Jacques and I said quietly, tentatively, "Jacques? Are you asleep?" A low tone voice came back, "No, but I am frozen!"

"Did you manage to sleep?" I went on, the talking helping me to come back into the physical reality. "Yes, a little, did you?" "A bit, but I am cold also, let's get up!" I answered, as I sprung up. After having been for several hours set into a foetus position, stretching felt wonderful and as the blood was beginning to flow freely through my limbs, it brought life back to all parts of my body. Jacques blew on the fire, to bring it to life; I looked east and saw that the sky was getting lighter, reviving all the colours that also had been resting through the night. We sat by the fire to discuss our next steps and decided, as we had no food left and as we now could see well enough, to go back down to the farm, take our bikes and go home. Making sure that the fire was completely out before we left, we covered it with flat stones, took our empty rucksacks and hopped over the rocks of the north face then promptly ran down and along the way we had come up.

Already, we were at the screed river, and having done it before on sand hills, I convinced Jacques to sit on one foot, the other in the front and let gravity do the rest. I knew that when we got up to a certain speed, it would stabilise, but the thing was to get off at the right moment, as sometimes the screed went into dangerous ravines. We set off, keeping balance with arms and hands and agreed to be next to each other, so as to avoid getting hit by stones that might have tumbled down. It was a real shortcut and the run was trouble free for about half an hour, when I suddenly saw that further down the screed simply disappeared into an abyss! I pointed the problem out to Jacques and we agreed to grab the first branch that would appear on his right side.

A robust looking pine tree was coming towards us; I grabbed Jacques hand as he rose to catch firmly our lifesaver. Then, he swung me round with his other hand, to the safe side of the mad screed river. Now we were in complete silence, without our weight the screed flow came magically to a standstill. We were both beaming with satisfaction; our skid had been a success and had taken us way down the mountain. We reached the woods along horizontally first and found the original path we had come up on. It took us to the stream, where we stopped and quenched our thirst with a long drink. Our ankles took some bashing; we took off our shoes and socks and rested our overheated feet into the clear cold stream. When we were back at the farm, it was the early part of the morning and the lady happened to be outside when we arrived. She greeted us with a large smile and then invited us to the kitchen where she served us each a bowl of fresh tepid milk. While we were drinking, she went to the large kitchen cupboard and took out a pot of the lavender honey she had given us the previous day. "Here my lads, take this back to your mother, it's a present!" She affectionately gave us each a kiss, I felt her soft rounded shiny cheekbone against my face and pick up a potent smell of goat mix with the particular scent of the Savon de Marseille. These earthy, healthy grounding odours made me feel close to the earth. We thanked her very much as we walked backwards to the barn to pick up our bicycles.

We arrived at Maison Martin, just in time for lunch. Maman was in the kitchen by the stove when she heard us come in and she turned round saying, "No, you've come back! How wonderful!" She obviously was so happy to see us; Sylvette came down from her bedroom and told us that they had been very worried the previous night, wondering where we were. We told them of our adventures, getting surprised by the night on top of the Lance and having to spend the night under the little tepee tree, both shown their amazement and Maman commented, "Gosh! You were wise not to try to come down in the dark and how kind of the farmer's wife to give you the honey!" These two days spent with Jacques, strengthened the bond between us and we discovered true friendship.

There were some details of our many expeditions that I did not share with my Maman; I did not want her to become unnecessarily anxious, especially when we went out on our speleology adventures. Millions of years ago, the region had gone through violent geological changes that had created all kinds of cracks and caves in the mountainous chalky countryside. We had spotted such a crack under a small cliff, off the road that led to Bourdeaux, north of Dieulefit. On a sunny Sunday morning in early June, Jacques, Sylvette, her friend and I set off with a small picnic and our two 'Wonder' battery torches. As we climbed up the steep sandy slope to the overhanging cliff, we found to our delight that the fruit of the wild cherry trees were ripe. While crunching the dark sharp/sweet fruit, we searched for the best hole to investigate. Some were really too small to get into, others gave the appearance of going somewhere but stopped within a few metres. Finally, we chose one that looked too small to get into but found that by removing some fine sand that obstructed the opening, we noticed a cold draught coming out and deducted that it was the right place to investigate.

Sylvette and her friend, fearing danger, did not want to join us in the adventure and said that they preferred to wait for us outside the cave. Jacques, in his quiet and confident cool manner, led the way.

157

Keeping his head low and with the help of his elbows pulled his body forward, his feet soon disappeared through the small entrance; I followed close behind feeling a little nervous. As soon that I was in complete darkness my sense of hearing, smelling and feeling heightened. The narrow passage was just over the width of our bodies, it was difficult to wiggle forward as there was not much space for movement. I felt now the coolness of the draught; it smelt of wet sand and mushrooms and heard Jacques struggling ahead of me, his breathing sounding heavier, every so often emitting a grunt expressing frustration but persistence. With my hand, a times, I would make sure that I could touch his foot, that feeling would comfort me a little in the pitch darkness. At times I would say, "You're okay?" A distant muted voice would come back with a reassuring, "Yes!" But unexpectedly, on one of these 'ok' exchanges, there was no reply and the tip of my fingers indicated that his foot had moved on, disappeared in the darkness…

A slight feeling of panic invaded me, what was I going to do? There was no way I could go backwards as the tunnel was too narrow and anyhow, even if I had been able to do that, I could not have left my friend in such a place. The only way was forward and I called again: "Jacques?" All I heard was my heart beating faster and my respiration, which sounded as if I was breathing in a metal bucket. I started to feel claustrophobic, my arms body and legs suddenly wanted to move freely in all directions, and my lungs wanted to take in fresh air. Also, I needed to wipe my mouth to clean up the sand that stuck on my lips. Remorse started to creep into my mind: You should not have gone into this cave"… and what about my sister waiting outside? And my Maman? As I thought of her, I saw her gentle smile looking at me with reassurance. This comforted me; I switched on my torch. The tunnel ahead had a slight curve to the right and seemed to open out slightly, hot and dribbling with sweat, I accelerated my crawl forward and it became easier as the tunnel widened. Suddenly I felt space around and stood up carefully; coming out of the darkness I could hear dripping water I called out quietly,

CHAPTER 3

"Jacques?" The sound of my voice echoed instantly telling me that I was in a smallish chamber. "Oh! Here you are. I was beginning to wonder if I'd lost you! Hey, look at that! Isn't this magnificent?"

He had sent a ray from his poor torchlight onto a group of pink-orange coloured stalactites and stalagmites that stood around us like the pipes of a cathedral's organ. As I walked towards them I almost tripped over, directing my torch to the uneven surface, I saw that it was due to the calcium agglomerations over millions of years of the budding stalagmites rising up from the ground. Also, we took care of our heads as there were stalactites coming down from the roof of the cave at different heights. We stood there speechless; my mouth dropped open as I was slowly directing the beam around this fairy-like room. The diversity of shapes and forms was breath taking. The scenery gave us the impression of being alive, with strange deep black shadowy beings that seemed to be running and jumping trying to catch the ray of my torch. Actually, these mad grotesque forms made me feel ill at ease, I directed the beam to the ceiling and all the strange creatures momentarily vanished.

Jacques's torch had gone so dim that he had turned it off; he borrowed mine and pointed it in a new direction that made the beam abruptly stop sending us its colourful messages. The reason was that it had gone into a too deeper space to find a surface to reflect on. Now, directing it at the ground, we moved in the direction of darkness, stopping at regular intervals to listen to the sweet melody of the drops of water falling from all the different heights, "It sounds as if there is a small lake over there!" I said in a whisper; Jacques kept silent. We had just discovered an enormous chamber of which we could see neither the ceiling nor the end. Finally he said: "I wish we had a stronger light, this is an incredible grotto! We've got to come back with the proper speleology gear." I agreed nodding my head and said not with out some humour, "Yes, but first let's find our way back to the daylight!"

We tried to locate the entrance into the first room but we found that there were many possibilities as there was more than one hole leading out of where we stood. I said to Jacques, remembering a Greek fairy-tale story told by our history teacher, of Theseus and Ariadne. "We are silly! We should have taken a ball of string with us, like this we could have found our way back to the entrance!" Jacques grunted in agreement and added, "Take hold of my shirt so that, at least, we wont' loose each other!" I did just that, while trying to push-away the anxiety that was creeping steadily inside my chest. The dim orange light of my torch gave up the ghost; my friend gave it back to me and I settled it in the depth of my pocket. We were now sitting on a sandy ground, resting our backs against some damp wall in total darkness. We stayed like this for quite some time, each lost in our thoughts. They were probably quite similar; I was feeling bad about causing anxiety to my sister who was waiting outside wondering anxiously where we were. Luckily the girls had come with us and could give the alarm if we did not find our way out, but this idea displeased me immensely.

Suddenly, like a wondering butterfly, an absolutely logical thought came to me, 'Surely, if one of these holes is connected to the outside, there should be a slight draught, or a different smell in the air current?' I turn my head round to Jacques, who was miles away, deep in his wonders and I spoke with much assurance, my voice took him by surprise, "I have an idea… any hole that is linked with the outside will carry fresh air and, maybe, a different smell? Follow me!" And without waiting for him, on all fours, I started my way back while touching with my hand the wall of the grotto. He grabbed loosely my sandal and followed. Like an underground insect in a lightless world with all my sensors out, ready to perceive any changes in the vertical rocks I was following or any draft that might come across in the heavy close atmosphere, I moved on. I stopped every so often to check a depression or hole in the sandy rock surface. Once I knocked my head and quickly learned to use my hand to check over my head before I moved forward, I then warned Jacques to mind his head too.

We had been going for quite a while; it was strange to discover that in total darkness one had absolutely no idea of time. Taken by surprise, I suddenly felt a slight coolness feathering my sandy sweaty face. Aware of the faint but delicious dry grassy smell coming from the weak air current that was coming from my right side, I exclaimed excitedly, "Jacques! I think I've found the way out! Over here to the right, follow me…"

My head was now in the new cavity and, stretching my body round to the right, I started to crawl forward, making sure that, my friend was following. It became more difficult to advance… and I thought, 'How on earth have we managed to move into such a narrow space?' The air became more soothing and I saw far into the distance a spot of bright blue light, a wonderful feeling invaded my whole being and I shouted allowing my joy out freely. "Jacques! I can see daylight! We're there!"

Blinded by the flooding brightness of the outside world, we were now standing under the cliff, brushing the sand off our clothes, beaming to our ears with the happy feeling created by our regained freedom. Sylvette and her friend were running up towards us looking angry and upset. "You are horrible! How can you be grinning like this? You were ages! It's 4:30pm and we were terribly worried and about to call for help!" Jacques looked at me and winked giving me a little wry smile, I understood immediately that we both would not tell the true story of us losing our way, but only of the marvellous time we had. "We're starving, any of the picnic left?" I said to change the conversation, Sylvette pointed to the basket with her head, "We have had ours, and the rest is for you!" While devouring our picnic, we told them of the marvellous things we had found in the magic cave.

Jacque invited me for Easter to his parent's small castle near Ganges on the Herault River, some month before they moved out of it. His uncle Eric had run a successful silk stocking factory in the town. After the war, the American nylon stockings flooded Europe forcing Eric's factory to close down and later to sell the large property. We travelled by train and were met at the Ganges station by Eric who had come with his black Light 11 Citroën. The ride to their small castle made me feel rather grand, I had always wished to ride in such a car. We were now going through gorges, along a large river; the road was full of bends and went steadily uphill. Finally the landscape widened into a small valley. We turned left on a narrow stone bridge crossing the Herault River, then over a narrow canal to arrive at their home. Immense plane and cedar trees surrounded the property and we parked under their shade. Jacques's mother, who was tall with auburn hair, red cheekbones and jet black eyes, greeted us warmly. I noticed that she was pregnant. After she enquired how our journey went, she took me to my bedroom. She wore slippers that flipped flapped on the circular stone staircase as she stepped up to a narrow well-waxed oak corridor. She pushed open a tall door and entered into what was to be my bedroom. It was square, with a high ceiling and one tall window opposite the door through which came a subdued green light. The high bed was on the right and I noticed a salmon-pink eiderdown, which was unusually puffy - I could not even see the top of it! She left me in the room saying with her soft clear voice, from which I detected an Alsatian accent, "When you hear the bell, come down as it'll be suppertime." As soon as she left, I could not wait to jump on top of this irresistible eiderdown; like a popped balloon, it flattened down slowly. I slipped off and watched it rise again to its original height and noticed there were no blankets on the bed. Looking out of the window I saw a paved courtyard surrounded with plants and trees and vines of all kinds; it was the sun coming through this green jungle that gave the strange green light in the bedroom making it feel rather spooky.

The bell rang. I rushed down to the dining room where I met the three sisters. As we exchange rapid hellos, my eyes caught the piercing and lively black eyes of Odile and I felt a heat in my heart as she gave me a little smile revealing her two large front teeth. Her dark hair was cut short, showing her elegant thin neck. She sat opposite me, I was terribly attracted by her gentle but witty presence and I found it difficult to bring to my attention the conversation that was held around the table. Jacques was being asked many questions

CHAPTER 3

about the term spent at school, about his grandparents and his aunt. I found uncle Eric likable. He had a lovely big smile and apparently he could put a tennis ball in his mouth and close his lips completely and I found that most impressive! Also he was kind and considerate, his voice was low and soft and he helped in the kitchen. I felt comfortable in his presence. Eric taught Jacques many things such as skiing, swimming, making canoes, fishing, climbing rocks and shooting with rifles. All these sports attracted me immensely and I looked forward to trying out the ones I had not done before.

I slept well under the huge eiderdown, and the proud sound of the cockerel coming from the farm woke me up early. After a bowl of milky coffee, slices of fresh bread spread with farm butter and homemade jam, Jacques and I left the kitchen hurriedly as there was so many things he wanted to show me on his domain. Through a small door at the back of the kitchen, we went down a narrow vertical stone staircase that led to an enormous cellar with vaulted ceilings; it went all the way under the castle to a double arch opening that gave onto the front courtyard. Jacques first went to the right corner where uncle Eric was building an Indian type canoe; the frame and ribs were made of ash, the body of a fine red mahogany ply. It was a fine looking boat to be, wide and long enough to take five people. Uncle Eric joined us and excitedly showed me the machine he made to produce the steam necessary to blend into shape the ribs of the canoe. It was an amazing contraption, which when the fire was lit, enabled Eric to bend under a jet of steam the very rigid white ash slats into the delicate curves of the boat's ribcage. Small brass nails would be pushed through and riveted on the ribs, not a drop of glue was used. Seeing that there was a nice workshop with a bench in the cellar, I asked Jacques if we could make bows and arrows, he agreed and we went out into the nearby woods armed with a small handsaw to look for the desired wood. We walked to the woods that banked the large river; there we found hazelnut trees, which were ideal for making bows. We cut two straight sticks, roughly the length of our height, then we looked for an elder tree to provide us the sticks for

163

the arrows, the branches were straight, the middle was hollow, which made them light. We spotted one and with our Opinel knife cut several branches and loaded with our new materials, walked back to the workshop. We enjoyed as much the making, as the fun of shooting. It was easy on the large workbench to shape the bows with the use of an old two handled tool that the barrel makers used to shape their oak barrels; either end were flattened out, leaving the centre part full for the handgrip. We used a strong linen thread for the string and by the end of the day we had finished our bows and started on the delicate job of making the arrows.

While Jacques went to his mother to ask her for some more linen thread, I went out through the courtyard where the chickens roosted to collect duvet feathers, as they helped to keep the arrow flying in a straight line. In the cellar was an World War II ammunition box still full of large bullets, taking great care in fixing the brass cartridge in the bench vice and with a pair of pliers we held its copper head and with a twisting, pulling out action, removed the head from the cartridge, making sure not to lose the precious black gunpowder to use later for some other games. With the pliers we held the bullet's head, over a candle flame to empty it of its lead content. This took some time, while we watched the magic flow of the liquid lead, shiny like a silver river, run out of its container on to the workbench in a big splash that reminded me of sliver stars.

With our Opinel, we now shaped the wood part of the arrow so that it would fit perfectly the bullet's head. Then came the notch at the other end to receive the string. Next, was applying the feathers, while I held them together around the arrow base, Jacques started binding them with the black linen thread. It was important to do a perfect binding, and we knew how to do that, starting with a loop and winding down tightly towards it, threading the last piece of thread through it and pulling the other end for it to slide underneath the binding, then it was cut off neatly. How exciting it was to go out with our bows and arrows and try them out in the open. They were powerful, and when we shot at the trunk of the horse chestnut tree, the arrows had stuck and vibrated.

Once, we found ourselves not too far from the farm and the farmer's wife had just come out to hang her washing on the clothesline. She unknowingly set out for us an exiting shooting range: hanging in the breeze were pink and white nickers, grey long johns and tea towels. Hiding in the tall grass at some 40- 50 metres, we drew our bows, and aimed in the direction of the washing line. I chose a pair of white knickers and released the taunt string... the aim was perfect and the arrow hit the middle of the panties, but it did not fall as the binding of the feathers acted as a brake stopping the arrow from dropping to the ground. We started to giggle, it was difficult to keep serious, but when Jacques had hit the tea towel, we became serious again as his arrow had gone right through and had flown passed on to the farm lawn, leaving a neat hole in the cloth. We did not want the farmers to find our arrow and come to the castle to complain to Jacques's parents about the naughty little boys. Identifying completely with red Indians, we crawled in the high grass without being seen. Finally we arrived to the edge of the finely cut lawn. We decided that I would go first, as my arrow was too obviously visible, then it would be Jacques's turn.

Making sure that there was no one, I shot out of the tall grass, grabbed the feather end of the arrow, pulled it out and in seconds was back in our hiding place. The task was more difficult for Jacques, so he decided to crawl like a hunting cat, and he did this very successfully, coming back towards me with a big grin and holding the arrow between his teeth.

The Easter holidays at Jacques's home had been good for me; they were a big change compared to our home. I experienced a different way of living, a different relationship between mother/father and children. Jacques's mother was not as affectionate as our mum, she was more distant and demanded much discipline from her children. Things had to go her way, and I soon noticed that Jacques much preferred to be out of the house than in. I witnessed how, the children, slightly feared their mother's temper and what she thought of their behaviour.

Uncle Eric left his wife to do the house discipline and order, now and then he would agree with her to give her support but when at home, he preferred to be working in his workshop on the canoes or other things that took his interest. I noticed how the house was kept immaculately clean, how Jacques's mother would spend much time polishing the wooden floors with special polishing slippers. Sometimes she gave the tasks to the children who happened to be standing by.

After they sold their castle, the family moved, high up into the Massif Central, to a village called the Chambon sur Lignon where they ran a Pension. I was invited there for the Christmas holiday once, Jacques and I had travelled by train and bus and arrived late on a dark cold night. The house, neatly pointed with apparent stones, was tall and narrow. Its entrance door was crowned by an orange glass scallop-shaped canopy and was flanked with tall, large windows and blue/grey shutters. The repetitive pattern of the windows and shutters on the three floors, gave it an orderly appearance. The high pointed roof, armed with snow retainers, projected out from the house and reminded me of the hat of some magical character in a fairy-tale. To the left were the fruit and vegetable gardens and to the right was a tall deep black forest of spruce and pines. The interior layout was straightforward: a central staircase served all the rooms on the three levels. The floors were of well-worn polished pine and they creaked as one walked on to them; central heating kept the house warm. Jacque and I shared a simply decorated second floor room that gave onto the garden.

When we woke up, we found to our great pleasure, that all was white, the snow had fallen heavily in the night. After breakfast, we went back to our bedroom Jacques wanted to share with me his latest discovery, a book of poems called 'Paroles', by Jacques Prevert. We read and discussed the poems all morning, indeed they were different from the French classics we had learnt at school, such as Verlaine, Victor Hugo or Lafontaine. The unexpected freedom in which Prevert had used words to create an off balance situation and broken the regular rhythms of classic poetry appealed enormously to our minds; it showed a way out of convention, out into a new space for expression, we recognized that some of the poems had been put into songs by our hero, Georges Brassens.

In the afternoon, Jacques invited me to join him to see an aunt, but tempted by the thick powdery snow, I chose to go into the woods by myself on a borrowed pair of skis. Jacques, the expert skier, passionately showed me his skis that he cherished, and promptly put them on. He then chose an older pair that would do for me. Now, dressed for the cold and well equipped for the snow, we went out through the back door of the pension. After a few 100 metres, we separated, he joined the main road down to the village; I turned left into the deep silent forest. I saw him gliding elegantly away, with his hands behind his back down the snow-covered lane.

I appreciated being alone in the forest, at first there was no noise, except the sound made by my skis sliding on the smooth powdery surface. Now and then, I would stop and listen… listening to what might come out of the silence? It was interested to notice that what seemed like a deep white stillness, was actually full of sounds, but they were more delicate, more refined, also more musical. The fall of the snowflakes made also different crystalline sounds, depending on where they fell. Heavily snowed up branches disturbed by the breeze that blew high up in the trees, suddenly unloaded their extra weight, sending down cascades of frozen crystals by the billions, giving the music of a delicate chime. The air drifting through the pine needles, made high harmonic sounds, I was enchanted by the magic world that surrounded my presence. At erratic moments I heard the absorbed 'thump' of a heavy lump of snow hitting the soft ground giving a spontaneous punctuations to the intricate orchestration.

On observing attentively the apparent bleakness, I discovered that actually there was no white anywhere! But just a multitude of refined tones and colours. I became aware of an array of tinted greys, depending on how the light and shade interplayed with the forms. Pink greys, green greys, pale blue greys, mauve greys, dark brown greys and, as I looked more deeply at any of them, I'd discover more hues, as if nature was telling me that nothing ever ended, but that there is always more, and that it is simply related to the broadness of my consciousness. This state of sharp expansive awareness continued... I was now standing by a large fir tree, looking at it's tall elevating powerful trunk and became fully absorbed by the colours of its rugged bark: tints of ochre pinks and aubergine browns, enhanced by the Nile green of the moss nested in its cracks... when a sudden shrieking squawk, possibly made by a Jay that my presence had disturbed, violently pulled me out from my inner post of observation, into the immediate physical reality of my standing on my skis in the middle of a snowed up forest.

It was still snowing lightly, and I decided to walk further on, in the direction that Jacques had pointed to find the ski run. After some time, I came to the big pine tree with a broken branch that he had mentioned, glancing up hill from it, I saw the perspective of the ski run going up steeply and disappearing into the snowy grey sky. I was not an experienced skier, nobody had ever taught me this sport and in Dieulefit, the very old wooden pair of skies I possessed were much too short for me and had an archaic leather strap system that wasn't efficient as they kept on coming off! I felt more comfortable on a toboggan.

Pointing my skis across the slope, I started going up by making large sidesteps with my left leg then dragging the right one up to it. And again, and again, until it became automatic, I could now leave my body to it and put my mind somewhere else... I remembered reading a book by James Oliver Curwood called 'The Grizzly King', a nature story about the great Canadian North, and another by Jack London, about a dog called 'White Fang'. So, filled with the stories of animal wildlife, forests and snow I methodically went up the hill. Being completely by myself and surrounded by forest, activated my imagination as if I really was in the great North, expecting at any moment White Fang to come towards me to protect me from the wolves, wagging its tail, its thick grey fur clotted with lumps of snow... my imagination had taken over my feelings. As I went up, I felt that I was being watched by the grizzly bear hiding in the thick forest. Although he was my friend, he was never the less wild and kept his distance.

Unexpectedly I came to a step where the ski run made a sudden rise, not a very high one, only 50 cm or so, but having not really done ski jumping before I decided to have a rest, while making the decision to try it or not. I was out of breath and puffing, feeling hot under my thick woollen clothes I turned round to see how far up I was. The snow was still falling, flakes were going on my eyelashes, tickling them, falling on my nose, on my lips, I turned my face to the sky, it was a pale ochre grey, swarming with speckles of darker grey flakes. I pulled out my steaming tongue and presented it to the sky... the feeling was strange, it was as if iced fairies were dancing on it and as soon as their cold feather light feet touched it, they vanished instantly, leaving no taste of their presence behind.

I decided to go up a little further, not too much, but just far enough to build up the speed I estimated I needed to make the small jump. Jacques had told me once that: "When ever you are about to go down a ski slope, you must shout loudly three times 'Piste, Piste, Piste', and listen... and if no sound is heard, look carefully to make sure that nobody is coming up before you start off."

Although I knew I was completely by myself, I obediently yelled three times the safety word and listened... no human response came up the ski run. As this part of the ski run was steep, I had to carefully turn round without skidding off into a tangent. I shifted my weight onto my right ski and was off. In seconds I had picked enough speed to face the jump, it came, no way I could change my mind now and I was off feeling weightless for an instant, concentrating fully on my knees to receive the impact of the landing. I landed smoothly, leaning forward I felt now like a real professional, pleased with myself, but the speed that I was picking up forced me to keep all my attention on what I was doing. Not quite imagining how I'd take the corner at the bottom, doubt and fear creped into my heart. How will I stop?

How did Jacques do what he called a 'Christiana', bringing your two skis perpendicular to the slope and putting your weight on to the ski closer to it? Thus creating a beautiful wave of snow. I could now see the large tree with a broken branch at the corner where I should either turn or stop. There was no time for thinking now and after doing a few quick hops on the skis trying to turn right, I suddenly let myself collapse onto the ski run, my arms, my legs, my body, one of my skis, my poles, all seemed to explode away from me, flying off in all directions! When I regained some quieter consciousness, I found that I'd just missed the tree by a few inches, and was resting my back against a sturdy bush.

My head was clear, I realised that I escaped a very near drama had I hit the big pine. Although one of my legs was badly bent with one ski half-caught in the bush, the rest of my body was fine, I notice that the other ski had come off my other foot, and was waiting for me some way further down. Unloading the strong spring that held my foot fast in the ski binding relieved me of the pain I felt in my knee. I struggled up in the deep snow, fetched the missing ski, collected the ski poles, shook off all the snow that had gone into my neck, and especially inside my sleeves and looked around me for the way to go. I did not have the time, but realised that it was getting late as the light was beginning to fade under the dark grey sky. I searched for the traces that I might have been left on my way up, but the snow that was now falling heavily had erased all marks. I skied on and on, every so often stopping by a tree to take my breath and look for the direction to go.

Night had fallen and I just manage to see my way with the help of the white snow that reflected any minute bit of light available. I began to develop a feeling of doubt, had I, after all, gone on too far from the house completely absorbed in my world and forgetting the other, the one that I was now desired so much to go back to? As I dragged my skies along, I imagined that I was in the house with Jacques's family around the dining table, sitting next to Odile, with a delicious hot soup waiting for me while I told my story of the ski slope. Anxiety crept undeniably into my usually sturdy self-assurance. I would have to make a shelter for myself, the branches covered in snow would make some kind of igloo where I could spend the night... I heard the long hoot of an owl somewhere ahead of me in the forest, it immediately made me feel reassured and I took it as a providential companion, instinctively I accelerated in the direction of the call. Again, the bird hooted as if to say, "Come, come... this way!" I decided to trust the invisible friend. From up there, I thought, it will have a better view of my situation so I followed the sound. Was I now dreaming or not? Had I seen some light in the depth of the woods? Forgetting my friend the owl, making straight for the twinkle, I quickened my glides. As I came nearer, I thought that the people of the house would be able to telephone and contact Jacques's parents, who by now must have been very worried. I was very tired, hungry, my knee was hurting and I was longing to receive care, attention and some compassion.

The house stood in a clearing, I had come to it from the back and walking around it looked for the front door. Well, it seemed familiar? I looked up and saw the orange glass scallop-shaped canopy! Greatly relieved I thought, incredible! I'm standing bang on the front door of the house I have been so longing to find, hurray! While I rested the skis and the poles by the side of the front door, I thanked the invisible owl that had led me back. With my numb fingers I untied with some difficulty the frozen bootlaces and finally managed to pull them off. The door opened and Jacques was standing there with a big smile, "What were you doing to be so late? We have been terribly anxious." Having been in the dark for such long time, the bright light of the hallway blinded me so much that it took me some time to adjust. "Quick, come in to the dining room, they are all waiting, Maman has kept you some supper." I did not reply to his question and followed him. "Here he is!" Jacques exclaimed enthusiastically as we entered. There was tension in the room; the children appeared dead serious and were looking down into their empty plates. Jacques's mother was obviously angry, but she contained her anger, her mouth tight, acting as if she did not want to see me.

Looking at me straight in the eyes, Uncle Eric spoke first, "Do you realise how late you are? That we have been looking for you everywhere? Are you aware of the anxiety you have caused the family?" The white of his eyes amplified the icy blueness of his iris, accentuating his disapproving feelings. I replied timidly, feeling ashamed, "I am sorry, I was caught by the night and couldn't find my way back to the Pension." Jacques's mother suddenly stood up, pushing back violently her chair with her legs, and said sharply, "You are to never go out of this house by yourself again! Think of how I would have felt towards your mother if you hadn't come back?" I was now feeling heavy, looking down at the table, my ears throbbing, my face bright red wishing not to be here, but knowing that there was no escape from the reality. She served me soup, its appetising vapour was soothing; I did not dare to look up but glanced to the side and caught Jacques's eye, the discrete wink he gave me reassured me. I looked the other way to see Odile who was too looking at me with a fraction of a smile and sparkling amusement in her eyes; the feeling of guilt evaporated. Uncle Eric, in his more usual warm manner, said auspiciously, "You won't do this again will you?" And without waiting for a reply added, "No, of course you won't, come on, have your soup and let's forget about it now." I finished my supper, Jacques stayed with me, as it was our night to wash up, and I told him all about my adventures, but not of my finer discovered realities about the infinity of sound and colour.

The rest of the holiday went smoothly, we had much fun together, especially in the evenings after supper, when together with his sisters, we took our sledges and went to the village to sledge down the kilometre plus main street of the Chambon sur Lignon.

Coming to terms with my own fears

One day, I came back from the Beauvallon School by myself; my sister had stayed at school for the night. It was in late autumn, the sky was heavily covered with dark clouds and I was walking briskly home absorbed by my thoughts. I passed the farm and the apple tree alley, the Alsatian dog was not there and I started to go down the hill under the very tall poplar trees. A strange feeling that I was being followed crept into my spine; I turned round but could not distinguish anything in the vanishing light. A gust of wind in the trees made a loud rustling noise as if a big hand was rushing through them over my head; goose pimples erupted all over my arms and legs. I felt uneasy as if there were horde of invisible beings watching me. I hurried my step and started running.

Now I was not in my dreamy thoughts any more, but all in my senses, hyper in my hearing and in my seeing. I heard a crack in the depth of the wood, looking in that direction I seemed to see a sombre shadow leaping from one tree to another. I accelerated my steps helped by the downhill slope; my legs were going so fast I lost control over them... somewhere deep inside, I felt that I was stupid to let this fear overtake me, but I couldn't help it; it was as if my whole body had decided to escape some incredible danger, similar to when a horse or cows react to a sudden fear.

Within myself I started a struggle to reach a decision, to either run faster, if that was at all possible, or be brave and face full on whichever monster it was! I chose that last option. I slowed down rapidly and suddenly stopped just before entering the wooden bridge. While puffing to catch my breath, and feeling my goose pimples erect as if I was about to be swallowed up by the horrific beings, I wheeled round to face the fear directly. My eyes watered with the strong emotion, my body all tensed up, I shouted inside, "Come on then!" Strangely, as I turned round, the feeling of panic magically changed into a state as if I contained an immense power - I felt indestructible! Before that instant I feared for my safety and my life to the point of feeling my legs melting under me, losing all my strength, even my voice; now my chest was blown out full of strength, standing with my arms and legs apart, my skin feeling as if it was an armour, I uttered a short feline growl "Grrrr"...

I felt immense with all my senses on the alert, yet, at the same time,

I was taken over by a deep sense of peace. I was facing the unknown in the semidarkness, the giant trees and the invisible beings that had caused my fears and panic. Although the wind was still blowing in the tall forest, although the river cascading made its usual monotonous music, although I could hear thunder in the distance, there was a silence and peace in my being. I notice that all the sounds I could hear now had become musically whole and soothingly harmonious.

I was now aware that the strange beings came into existence because of my fears, and that my self-assurance had pushed them back deep into the obscure nests of my diffidence. The sense of power and of indestructability diminished slowly as I turned round and started to walk in the direction of home. I was feeling happy now, quiet inside myself; I thought that I knew what to do when fear came, so I felt well and confident. A thought popped in my mind that actually there might be somebody following me. To test what I had just experienced was real, this time, I did not run but turned around quietly, again I felt peaceful and happy and saw that there was no danger. I repeated this experiment and reassured, accelerated my steps with a big smile of satisfaction on my face. It was very dark when I got into our warm kitchen scented by a delicious leek and potato soup. After a kiss and a hug, I described to Maman what had happened on my journey home. She listened carefully, frowning and looking anxious when I was telling her about the beings and the wind following me, followed by my desperate running. She smiled with a sense of relief, when I told her that I had suddenly turned around to face what was frightening me. Her eyes became watery and she looked at me with an expression admiration and intense love. I felt she had understood that her little man had gone one step further towards self-confidence.

The farmer, Monsieur Reboule, had a black alpine goat crested with a sharp pair of horns curled back over its long ears that moved about like a weather-vane in the wind; when full of milk, it's large udders would stick out prominently on either side of her silhouette. Every so often, Monsieur Reboule would change the grazing spot by hammering a rusty metal post into the ground, attached with a long antique wrought iron chain. Unfortunately, often the chain came across our path making it impossible to pass without confronting the goat. On our way to school, Sylvette, usually walk ahead of me, I supposed it was to entice me to walk faster as I was continuously distracted by the plants and the wildlife that surrounded us. Invariably when we came to the tricky bits when we met either the dog, the geese or the goat, I was always the one left behind!

The horned animal never charged my sister, but would stop grazing as she walked by letting her through graciously. Then would concentrate all its attention by staring at me with its enigmatic eyes, its goat's brain working out how best to thump me. Between us, it was war... there was a strategy that both the goat and I had to work out to either give the blow or, in my case, to avoid the confrontation and escape. My sister use to wait for me in the safe zone amused by the scene, while I made up my mind what to do. Usually, aiming at the shortest route, depending of course where the animal was at that moment. I knew that speed was the thing, but twice the black hoofed devil made a better estimate than mine and thumped violently my backside. Once, it was because I tripped over a stone and, as I got up, it hit me flat on my bony bum and left painful bruises. For some reason, Sylvette found these episodes very funny and she had fits of giggles as she saw me working out my strategies. I felt a bit like the early Christians in the arena of the Coliseum in Rome, having to face the wild beasts. Sometime, to my great relief, the goat had wrapped itself tight around its own post and was stupidly caught there looking at me helplessly. I would then dance and clown around it knowing that it could not catch me.

Once, on a warm spring day coming back from school on my own, my persecutor was there, waiting for me. Its head slightly down pointing its sharp horns, its front legs apart, the slit iris of its pale eyes focusing intensely at my lower parts, obviously trying to work out which strategy I would choose. This time my challenger had carefully prepared it and no way I could go through without being

175

caught. I felt annoyed; it was somehow unjust that I should be confronted to these fears on my path so often. I decided to fool the beast, not to try to avoid it or to run away as I usually did, but to stand firm until it came right up to me. The black devil charged and, like a Spanish torero, giving a slight twist of my right hip, made the horns just miss my body while I grabbed them as they passed. I got a good grip just over the head where the horns take root. The mass of the body of the goat pulled itself round as I drew its head against my hip, keeping my arms tightly against my ribcage, and tried to let my weight do the rest to force it down. But my challenger was resisting fiercely, pulling back on its four skinny legs and giving violent jerks with its head in the hope that I might let go. But that wasn't my intention at all and I went on turning its head round clockwise. I could now hear its heavy breathing; its eye met mine for an instant and I noticed the distant cool animal anger that resided in the goat. It resisted once more, giving a wild last struggle, I could feel its body beginning to tremble, I increased the screw effect to bring its muzzle right round. Then came a sudden abandon of resistance, the fight was over... Badaboum! The black alpine goat was lying on its flank, motionless.

Hurray! I was on top, the goat under and it felt good. It obviously was now waiting for me to do the next move. I suddenly admired its intelligence and unemotional presence; something in me shifted and I began to be really fond of this animal. Our heads were now almost touching, I could smell its strong odour, its lower jaw slightly to the side revealed a neat row of small yellow teeth, the rounded wet muzzle was covered in soft white hair, some with tiny pearls of water as if it had been exposed to the dew. Our eyes met again, actually only one of the eyes met the other, its almond shape was neat, the iris was a deep yellow-orange, a flaming colour and flecked with tiny red-brown and pale green spots. I looked into its rectangular shape lens, trying to explore the distant darkness of the animal universe; it absorbed me like a bottomless pit, at times flashes of iridescent lights appeared to come out of it. A raucous grunt pulled me out of my observation and reminded me that we could not stay like this forever. The problem was that I wanted to be sure that the goat would not go for me as soon as I let go of its horns; when I fought with the boys at school, I used to say, "Promise me that you won't do it again? "Or "promise me that you won't say this again!"

But with this hoofed creature, how could it understand? I looked at the eye once again, this time with my feelings widely open and I saw in the eye an acceptance, gentleness, the anger, the resistance had vanished, the goat was now looking at me with a kind of respect. This triggered in me a deep feeling of love for the creature; equally I felt respect for the animal's realisation that the fair-headed skinny two-legged being was to be left alone. I slowly let go of my grip, until my hands felt as if there were one with the horns; I stayed like this for a while, until no more resistance was felt. Peace descended, uniting us, making us friends. Affectionately I rubbed my nose gently on its soft muzzle, and my face broke into a huge smile. I felt radiant as I rose, the goat respectfully waited for me to be fully standing when it decided to stand too. Then it walked away some distance, stopped, lifted up its little triangle flap of a tail, revealing its pink private parts, and proceeded to evacuate a necklace of dark green olive shaped pebbles as if to say,

"Okay, every thing is fine between us now." Then it proceeded to nibble the grass and it never chased or aggressed me again.

Faced with the sexual realities of male/female attraction

Fonsou had served his 12-month prison sentence and had come back home. Our mother had visited him several times in Valence, each time bringing tasty food and cigarettes; she left very early in the morning and returned in a day. We were relatively happy to see him back, but deep down there was a slight resentment, we had managed very well without him, we knew that his return was going to change the atmosphere of our house drastically.

His pottery took him back and he soon fell back in his old routines:

off at half past seven in the morning, back at 20 past 12 for his lunch mother always had ready for him on time… off to work again at 1.30 pm to return half past six or seven depending on the days and what had to be finish at the pottery. His stay in prison had somewhat silenced him, mind you he had never been a great talker. He seemed to spend much time in a semi-absent state, often looking far into the distance with a serious expression, as if he was thinking about something very important. Maman, with her caring nature, did all she could to keep a kind of harmony between us all, always trying to bring back a balanced situation, softening the corners when ever she could. She'd often say, "No, they're not like that, they will be fine." And to us, "No, he's not so bad, he loves you really…"

One sunny spring mid-day, we finished lunch and Sylvette and I went outside to sit in the sun. After some time, a beautiful green lizard appeared by the doorway, it came to sit with us to be warmed by the heat of the sun, its mouth open with a slight smile expressing joy. The moment was so beautiful that we wanted to share it with our Maman; the entrance door had been left open and, as we stepped in, we realised that the kitchen door was closed. While we tried to open it, we heard rhythmic squeaking and creaking sounds; they came obviously from the kitchen table. The door had been blocked from inside, probably with a chair as the door had no lock; my sister looked very angry and walked out! The table was now quickening its rhythmic sounds, the intervals became shorter as the table complained, I cried out, "Maman! Let us in, what are you doing in there?" In an unusual, strange strangled voice she replied, "Yes, in a minute! Won't be long now!" It was the first time that our mother closed a door on us; we felt strangely separated from her… how could she do that to us, she always shared things with us. I stuck by the door, intrigued and worried by our mother's behaviour. The table was creaking almost continuously now; I heard Fonsou's heavy breathing mixed with a strange grunting sound. Then, suddenly there was silence… I felt heavy in my heart; I wasn't thinking but just trying to sort out my feelings, where was I in all this? I felt lost and didn't know how to be in myself. I stepped back from the door into the hallway. Then, I heard Fonsou's voice say in his usual routine manner say, "See you this evening then…"

The door opened, he appeared in his old grey shorts and sandals, his face was red, his mouth showing a very slight smile, he didn't look at me, although I knew he was aware of my presence, and as he passed by rapidly to go to work, I smelt his sweaty odour mixed with mother's perfume. I stood there, realising that what had just happened between Fonsou and my mother was something they didn't want to share with me; it must have been sexual for it to be so hidden, but why in the kitchen? Why in the daytime when we were around? I did not like the thought of this and quickly buried it away.

It triggered my thoughts about sex and I re-lived for a moment what had happened at the school's farm once. One morning on our way to school, as we arrived at the cow shed, we saw a silent group of people standing around the liquid manure pit. They seemed to be watching with much attention something that obviously captivated them. The pit, just across the road from the farm, was surrounded on three sides by a sturdy concrete wall, its floor sloping to the deeper end where the dark brown liquid manure resided. At the top end, the manure was dumped and with the rain created the precious fertiliser. We came into the crowd too absorbed to be aware of our presence and we ploughed our passage to the front. Our curiosity was quickly rewarded when we saw the scene. The farm neighbour's young and vigorous black bull had too shorter legs to mount the handsome tall, placid brown and white cow that was presented to him. So, an old oak door was placed against the wall half way up the pit to serve as a gangplank. The cow, ready for mating, was waiting transversely in the pit, presenting her appealing backside to the agitated bull with only half her body visible from where we stood. The bull was already on the gangplank when we arrived; obviously it wasn't the first time it had been doing this exercise that morning; it knew exactly what to do. Rushing awkwardly on the gangplank, the fervent black male lifted its weight over the backside of the waiting cow. The farm boy had his role to play and was standing proudly on the concrete wall, ready to execute his important role, which we were about to discover. When the black bull, lifted its body on its hind legs, I saw his glistening long pointed bright pink thing. The farm boy instantly grabbed it with his two hands and put it into the backside of the waiting cow. I do not know if the loud bellowing sound that came from the cow was from pain or satisfaction, but the watching crowd cheered enthusiastically, clapping their hands. The farm boy, with a large grin on his face, was wiping his hands on a dirty old towel. It all happened extremely quickly, the black bull was now breathing heavily as he was pushed away by the farm boy backwards down the gangplank. Apparently that morning, the whole herd of twelve cows had been fertilised that way by the short-legged young male all with the help of the farm boy. Sylvette, who had been holding my hand, pulled me out of my reveries unexpectedly and reminded me that we were on our way to school and that we were late. I'd like to have stayed to watch the next, but on her insistent pulling, I followed her.

My sister had come back into the house, pulling me out of my flashback memories; I had waited for her on the step before going back into the kitchen. Maman was washing up the lunch dishes and we sat down quietly not knowing how to express how we felt when we discovered that the door had been blocked. She was facing the sink, a cigarette in her mouth, wearing her dark blue and black Provençal apron neatly tied round her narrow waist. She cleared her throat, as she often did when she came to a sensitive subject, then took out her soapy right hand from the hot water and held the half smoked Gauloise between her thumb and her index trying not to make it too wet. She was smiling gently and looking at us said, "I'm sorry for this my darlings, I promise, it won't happen again!" "You've never locked the door on us before Maman," I said reproaching and Sylvette added in an angry tone, "I know what you were doing with him, its horrible Maman, disgusting!" During the long silence that followed, I realised that our mother was not entirely for us, but somehow had to be shared with Fonsou and this was a painful realisation.

CHAPTER 3

I missed my father immensely, that night I cried at length.

Pain separates consciousness

There were many happy moments in my young life when I felt clear, when my awareness found inside myself a place of joy, usually it was when I was alone absorbed by the nature that surrounded me. Or when I created music on my mouth organ walking through the nearby wooded hills. Also when my sister took care of me when we played together. Being with our Maman painting or doing sculpture with the clay that she had brought back from the pottery. I liked it very much when we went to discover new places. The happiest moments I had at school were when I was doing sports, whether playing football, basketball, volleyball or doing athletics, like running or high jump, these activities made me feel at one with my body. I enjoyed feeling it, obeying to my wish to get more out of it, to make it faster, go higher, pushed by the strong desire of competitiveness. I suppose it was because, except for the arts, I was not so brilliant in the classrooms. My dyslexia had interfered with my reading, writing and mathematics making it all too difficult to get any satisfaction or to feel progress. Any activities when nothing was in the way was a delight, I felt then I had the capacity to get the maximum out of my self and to discover who I was in the harmonious process of play.

Something unusual happened once, it was caused by a small accident I had at school: just before going into the classroom waiting for the bell to ring I was skidding on the ice in the front of the main building, when I violently hit the one foot high concrete wall that formed the courtyard. It cut deeply and bruised my right shin through my long woolly socks. It was very painful, but I was quite tough and just pulled up my sock over the wound and left it at that. In the evening when I got home I felt it painfully and as I entered the kitchen I showed it to Maman. The problem was that the sock had stuck firmly to my bruised skin and couldn't be pulled off without an excruciating pain. Finally we managed, by wetting the dried blood with warm water, to discover that there was an infection; the whole area was hot and of a dark red colour. Mother did the usual trick of dressing it with a wet compress of calendula and bandaged it up. I woke up several times in the night feeling much throbbing pain. In the morning I felt feverish and did not go down, as I normally did for breakfast. Mother came up to find me in bed burning hot, weak and distant; she decided that I should stay at home and Sylvette went to school by herself.

My appetite went, the throbbing pain increased although my mother changed the bandage and cleaned the wound. She discovered that the infection was now deeper and that it had eaten into the bone. The pain did not leave me; I tried to escape it, to find a place somewhere in myself where it did not reside, but like a convict attached to his chains, its intensity kept me right in it. I lay on my back, moving was too painful; Maman put a few cushions behind me and brought some books and comics for me to look at.

After several days the family became worried and it was decided that my bed be taken downstairs and put it into my mother's and Fonsou's room so that they could keep a closer eye on me. The large round cast iron stove was filled with coal and kept the bedroom warm, I felt safer there and from my bed I could see the kitchen door open and hear my mother busy in the kitchen. It was then that a strange experience happened. While my whole body ached unbearably, I kept on closing and opening my eyes trying to find where to put my consciousness. Suddenly I saw crawling up on my chest something that looked like Donald Duck, dancing and talking all the time and making me laugh. Then I saw that there were many of these small beings, they looked a bit like Walt Disney characters and were very much my friends, they had come to distract me, to entertain and take me away from my pain. They were terribly funny, so much so that they would make me laugh and I began to love them as they were giving me such a relief and joy. Mother became worried when I told her that I wasn't alone and that I was surrounded by many little beings that amused me and made me laugh, I had asked her if she had seen them around my bed? "No my darling, I can't see them, but I'm glad that they are making you happy." I went on talking, "They are similar to the characters in my comics but they really talk! And they move about quickly, they dance too, and can do funny things…"

The doctor arrived some time later, with a brown cardboard briefcase from which he pulled out strange instruments. His cold hands pressed gently under my jaws, on my tummy, my body was fiery hot. He removed the damp bandage off my shin; a small acorn could have filled the hole in my tibia bone! He appeared worried and talked to Maman in a low voice, I stretched my ears, "It could be the start of gangrene, we have to give him some sulphonamide and hope that it will clear it, otherwise we might need to amputate." I didn't know what these words meant but noticed the tightening expression on my mother's face. The doctor left leaving on the table some large tablets that I should take twice a day adding that we should let him know rapidly if it worsened.

After the doctor left, I quickly returned to my active companions, they were there waiting to distract me by chatting and laughing, taking me far away from my pains; their expressions were so hilarious that their seriousness made them even more amusing. The one that had first appeared to me, the Donald Duck character, I felt the closest to. When my knees were up, he'd come right up, sit on one of them and talk to me, telling me nonsense stories, I could feel his weight on my skin as he changed his weight from one foot to the other or dance around like a happy monkey. It seemed, that I could switch their presence on and off just through wishing; it depended on where I put my attention. I could see them even with my eyes closed but not quite so clearly as when my eyes were open.

Gradually, my situation improved, the hole in my leg slowly healed up and the pain lessened. From this experience I discovered another thing within myself, that was that by disconnecting from one place of being I could plug into another and live a different reality as real and as valid as my ordinary state. After this accident I realised that there were different ways of seeing, different worlds, all happening at the same time, but not everybody could see the same realities. Also, this made me find new friends and I knew that to find them, I had first to disconnect from the everyday doings. When I talked to my mother about these beings, how they helped me, how caring they were, she did not refute it, on the contrary she believed me and seemed very interested but added that she could not see them herself.

It had been a very cold winter, probably in 1947, when I woke up at 6:15 one morning, to find that I did not hear my mother in the kitchen below preparing breakfast and lighting the fire as she usually did. I dressed rapidly, ran down the stairs two by two, flew into the kitchen to find it cold and empty, then I dashed into their large bedroom to discover that Maman and Fonsou were still in bed. There was an unusual passive atmosphere in the room and the cast-iron fire was out. She always slept by the window's side, as I came closer to her I became aware that something was really wrong! The half of her face that I could see, was as white as the sheet, she seemed not to be breathing properly... I touched her, her body was not warm and feeling anxious I called her, "Maman! Maman! You're okay?" After some time, she sort of mumbled, I couldn't make out what she was saying, one eye opened slightly and it seemed to be such a big effort for her just to do that. "Quick, fetch Doc…" She managed to utter. An electric jerk went through my body; I understood the urgency and ran out to fetch my sister. She was getting up, "Where is Maman?" I told her how I had found Maman half conscious and Fonsou not moving. I hurriedly put on my thick socks and snow boots, as it had been snowing for a few days and the mistral had created many snowdrifts. Sylvette stayed in the house to look after them and relight the fires, I rushed out into the dark and freezing early morning in the direction of the Rouvières.

By foot across the fields, the doctor lived at some 3 km's distance from Maison Martin. I walked as fast as I could, stumbling in and out of snowdrifts, climbed slippery slopes, running on the hard soil where the mistral had removed the snow, my nose and my cheeks were now burning hot and felt as if they were about to crack open. My mind was very active – pictures of my mother looking so ill kept coming up, flashes of thoughts of losing her appeared unexpectedly, flooding my chest with emotions adding more tears to my eyes that were already crying from the cold wind. I accelerated my running across the flat fields; I could hear my loud breathing mixed with a thumping heart and the sound of my steps in the frozen snow. There was such a racket of sounds inside me, accentuated by the stillness outside. I was living a nightmare, and never had all my sensors been so acute, yet my feelings were so confused not knowing what the outcome of this drama would be? I ducked under the barbed wires of the fields; in the rush, I had forgotten my gloves and my hands were numb with frost. Finally I came to the little road on top of the plateau of the Rouvières, which led to the doctor's house. Although normally I would not have dared to go in by myself, because of the sign "beware, nasty dog!" My safety seemed like nothing compared to the urgency and I rushed in, crossed the yard and knocked loudly using the green bronze knocker. Fierce, deep barking, growling and scratching came through the closed door. Ignoring the aggressive behaviour of the Alsatian monster, I waited, trying to force down my heavy breathing and emotions so as to find speech. I heard the doctor's voice overriding the dog's barks, shouting with much authority, "Go to sleep... come on, go!" Hesitantly the doctor's nose appeared first, and then his thick glasses behind which I saw two tiny blue eyes looking over my head, probably for an adult that he did not find, he then focussed down and looked at me. There was a kindness mixed with intrigue in his look; I picked up the strong odour of the Alsatian bitch and felt the heat of the house coming out through the narrow opening of the door. "Quick, my mother looks dead! Come and help!" I said hurriedly. He asked me to describe the situation, and rapidly understood the cause of the urgency, "Just wait a second for me, I'll get ready and will' go in the car!" He said in a whisper, closed the door... and I waited. While driving in his small Simca, I was able to explain more about the bedroom and the coal stove, he explained that carbon monoxide probably was the cause and that it was urgent that we get to them as soon as possible. We arrived at M. Reboule's barn and parked, he took out of the car his brown cardboard case and we hurried up the riverbed in the thick snow to our house.

Sylvette was so relieved to see us arriving; she had been waiting anxiously looking through the kitchen window for us to appear. The doctor went straight to the back bedroom and to the window that he immediately opened wide, while asking Sylvette to open fully the front door to create a draft. He first attended to our mother, listening to her heart and lungs with his stethoscope and then put his attention to Fonsou, forcing him to sit up, calling him to open his eyes, tapping gently his cheeks. With gravity he turned to us, "You will have to look after them for a few days, but do not worry, they will be all right, make sure they take these medicine twice a day." Upon which he put his medical tools back in his brown case, said goodbye and left.

Maman scrambled up the next day, feeling poorly with a very bad headache but determined to be our active, loving Maman again, Fonsou stayed in bed another three days before he got up and returned to work.

I had taken my mother, in some way, for granted before this accident, but now realised how precious she was to us, how much we loved her and needed her. To see her pottering about in the house again, to hear her voice singing in the kitchen filled me with enormous joy and gave me the reassurance that all was as normal, but from now on, there was a difference in my appreciation of her motherly presence.

CHAPTER 3

Lena, Fonsou, Maman and myself

Maman at Maison Martin 1947

Painting Easter eggs soon after the move

187

WALNUTS & GOAT CHEESE

The golf trousers, the view beyond

At the back of Maison Martin

Chapter 4

Return to the Île du Levant 1948 – 1953

I do not remember when mother told me about our brother Philippe, although she might have mentioned him to Sylvette at the time when she enquired about her dad. Our brother, in reality my half brother, was born in Gisors in Normandy, on the third of December 1926. In 1936 when his father Mano came to the island to take him away, Maman buried her pain deep down, and concentrated all her attention on Sylvette and her life on the island. Because of the war it was not possible to travel or to receive letters, and therefore she did not receive news, nor could she contact her beloved son any more.

When the Post Office re-opened in 1946, 10 years later, she was able to correspond with Mano. He started sending her a monthly postal order of 300 French Francs (equivalent of about £30.00) to help towards our financial situation. In the spring of 1948, after having read a recent letter from him, Maman announced joyfully that we were to go and meet Mano and Philippe on the Île du Levant, to spend our next summer holidays together. Sylvette and I were very excited at the prospect of meeting our brother.

The lavender came into blossom again and once more we had to cut it, to sell to the lavender oil press in the village. It was hot in early

July and dealing with the lavender was very hard work, but we needed the money to fund our journey to the Lavandou. To my sister's and my surprise, Fonsou was to come with us. I did not express it, but inside I felt, 'Why does he have to come with us? It's not his brother or his father we're going to meet.' I'm sure Sylvette felt the same, but my mother had her reasons to invite him… perhaps she was frightened that he might be jealous of Mano? Fonsou gathered up our camping equipment and we travelled by bus, train and bus again. The journey was long and tiring in the great heat. When we reached the Lavandou, the incomparable scent of the sea reminded me that it had been over six years ago, in the winter of 1942, that we had hurriedly left the island.

I filled my lungs deeply, almost voraciously, until they were full to the brim with the sea air. It was for me a precious perfume that I so adored. Its salty iodine odour mixed with the wet sand and dried algae, together with the melodious music created by the small waves dying on the beach, nourished me and satisfied my soul. I could just distinguish the island through the beautiful, hazy, pale blue light, stretching out in the heat like a sleeping cat on the far horizon; it gave me a feeling of unreal eternity.

We walked several kilometres on the white sandy beach to a small hill crested with maritime pines, protruding east into the shallow turquoise waters. The camping site already had many campers, but we found a space to pitch our two tents: one for Maman and Fonsou, the other for Sylvette and me. Longing for a swim, Sylvette and I put on our bathing costumes and ran down to the dry seaweed and sand beach, the smell of the rotting algae powerful, the water calling. Immersing myself in the clear salty sea was like a huge relief, a reunion and a communion. I felt deeply appeased.

It was late in the afternoon and our mother had asked us not to be too long, as Philippe was due to arrive to meet us at any moment. Both Sylvette and I were highly excited at the prospect of discovering the brother who had vanished from our memories. When we got back to the camp more people had arrived. I did not like the feeling of the noisy place very much, the radios belching out cacophonous sounds, campers talking loudly to make themselves heard, children screaming and shouting, some crying. We were not used to this in our peaceful and quiet Maison Martin. Here all this noise made me feel slightly nervous. Or perhaps it was the apprehension of the meeting with my half brother that made me feel so tense. When we reached our tents, Maman and Philippe were already sitting on a blanket talking, and as we approached, they stood up. Fonsou was slightly behind them, shyly respecting their intimacy. This unusual occasion gave him a joyful expression, which revealed his chrome teeth. Maman was scrutinising us, a hesitant smile showing signs of a slight anxiety.

We stood there, our salty bodies feeling prickly as the sea water evaporated off our skins. With beaming faces we looked at our brother. All my senses opened positively, to absorb the maximum information about him in the short time we would be together. The first things I noticed were the navy-blue sea captain's cap he was wearing, a fine gold chain around his neck, and, on his right wrist, a loose twisty silver bracelet with a flat label. On the other wrist was a complicated watch full of buttons and knobs. He wore a short-sleeved, green and yellow tartan shirt that was unbuttoned to reveal his soft and hairless brown body. Philippe's hair was dark brown and his eyes a hazel colour. The long navy-blue shorts he wore went almost to his knees; in Dieulefit people wore them much, much shorter. I recognized familiar sandals and this gave me a feeling of warmth in my heart: they were the leather Sparciatte made only on the island by a M. Parcenot, and we all had a pair.

He had a gentle smile, and through his eyes I saw him as fragile, hesitant and secretive; he spoke clearly and softly. Leaning towards Sylvette he rapidly gave her a kiss on both cheeks and exclaimed, "Qu'elle est belle!" while at the same time the fingers of his left hand were warmly massaging the top of my head. I loved him instantly, yet I felt strangely distant from him, as if he had come from another world of which I knew nothing. I noticed that he was totally ignoring

Fonsou, neither looking at nor talking to him. I deduced that this was because he had not seen his mother and sister for 9 years, or indeed his half brother at all. There surfaced in me the strangest of feelings, which I did not recognise: the intricacies of relationships created by the mix of heredity in my family. This was a realisation that brought about a change in my inner space - it ruffled, stretched and confused my emotions. He looked at his impressive watch and said, "My God! I'm going to miss the last boat to the Island. I must go now!" He then gave his mother and sister a brief kiss, and, leaning towards me, took my face in his hands, as if deciding whether to kiss me, and smiled. Then he left hurriedly.

His short visit had the effect of a tornado invading my feelings and leaving them full of questions and frustrations. The sudden departure left a deep silence among us; no one spoke. Mother went to prepare supper on the little camping gas cooker, Sylvette disappeared into our small tent, Fonsou turned to the east and scrutinised the horizon as if he was looking for something he could not find. I stood there, feeling happy to have found an older brother, but not knowing where to put myself in relation to him. Was I in his heart as much as he was in mine? I felt a slight feeling of pain that I quickly buried; he was my brother after all and I wanted to have a good feeling of him inside myself. I became distracted by a tune, playing on a radio somewhere in the camp. It took me away into the world of nostalgia; I recognized the voice of Edith Piaf. I liked her dense vibrations so full of feelings, with the accordion that accompanied her.

The sun had gone down behind the hills, different cooking smells came up from the campers preparing their supper, and candles had been lit in preparation for the night to come. I was hungry and found that Maman had prepared supper. During the meal she told us that at 10:30 the next morning we would take the boat to the island and stay at La Cigale for the whole summer with Philippe and Mano. He would pay for everything because he had invited us. Sylvette and I were delighted at the thought of meeting Mano and being with our brother for two months. In the tent that night, we talked for a long time; I had so many questions to ask and my sister replied to a few, but for many she had no answer. Finally she said, "Come on, let's go to sleep now!"

I turned my back to her, trying to find comfort on the hard and irregular ground, hoping that this would stop the flow of questions that remained unanswered in my mind, but it didn't. What was it that confused me? Why had he not kissed me like he had my sister? Why had he not talked to Fonsou? Why did he wear such a big watch with all those knobs? What was their use? Then I saw his hazel eyes looking at me... why did they hold so much back? Then his smile, it was similar to my mother's, same nose, same mouth even to a small bump on the right side, just on the edge of the lower lip. I liked that detail, which really made me feel that we had the same mother, and this made me feel closer to him.

We rose early the next morning with a deep blue sky, which usually meant that the mistral was blowing on the open ultramarine waters. The Cap Bénat, a long arm of hilly land that protruded south into the sea, protected the Lavandou from the mistral. The cicadas, warmed up by the already hot sun, were joyfully blasting out their monotonous scratchy sounds. I felt fizzy with excitement.

After a short breakfast, we packed up tents and belongings and started the long walk along the sandy beach to the jetty. Fonsou carried the heavy tents, Maman two well loaded baskets, Sylvette and I towels and beddings. It was hot, and the white sand reflected so much glare from the sun that I kept my eyes almost closed. I walked in the transparent waters to keep my feet cool. On the horizon I noticed a white spot tossed up and down by the white waves. "Maman, Maman! Look over there, the boat is coming!"

"Yes, it is. Its probably Loulou; he'll be on time!" She had told me about Loulou: how, when he was 17, he had held me in his arms on the crossing to the island, a few days after my birth. He was the only son of the Père Pégliasco who lived in the small house by the beach of the Grand Avis. It was also Loulou's father who had brought our grandfather back to life many years ago. She had told me what good sailors they were, and that they had never been to school, could not read nor write, and how all the women fell for Loulou because he was so handsome.

The small harbour had one single jetty surrounded by colourful dancing fishing boats. From Loulou's pale blue boat someone threw a heavy rusty anchor into the turquoise waters, its chain making a metallic sound as it coasted gently against the jetty. Only two or three people came off the gangplank and it was now waiting for its new passengers to come on board. We unloaded our belongings on the wooden quayside; looking through the spaces between the planks into the clear waters, I could see mullets with their flat dark blue noses swimming around just under the surface in search for food. They were like old friends I had not seen for six years, and my impatience to swim amongst them in the sea increased.

Maman and Sylvette had gone up the quay towards the café, leaving Fonsou to keep an eye on the luggage. I ran up to them, and as we reached the bar there sat Loulou on a tall stool in front of a cup of coffee… when he saw our mother he exclaimed enthusiastically "Honor!" Revealing a perfect set of white teeth. He was obviously surprised and pleased to see her after six years. I was looking at him with interest— there sat the man she had told me so much about, who was almost totally naked but for a red handkerchief tied tightly round his head and a pair of very small blue shorts. In the centre of his belt, he had tucked a shiny, worn, black leather wallet bulging with bank notes, which hid his belly button. His bare feet were wide and steady; he obviously never wore shoes, for the soles of his feet were thick, and cracked at the heels. When he stood up I noticed that he was smaller than my mother; I was impressed by his brown lean body, with well defined muscles that looked like a nicely laid out pattern of pebbles on a wet sandy beach. I could not see his hair under the red scarf; just his long dark sideburns and his square and unshaven jaw. Thick black eyebrows made a continuous straight line across his forehead and over his sunken piercing brown eyes, and he

CHAPTER 4

looked at me for a brief instant. I noticed something that looked like an animal presence in them as he showed me an evasive smile.

We sat on benches round the front deck of Loulou's large, recently purchased boat called Les Iles d'Or. The diesel engine was purring, a young lad was passing Loulou boxes of fruit and vegetables and all kinds of other goods, including a heavy double spring mattress. All the goods were neatly arranged right behind the cabin. Loulou moved about like a cat, fast, neatly and silently. The 15 passengers became the spectators of the loading activities and preparations before departure, the ladies not missing any of his graceful and precise movements, obviously enjoying looking at the captain.

He went into his cabin to fetch a huge conch, which he brought to his lips and, taking a deep breath, blew like a trumpet in the direction of the small harbour. The sound that came out of the seashell was loud, round, and with a low rich tone that carried me into long ago times. Into my mind came clichés of the period when busy Phoenicians traded in these waters, or when, in the not so distant past, fishermen announced their return to harbour by blowing into a similar shell. The hills behind the Lavandou faintly echoed the generous sound back to us, as if the land was saying goodbye. Loulou gave a last glance at the jetty to make sure that there was no latecomer, while his young mate untied the ropes and jumped into the boat, and we were off! Loulou pointed the ship in the direction of the Cap Bénat and gave full throttle.

Snuggled against my mother, feeling eternity, I was not in my thoughts but in a space of simply being, all my senses attentive, letting the multitude of impressions that surrounded us go by freely. I looked at the rear of the boat, where the red, blue and white flag was snapping in the turbulence of the air currents; a trail of white froth followed us, making a long bubbly boulevard that led to the speckled pink and ochre colours of the disappearing Lavandou.

Loulou had collected the money for the crossing and the leather wallet was now much thicker and tight against his abdomen. He had a short chat with each passenger, checking to make sure that they were okay. Back in his cabin now, he looked serious, concentrating on the horizon as the boat started to rise up and down, and I now turned my attention towards the open sea. Holding on tight to the parapet I realised that we were close to the extreme end of Cap Bénat. Large waves were crashing onto the rugged rocks in an explosion of rainbow droplets. Ahead of us the sea was littered with white horses galloping away, chased by the mistral. I was completely absorbed by the interplay of the elements, feeling at one with the boat and the sea. Suddenly I was brought back to reality as the prow of our small vessel came down violently into an incoming wave, creating a huge spray that completely soaked us. Loulou and Sylvette were laughing and so Maman and I left our precarious spot, holding on tight to whatever we could find, to reach the back of the boat, where Fonsou was sitting quietly. It was his first time at sea and he was not feeling so good, hiding his anxiety. Wet and salty, I was now shivering. Maman slipped a pullover over me, but I wanted more thrills, and shouted over the sounds of the elements: "Maman, can I go to join Sylvette in front?" She agreed, asking me to be careful and to hold on tight.

All our attention was ahead of us; the coastline was disappearing in the distance as the boat pointed South West in the direction of Bagaud, the smallest of the string of islands called Les Iles d'Hyères. Now in the full blow of the mistral, Sylvette and I had adapted our bodies to the rise and fall of the waves, and delighted in feeling their power lifting our boat up to the heights and then just abandoning it all to gravity. The sea had become silver as the sun was reaching its zenith; Bagaud was now close enough to see its rock formation and the ruins of the old fort half-hidden behind the pine trees.

Les Iles d'Or turned its back to the mistral and headed southeast towards the protected bay of the island of Port Cros, with the waves pushing us forward in long leaps until the boat finally came into the calmer waters of the bay. Loulou brought down the throttle, and we glided into the peaceful harbour, to deliver goods to the few inhabitants. The Bay of Port Cros has the shape of a crab with one of its large pincers out. Dominating the small harbour and built on high dark granite rock is a fortified house. Many tall agaves surrounded the fort's high wall, their long, olive-green serrated leaves pointing their violet prickles in different directions, towards the sky. Opposite the jetty was a row of small fishermens' houses, painted pink and ochre with brown shutters. Although the engine was ticking over, I could still hear the wonderful sounds of the wind in the pines, and the frantic noise of the cicadas reminding us of their presence.

After a few minutes unloading, Loulou was back at the tiller, and turning round in a perfect curve, pointed us west. To appease our hunger, Maman had given us a torn part of a baguette, a lump of dried goat cheese and a tomato each, which Sylvette and I ate sitting at the prow. Ahead of us, and now looking east, we noticed many flat rocks that looked like square lumps of chocolate put together haphazardly, and remembered that it was called La Galère and that it was an important marker on the sailing route. We had to go wide by some hundred metres to avoid its shallow reef. Then the boat went south to towards the Ile du Levant's new harbour, called l'Aygade.

We could now see the island that we loved so much - it was as if it had been waiting for us all these years. Every detail we knew was clearly defined and we enjoyed pointing out the different houses and places where we used to fish and swim. Maman came and, standing between us, gently placed her hands round our waists, pressing our bodies against hers. We felt as one being, full of joy, all together in that instant.

"Look! Over there, La Cigale!" Sylvette exclaimed excitedly, pointing her finger to the perspective, the great flat stone staircase leading up to the fort of Napoleon. There it was: the house built by my Dad Marcel Lassalle, where we had spent the happy first years of our lives. Suddenly I remembered him, and as my throat tightened, my nostrils swelled and my eyes watered, I quickly wiped them dry with the back of my hands. It wasn't the place nor the time to cry, as I did not want Sylvette or Maman to be aware of my tears in such a joyful moment, so I swallowed my sad feelings bravely.

197

"Look! l'Ayguade, how it's changed!" My sister exclaimed, "A boat has been sunk just in front of it!" Obviously she was very excited, as she was going to meet her real dad, and I understood her excitement in silence. The dramatic events of our lives had created a hidden separation in the feelings of Philippe, Sylvette and me. We each experienced very differently the same shared moments; none of us really knew how the others felt inside. I kept my feelings to myself.

To protect the harbour from the mistral, an old rusty cargo boat had been dumped there. Its huge rusty body lay partly on the rocks, partly in the sea and reminded me of an old seal baking in the sun. Loulou manoeuvred Les Iles d'Or backwards alongside the quay, so as to be in a position for an immediate departure in case the weather worsened. I noticed on the pebbled beach, the small, green flat-bottomed rowboat, and remembered Victor, the old Portuguese, (or was he Italian?) fisherman who had first seen Grandfather Gell floating unconscious near Portman, and had notified it to a nearby fishing boat.

Discovering the complex behaviour of adults

There were many people on the wooden quay, either waiting for their goods or meeting someone. In the suntanned crowd I recognize Philippe, who was totally naked but for a yellow minimum slip that everybody present wore. It was a triangular piece of fabric, flat for the ladies or in pocket form for the men, one corner of which became a ribbon that passed between the legs to make a loop at the back through which one tied it to the other two extended corners. The ladies, like the men, were topless.

Les Iles d'Or was now tightly secured against the car tyres that protected the quay, emitting creaky sounds as the boat moved up and down, tossed by the waves. The cicadas were singing loudly here too, and the heat reflected off the rocks. The wind had almost stopped but the sea was still rough, so it was difficult for the passengers to walk off the boat. I heard my mother call "Sounet!" "Sounet!" I found her near our bags, Fonsou already picking them up, and Sylvette, now gone shy, standing right next to Maman. In a gentlemanly manner, Loulou, with one foot in the boat and one on the gangplank, was helping every passenger safely onto the jetty. In a flash he picked me up and settled me onto the quay. Sylvette came immediately after, and then elegantly holding our mother's hand, he led her all the way to safety.

Philippe greeted Maman with a quick kiss, Sylvette received one too and, as I had experienced in the Lavandou the previous day, I received a quick rub of his hand on my blonde hair. Today he wore a different watch, but the same gold chain around his neck, this time I saw a little gold cross on it, and the same silver bracelet around his wrist. He led us through the crowd to meet Mano, who was waiting for us at the end of the jetty.

My sister's father was plump, his round face and brown eyes were smiling, and he gave me the impression of being a gentle and kind man. I noticed too his generous, slightly hooked nose, his chestnut hair neatly pulled back from his large forehead, a pair of Sparciatte sandals, a faded pale green minimum. He wore no jewellery nor watch. I saw him put his hands on Maman's shoulders kissing her rapidly on either cheek and pushing her back, to show that he wanted to be in control of who was to receive and give affection. He was obviously longing to look at my sister, the daughter he had not seen since she was two.

She was now thirteen and I had noticed how men kept looking at her. She was pretty, with her plaited silver-blonde hair and her green eyes, high cheekbones and a well-proportioned face set on her long neck and square shoulders. Always standing with her back perfectly straight, her posture revealing dignity. In one long glance Mano devoured her from head to foot, as if he wanted to absorb in one gulp all the years that he hadn't seen his daughter. Then he gave her two short absent kisses and turned to Maman saying, "My God! Isn't she beautiful!" He finally turned towards me, held my face in his large and extremely soft hands, looked into my eyes, and said, "Are you a good boy?" I replied a shy "yes", not knowing what else to say. He looked at me absently when our eyes met; I did not sense his presence and this left me with a strange, unresolved feeling.

Like ants carrying their burdens, the small crowd slowly dispersed from the quay, leaving behind only Fonsou standing next to our luggage, and the huge double mattress that I had seen at the Lavandou.

Mano, probably thinking that he was a local porter, asked him, "Would you mind carrying this mattress up to La Cigale for me?" And without giving him time to reply, he added, "Just follow us, if you don't know the way." Looking a bit mystified, Fonsou put the heavy awkward object on its longer side, turned his back and grabbing the thin ropes that held its wrappers, lifted it onto his back and waited, leaning slightly forward with his strong legs firmly apart.

We divided out the rest of the luggage and proceeded on the long climb. It was around one o'clock, the sun was at its maximum height and soon we were all sweating. Remembering the way, Sylvette and I climbed ahead, followed by Philippe, Mano and Maman, chatting, and Fonsou behind, following in silence.

We all heard from down below, the long cry of Loulou's conch, calling before his departure back to the Lavandou. Sylvette and I walked faster and were quite ahead of the others; we turned around and sat down on a rock to admire the view, under the shade of a tall Chinese strawberry tree. It had not changed, except for the rusty cargo ship flung across l' Ayguade's harbour. It was still as magnificent as we had left it. The maquis surrounded us; small gusts of hot air picked up the strong scents that came from the many aromatic plants. At our feet, the hot mica sand glittered like gold flakes, the sounds of the light wind going through the briar and Chinese strawberry trees, together with the ever chatty cicadas, lifted my soul up to a high place in the heavens. Sylvette and I stayed there silent, overcome by the enchantment of the magic island.

Our brother caught up and joined us in our admiration of the view.

"Isn't it beautiful?" he said, a little out of breath; we nodded silently. Emerging from the path far below, we saw Mano and Maman still talking, then the mattress coming up as if climbing by itself, Fonsou under the heavy weight steadily following. Not giving them time to stop for a rest, we moved on along the wider road, our brother walking between us, talking. He had lots of interesting things to say - how much he was longing to go fishing and swimming with us.

We were now nearing La Cigale. I noticed that the trees had grown taller, so had the agaves and one was even in bloom! Thrilled, I ran up the path leading to the kitchen of the house. Now the briar and the Chinese strawberries trees created a long dark tunnel, at the end of which very tall geraniums displayed their splash of colourful reds. I dashed round the corner; the pump was still there and so was the old rusty tin can with water inside for priming it. I activated the handle, while pouring the water into the cylindrical top… and out of its nozzle came the cool, soft rainwater. "Please Sylvette, can you pump for me?" I said, hurriedly taking all my clothes off and sitting underneath its spout.

I was her young brother, and my eccentric behaviour in the front of others and especially our new big brother was embarrassing for her. She wore a shy smile with an expression as if saying, "He is my little brother, he behaves in funny ways some time. You have to excuse him." I knew of her embarrassment and I must say that it enticed me to clown more. She started pumping, the nozzle letting the flow of soft water onto my head and body; it was cold compared to the outside heat, and for an instant it forced my breath out and I shrieked in delight. "Now it's your turn!" I said as I stood up, my body refreshed and glittering in the brilliant sunlight. "No! I don't want to, I haven't got my bathing costume with me!"

We heard voices coming up the lane. The rest of the family arrived, hot and puffing. Fonsou had put down the mattress that would not go through the tunnel of branches and leaves, so he turned it sideways and finally laid it against the dry flat stone wall; then he leaned against it to rest and recover his breath. Mano took out from his canvas basket a wad of banknotes and turning towards the exhausted Fonsou and exposing a kind smile said,

"Thank you very much. Thank God you were there! I couldn't have carried it myself! Tell me, how much do I owe you?" A tense silence followed: Fonsou, red-faced and soaked by his Herculean efforts, looked perplexed and could not find the words to answer Mano. He turned to Maman who said, as if all was perfectly normal, "Oh! By the way, let me introduce to you my companion… Fonsou…"

No one had told Mano that Fonsou would come on this holiday, or even who he was. I noticed anger and irritation in his eyes and, although he was smiling, he was surprised. Mano pulled out his hand and said politely, "Pleased to meet you. All my apologies for the mattress, I did not realise…" Maman's partner managed to show a timid smile and offered an inert hand for Mano to shake. Philippe had disappeared somewhere in the house, obviously not wanting to be part of that awkward moment.

Fonsou and Maman went off to the Coccinelle, a hut grandpa Gell had built to use when he needed to be completely alone. The hut consisted of a concrete slab floor on which stood a fixed wooden frame covered with ochre/red interlocking aluminium sides decorated with embossed lozenges and a corrugated iron roof that sloped down towards the hill behind. It was totally hidden by the tall maquis, some fifty metres away from La Cigale. Mano walked up to the Carré where he stayed during his holidays. It was a square stone building in the shape of a perfect cube that was between La Cigale and the Coccinelle. Originally Edward and GG had had it built by my dad, to use as a reading and rest room.

I ran into La Cigale and saw that things had changed. The war had left its mark—everything had been stolen except for two exceptionally heavy wooden chairs with straw seats. I inspected every corner of the kitchen and dining room, which brought back memories, as I felt my dad's presence everywhere. On seeing the now-broken food cupboard in the tiny kitchen, I remembered how our mother had seen Sylvette and me standing on a chair reaching for the top of the

CHAPTER 4

cupboard, where she had hidden the sweet can of Nestles condensed milk.

"Naughty children, will you get down? You are terrible, I have no more hiding places now!" She had said, with amusement in her voice. After that incident she had stopped hiding the sweet milk. I went into the dining room, which felt different and bear, then reflected, "It's awful to go into peoples' homes like this and steal everything!"

Looking at the wall opposite the large windows I saw, scratched into the white plaster and heightened with watercolours, an exciting and colourful mural depicting an underwater scene, with small waves cresting the top, and sea life below. Fish of all kinds and shapes caught by Philippe and Mano were depicted, and under each catch was the date, and the name of the person who caught it. I recognized instantly the types of fish in this vigorous and precise drawing full of humour; even air bubbles emerged from the fishes' amusing mouths; their eyes were expressive and seemed to look at me. On the lower part of the wall Mano had drawn the seabed with seaweed, red starfishes, sea urchins, octopi, shells and crabs of all types. I was lost deep in the inspection of the details of this underwater world when Mano came in and asked amusedly, "You like it?" "Yes, I do!" He rested his gentle, heavy hand on my shoulder and pointing at a large silvery pink fish with sharp teeth, said, "Look at this big one, it's called a Denti, hard to catch… it's carnivorous and lives at a depth of 10 to 30 meters. Your brother caught it!" Mano used his lively hands and made facial expressions together with sounds to accompany his funny gestures. He added with less enthusiasm, "In fact, when I look at the wall, I realise sadly that all the larger fish have been caught by Philippe!"

After a quick search, he pointed at a dark green and orange fish hidden in the seaweed, "Here, look, I caught this one! It's called a Rouquier, poor fellow; I did not give him much of a chance! My harpoon went through just behind its gills!

When we were with Mano, he did most of the talking, and it was difficult to find the space to say anything; but what he said was always interesting, and I soon discovered that he was a wonderful storyteller. "First fish you'll catch, we'll have it on the wall, look! You see…"

And putting his large hand flat on the wall, he took the blunt end of a pencil and drew a contour around it. I noticed that bits of skin had been pulled out around his fingernails giving them an untidy appearance.

"We trace round the fish, like this… so as to have the true size." Mano sharpened my appetite; I was longing to go into the sea to harpoon a fish, so that I could have my catch added to the fresco. Maman, who had just prepared lunch, was calling us to sit at the table, but I went on with my inspection of the house.

Getting to know my brother

I passed through the dining room into a long bedroom that led to the round tower. Our grandfather who loved singing had designed it as a place to exercise his powerful voice. Before we arrived, Philippe had installed himself on the long, low built-in bed by the window that gave onto the courtyard. The bed was a large piece of furniture, with one end raised to become a bookshelf; I imagined it was too heavy and cumbersome to steal like the rest of mum's furniture. To the left were three short steps leading up to a platform from where Maman's double bed had been stolen. Through the round window I checked rapidly the view of Port Cros, as if it might have been stolen too, like all the nice things in our house. Opposite the fitted bed, was a long narrow window looking onto the north view of the distant coastline and the Cap Bénat. At the foot of the fitted bed was the chimney, which fascinated me because it had three adjustable metal panels that could be fully opened, fully closed or adjusted, to control the draught. Except for the bookshelves and the fitted bed, everything had been stolen and I felt a large part of my past had vanished.

All the flat surfaces, the head of the bed, the raised platform, the steps, the floor under the North window and the top of the black marble fire surround, were now covered with an array of objects - tools, scissors, nail clippers, spanners and hammers, guitar, harpoon guns, flippers and masks, clocks, magnificent cameras and cine-cameras, many different types of knives laid out according to size, daggers, and even guns and bullets! I was discovering my brother's habits, hobbies, interests, science fiction and detective books, and his passion for photography and underwater filming.

At the Maison Martin, the only tools we had were an old-fashioned bow saw for cutting the logs, a pair of pincers, a hammer, a screwdriver and an axe for splitting the wood! Our camera was just a Kodak pinhole box; it didn't even have a lens, but it nevertheless took jolly good photographs. The room had been taken over by my brother. However, there was so much to discover with his display of material objects, which kind of frightened me. I simply stood there looking, not wanting to let their attractive force invade me. I did not touch anything, but turned to my brother who was lying on the bed, scratching his feet while reading a thriller.

"Come in. We will sleep in here together, but first, I will have to remove some of my things." He then pointed to the bottom of the room near the chimney corner, and went on, "I found some army camp beds in the shed by the pump where Sylvette will sleep; we'll take one out and bring it in here for you: you'll see, they are quite comfortable. Later, I will order a double bed and put it up on the platform, and then you will be able to sleep in this one." My brother did not know that before the war I used to sleep in the very same bed he was lying on. He forgot that I had lived on the island before, and it had been my island and home too. The bed reminded me of my papa carrying me while I was almost asleep, and how Maman used to rub my aching tummy in a circular motion to help me to settle down. Of course Maman must have rubbed his tummy too, must have snuggled him to sleep too. But we knew nothing of each other really, and we were individually too preoccupied with ourselves to be aware of each other's feelings. I felt high, and did not really know what to do with myself. So much new information was poring in, so many new feelings to deal with. A code of existence functioned between Sylvette, Maman, Fonsou and I; we knew how to be, what to do and what not to do to keep the harmony between us. Now, everything had greatly changed and I found it difficult to adjust. Maman called again for lunch, and we left the bedroom.

"Please Philippe, can we go to les Pierres-Plattes for a quick swim?" He answered without much enthusiasm, but on seeing my excitement said, "Okay then, let's just take goggles and flippers. I think I'll find a pair for you and Sylvette." I was so excited at the prospect of swimming from these lovely rocks again. I ran round the corner to fetch my sister who was equally delighted. We set off with our light equipment overwhelmingly happy to be with our brother. Like a goat that had been kept in a shed all winter and was suddenly let out in the spring, I ran ahead on the narrow footpath down the steep hill, jumping over root stumps and rocks, my young emotional ego wanting to show my brother that I knew the way perfectly well. I waited for them at places where there was a clearing with a good view. The sea had quietened down since the morning and as we approached it, I began to see the wonderful array of colours made by the seaweeds through the clear water - the ochre, the pinks, the browns, the reds and purples contrasted by the almost fluorescent light greens of the sea salad that grew on the rocks along the water's edge. Looking further out were large patches of turquoise, showing a sandy seabed, encircled by deep ultramarine blues created by tall algae. As I came out of the maquis onto the rocky cliff, my nose picked up the distinct range of smells, carried up by the warm sea breeze. There was a definite change from the aromatic scent of the maquis to the scent of the plants that lived on the edge of the water.

I was brought out of my contemplation by voices suddenly emerging out of the maquis; Philippe and Sylvette stood by me for some time in silence, a silence similar to the one that descends at a dining table when everyone is savouring a delicious meal. Now filled by the beauty of the scenery, we proceeded to climb down the perilous rocks. The place was called Les Pierres-Plattes because of the large mica sandstone slabs, encrusted with lumps of iron ore and embellished by white and red stripes of sharp flints, resembling frozen packs of cards. As we approached the water the slabs came out of the sea almost vertically. Crouching and facing the sea, with our toes licked by the waves, our brother sat between us and gave us a demonstration of how to put on the goggles. Before the war this type of snorkel didn't exist, he explained, "A sea captain called Jacques-Yves Cousteau developed these snorkels to explore the seabed." He pulled out a handful of fluffy brown algae; "You can use this seaweed to clean the glass by rubbing it together with your spit, or even your own pee." There was much conviction in his voice, "Because the acid of the urine takes all the greasy marks away and gives you a perfectly clear glass…"

As I was naked, I promptly peed into my goggles enjoying the hot liquid on my fingers in contrast to the cool seawater and I rubbed the glass thoroughly with the seaweed.

"Now, immerse the goggles in the water so that the temperature of the glass becomes the same as the sea. Wet your face with your hand, making sure all the hair of your forehead is pushed back." I noticed how much he enjoyed explaining things, giving the maximum information, and I liked that because I liked to understand things. With both thumbs he pulled back the black flexible rubber sides and applied the goggles to his wet face creating a snappy sound. By turning his head to Sylvette and then to me, he demonstrated how the suction kept the goggles squashed onto his face without using the strap. He looked funny with his upper lip slightly turned round and up. With his round eyes and squashed nose he reminded me of some strange deep-sea fish. The next thing was to pull on the strap over one's head to fix the whole contraption into position. Satisfied that his demonstration had been understood, he said in a strange, scanty voice, similar to when you talk while pinching your nose, "Very good, you see, it's easy!" With his flippers on, he slipped into the water silently, and, like baby otters following their mum, Sylvette and I went in after him.

I was taken by surprise by the many impressions and emotions that came tumbling down into my chest. First, was the feeling of the cool water surrounding my body; there was not one part of it that did not feel the immersion. The second thing was the clarity of the water, revealing such a diversity of life: there was so much to look at that my eyes could not properly focus on one thing. The third was the strange sensation of floating while looking down several metres below and realising that I could relax without having to move to keep afloat. The sound world was different, sounds that I could not distinguish. Sylvette was swimming beneath me, her long fair hair a silvery pale green undulating out, and at each breast-stroke gathering into a bouquet. Although I still wanted to look around, I couldn't hold my breath any longer and I came to the surface to breathe. Sylvette and Philippe were still below. I took in as much air as my lungs could contain and dived down again towards the top of a rock where I had seen a silver fish with a black ring round its tail. I swam deeper to observe more closely its silvery coat; it was almost transparent and like a mirror, reflecting its surroundings; its large round eye was looking at me intensely. As I came closer, it took fright and, with a flick of its tail, propelled itself some 20 meters, where it stopped as suddenly as it had taken off, letting itself quietly float. Then I saw a beautiful sea urchin, mauve with pale white spots along its prickles; they were not the edible types like the dark green and purple almost black ones that had dangerous sharp needles that one had to avoid. I remembered that when they were dead, their pale mauve or pale green tomato shaped skeletons were exquisite, with their sea star design amplified by fine raised green or violet dots. There was one! Resting on the bottom of a sandy patch; I dived for it… but before my hand could reach it, I felt a sharp pain in my ears and, abandoning my descent, I surfaced.

We had only been in the water 10 minutes, but feeling cold I swam to the rocks to climb out, taking great care where I put my feet, to avoid the sea urchins. It was easy with these wonderful goggles acting like a magnifying glass, and everything looked big, sharp and clear. Finding a smooth rock for my feet, I crouched down into a ball put my arms round my knees to keep warm and watched my brother and sister. Although I was trembling with cold, I was immensely happy to be reunited with the sea world, with the island and with my brother and sister. They were still in the water, talking and laughing with their goggles on, exchanging impressions, and then disappearing under the surface again. When they finally came out, they carried in their hands their finds from the open treasure box of the seabed. Opening their frozen white fingers I saw different types of sea shells, some in the shape of a pierced ear and sparkling with wonderful fluorescent pearl colours, a powerful crabs' clamp, one little pink flat shell in the shape of a heart, another one the shape of a large snail striped with dark green and white lines. Philippe talked all the way home, mostly about his fishing exploits. He showed me a nip on his forearm, and explained, "I was playing with a fair sized octopus in open waters, it stuck to my arm while I swam… suddenly I felt a pain! It had nipped me with its sharp beak!" I was fascinated by his sea stories and they made me long to go back in the water with the all the proper underwater equipment.

Mano and Philippe really took all the space when we were together round the dining table. Fonsou made himself discreet and did not engage in conversation, for he was a communist and strongly believed that the rich were the cause of all the problems. Mano on the other hand, was a royalist and had extreme right-wing ideas, believing in the death penalty, and that Stalin and the Communists were the expression of the devil.

I knew Fonsou well enough to read from the expressions on his face what went on inside him; he found it very difficult sometimes not to express his anger at what he was hearing from Mano or Philippe. He could not find the words to communicate his understanding and beliefs, as he was too self-conscious of his poor vocabulary and education to start an argument with Mano. He was also embarrassed by his table manners: how to hold a knife and fork to cut meat, how to eat soup; even cutting bread was done differently. I became aware of all the different customs that separated our society: what distinguished us from each other. What was considered proper conduct by the bourgeois society was not by the workmen or farmers.

Maman, on the other hand, was much more free, she had been brought up by the English upper class, lived in the bourgeois atmosphere of her Parisian life and was now living with a workman, himself brought up as a farmer. So like a butterfly that haphazardly chooses its flower, she flew from one set of arguments to another, often laughing, almost teasing when the conversation was getting too serious. She liked to upset manners, to round off the edges in a conversation, to smooth things to make them as equal as possible, to find the opposite argument to a debate. I was silently observing the adults playing their games, and chose for myself the parts of the conversation that I felt were most truthful. Mano certainly knew a lot of things and how to communicate them; whether it was about the arts (he was an art dealer), whether it was about politics, national or international, or whether it was star gossip which he seemed to enjoy very much, as he bought all kinds of magazines to read during his siesta in the Carré.

Philippe enjoyed mother's food, as we all did actually, and during meals he would let Mano do all the talking, except for the odd occasion when he added a few words to Mano's point of view. He avoided confrontation, did not enjoy arguments or comparing his ideas to someone else's. He preferred to talk without challenge, to share the book he had read, to talk about his girlfriends or what we would do the next day. Maman knew Fonsou and Mano well, she was able to mingle delicately between their convictions, and when she talked with Mano in Fonsou's presence, she spoke for him, defending the arguments that she knew were in his mind. Sometime during the siesta by the Coccinelle, I could hear Fonsou's loud shouting to decompress what he had bottled up during the meal times!

It could not have been easy for Maman, but she never showed or shared with us any of her suffering.

Fonsou stayed only two weeks with us. He had to return to Dieulefit to work in the pottery and it was not surprising to see how the dynamics changed when Fonsou took the boat back to the coast. The atmosphere lightened up and I noticed how everyone behaved differently after his departure. Sylvette was much happier; Philippe talked more and did not escape into his thrillers so often. Mano no longer talked about politics, but instead would remember the times when he and Maman lived together in Normandy or in Paris, driving down to Provence in their Renault. The times they studied at the Académie Julian where they had first met - it was clear that he still loved her. He would often say to me, "Your mother is completely mad, but a mad Saint! She is a crazy Saint!"

I did agree about the Saint part, but not that she was mad or crazy, because to me she seemed extremely sane. From hearing the way he talked about people I sometimes thought that it was he who was mad.

Mano was a very generous man. He looked after everybody for two and a half months taking care of all our material needs; large brand new banknotes would flow out of his back pocket as if it was natural. Maman had no money worries during our summer holidays. His holiday was shorter than ours, and after four weeks he would join his Sudanese wife, Gany, and his mother in the village of Camaret.

In the late 1940s and early 1950s the island was still pretty wild. The French Navy had not yet taken possession of it and we went for long walks with our picnic baskets to its many beautiful beaches. Sylvette and I particularly liked the beach of Rioufrède, which was about an hour's walk away. We accessed it by climbing down a steep path among tall pine trees; looking down through their large rose brown trunks, we would suddenly discover its crescent shaped, white and pink pebbled beach and its crystal clear azure water. From that moment, we accelerated our steps until we ran to see who would be first in the sea. We went to this beach on the days the Mistral blew, for it was completely sheltered from the wind that guaranteed us a blue sky.

With the newly discovered snorkels, Sylvette and I found an amazing underwater rock that had a long slightly curved hole through it. It lay two to three metres down, on the fine, white, pebbled floor, with no sea urchins; it was only covered by a light-brown soft algae that reminded us of velvet. The hole was large enough for our slim bodies to go through from one end on the sea floor up to the other, nearer the surface. Behaving like fishes, we kept our arms alongside our bodies to propel ourselves through the long tunnel using our new flippers. Looking down from the top of the narrow tunnel, reflected light-rays of pale green gold-orange took our breath away. I watched my sister come through the hole and made monkey faces at her until she burst out laughing in an explosion of bubbles making her mask come off.

It was at Rioufrède, that I discovered what fun it was to follow my brother when he went fishing with his impressive, 2-metre long, harpoon gun. His preparation was a ritual, with all his hunting equipment first laid out flat on a rock in an orderly fashion. He then attached a nylon belt to his waist to hold a brown Bakelite sheath with a cork handled dagger, and a large circular slip-hook to hang the eventual prey.

"Why do you wear a dagger when you go swimming?" I had visions of my brother, like the Tarzan fighting with a large shark. "I carry it in case I have a problem, for instance if I capture a large fish, and it pulls my harpoon away. I'll cut off the nylon thread so not to lose my harpoon gun, only the arrow. If in the struggle I lose my knife, then no problem: with its cork handle, it will float!" Then came the large black flippers, then the goggles thoroughly washed with urine and seaweed, rinsed and then cooled in the seawater.

"These are Italian, they are the best you can buy, the glass is very strong; it is safe to go down up to 100 metres with them!" Once the flippers, the goggles and the snorkel were on, he took the pale blue aluminium harpoon. He then slipped silently into the appealing water, fitted the rubber mouthpiece into his mouth, inserted the harpoon into the nozzle of his gun, and with a sudden effort, forced the arrow down until it clicked to safety. When the gun was loaded, he began to move forward, floating quietly like a bird of prey.

Now it was time for me to practice my talents as a mountain goat. The coastline was very rocky and uneven, with deep crevices, and at times vertical cliffs forced me into the water to swim round the difficult parts. While climbing, jumping, and calculating my next move, I constantly kept an eye on my brother's whereabouts. When I saw him dive, I held my breath to see if I was able to hold it as long as him, but I never could. If his disappearance was too long, I started to feel anxious and searched the surface for any ripple or bubble that might give me a clue to his whereabouts. At times, he would unexpectedly swim out to sea, following some large fish, perhaps a tuna. If he came zigzagging towards the rocks, it meant that he was cornering a sea bass or a golden Royale sea bream. Sometimes I heard his breathing stop; he would be reloading his harpoon gun, or watching a captivating fish or getting ready for a dive. I would then stop my leaps and bounds and watch his body lose its shape and colours as he descended into the depth. Like a faithful dog, I waited attentively for any sign that might reveal information about what he was doing.

Sometime, he popped his head out of the water and removing the snorkel said, "It was a big one!" or, "I've just missed it!" On rare occasions, as he came up from the depths, I saw flashes of light coming up with him, indicating that he had caught his prey. He then swam rapidly to the shore, and passed me the gun with the harpoon and the fish madly flapping, desperately expressing its agony. Philippe then came out to warm himself on the hot rocks. Still trembling from the cold, he told me with precise details all about his underworld adventures. Once rested and appeased by the generous sun rays, he would go back in the water with the fish floating behind him, secured on the slipknot wire ring.

The day came when Mano allowed me to use one of his small harpoon guns. It was short, just over the length of the harpoon, and was activated by two powerful rubber bands held together by a wire hooked onto a notch on the arrow. I could unscrew the harpoon's head and replace it with a Neptune fork used for catching rockfish. From then on, Maman and the others would not see much of me, as I would spend most of my time fishing with my goggles, snorkel, flippers and harpoon gun.

I felt so good floating in this beautiful crystal clear water, looking onto the magic world below; there was so much to absorb and discover, every rock or algae or patch of sand was hiding something. As I dived down to investigate, it would reveal unexpected secrets: an octopus's garden, well arranged with carefully chosen pebbles, the eyes of a sole looking up at me from the sandy bottom, or under a rock, the silver bellies of fish moving gently as they rubbed against each other. Sometimes I came nose to nose with a Moray eel, its mouth partly open revealing lethal, grey teeth. Had I not had to come up for a breath of air, I would have stayed in the depths for ever, but the infallible laws of nature make sure that each species lives in the world for which it was destined.

My first catch in the shallow waters was a very prickly, pinkish brown rockfish. I came out excitedly and made sure that all the people sunbathing on the nearby rocks saw my catch. There was applause as I arrived triumphantly with my prey. Mano looked very impressed, and that pleased me, "Hey, this boy is gifted! Catching a rockfish is not easy, for it is difficult to distinguish it from the seaweed and rocks. This one will have to go on the mural in the dining room!" His remarks boosted my self-confidence and swelled a little more the timid I of my ego.

My brother often talked to me about his sexual exploits, but only when we were in our respective beds and in the dark. I had never heard such stories before, and one warm night he said that apparently black women had extra soft skin. "When you caress them, especially on certain places!" Adding a little grunt of delight, "It is much softer than silk, and their body odours..." Then a little squeak of pleasure, "Its like the rich scent of a tropical flower... and their hands with their smooth long fingers!"

I would desperately try to imagine the rich smells of the tropical flowers that I had never seen or smelt, as for the silk, yes, I knew that it was soft, warm and slippery to touch. But by that time I was usually dropping off to sleep. Once in complete darkness he perplexed me by suddenly saying with authority, "You know, it's very dangerous to masturbate!" Already half in my sleep I murmured, "What does it mean to masturbate?" Surprised, he tried to explain, "You know, when you touch and play with your thing..."

This I understood better as I had already discovered, in all simplicity, the pleasures of touching 'my thing' as he had put it. Intrigued, and wanting to know, I queried, "Why?" "Because, when you masturbate, the energy you create returns back into you, it doesn't flow out and can bring about a bad illness." "What kind of bad illness?" "Oh, you get the shakes, you tremble and you can even get convulsions!" I didn't reply to his strange explanation, for to me it did not make sense that such a simple pleasurable act could be dangerous. When he told me that story, I was just creeping into puberty and had not yet experienced the full cycle of masturbation. Nevertheless, for many years to come I would hear my brother's comments each time I investigated the exciting world of sexual feelings.

Some days everyone rested at La Cigale and there would be silence while the adults took a nap or read in their respective bedrooms. On rare occasions my brother agreed to do some shooting with his 22mm rifles and 22mm pistols. Once again I tried to listen to the detailed security precautions he recommended. He seemed to forget that he had already told them to me, but I did not remind him because I did not want to upset him, in case he changed his mind and called it off. I liked the round metal tin heavy with the small bullets; my brother carried the gun and pistol making sure they pointed to the ground. We would find a safe spot, usually in the courtyard with our backs to the house, protected from the wind, facing the high rocky embankment. It was an extra security to put up a plank to pin up the cardboard targets. I tried to share with him my shooting experience in the cellars of Jacques's castle, but he brushed it off by taking over the conversation,

"Oh yes, a Mauser, yes, they're very good guns, I've got one in Camaret. I found it just after the war, with a whole lot of machine-gun ammunition near the airport, hidden in a blanket under a green-oak tree." I'd stand next to him quietly but with some impatience while he explained how to hold a gun, where to put the hands, the cross tight against the shoulder and cheek… he was good at shooting and his first shot got very close to the centre.

"Hey! That's not bad for a first go! Isn't it?" Before I had time to express my congratulations he continued, "I'll do a few more on this target, and then I will let you have a go on a new one." I was impressed by the accuracy of his shots… my turn came and I ran up to the plank, removed the pierced cardboard, examined the damage caused to the plank by the lead bullets and put up mine. I now sat on the stool, took the light rifle, held it sturdily and aimed. Again I found it difficult not to move, the aim at the end of the barrel seemed to travel from right to left across the white target, I decided to press the trigger when the barrel seemed to be the closest to the centre of the printed rings. The shot went off! I found pleasant the smell of the blue smoke that came out of the barrel,

"Well that's not too bad for a first shot." My brother said positively, "Here, have another try." He handed me another bullet and I felt reassured. Surely this 22 rifle was easier to handle than the big German army gun I had previously held when on holiday with Jacques.

Good weather was almost guaranteed for the three months in the summer and we enjoyed going for picnics as often as possible. Where to go was never a problem, for the 11 km stretch of the island gave us so much attractive coastline to choose from. Together at breakfast we decided on the ideal place. If the Mistral blew from the northwest, we chose the south coast where beaches like Rioufrède or les Pierres de Fer (Iron Stones) with its huge boulders that rang like bells when hit with a stone, and where the sea was deep. If the wind blew from the south, we went to the north side, to the Petit Avis with its white sandy beach, or to les Moines, a cosy sheltered spot a 20-minute walk from La Cigale.

I loved these long early morning walks on the narrow paths through the dense maquis, one behind the other, each carrying something. I usually carried goggles and flippers. As I walked, my awareness would fluctuate between my inner feelings and my outer ones. Many places we walked through brought back to me the presence of my dad, and I would retrace in my memory parts of the precious short times we had spent together. These were happy memories where for an instant I met his love and affection. There were moments of just inner silence, when my awareness simply pulsated in space and then merged into the present. I always walked barefoot, forcing me to constantly look out for the next tree stump, root and sharp stone. I found it amusing to look at the back of the person ahead of me, each body displayed such a different show. What amused me was the way each step produced a pendulum effect at the base of the spine, it clicked one way then the other, as the right or left heel hit the ground creating vibrations up through the skin up to the neck or down to the calf. Being round and podgy, at each move of Mano's pendulum his right or left buttock would shake like a well-set jelly, and then move down to give his calf a little tremor. He normally wore a pale-blue, striped cotton hat and carried a small rucksack with some of the picnic.

With Maman the scene was very different; her body was usually suntanned and shiny with nice smelly oils. Being very slim, I could see her spine clearly, especially at the base where the vertebrae made a zigzag, and the pendulum effect was more definite than on Mano's back.

"Why is there a kink at the base of your back Maman?" She stopped walking and turning round mimed with her hands and arms, "Before the war when Sylvette was a baby, I was carrying her in my arms when I hit a stump as I came down a steep cliff, near Rioufrède actually. To protect her I kept her tightly on my bosom with both hands and, not being able to grab or hold anything during the fall, I hit and scraped my back all the way down. Thank God Sylvette was fine, but since then I have problems there."

Often friends joined us on our picnics. Maurice and Monette owned a tiny one-room house completely hidden in the maquis at a few minutes walk down from La Cigale. Maurice had been a chemist but now with Mano's help and knowledge of art, he found it more lucrative to sell modern paintings in Paris and around Europe. He worked hard during the winter and would spend the other six months on the Island with Monette. So when we arrived, their skin was already a beautiful colour. Hers was a deep reddish brown and complemented her long dark red chestnut hair; he was fair with a crew-cut and every part of his skin was a light copper colour, and completely covered in short curly pale yellow hair, always glittering with either sweat or suntan oil. The paths through the maquis were narrow and I would work out my timing to be in the queue just behind Monette, often walking between her and Maurice. She was slender, her long legs emerging from her short torso, which had enormous round and heavy breasts held up by a minimum flowery top bra. As she walked, they would suddenly appear on the right, then on the left of her thin arms. I liked walking behind Monette with her delicate honeysuckle perfume that satisfied my acute sense of smell. She generally wore her hair on top of her head in a decorative arrangement similar to some early Greek statues of goddesses I had seen in one of my mother's art books. In fact her whole body reminded me of these early Greek Tanagra statuettes with their long necks and narrow waist and shoulders amplifying their round bosom. Although frail looking, she was very strong. She always took the maximum weight in the largest baskets carried by her graceful hands, and this had the effect of lowering the shoulder, lengthening her attractive neck even more. Around her left ankle was a tiny gold chain that sparkled as she walked silently… never talking except for the bare necessities and always obeying Maurice. The click clack of her spine pendulum was not so obvious, as it moved imperceptibly in the opposite direction to the upper part of her body.

Some times I found myself behind the robust body of Maurice, with his square shoulders his lower back muscles giving the impression that his spine was buried at the bottom of a deep gorge, the movement of his pendulum was rhythmic and clear over his solid buttocks. He usually carried all his underwater fishing equipment, including the very long harpoon gun, which sometimes got caught when the maquis became too dense. He then swore while untangling it, giving me a look that carried humour in the depth of his flaming eyes. Maurice was a joker; he laughed a lot and took great pleasure in teasing me, especially with regard to women. He would laugh at my embarrassment, "Come on François! Go and give her a kiss, isn't she beautiful? Don't be so shy! Come on…" It was not possible for me to join in the general laughter sparked by his cruel jokes and I did not know what expression to adopt. I would usually turn bright red, look to the ground and try to show a smiling face when I really felt like crying, even though I knew that his teasing was his way of expressing his fondness for me. He was a tremendous swimmer, staying in for what seemed like hours and coming back with enormous fish. In the war he earned a meagre living by fishing with his handmade harpoon gun and goggles. He reminded me once in his husky smokers' voice, "Do you remember how during the war you and Sylvette used to set off my bird traps hidden in the maquis? And making them jump by throwing stones at them?" He then looked into my eyes, "And how angry I was when I came to La Cigale to tell your mother off? It was you and Sylvette, wasn't it?" I nodded slowly in agreement, grinning and answered, "We were hiding in the maquis when you came, but were too frightened to come out!" "I am glad you didn't! Otherwise I might have strangled you!"

Now we all laughed together, but I knew that the motives for our laughter were very different: Sylvette and I found it terribly funny that we had not been caught in our 'save the little birds campaign'; Maman laughed because she thought how clever it was of her two little children to hide in the maquis to escape the angry man; Maurice laughed when finding out that his guess was correct - it was Honor's little brats who had been the cause. Now he had become Mano's and Philippe's closest friend and as I got to know him better through the years, I became fond of him and enjoyed his company.

That year, our brother bought several books on sailing and long pieces of white ropes to practice making sailing knots. He spent much of his time reading and talking to people who had sailing experience. He told me how in the winter and spring, he had gone to sailing school in Brittany. Maurice and Monette had bought a Canadian mahogany canoe, and they paddled off with their swimming and fishing gear for the day. Sometimes we arranged to meet them on a particular beach. They canoed everywhere and when the weather unexpectedly became too rough, they left their canoe in some creek and walked home with us.

A newcomer

The following year we had only been on the island for a week when one morning Philippe and Maurice went off early to Toulon, to fetch his newly acquired second-hand sailing boat. For Sylvette and me it was exciting to know that in the late afternoon Philippe's sailing boat would be moored at l'Ayguade. I found it difficult to put that thought out of my mind, and throughout the day I glanced at the horizon hoping to be the first to see a little white sail coming from Toulon. It was evening when I saw a white dot off the Galère and ran into the house excitedly shouting, "They are here! They are here! Who's coming to l'Aygade with me?" Sylvette went to the window of the dining room, and seemed dubious, "How do you know if it is them? It could be anybody!" I did not have an answer but heard Maman say from the kitchen, "Yes, they should not be long now, why don't you go down and see, while I prepare supper?"

CHAPTER 4

We ran all the way down to the small harbour, stopping every so often to see if we could distinguish who the sailors were on that small white sailing boat. It was only when we climbed down the last rocks on the path that we noticed two men. the one standing on the foredeck was Maurice for he was suntanned and naked but for his minimum. The other at the rudder was wearing a short-sleeved shirt and a worn captain's cap—our brother. As we ran down we saw Monette on the shore standing against the light of the lowering sun, arms crossed and facing the sea wearing a crochet pink linen cardigan. She turned her head towards us and gave a warm smile as she bent down to kiss us, then we all waved to them enthusiastically. I started running up and down the small pebble beach waving my arms expressing bubbly joy.

Our sailors were too preoccupied to wave back. Maurice was taking the sails down in a messy heap on the foredeck and cabin roof. Then he tried to catch the mooring buoy with a long hooked pole, while shouting instructions at our brother who was now standing, holding the rudder with his right foot, trying to see over the cabin for the buoy. This type of boat was a Beluga, made of thick marine plywood painted white, while the mast, deck and the cabin were made of mahogany. The rear was flat and fixed with a rudder and a tiny outboard motor. I could not wait any longer to go on board and swam to it. When I got there, I found that I could not climb onto it by myself, so I hung onto the buoy that secured the boat and watched the sailors. On the deck our brother was folding the mainsail, tying it neatly to the beam, while Maurice was putting the jib into a long white bag. Philippe saw me and smiled, and turned around and grabbed a bright orange rubber dinghy, which he threw towards me, loosely tying the rope to the side of the boat. In no time I was sitting in it and found I couldn't stand up, as the bottom sheet was elastic like a trampoline. It had two small aluminium oars that I put through the strong rubber loops. Pulling gently on the string brought me up to the Beluga and I climbed on board. I started to investigate the newcomer; normally I would have gone up to them to give them a

221

kiss as it was custom, but knowing how busy they were, I felt it better not to get in their way. I went down the few steps that led into the cabin. On either side were two cherry-red canvas mattresses rimmed with a white cording with many shelves and cupboards above. In the middle was a funny looking folding table. My brother came in and said,

"Isn't it great? We can sleep two people on the bunks; what you're looking at is actually also a folding keel, to moor in shallow waters, look! You pull it up like this and push the pin through to hold it up in place." A big flat metal keel appeared from between the table flaps, "But we will leave it down as we are in the harbour and it gives the boat much more stability!"

I opened two small mahogany doors and discovered a confined triangular space where the spare sails, fishing baskets, ropes, cables and fishing lines, wound round cork slabs with fishing hooks inserted, were kept. With the mixed smells of varnish and paint, I began to feel slightly sick, so I closed the doors and quickly went out of the cabin to breathe the fresh air. Maurice and Philippe had finished their tidying up and everything was now in order,

"François! You jump in the dinghy and take Maurice to the shore, then come back and fetch me, okay?"

I felt wonderful! It was such a nice feeling to be asked to participate in such an important moment. "Yes okay!" I jumped into the little orange shell and, grabbing the oars, guided it towards Maurice. Feeling nervous and unsure, squeezing his small white canvas bag between his knees, his arms and hands out holding either sides of the inflated orange raft, he said in his raucous voice and with a suspicious smile on his face,

"Watch it! Do not do anything silly François, remember, I do not want to get wet!" I could not hold my laughter – there he was, at the mercy of my rowing! I dominated the situation and it felt wonderful and wanting to impress him, I rowed as smoothly as I could to the pebbly beach. "Good, you've done a good job, thank you!"

I went back to fetch my brother, I was beginning to understand how to handle this light craft, in two strokes I had turned it round so that my brother could climb down. He too did not feel sure about my piloting, and as he sat down placing his bag between his feet, he said, "Be careful, I've got my cameras, they absolutely must not get wet! Also, take me to the rocky jetty I will tie this rope round the rocks to secure the Beluga."

I guided the rubber boat to the rocks with great care, he passed his heavy bag to Sylvette who had come round to help and before he climbed out, said to me, "Take the dinghy to the beach, we'll drag it out, and tie it to the old heavy wooden boat over there."

We started the long climb back to La Cigale; I had a question in my head that I was dying to ask, What is it that holds the buoy in place when the Beluga pulls on it? But there was no space for my question, as he was conversing with Maurice and Monette. I waited patiently until we reached the road that led to their home where we parted. I now found a better way of asking my question, "What makes the buoy so steady Philippe?"

"Each boat that moors in the harbour has its own buoy. Each is connected to a small chain that is tied to a very heavy chain that lies on the seafloor. The very big chain is itself attached at either end to enormous concrete blocks, making the whole thing completely steady."

I was satisfied by his clear answer. Understanding things gave me a sense of security and added another link to the development of my knowledge of material things.

After that new arrival, things changed at la Cigale, not only in the fact that we did not go for long walks any more, for with the Beluga our brother had acquired a needy child. The sailboat brought a new dynamic into the family, for Philippe could not stop thinking and talking about his boat. Every evening and morning, he tapped on the barometer in the dining room to see whether the pressure would be high or low, windy or not windy. When the weather was bad he sometimes got up in the night and with a torch, walked all the way down to l'Ayguade to check to make sure his Beluga was still safely attached to the buoy. Every morning before breakfast he put his nose in the air to see what the weather had brought and where the wind came from. Once, intrigued by this tapping on the barometer I asked, "Why do you tap the glass of the barometer every morning?" While turning the little knob that stood in the middle of the protective glass he explained, "You see, when I tap the glass, the vibrations loosen the hand into the latest position of the pressure, then I turn this knob to adjust the manual hand over the other. It makes it easier, later on, to see whether the pressure has gone up or down. This instrument started to fascinate me. I could not resist looking at it several times a day and enjoyed telling my brother of the changes before he saw them himself.

The whole family adapted joyfully to the new arrival. When the sea was quiet, Sylvette sat with her back against the mast and sang gently to herself, or went into her dreams while looking at the sea. Maman, with a smile on her face and completely relaxed, sat in the well at the back of the boat, opening her eyes at times to look at her eldest son with admiration. When Mano was present, he sat on the other side, always slightly anxious, holding on tight in case something might go wrong. The wind rising, dark clouds coming, the outboard motor breaking down… in a worried voice he would say, "Philippe! Are you sure it's all right? Are we safe? Shouldn't we go back?" Philippe would reassure him saying, "Yes, don't worry, all is fine."

I became the shipmate and did everything my brother asked me to with delight, whether putting up or taking down the jib, coiling up the ropes, throwing the anchor into the depth, transporting passengers and picnic bags in the orange dingy to the beach and back. There was so much to do, I simply did not stop running around attending to my many tasks. I had time to myself when the Beluga was moored and the adults were resting or talking, and went fishing with my harpoon gun, or with a fishing line from the boat. This method, called in Provençal la palangrotte, consisted of a long nylon line wound round a flat piece of cork at the end of which was tied one, two or three hooks, followed by a pear shaped lead weight. Usually I started fishing with the harpoon gun until I trembled with cold; I then came out of the water, threw my gear into the dinghy and looked for rock seaweed where the precious fishing worms hid. I filled my goggles with as many as I needed. With the hot sun on my back, my hands in the cool water, the smell of seaweed, and my mind and emotions resting, I felt whole and at home in the placenta of creation.

Then I rowed back to the Beluga, my thoughts already preparing the palangrotte. Fishing with my right index finger directly holding the line and feeling the fish nibbling the bait made my response immediate. With a flick of the wrist, the baited hook dug itself into the lip of the fish and I pulled up the nylon thread. Then the great thrill of dragging up the fish started, quickly winding up the length of the line until silver flashes appeared, as the resisting victim came closer to the surface. When the fish was out of the water, I gave the line a final jerk, sending my prey onto the deck; I carefully slid my left hand into its mouth, taking great care to free the steel hook, and instantly taking away its life, by breaking its neck with my thumbs. Every time I did this act, I felt for the animal and told it that it was for our supper. I then studied and examined its beauty; I felt its texture, and admired its glowing colours and harmonious lines. What gave me satisfaction was the thought of presenting my catch to the adults later, and especially to my mother, as she would cook it for supper. There was no fridge at la Cigale and what was caught that day was eaten at the evening meal.

A traumatic realisation brings about an identity change

It was on such an occasion that something profoundly disturbing transformed me. It was to deeply change my emotional balance: all the seats of my inner landmarks were reshuffled, providing me with a new perspective. I had not realised that my emotions were so precarious and sensitive within me. From that evening on, my whole emotional world shifted.

It was Mano and Philippe's last evening of their holiday on the island for that year of 1953. We had spent a big sailing day on the Beluga, and feeling very tired, I ate with my elbows on the dining table, holding my head with the left hand and eating my fish soup with the right without lifting my arm. Not listening to the conversation that was going round the table, I was in my own world with my dad and greatly missing his presence. Suddenly I heard Mano say sharply to Maman, "If that boy had a father, he would not be eating with such bad manners!"

These raw and insensitive words threw me as if I had been hit by a thunderbolt! I felt totally desolate and naked. An indescribable pain rose from within my depth, tears started to flow as I rose, pushed away my chair and walked to the door of the bedroom. As I opened it, I heard Mano again: "What's the matter with him?" I did not want to hear the answer, and slamming the door behind me, I collapsed on my bed letting the tears flow without restraint. After some time, my mother came in quietly and sat on my bed and said in a soft voice, "Sounet, my darling, Mano didn't mean to hurt you… you know that."

I turned away from her to face the wall, took a foetus position and wailed sorrowfully. Something I could not control overtook me. I could not stop my lamentations, which came like powerful waves from my profound despair, tossing me about aimlessly! I felt Maman's soft hand stroking my forehead and now from far in the distance I heard her caring voice, "Come on Sounet, come and finish your supper, it's going to be all right." But I was already too far away on my ocean of sorrow, drowning in my tears, trying desperately to find my breath, I was unable to find words. There was a no more vocabulary in my mind. Maman had not fully realised how much I missed my father and did not know how almost every night I cried in my bed thinking of him. She quietly left the room after having kissed me on the forehead; I turned on my back and went on crying for what seemed hours, letting the hot salty water run down my temples into my neck, soaking my pillow. My eyes were puffed, my cheeks were burning, I turned my pillow around the other way and the coolness of the smooth linen appeased me from the turbulent waters I was caught in and I fell into a profound sleep.

When I woke up the next morning the house was quiet, Philippe had left very early to meet Maurice on the Beluga. They were to sail to the Lavandou where the boat would be parked on somebody's land until the following year. Mano had gone down to catch the ferry to the coast where they would meet and drive to Camaret to continue their holiday. I was in a strange place inside myself, feeling drained, lying in bed awake but with my eyes closed, floating as if in between sombre waters, my consciousness feeling around in the darkness to find anything firm that could help me back to my shore. A black and white passport sized photo of Marcel appeared in my mind. He was wearing his brown leather jacket with an open white shirt underneath; his full face was smiling gently at me. I had seen that picture in my mother's papers and secretly looked at it when I missed him. Tears immediately rolled out again, why had my Papa left us? Why could he not be next to me now? I found no answers to these simple questions, and went back to him again. I let myself slide into the time when I was in his yellow lorry, listening to the singing of the engine as he changed gears, looking up through the windscreen and seeing the upside-down sky with the pine trees going by.

Maman came into the bedroom holding a tray with breakfast, she said with a big smile, "I thought you'd like breakfast in bed this morning. Sylvette is in her room reading; they have all gone back to Camaret." She put the tray on the shelf behind the bed, sat on the edge and kissed me. I could feel that her eyes were searching for mine, but they were too swollen and full of tears, I didn't want to look into hers and turned my head away, and then said harshly, "I don't want any breakfast! I don't want to get up! I want to be left alone!"

She sat by my side for quite some time, in silence, with her hand on my shoulder. I did like my Maman being there, saying nothing, the warmth of her hand making a loving contact; I was now in a place of stillness, away from my emotions, feeling my body in the bed and my cheek sticking to the wet pillow. I lifted slightly the linen cover of the pillow stuck to it and this created a pleasant coolness. Hearing my mother's voice brought my attention back to her, "Here, give me your pillow it's all wet, I'll change it." She changed the wet pillow, took the tray with the cold breakfast and left the room.

Alternating between sleep and tears the day went by, I did not want lunch nor supper and only went to pee outside the back of the house where I knew I would meet no one. I was much too disorganized in myself to be able to face anyone, although I appreciated my mother's discreet interventions when she proposed food or changed my pillows. I did not sleep much that following night, I was reliving all the loving moments I had spent with my Dad, not like dreaming, but living through these precious moments again, as if the past had become present. I was with him at the quarry, getting stones for building, helping him by carrying some myself, trying to lift the bigger ones to show him how strong his son was. Being on his shoulders, my hands in the thickness of his black curly hair, my legs sticking to his sweaty body, creating no separation between us - just as if we were one. Putting me to bed, hearing his kind voice saying goodnight, then from the tip of his lips, the comforting kiss on my forehead. I was absorbed in a world of feelings, floating, not connected to the ground, which was not of importance any more.

I opened my swollen burning eyes slightly, to see it was morning, with the light so blaring that I closed them again. As tears came again, washing the soreness away, I heard the door open and Sylvette enter; she stood by the bed, looking at me and said in a positive way, "Are you okay? Come to breakfast. It's lovely outside!" I wasn't ready to get up, so my body did not move, as I answered, half opening my watery eyes, "No I won't, I'm not well." She was standing there, against the light of the north window, with her plats sticking out on either side of her head. The whole image wavered as if a mirage and I noticed the anxiety on her face, "Don't worry." I emphasised the word worry and tried to comfort her, "I'll get better soon." She left the room.

For two summers, Philippe had been sleeping on the platform under the round window in his new double bed. It rested on four wooden olive-shaped short legs, holding a painted metal frame with a fine springy wire mesh. A thick white mattress with grey lines lay on top. Maman came in, carrying sheets and pillows and, while putting her hand on my forehead, said positively, "Bonjour Sounet, I'm going to make your bed up here, you'll be more comfortable… how are you feeling? Your forehead is hot, but I think it's because you've been crying so much, I don't think you have a high temperature."

Moving into this big bed was pleasant for it took me out of my world of day dreams for a moment and returned me into my physical body; sensing the coolness of the sheets, my legs discovered the corners of the large new space. Looking around the room was different too, a new angle, more open and less boxed in like I felt in the old bed. My eyes went to the round window where I saw the cobalt blue sky framed by the crescent of the stones wall. Then I suddenly felt that I was abandoning my father, not being fair to him when l let myself be distracted by the outside world. I closed my burning red eyes and searched for him in my inner darkness.

I had probably fallen asleep when I was woken by the sound of the door opening, Maman had entered the room; I heard her walking quietly up the two small steps and felt her weight as she sat on the edge of the mattress. The warmth of her hand settled on mine, and she called quietly, hesitantly, "Sounet?" I let the silence flow in between us… and, finally answered distantly, "Yes?" She cleared her throat, "I have something important to tell you, it's a big secret…"

I opened my eyes slightly, the beam of light coming from the round window was lighting one side of her face, revealing the weight of her secret. Our eyes met and I saw a great uncertainty in them, together with fragility, her mouth showing the tension inside her. She left my hand, straightened her back, cleared her throat again and said almost loudly, "Sounet... for a long time now I have been hesitating to tell you... but now I feel that I have to share this secret with you."

"What is it Maman?" I wondered what it could really be as I believed she had always shared everything with us. She spoke matter-of-factly and cleared her throat once more, "Well... actually you have a father!" I hoped that I had not heard her properly.

"What did you say?"

"You actually have a father, he is a painter called Henry Valensi; he is Jewish and lives in Paris."

She confirmed this with now more sensitivity in her voice, revealing a slight smile. "Yes Sounet, your genetic father is alive."

Similar to the game of snakes and ladders, this unexpected bombshell, sent me far back into the depth of myself, somewhere before consciousness, where there was only darkness, no trace of structure, or reference to any experience of being. I suddenly felt cheated and thought to myself... How can I handle all these years of crying for my father who, in truth, was not mine? What was I to do with this devastating information? Why had she not told me this before, when I was much younger? How could she have held such a secret for such a long time?

The hot lava of my inner volcano was about to force itself out. I became one with anger. Tightening my abdominal muscles, I raised the upper part of my body and, resting it on my right elbow, looked straight into my mother's fragile blue eyes that I had loved limitlessly. The lava suddenly turned into freezing ice and through my stare, I allowed this violent electricity flow to go straight into her heart. It was the first time that I did not mind seeing her suffer, for my anger felt justified.

"You're a prostitute!" I said in a cold monotone, "How could you have done that? Poor Papa!" She could not take my stare any longer. Her eyes went pink and watery and looked down, deeply wounded, turning her head away silently. A quiet space followed as we both returned to ourselves, not quite knowing how to go from there. My strong anger dissipated rapidly and I felt a change within myself, which is hard to describe... yes, it was like a kind of new beginning. I could now throw my anchor into the depths of my being and feel somehow moored, although I did not know to what.

I sat up in a lotus position and now wanted my mother to empty the bottom of her bag and tell me all the things that she had kept away from me. Questions started to come from all parts of myself, "If you loved Papa so much, why didn't you have me with him?" She wiped the tears off her cheeks, and looking at me absently, almost whispering she said, "Marcel could not have children, actually I came to realise that he was infertile..." A silence followed while my mind was trying to sort out my disturbed emotions; but I wanted to know more, she felt it and went on, "You see, I began to feel terribly low after Mano came to take Philippe away from us. He decided to put him in a Jesuit school in Avignon... I was just left with Sylvette and craved another boy. So, with Marcel, we tried, and tried, and tried but you wouldn't come! Finally, I decided secretly to find a seed somewhere else... and went to Paris in late February of 1937." She paused, searching for the best words to explain her actions.

"I decided to find somebody interesting, somebody I really admired, and liked and respected, intelligent... you know. When I studied in Paris I was friendly with a girl called Denise who had posed for me and she was very keen to introduce me to an artist called Henry Valensi who was in fact her uncle. So Denise fixed a date and I met him in his large studio, in the Porte Champeret. Henry was 25 years older than me, I was impressed by his work and his personality; I admired his intellectual capacity and erudition..."

"What does 'erudition' mean?" I did not want to misunderstand any part of this important revelation.

"It means that he is well read, scholarly. And he is very kind, and he is married, but his wife cannot have children." Maman paused as if looking for her words, then continued, "So, I decided that Henry Valensi would give a good seed for the boy I wanted and, taking Sylvette with me, we left for Paris. I left your sister who was two and a half with my very close friend Line Viala, and went to his painting

231

studio on a rendezvous fixed by Denise, his niece. Actually to be honest, I went there twice, two days running. But as soon as I felt that you were inside me, I returned to the island."

While she was explaining her escapade to Paris to conceive me, I noticed her face relaxed and carried an affectionate smile.

"What happened when you came back, how did my Papa react then?" I remembered he had a quick temper.

"I did not tell him right away, but finally when my tummy began to swell I had to… and it made him very, very angry. His violent temper frightened me and, while he went out in a blind fury, I locked all the doors and shutters to keep him out. When he returned later, he broke one of the dining room shutters and came in through the window! But things finally quietened down… and when you were born in a clinic in Nice, he took you in his arms to the Mairie to declare your birth to the authorities. Nobody knows that you are not his own son except Mano, whom I told right away, Line Viala and Myrette, a Parisian friend."

Feeling strange, separated somehow from myself and from my mother, I sat on the edge of the bed, with no more questions. Maman came close to me and hugged me, but I stayed absolutely rigid and distant, unable to receive her affection. I felt as if I had been uprooted from the earth and replanted into a garden pot.

I changed into a teenager, life unfolded…

Our holidays on the island continued, thanks to Mano's generosity. He pointed out that he preferred Fonsou not to be there, so Maman's friend came only when the others had left. Philippe became very confident in sailing the Beluga; we had been round all the islands, l'Ile du Levant, Port Cros and even Bagaud, exploring every one of their beaches and creeks and, as Mano had pointed out, I had become his indispensable shipmate. Philippe arrived at l'Ayguade one summer in a smooth looking, Italian mahogany speedboat. He had sold the Beluga and replaced it with this powerful outboard motor, with a large white bakelite car wheel and a dashboard with chrome circular dials. With its low, rounded windscreen, it resembled a sports car without wheels. It could go very fast, and a pair of nautical skis was tucked under its long back seat.

He took us out on it a few times, but this newcomer marked a turning point in our summer holidays. Our brother had really bought the speedboat to take out his beautifully sun-tanned girlfriend called Claude, and his Parisian friends. Mano had told us that his wife Gany did not like him spending too much time with us on the island, and so he came less often and for shorter periods.

The few years spent with him on the island had a definite influence on my life. He had a great ability to tell stories and his use of words was accurate, powerful and contained much humour. He was a famous salesman in the art world, and when he realised that I wanted to make painting my profession, he said, raising his index finger to the sky, "Today, there are 60,000 painters in Paris, only ONE will make it in a lifetime! You will not have a chance. Paint, yes! But for yourself only, do not try to make a living out of it! Do something else... for instance advertising... with that profession at least you have a chance to make money. Look at Savignac, Villemot, Paul Colin, Cassandre - they have all made a fortune with their posters!" It was an important thing for Mano to become a rich man.

In truth, his words deeply hurt me. He did not realise this of course, but I felt he tried to take away from me my raison d'être. I had always wanted to be a painter and had no doubt that this was the talent I needed to cultivate in myself. Art interested me – I would often go into my mother's art books and I was fascinated by Mano's stories that he told me about the painters whom he met in his posh art gallery, at 52, Faubourg St Honoré in Paris. Many times when Mano found that he was alone with me, he would repeat, "You know something, it is with your mother that I spent the happiest moments of my life. She is a real saint but completely mad!"

When he spoke like this, I knew inside myself that he still loved her immensely.

WALNUTS & GOAT CHEESE

Arriving at the Ile du Levant

The Beluga, Philippe, François, Maurice and Monette (in the water)

CHAPTER 4

François, Maman, Philippe and Sylvette outside the Cigale

Henry Valensi, my genetic father

235

Chapter 5

Summerhill School 1951-1953

Lena Münz, Maman's close friend, was visiting for a few days. At breakfast, we found them talking passionately in English, a tongue we could not speak but which we'd heard many times before. I realised that they were talking about education because I recognized a few words like A.S. Neill and Summerhill. Probably due to the war, Maman had only spoken our native tongue to us.

Unexpectedly, one day in the early part of summer 1951, Maman said positively while we were having lunch, "Darlings... how would you like it if you were to go to school in England?... To Summerhill School? You know, the school where Lena went, when she was your age."

We were unprepared for such a question, it created a long silence, which Sylvette finally broke, "But we won't be able to understand what the teachers will be saying in the classroom! And anyhow, where will you be staying?" Maman's reply carried a feeling of hesitation. "You will be boarders, like all the other children at the Beauvallon school, as for understanding the teachers... well, you will soon pick up the English language. I will remain here in Dieulefit... but you will come down for the holidays of course!" And noticing our discomfort filled with dubiety, she added, "And you will be near

GG, Ralph and Tony who will come to visit you at half-term."

I had not been so happy at the Beauvallon School. It was a place that had given me more suffering than joy and the thought of not going back made me feel light and free. Just to think no more of this horrid homework pleased me immensely, especially Latin and mathematics, which used to take the best part of my Saturday afternoons and Sunday mornings. No more annoying teasing which so often ended in fights leaving me with my emotions all stirred up, and my body trembling like a leaf in the wind. Also, the idea of going to England and seeing GG, Ralph and Tony was appealing, as I had liked them very much when we had visited five years previously.

"How can we afford it? And who will we pay for the school?" Sylvette queried and Maman replied, "You're daddy will (Sylvette and I called Mano daddy)… Do you remember the man with the beard we met on the train in 1946? The one who bought us a meal on the way to London – do you remember him?" Maman was feeling that her plan was beginning to take root. My sister and I nodded… how could we forget the nice man who satisfied our great hunger by offering us a meal on the train from Newhaven to Victoria? "Well, he has agreed to pay for Sylvette's fees in sterling, that is in English money, and Mano will reimburse him in Paris, in francs. He says that he needs francs for when he comes to France." She turned to me, leaving no space for me to feel left out, "As for you, GG says that she has some money set aside, which she can use to pay for your educational fees. Also Mr Neill has kindly reduced the fees for us. You will start together in September." Maman had actually taken all the decisions and arranged everything before speaking about it with us. It was a fait accompli and this new perspective did not displease me, although we were not sure about being so far away from her loving presence.

My consciousness of the outside world and my relation to it was getting wider and clearer. I had not been aware before that my English grandmother actually cared for me so much as to pay for my school fees, and for our uncles to come to see us at half term. Sylvette had her daddy to look after her financially and that was fine. But to know that GG was ready to help with financing my school fees, stabilized something in me: GG's interest in my education reassured me greatly and I began to realise that my family was larger than I had been aware of. Before this it was just Maman, Sylvette and I.

During the summer holidays of 1951, Maman told Mano in La Cigale about her decision to send us to Summerhill School. He was absolutely delighted and said, "That's great, for once you're making an intelligent decision! It will be excellent for both of them." He went on and lamented, "How I miss not speaking English… I come up against it all the time with my clients at the galerie, I wish that I'd had such an opportunity in my youth!" Mano and Philippe were Anglophiles with great respect for the English and their education system: that is, the English public school system. They had no idea what kind of a school Summerhill truly was! To Mano's reasoning, 'out of an English school comes a gentleman!' Our mother carefully avoided giving him any details of the way Summerhill was run.

We came back from the Ile du Levant in early September to prepare our bags; Sylvette was arranging her small suitcase deciding on what to take and what not to take. I had seen the French sailor's in Toulon station and I liked the way they looked. I had noticed that they didn't have suitcases, but long white kitbags with a padlock at one end. I had seen how they carried it on their shoulders, holding it up there with one hand and how, when they were tired, they sat on it like on a soft cushion. I had seen such a bag in our house; my mother told me it had belonged to her father when he was in the army; after some searching, she finally found it, and it became my suitcase.

We took the train from Montélimar one evening; this time we had a proper couchette each, as sleeper carriages were back in circulation. This trip was more comfortable than the previous one in 1946 and Maman had money in her purse! We were able to have breakfast in the Gare de Lyon before crossing Paris to catch the next train from Gare St Lazare to Dieppe. Then we sailed the four and a half hour long cruise to Newhaven and finally reached Victoria Station where our mother's bearded friend from1946 met us. He showed much joy in seeing us again, especially our mother. Then he took us to Liverpool Street Station, for the train to Saxmundham where we changed for Leiston, the village of our destination. Apparently Summerhill School was right next to the railway station, but our mother told us that it was too late to turn up at the school and we would stay in a bed and breakfast near the station for the night.

As we came out of the train, I saw all the lights were of an orange colour and I wondered why they gave such a feeble light? "Apparently," mother said, "they have been designed to penetrate the fog." I'd woken up and went on with my questions, "Maman, why do these lights make all the colours disappear?" After a short silence she replied, "I don't really know my darling." I realised that her mind was somewhere else, probably wondering where the place we were to stay was. All the walls of buildings, including our railway station were made of red bricks… red bricks everywhere! Another thing that impressed me was how damp and cold it was, although we were only in mid-September. Everything seemed to be dripping wet, each drop shining like a black pearl under the orange lights. We came to the railway crossing and to the left stood a white painted cafe that was still open and over it in red letters, 'Tufford's Café'. Next to it stood our small hotel. We rang the bell… a bent, elderly lady, holding a cigarette close to her face, appeared in the half open door. I immediately smelt a dense odour of fried bacon and cold sweet Virginia tobacco that came from the small opening of her world. Mother said a few words in English and she immediately let us in.

A reddish-brown, fitted carpet patterned by large black and white leaves and flowers covered the floors and stairs. We were shown to a strange, large bedroom; the lugubrious orange lights coming through the windows accentuated the morbid atmosphere. Still puffing on her cigarette the lady of the house switched on a feeble light hanging from the ceiling inside a yellow, dusty lampshade. The toilet and bathroom were at the end of the corridor and a tap over a corner sink supplied the bedroom with cold water. Three small beds, covered in grey-blue satin duvets stood side by side; under the light was a low round table, its edges burnt by cigarettes. Three bentwood armchairs with large brown cushions completed the furniture. The room carried a similar smell to the rest of the house and gave a view onto the railway tracks and the station beyond. We were exhausted and crept into our cold, damp beds, and I was soon overtaken by sleep.

The next morning I rushed to the window to see that the orange lights and the cold, damp mist were gone, replaced by brilliant sunshine. Opposite I could see a red brick curved wall, Maman came up behind me, "I think this is the entrance to the school, but first, we are going to have breakfast in the café, you know, the one that we saw last night?"

Tufford's cafe was a prefabricated, large wooden shed with two steamed up glass windows on each side of its entrance door. A buzzer announced our arrival; I was instantly struck by the powerful smell of fried pork, burnt toast unpleasantly mixed with cigarette smoke and sweet tea. Formica topped, chromed legged tables and chairs filled the room, one was taken up by a workman busy eating off a plate bulging with fried sausages, thick chips, red beans in tomato sauce crested by a couple of fried eggs!

Across the end of the cafe was a long counter partly covered by a glass food cabinet filled with sandwiches, doughnuts, Danish pastries and what looked like - chocolate things wrapped up in colourful silver paper. Behind it all was a short man with a fat round nose supporting a thin pair of wire glasses. He wore dirty, pale grey overalls and I thought that he must be the Mr Tufford. Behind him were shelves and worktops, with the till and a steaming, tall, chrome cylinder, with a tap with a black handle, under which hung a tin can to collect the drips. A toaster jumped noisily with a clang, expelling into the air four golden pieces of toast.

After a short consultation with Mr Tufford, Maman ordered tea with toast, butter and marmalade. Sylvette and I liked this English, white, toasted bread covered with salty New Zealand butter and marmalade so clear it showed hair-fine slices of orange peel. But for my taste the tea was too strong and I added sugar to make it drinkable. Maman was looking at us smiling; I could read in her eyes an expression of excitement but it carried a certain sadness as well. Our mum's excitement probably came from her anticipation of meeting A.S. Neill, the man she admired. I knew what the sadness was and I didn't want it to meet my own, so I looked away.

We left Tufford's cafe and walked the short distance to the opening in the curved brick wall leading into the property. To the left in a small, dark, clinker-built garden shed was a sweet and cigarette shop, cleverly placed at the entrance to the school. Ahead of us was a low wooden fence separating us from a back garden. Fine beach pebbles crunched under our feet covering the path. As we turned left to enter the grounds, a diversity of mature trees, silver birch, beech, horse chestnuts, and immensely tall cedars and pines. The place gave me a feeling of space with buildings scattered amongst the trees, and a large vegetable garden backed by greenhouses on the right. Through the trees Summerhill School's main building appeared, built of red bricks, the window and door frames painted white, and with the decorative skirting of the pointed roofs accentuating its irregular shapes.

All my senses were out, looking attentively at everything, smelling the air to see if I could recognize any odours, listening to the new sounds, certainly they were different from the ones at Beauvallon. Here it was much quieter. There was silence in my thoughts too; I could just feel my emotional heart slowly thumping inside my chest. We were now in the courtyard in front of the building; children of all ages played peacefully, and did not seem to notice us arriving with our luggage. We walked to the entrance porch where we left our suitcases. A scruffy looking young boy, later I learned he was called Storm, came up to our mother and said plainly, "Are you looking for Neill?" "Yes, we are, thank you!" Our mother replied as the boy ran off in the opposite direction to the school under the darkness of the cedars.

A tall lanky figure emerged from under the trees. He wore big black shoes that curved inwards and he swayed as he walked towards us in a baggy brown pair of corduroy trousers. His jacket was a red, blue and white tartan type Canadian jacket, his head was large with red skin, and sparse white hair rose into a kind of crew cut. A pronounced nose carried a pair of circular, tortoise-shell glasses. He took no notice of us children whatsoever and went straightaway into conversation with our mother. Neill then invited her up to his office on the first floor of the main building, leaving us downstairs near our luggage.

Sylvette and I were sitting on our suitcases, waiting for Maman's return, when a jolly faced lady with protruding round cheekbones and deeply sunken blue eyes, came up to us and to our surprise said in a soft voice in French with a strong German accent, "Hello, my name is Ulla, I will be your house mother. That means you can at any time come and see me and talk and ask me anything, and also bring me your socks if they have holes in them so I can mend them... or missing buttons or whatever!" She let the silence float, while she looked into our eyes smiling, to check whether we understood what she said. Once satisfied, Ulla went on, "I will show Sylvette her bedroom first, so that she can install herself, take your case now and follow me." She then turned to me; "I will come and fetch you straight after, François, to take you to Daphne who looks after the carriages where your bedroom is." As I sat at the bottom of the main staircase in the large oak panelled hall, I wondered if I was going to be put into a train? Looking around, I noticed how everything was worn and well used, including the oak floorboards with all kinds of patterns in the grain. Large French windows gave onto a green, and in the corner to the right, high up from the ground, stood a boxed platform accessed by a ladder. On a low shelf stood an electric gramophone.

Ulla was quick to return. Behind me the large stairs of the hallway creaked, and as she passed I rose with my kitbag. She explained, "This is the assembly room. We meet here every Saturday afternoon, and use it for dancing in the evening." She turned right and

I followed her down a long corridor at the end of which was daylight. We went past an art room, a dining room, a kitchen and then into a small anti-chamber into a small courtyard. On the right stood a rather dilapidated brick building with an old external wooden staircase. To the left was a long row of huts with gentle sloping roofs resting against a high brick wall. Ulla stopped for an instant, smiled to revealed large yellow teeth, and pointed to the building on the right saying positively, "Upstairs is the ping-pong room; downstairs the boys like to play football when it is raining." Then showing me the row of huts, she went on, "At the corner, here, we have the pottery which is run by Peter Wood, next to it we have the science labs run by Mr Corkhill, the children call him Corky!" She giggled.

We walked under a brick arch to find many dustbins; several cats were sitting on and around them and I reflected to myself," I'll make friends with them." A group of white and grey geese with reddish orange beaks reminded me of the ones I had had to face on my way to Beauvallon School. Ahead of us lay a long straight path made of large concrete slabs; to the right was a field of apple trees heavy with green apples. I had never seen such large ones and Ulla told me they were called Bramley, grown mainly for cooking. A small brick house stood along the right of the path. We walked round the back and found a plump woman with very short, black, shiny hair. She was dressed just like a man, wearing a pair of tight pale grey corduroys and a navy blue lumber jacket and was feeding many more cats. Daphne lived there with her feline friends. Ulla introduced us rapidly and turning to me said, "If you're in need of anything do not hesitate to come and see me in my room, upstairs in the main building." And she promptly left us.

Daphne talked but I could not understand her; I picked up the word 'carriages' again. She was a youngish woman with a square face, always smiling to display a row of perfect teeth, and her eyes were piercing, jet black, appearing like slits through her podgy features. We left her cats gulping up their food and walked down the concrete slab path towards a wide, low, dark brown wooden shed centred by two concrete steps leading up to a glazed door. Daphne talked all the way, still not realising that I could not speak her language. She opened the door and we entered a wide, unlit space with a rusty metal bench behind which stood an old, silver painted coke boiler. I stopped and looked around... To my surprise, three of the walls of the room were actually 3 railway carriages! I instantly understood what that word meant. Each was a bedroom with its own railway carriage door. She went to the first one to the right, still talking and smiling, turned its large brass handle and swung it open without going in. Holding the inside knob, her short body half blocking the narrow entrance, she announced with some glory, "And here is your room!" Her round shape almost filled the entrance and I could not help but feel her protruding breasts as I squeezed past them.

It was a real railway carriage, painted in a creamy colour, with the bed immediately to the right and a curved ceiling with a small light bulb in the centre. Embossed scrolls and leaf patterns paper decorated the walls. Opposite the bed were three carriage windows and to my delight, the middle one had a window that opened by pulling up on a thick leather strap, just as I had seen on the train from Newhaven to London back in 1946. Immediately to the left were railway coat hangers; the wall was plain except for a luggage rack and an oval mirror etched with the letters B.R. I felt happy with my room, threw my kitbag onto the already made bed, and went to open the leather belt window. I could not walk outside if I opened the door, for it led to an overgrown, damp and unfriendly looking field that was covered in tall grass and stinging nettles. Far to the right was a football pitch where I could hear boys playing. Daphne popped her head through the door again and talked to me, indicating with her bent index finger to follow her. She pointed to the stove in the middle of the hallway and then to the cast iron pipes, walked to a primitive wooden staircase leading to a dilapidated bathroom above. I understood what she was trying to explain: in order to have a hot bath, I first had to light the fire down below to heat the water!

CHAPTER 5

Leaving my kitbag in my room, I walked back to the main building to look for Sylvette and my mum wondering what they were up to. On my way there was a row of bushes covered in white balls the size of marbles, I stopped to feel them, and found they were cool and squishy and smelt like bitter rubber. Behind the bushes were tall maple and oak trees that seemed to be part of a small forest. Ahead was a greenhouse stuck to the back of the main building; an opened window and steam escaping smelt of boiled cabbage, which made me think about lunch and I felt hungry. Maman and Sylvette were in the assembly room chatting, my sister was obviously curious about where I had been, "Where were you all that time?"

"I was in the carriages where my bedroom is; I am in a railway sleeper... all by myself!"

She could not take me seriously, "You're telling me a fib... I know." Delighted that she didn't believe me, I went on "and I have a railway window with a leather strap, and if I want a bath, I have to light the boiler to warm up the water!" And I exploded with laughter! She shrugged her shoulders and said, "Well, I am upstairs and I share a bedroom with three girls, actually, there is room for five but there are only three. I've met two of them and they're very nice." Maman came into the conversation and talked with excitement, she seemed elated, "I was just telling Sylvette - I was in Neill's office all that time and we had a very interesting conversation; we talked about all kinds of things: education, politics, art. He is such a nice man!" From the tone of her voice I could hear how much she had appreciated this interview and feel the enormous respect and admiration she had for him.

From the corner of my eye I had seen quite a few of the children, but they went about without taking any notice of me, as if I had always been there. Had this been in my last school, staring silent children would have surrounded us, for newcomers were always observed with suspicion and defiance. With the sound of a ringing hand bell, we heard running upstairs and saw children leaping down the wide staircase and running through the entrance porch into the Assembly Hall and down the long corridor.

245

"Neill told me that I could have lunch with you in the dining room, but then we must eat quickly. I want to see your bedrooms before I catch my train at 2.30." I felt that she liked the place already and this reassured me, but I didn't like the idea of her leaving.

At the end of the long corridor was a pale blue door and next to it, from a hatch came a damp, tepid draught that carried a mix of smells from the kitchens. Along the wall was a queue of chatty Summerhillians. There was a harmonious chaos; most children were talking to each other, and although I did not understand what they were saying, I detected no fear or aggression in their voices; I felt comfortable among them. As I caught the eyes of boys or girls of my age, I noticed no dominance, just gentle equal observation. Maman was talking to an older boy asking him questions about the school in English. Sylvette was silently observing the children on either side of us, probably like me, searching for the one she would like to associate with. Some adults joined the queue who didn't look like teachers: some looked scruffy, one was smoking a smelly worn out pipe, another had a light-coloured goat's beard, very round blue eyes, and carried a newspaper under his arm. He was talking with a 16-year-old, fair-haired boy; they were obviously having fun as, after each sentence, the teacher would bend his body backwards and laugh.

The queue was moving forward and it was my turn to look into the hatch. A lady's face appeared with black hair, crescent shaped eyebrows in a questioning position over large brown eyes looking at me. She talked from the side of her tortured mouth, for on the left where the jaw met the neck, was a deep scar. Realising that I was the new French boy, she gave me a kind side smile, and pushed through a steaming hot plate followed by another sweet smelling one, "Your pudding!" She said still half smiling.

The dining room was a few feet away on the opposite side and I took my plates and stood by the entrance. It was a large room with scrubbed, ash top tables and wooden benches to the left and right. The pale blue room was extremely light with many windows facing east and south; the children chose their places according to their

CHAPTER 5

fancy, but most of them seemed to go to the left side. Sylvette was now behind me and edged me forward into the room. We chose a table on the right side by a window, its surface heated by the sun; putting my plates down I felt the heat with the flatness of my hands, smelt them and detected bleach. The cutlery, glasses and water were on a separate table. Maman came to join us, as she sat down she murmured, "The lady at the hatch is Neill's wife, she's called Ena, she's very nice."

I had never encountered such food. From the thick white plate different scents rose, dominated by strongly flavoured cooked meat covered by a slab of thick pastry. Two perfectly white round mounds that sat in a dark brown sauce reminded me of ice cream. They were mashed potatoes, surrounded by extra large brilliant green peas and few grey-looking Brussels sprouts sitting in a brown sauce.

"It's called steak and kidney pie, my darlings, you'll see it's very nice! And the dessert is called steamed pudding served with what we call custard. In France we call it crème Anglaise. It's actually egg, milk, sugar and cornflour." With my fork, I dug into one of the potato mounds, and as I pulled my loaded fork away from the peas, I saw the brilliant green had tinted the potatoes! "Why are my potatoes green Maman?" She looked suspiciously at my plate, "Oh yes, I don't know… it must come from the bright peas, I suppose they've been dyed!" She laughed and Sylvette joined her saying, "Just eat and don't be so fussy!"

By now the dining room was full; the teachers sat together at a table in the right corner of the room, there was much lively conversation going on around us; we were silent. I was experiencing new food, new tastes and was missing my baguette.

"Is there any bread?" "Yes, I have seen children getting it from that table over there." I felt a little self-conscious standing up and walking through the dining room to fetch my bread, but I did it and noticed how no one took any notice. The rectangular loaf was half wrapped in a shiny smooth red and white paper; I touched the already cut, very soft white slices and, as I took two, there was no resistance and

247

they limped away from my fingers as if without life. The slices did not have a crust, but instead a very thin pale brown rubbery cover. As I walked back to my bench, I brought them up to my nose and detected a faded smell of flour and yeast. "Why is the bread without crust Maman?"

"Because it's made differently over here. In Provence the bread is baked in a hot wood oven, here I think that it is steamed in a mould." She was always ready to explain what she knew.

"Come and see our bedrooms quickly before you go Maman!" urged Sylvette as we got up from our dining room benches. My sister, who was going to be 16 on the 14th of November, was in a large bedroom upstairs with the older girls. The luminous south bedroom was over the art room, and had a view onto the courtyard with the cedars to the right and the great beech tree to the left. The distribution of spaces was similar to downstairs: a long corridor linked bedrooms, two bathrooms and toilets as well as walk-in linen cupboards. We walked down to the end of the corridor where a small, steep staircase led down the back entrance of the school. I now proudly led them to my digs, happily dancing ahead of them, pointing and explaining, as we passed, the dustbins, the cats, the geese, the Bramley apple trees and Daphne's house. As we entered the carriages, Sylvette remarked, "Weird place this is! Are you going to sleep in here?"

I did not reply but passed the boiler rapidly and triumphantly opened my carriage door. They poked their heads into what was going to be my space and my sister shared aloud her realisation, "Oh yes, it's true, it's a railway carriage! You are jolly lucky to have a room of your own, I wish I had one…" Maman felt the blankets on my bed, "I hope you will be warm enough? At least you have a stove, which you can light if it gets too cold. It's nice for you to have your own bedroom, isn't it?" I was comforted by the fact that my mother had seen the sleeping corner of my world and she'd approved it.

We were back outside the main building and it was time for Maman to go. She was standing between us with her hands on our shoulders hugging us gently, "Don't come to the station with me, it's not necessary. I'm glad you're here; you'll be all right. And I will write often, I promise… You will too, won't you? I'll be longing to know how you are getting on." Sylvette answered positively, "Yes, we'll be all right, don't worry Maman." I had an emotional lump in my throat and could not speak; I abandoned myself completely into the last hug, and filled my lungs with the last drift of her delicate scent. It was the first time we were separated from our mother, but I did not feel insecure and let her go without any resistance. We stood there silently, watching her walk away with her small suitcase until she reached the corner that led to the sweet shop. She turned round, waved to us smiling… and suddenly she was gone.

Life without maternal presence

I turned towards my sister and questioned her, "What are you going to do now?" "I don't know. I am going to my bedroom to arrange my things. You don't have to follow me!" I understood that she wanted to be alone and we parted.

I walked back slowly to my room and did not go into the big house but round it. I felt a vast space inside myself that I had not felt before, a space that Maman had filled by almost 13 years of continuous close presence. I became aware that from now on, I would be totally on my own. She had been my satellite, always there; but now had gone into her own orbit, somewhere in her own universe. I felt as if a second umbilical chord had been severed, an emotional one, the one that I could plug into daily to receive the love, the compassion and comfort I needed. I took a big breath, and felt, for the first time, the young man I had suddenly become.

I stood by the empty ping-pong house and heard stomping sounds coming from the upper floor together with much laughter and thought some guys must be playing ping-pong up there. But I did not go up and went on through the arch to the carriages.

I enjoyed arranging what was to become my very own space for the next two years. I emptied the kitbag on the bed, checked with a blind hand that there was nothing left in it and, not forgetting to slip the lock back through its brass eyelets, I threw it under the bed. I saw my Opinel pocketknife and promptly put it into the right pocket of my grey corduroy trousers. Behind the bed I shelved the three books I brought with me: "The Grizzly", by James Oliver Curwood (I was fond of all the stories about the Canadian great North) and two Biggles as I enjoyed reading the many war adventures of this RAF pilot. My few shirts, jerseys and underwear went into the rickety old two-drawer chest, which stood on the left side by the entrance. My blue ink bottle, pen, writing paper and envelopes, I kept on the top of the chest of drawers; my passport went under my woollies.

The bed was a simple metal frame with four straight metal legs and stretched apart lozenge shaped wire netting. The firm mattress seemed to be made of horsehair, the sheets white cotton and the thick, heavy blankets were dark grey with a cherry red line at either end that reminded me of army blankets. I lay on the bed with my hands behind my head, looking at the ceiling and thought of my mum. She was on the train, going back to London where she would meet Tony. Early the next day she would be catching a train from Victoria Station called the 'Golden Arrow' to take her to Newhaven, then on to the ferry across the pale grey sea... Paris and eventually, the following morning, she'd arrive in Montélimar. Certainly Dieulefit was a long way from here, but I had no wish to return to Beauvallon; I felt I could be myself here without any pressure, ought or must.

I heard loud steps bouncing on the springy wooden floor of the carriages' communal space, and croaky, young manly voices chatting. They went across the communal space to the bottom left corner, a carriage door creaked open, followed by a slam and then silence. But it was not long before I detected the voice of a languishing blues singer accompanied by a guitar. I wanted to go and say hello to them but felt that I would intrude on their privacy, and anyhow, I had no means of communicating with them. So I relaxed listening to the music; I learned, some weeks later that the singer was Josh White, a blues singer from New Orleans.

I looked at my watch - 4 p.m. and remembered that during the summer holidays on the island, my brother had given me this old doctor's Swiss wristwatch: "You like it? I had it given to me when I was a young boy and it was already ancient at that time! It works well. Here look! When you press this small button and count 30 pulsations of your blood pulse, and then press again... the hand stops and points to a number which tells you if you're ill or not." I was most impressed and delighted to receive such a precious present, but I never managed to understand what the complicated numbers referred to... I heard a bell ringing from the big house, I wondered what it was for and went to investigate.

As I entered the main building I met Jimmy East, the teacher I had seen in the queue with the bright blue eyes. He looked at me smiling and talked in French with a very pronounced English accent, "Are you coming with us? Saturday afternoon is when we hold our general meetings in the great hall. Everybody goes." When he was speaking, his head jerked about on his thin neck making him look like a strange bird. "After the meeting, you'll queue up to receive your pocket money, then we have supper and after, for the ones who like it, they can dance until midnight!" He concluded with a short nervous laugh while patting the head of Vladimir, his powerful golden boxer who responded by looking up at his master, displaying the white of his eyes, wagging his tail and noisily licking his dark heavy flews. I patted the dog in turn but it took no notice of me.

The assembly room was already crowded; all the teachers rested against the wall on the right side and stayed together. I saw A.S. Neill right at the back, leaning on the ladder that led up to the music box. There were no chairs in the room except one on the left near the fireplace on which was sitting a blonde teenage girl with a writing pad and a pencil; next to her resting an elbow on the fireplace, was an older pupil obviously trying to catch her attention. Everybody seemed to be looking for places with a backrest, leaving the middle of the room completely empty. Up to its first landing, the large wooden staircase was a favourite place to sit. As it was already full,

I found a place against the newel post and searched for my sister. I eventually found her sitting above me, further up, near the landing, and we exchanged smiles. What an interesting incongruous crowd it was! A mixture of all shapes and sizes, clean looking, scruffy looking, each one was a true individual, affirming his or her own personality. I could not help but compare this assembly to the ones in Beauvallon... where every child according to age and size, sat cross legged on the cold concrete floor, the teachers on chairs, facing us, ready to point a finger at the one who was out of line with the rules and regulations of the school. Summerhill was not like 'school' as I knew it, where structure took away most of your responsibilities. Here it was more like life really is, where the pupils learned to take their own decisions about every instant of their lives.

The older pupil leaning against the fireplace finally called the attention of the assembly by knocking his metal lighter on the mantelpiece. I realised that he was the chairman and turned my attention to him. He was tall, wore a dark green jersey with long, baggy, brown trousers and well polished shoes; his dark brown hair kept sliding into his right eye and, with his right hand, he regularly pushed the forelock back into its original position. He was slightly plump, his voice gentle and smooth, yet it carried authority. I thought he was amazingly relaxed having to face that crowd of individuals. As the meeting continued, I heard that his name was Carlos; he was patient and fair in allocating speaking time to the many pupils who had something to say. The secretary was taking notes of the different resolutions being passed, when at times people were asked to put their hands up to vote. The teachers very rarely contributed to the discussions; Neill watched silently. The children freely participated in the discussions, and seemed attentive to what was being said and decided.

Creaky noises came from the porch entrance door; two latecomers were arriving and nobody took any notice... I felt instant sympathy for them as they entered the meeting hall. One had fair hair drawn back, glasses and looked quite neat in his chequered red/grey woolly shirt and brown corduroy trousers. The other was scruffier, with a big lock of brown curly hair rising from his large forehead; thick eyebrows sheltered kind blue eyes, and an unlit cigarette hung from his mouth; his white shirt hung out of baggy trousers that were turned up at different heights. I learned later that they were called Tony and John, better known as 'Brum'. John had slightly protruding ears, similar to but smaller than mine. The meeting terminated when Carlos, looking round rapidly to make sure that all subjects were covered, declared the assembly over.

At the bottom of the stairs pupils were queuing up behind a table, and I remembered what Jimmy told me earlier - it was time to receive pocket money. Ulla came down the stairs with the money box, a pencil and a large notebook with all the names of the pupils; putting her glasses on, she proceeded to allocate a different amount to each child according to their age and, I learned later, according to whether there had been a fine decided by the assembly against a specific child. It was the way the assembly sanctioned the ones who had been unsociable towards the community. Ulla methodically wrote down each amount; often she asked a younger child to hold the moneybox while she counted the shillings and pence.

A young boy who I had noticed in the queue came up to me with a smile obviously wanting to be nice; his deep dark brown eyes looked at me intensely as if asking for friendship. He must have been two years younger than I; nature had given him a delicate long face with fine almost feminine features. Uncombed fair hair fell forward covering his forehead; he was wiry and dressed in a grey shirt and shorts. He pointed to himself and said, "Philip!" Then the same finger was directed to my chest and he said in a honeyed voice, "What's your name?" "François" I made sure that my reply was clear. He repeated it, putting much effort to mimic exactly my answer, "François?" I replied affirmatively by nodding my head. The bell rang, Philip pointed to his mouth, "Eat, eat... supper?" It was obvious he meant it was time to eat, but I didn't want to go down the corridor with him, as I wanted to be with my sister. I looked around for her in the great hall, up the stairwell, but she wasn't around, Philip was pulling on my sleeve, so I gave in and followed him to join the queue, wondering where she was… "Why isn't she here, in the queue with us?"

The feeling to search for her and to tell her that supper was ready came, but was quickly taken by another that I should not disturb her and should be more independent. Philip was tapping on my arm wanting my attention; I looked at him and his face was hiding a smile, and his hand was pointing to a group of three older girls coming up the corridor. They were chatting and laughing like girls know how to, making the boys wonder what they're laughing about. One of them had already stirred my feelings when my eyes met hers during the assembly. I felt I had been caught by her femininity and lively spirit like a fish at the end of a line. As they walked by us, I noticed in a fraction of a flash, that she had seen me but did not want me to know, and how suddenly she became serious and distant. I felt embarrassed by Philip's behaviour trying to draw the attention of the girls towards me, and I blushed as they went by, anxiously wondering if they'd noticed it.

Philip was at it again, enumerating their names by counting on his fingers into the hollow of his scruffy left palm, "Mary, Jill, Tessa!" He grinned at me while wiggling the finger allocated to Mary. Jill was the girl who took notes for Carlos during the assembly. Philip's games were getting too much for me and to divert his attention I desperately pointed to the hatch, as we were practically under it. Determined to keep my attention away from him, I looked elsewhere down the corridor.

As I entered the dining room with my steaming plate, I glanced around rapidly to see if Sylvette was there and, as she wasn't, I made sure to sit where I could watch the entrance. Philip was determined to teach me English, pointing at the different parts of food and pronouncing each word slowly for me to repeat, not giving me a moment to myself. As I started on my rice pudding, to my extreme delight, I saw my sister, looking radiant, entering the room between two older boys. They were both fair, both frisky, their faces reflecting joy and excitement. The one in front was shorter with pale blue eyes and looked around for a place to sit. The one behind was taller with green eyes, he carried a book under his arm - both wore tweed jackets. I soon learned from my young friend, who had seen my attention going to them, that the taller was called Martin and the other Toby. I realised how much I had missed my sister through the day, her dignified svelte appearance comforted me; yet I could feel in my heart a slight pinch from my animal sheepdog possessiveness. It felt justified, wasn't she my sister after all? Sylvette was somewhere else and she had not seen me. Toby chose a table at the other end of the dining room out of my sight.

Philip, with his mouth full of rice pudding, grinned at me putting his thumb up said, "Your sister very pretty, boys like!" I smiled for an instant feeling proud to be the brother of such an attractive sister but, at the same time, I felt irritated by the relentless attention Philip was giving me. Did he not have other friends? Could he stop invading my space? There was no way I could communicate these feelings verbally and I decided to let go of them.

I heard music coming down through the corridor. As I stood up I glanced to the far corner of the dining room and saw my sister with her two friends laughing. I longed to join them in whatever joy they were sharing, but at the same time felt that I would be one too many at the table. I looked to the other corner, Tessa, Gill and Mary had not finished their pudding and the sight of them was enough to make my heart feel perky. I left the dining room and walked down the corridor to the assembly room closely followed by my clinging companion.

Night had fallen, and the vast panelled room was poorly lit by a single ceiling bulb and from a tiny one that faintly lit the top right corner of the turntable platform where an elder boy was choosing the next 78 record. Some younger children were noisily having great fun rushing about the empty room. I walked across the shiny worn floor to the fireplace, rested my shoulder against the mantelpiece, and listened to the swinging rhythms of the New Orleans players. This kind of music appealed to me very much, I had heard it once or twice on the radio in France and had not been able to hear more. I was fully immersed in it when Philip pulled my arm gently wanting me to follow him, but I said no, moving my head slowly from side to side. He insisted and made a sad face, but I repeated my head movements pointing my finger to the music perch and then to my ears, to show him that I wanted to listen. He finally respected me and disappeared.

Now vibrant clarinet playing filled my chest, and the music carried me to a place in myself where I had not really been before. It was as if I became the sound itself, going up and round and down as if one with it; I had the strange feeling that I already knew what the next notes would be; my foot was following the rhythm discreetly, tapping the wooden floor. There was no thought in my mind and the lively melodies filled my whole being.

The room started to fill. Mary, Jill and Tessa walked rapidly by me and entered the room to my left, which I discovered later was their bedroom. After some time they came out looking pretty after changing their clothes and doing their hair, tinting their eye lids and colouring their lips. My heart pulse changed as I saw Mary nonchalantly walk by, looking attractive in her white shirt tucked into a wide belt, narrowing her waist and accentuating her hips and holding in place her full white and pale blue chequered skirt.

Some older boys came with more records and climbed up the ladder to the music corner; I realised then that the 78s we were hearing came from the pupils' own collections. A group of three teachers came in to hear the music, talking to each other looking relaxed and joyful. Couples of all ages teamed up to dance, girls also danced together. I had never seen children dance together like this; on the 14th of July in the Dieulefit Town Square, all the dancers were adults and a few very young ones who jumped around, but self-conscious teenagers never!

Tessa, who I felt had a generous heart, came smiling towards me with her head slightly tilted and invited me to dance. She was petite, with dark wavy hair covering half her forehead; her relaxed smile revealed a large gap between her slightly protruding front teeth, "Dance?" She looked straight at me invitingly with her dark hazelnut eyes. A whirlwind of confusion suddenly exploded in my chest, I did not know how to respond to this unexpected invitation. I had never danced with a girl before and did not know how. With a nervous smile I declined shaking my head imperceptibly, and suddenly felt terribly self-conscious as my legs weakened and blushed till my ears throbbed.

She danced away as lightly as she had come, to find another more willing partner. Mary and Jill were dancing together and I wondered if they had seen the incident. The music had now become distant, I was in a place in myself that I knew well and found so uncomfortable. I felt fooled by myself, lonely, angry with my shyness, and wished I could have been more manly; in an instant I had lost my self-assurance: my happiness had vanished just because a girl had asked me to dance... this was stupid. I left the fireplace to find a darker corner where I could hide my embarrassment, and went under the dark shadow of the music box.

Neill came in, carrying a HMV record under his arm, wiggled carefully through the dancers and waited by the ladder until the jazzy music stopped. He then addressed the teenage jockey up in the music box: "Would you mind putting on this tango for me, please?"

Neill adored tangos and as soon as he heard the accordion, he selected a teenage girl and was off onto the floor, performing. His right-hand was hardly touching the girl's shoulder blade; his left was holding his partner's with only two fingers that he held right up in the air while the other two pointed to the ceiling. His slightly hunch-backed heavy body and clumsy feet suddenly became light, perky and moved about with a kind of elegance. I noticed how Neill was loved and respected by the pupils. The floor had almost cleared except for a couple of very young children and Harry, the German art teacher, who was dancing with Ena. It was like an interval, a break, when the children left the floor to watch Neill and the adults dance to their music. As soon as the tango was over, the New Orleans jazz was back on full and the floor crowded again.

There was no light under the music box and I felt comfortable, unseen and able to observe. The tango episode helped me to dissipate my embarrassment; I was now in a much better place in myself, back into the music and enjoying watching the children dance. I learnt later that the dances were called 'swing' when the rhythm was fast and 'slow' when it was more languorous. The lively swing seemed to force the partners apart, when suddenly the females freely escaped in a few twists and twirls, while the boys concentrated on moving their hips and feet. At intervals only known to them, with a jerk they would draw their partner back close to themselves... but only for an instant, as the girls escaped again as if pushed by the whirlwinds of the unrestrained rhythms. The slow dances called blues were very different; the couples stayed close together and moved slowly on the floor swaying slightly...

I was reflecting that this dance seemed easier to perform for a debutant like myself, when I saw my sister coming down the stairs followed closely by Toby. She stood out from the Summerhill crowd with her straight self-conscious stature. As they came onto the floor, Toby took her gently by the waist with his right hand, and with his left drew her decisively into the slow dance. His serious expression was undoubtedly trying to cover the immense joy and pride that resided within him, and as they started to move on the floor, an imperceptible smile settled on his face. Sylvette, looking happy yet highly conscious of all the avid eyes looking at them, was the French girl dancing in Toby's arms, so she was doing all she could to be natural and let her partner guide her across the dance arena. Someone of his own age made a remark which, although I could not quite understand the words, made Toby burst into a short laugh which released the tension that had been building up in him; he was now more relaxed and smiling up to his ears. The teasing did not go on, there was a kind of respect for the newly discovered couple who were living a new relationship. Toby had his own very individual style of dancing and Sylvette was picking it up pretty quickly; I saw how everyone dancing moved differently, very much according to how free they were inside, and wondered how I would move if I was courageous enough to dance.

They had not been aware of me there in the dark corner, and I suddenly felt terribly alone… left out. I became disconnected from the atmosphere of the room and went into an empty space in myself where there was sadness. Seeing Toby dancing with my sister made me feel as if he had taken her away from me; she did not need me to protect her any more. I could see that she was in a different world, a world in which I would have only a very small role. I was now standing on my own, only myself was aware that, from now on, my relationship with my sister would be different. The attention she gave me daily would now go to her boyfriend. I understood, but not in my head, rather in my feelings, that the strong love they had discovered for each other was going to totally change the dynamics of our relationship.

I wanted desperately to go to my bedroom and be by myself, but could not face walking across the dance floor nor did I want to let my sister know that I had seen them dancing, as I thought that it might embarrass her and also I would not know how to face Toby. So I waited in my hideout until they left the assembly Hall, and walked down the long corridor towards the carriages. When I came out of the main building I was struck by the dampness and the thick fog that had descended, it seemed attached to the ground. It was very dark, as the outside lights could not show their usual brightness. After feeling my way in the dense pea soup, I felt reassured when I saw the faint light over the entrance door of the carriage. I felt transpierced by the cold damp air and was shivering when I opened my bedroom door. No one had lit the fire in the hall, so there would be no hot water in the bathroom and the only warm place would be the one I'd create once in bed under my blankets. I quickly ran upstairs with my toothbrush and toothpaste, brushed my teeth and rapidly came back down, took my clothes off except my woolly vest, and slid into the freezing damp bed.

I rolled up into the foetus position and waited for my body to create a warm air pocket. The awareness of being alone came back. My mother was in her world with her Fonsou far away in Provence, my sister with her father and Philippe, and now Toby was with her. And I was just by myself... curled up in my bed, searching for my world. What had it become? Where was it?

The presence of my deceased father, Marcel Lassalle, came to me, but he wasn't in my bed with me, no, he was over there somewhere far away... yet near by being inside my emotional memory. I missed his physical presence terribly, and I started to cry. The tears were like a flowing river, soothing my feelings, relaxing and comforting me. The day had been a long one since my mother left that morning; I was really exhausted and fell into a deep sleep.

I woke up the next morning wondering where I was and let my eyes scan the carriage room slowly; from my bed I could see that the uncultivated field was glittering with white frost, the sun was rising and one of its rays gave the scene a pink sheen, as it caressed the uneven surface of the frost bitten plants. Condensation of white frozen webs blurred the window corners, framing them like a romantic picture postcard. I was warm in my bed and did not feel like getting up yet, so I let my mind meander freely into whatever sphere it fancied.

The first picture that came up was when I had stood in the queue for supper the previous day when Mary, Jill and Tessa walked by. Mary did attract me very much but the shyness in me was amplified by her provocative femininity. I had noticed, as they walked past, Jill's slightly large, pale blue eyes absorbing me, as if she had decided to take me into her orbit. This image instantly brought back to me the wiry face of Philip with his naughty grin and the knowing look that had so irritated me, I promptly changed this flashback by transferring it to the assembly Hall... Neill dancing his tango, Tessa coming to me and sweetly offering me the dance which I'd turned down...

I heard the ring of a bell. It came from the main house reminding me that it announced breakfast; I was hungry for a copious English breakfast. I rose to my feet feeling bright and happy, ready to tackle the day, dressed rapidly and then popped up to the bathroom to immerse my face in the breathtakingly cool water. Seeing myself in the broken piece of mirror that stood on the small shelf over the washbasin, I smiled to myself as I combed my hair. I was conscious of the impression I gave others, my clothes were clean, the same with my fingernails and seeing that all was in order, I rushed downstairs, hung my towel on the back of the chair, put on my jacket and walked out into the fresh air.

It was twenty to nine, yet there was no queue at the hatch, probably because it was Sunday I thought. A white oval face, framed untidily by greasy black hair, appeared in the blue frame of the hatch. A pair of empty, tiny, almond-shape black eyes flickered rapidly as they queried…. the kitchen girl grumbled, "Toast? Cereals? Tea!" I learned later, that the pupils called her Greasy Grace and that grumbling was her way of expression; I replied proudly my first English word, "Toast!" She pushed through the hatch first two large white bread toasts on a plate with a square of bright yellow New Zealand salty butter and a spoonful of chunky marmalade, then a largish cup of dark milky hot tea on a saucer on which some white sugar had been carelessly dumped.

There were few people in the dining room and I chose to sit on the left, near the end of the table where the three girls had sat on the previous day. The scrubbed tabletop emanated its bleach scent as I sat down and proceeded to spread half of the butter onto one of the slices of toast. I was not used to having salty butter, but its melted odour together with the toast was appetizing. I decided to have the first one with butter, the other only with marmalade. While I stirred the sugar in my teacup, I looked around the dining room quietly; there were no pictures on the walls, the space under the pale blue dado line all around the room was covered in large white glazed tiles. I looked up to the ceiling and to my amused surprise it was decorated haphazardly with rectangular lumps of butter at different stages of rancidness, their colour changed from a dark yellow to transparent grey white. This was fascinating, some were very well stuck, flattened by the impact, others were just hanging on, about to come down, pulled by the immutable law of gravity. As I wondered how they'd arrived up there, I noticed a boy, slightly younger than myself, looking at me grinning. He held a white Bakelite handled knife in his right hand; its blade carried a lump of New Zealand butter that was about to reach its final destination. Pointing the blade to his chest, his thumb curved under acting as a pivot. His other retained back the power while he aimed at the ceiling towards a clear space. Still grinning, he let go the catapult and in a muted thump the ceiling received one more of its greasy decorative items. I smiled, wondering whether one day, I would be free enough in myself to do the same?

Groups of older pupils came in, I watched them choosing their seats, and then Mary and Jill appeared at the door carrying their breakfast and searching for where to sit, when they noticed me at the end of their usual table. After a short hesitation, Mary came and sat to my right, Jill sat opposite her. I instantly became self-conscious and looked into my cup of tea where I had seen a tea leaf floating. This leaf became my raft, my excuse for not engaging in any situation that might reveal my clumsiness with the opposite sex.

"Good morning!" I heard them say in unison; I promptly replied faintly, "Good morning…" not leaving for an instant the concentrated attention that I had chosen to give to the leaf. I took my spoon and with accuracy cornered my raft and dragged it out on to the rim of the cup. Mary and Jill went into a giggle and in a herculean effort, I looked up and smiled, catching for an instant Jill's pale blue birdlike gaze and saw that her separated dark pink lips revealing two attractive large front teeth. I then rapidly brought the teacup to my lips and sipped my tea, keeping my eyes in the cup. Tessa came in with two other girls; she sat next to Mary, the other two opposite next to Jill. She automatically gave her sugar portion to Mary, and I registered that Mary had a soft spot for sweetness. As if they had

CHAPTER 5

forgotten my presence they started chatting and laughing together, I enjoyed the music of their voices and like a snail coming out of his shell, I was able to let my feelings and awareness extend beyond my self-consciousness. I dared to turn my head to Mary; she was closer than I'd realised and I found myself looking into her hair: it was thick and carried big curly waves reaching down to her narrow shoulders - the rich auburn colour when caught by the light reflected golden hues at times; a whiff of her shampoo reached my nostrils and I secretly breathed it in. I became aware of her territory, of the space around her person that was hers and I respected that space, I moved slightly to the left trying to separate myself from the powerful attraction. When I suddenly realised that I was the only boy sitting at the girl's table, it prompted me to get up and leave the room without looking behind.

As I passed by the kitchen hatch, I saw it was closed. There seemed to be no one around outside and I decided to walk around, to investigate the school grounds. Straight across the back door, in the distance was the vegetable garden backed by a tall red brick wall.

In front were lean-to greenhouses, to the left were wooden huts, each with a window and a door. I learnt later that several teachers lived there. On my right was the dilapidated ping-pong building, and I decided to walk down along its side. I walked round inspecting everything. I was feeling happy and positive, in harmony with the place as I came round to join another path that led to the front of the main building. Coming down from the main entrance was Tony, who I had seen entering the assembly hall with John Brum. I wondered where he was arriving from and remembered, as I walked in his direction, that I had not yet seen him in the dining room. Coming up to him, I gave a beaming smile, he responded with another, but more reserved, and pushed his glasses further up the bridge of his nose. I saw that his index and middle fingers were orange coloured with nicotine. I felt like engaging in conversation with him and he obviously with me, but neither of us knew how to start and we laughed. He searched in the pocket of his corduroy trousers and pulled out a packet of 10 Players Navy Cut cigarettes; offering me one he said in a warm mature voice, "You smoke?" I appreciated his sharing gesture, but declined the offer by saying, "No, thanks." I had already learned that one could say 'thank you' or more familiarly 'thanks'. I terribly wanted to converse and all my senses of perception were attentive, ready to learn new words to add to my so limited vocabulary.

Tony stuck the cigarette in the corner of his mouth, and pulled out a wide flat green and yellow box of bright pink matches. He struck one on the sandpaper side of the box and it instantly flared, giving a strong smell of sulphur; I read on the box 'Swan's safety matches'. It reminded me that, when on the island, I used to enjoy playing with sulphur matches by covering the pink part tightly with aluminium foil. Then, with a flame, I would heat up the prepared end that rested on a stone until a loud explosion occurred, catapulting the silver matchstick some distance in a wavy trail of smoke. I had noticed that by my new companion's feet lay the remains of a Polo Peppermint packet, the wrapper of which was a very strong tinfoil. I pointed to his pocket saying, "Matches?" He immediately gave me the box. With great speed, I bent down, picked up the silver paper, carefully flattened it on my bent knee and tore a strip out of it. Then, wrapped the pink end tightly with it and set the match in equilibrium on a stone and proceeded with my demonstration. Tony, holding his cigarette, was looking at me, amused, and guessing what I was about to do. The explosion came, the match stick shot into the hedge and we laughed.

I understood from Tony's gestured explanations that he was not a boarder, but that he lived with his mother in a small flat in the house adjacent to the B&B we had previously stayed in. He came to Summerhill every day, but went back home for his meals.

"Do you want a game of ping-pong?" He proposed, mimicking as if he was holding a bat and serving with an invisible ball. "Yes!" I was excited by the thought of playing a sport I had never played. We walked back to the dilapidated building and up the outside wooden broken staircase. The room was completely empty, but for the large well used professional size table tennis table with its taut, dark green net. Many of the glass windows were broken; the wooden floor was dusty and well worn. On the window ledge was an array of bats, some rather battered with their surfaces half torn off, others with no covers at all. Tony quickly chose the best two, offered me one and went to the end of the room ready to serve. I soon discovered that he was an excellent player: his spins were terribly difficult to return and his smash was as fast as lightning. He realised that I was a beginner and patiently proceeded to teach me the finesses of the game: how to slice the ball to give it a spin, how to hold the bat and what angle to give it to deliver a smash. Tony became a good friend, took me to his flat to meet his mother and later to Ipswich where they had a permanent residence. There was no sign of a father around him, and although we did not talk about it, we somehow instinctively recognized the lack of one in each other's life.

Summerhill was a very different school from my previous one, where the pupils were asked to listen to the orders given and to carry them out without a murmur. Here, for instance, one morning I did not get up in time for breakfast and came running up to the hatch a minute after nine to find it locked. I opened the kitchen door and put my head in to see if I could get my breakfast, but was sharply shouted at by Greasy Grace,

"Get out of the kitchen!" I understood that it was my responsibility if I wanted food, to be there on time. Similarly, for going to lessons nobody made any remarks if you didn't attend them, not even the teacher! It was up to you to decide to attend or not. All the children at the time I was in Summerhill went to the classrooms with one exception - an American boy called Jimmy Richards.

Jimmy looked just like a miniature cowboy, with Texan decorated high-heeled boots, and dressed in Levi trousers, chequered shirts and a denim jacket. He stayed outside all day; often, when looking through the Jimmy's class window I saw him running about playing with Vladimir. Probably because I was French and could not yet express myself in English, he took pleasure in teasing me, and he waited for when I came out of lessons and then nagged me by making faces or pushing my shoulder and saying things which I could not understand except the word 'Frenchy'. For several days I ignored his incessant nagging but resentment started to build up inside me and after a few weeks of his teasing, I exploded with an anger that I could not control and ran after him. He probably thought I could not catch him, but I finally did, at the back of the school, near the dustbins. Fighting was something I had experience of, and in no time he was on his back, with me sitting on top of him punching his face. In between each blow he exclaimed: "Frenchy asshole!" I had been in the UK long enough to acquire enough English/American to understand what it meant. Overtaken by anger, I did not realise that a ring of silent children were looking down at us with great concern. One of them came out of the circle towards me, he must have been two years younger, and he said gently, "Do you know François, this is the first time we have seen a fight in our School?" These few words said so simply without a hint of criticism had a tremendous impact, and echoed in the darkness of the dark cave I was in. Tears flooded my eyes, while all the aggression and anger that had filled my being was dissipating rapidly. I felt limp and weak as I rose and heard myself say in a feeble murmur, "I am sorry…" The stunned Jimmy got up and without a word walked off slowly towards the back of the assembly room. The ring of children opened and I walked towards the carriages, crying desperately.

As I lay on my bed still in tears, I realised that the reason of my feeling so vulnerable came from not having dealt with, in myself, the death of my father Marcel Lassalle. But I could not let go of him; I was stuck to the father figure that I missed so much. The care and love of the non-judgmental children, who had witnessed the fight, had a kind of miraculous, cleansing effect. As I rested on my back all in my feelings, I noticed that the anger and aggression had left me, evaporated, leaving me in a deep peaceful state.

This fight with Jimmy was a valuable incident for me; it changed my life and from then on, I have never fought nor hit anyone. Probably because of this radical change in me, Jimmy never teased me again, and we were able to have a normal friendly relationship.

This autumn of 1951 was particularly cold and damp; low fog came off the North Sea and crept silently at night into the grounds of Summerhill and into the bones of my body, especially my ankles. One Sunday afternoon, I heard that some of the boys had gone to play football on the village football ground so I ran up to the field to join them, as it was a sport I liked playing. I brought with me my well used French football boots, and keenly put them on; our team needed a left wing and they put me there, although I was not left footed; we were playing against some teenagers of the village. It was cold on that wet field; I was not getting the ball, and began to feel the damp rising into my bones. Unexpectedly the leather ball came to me and I started running with it in the direction of the village boys' goal; I managed to dribble to avoid an opponent, and passed the ball to a Summerhillian. It was then I felt tremendous pains in my ankles and sat on the ground rubbing them. My face must have shown my agony, but I wanted to show that I was good at the game, and went on running until halfway through the first half. To my dismay, I had to sit down and stop playing as the sharp pains amplified. A teammate came running up to me, asking what was the matter. I explained in my pigeon English that I could not walk because something was wrong with my now swollen ankles. In great pain, I walked off the field as the game continued, and took the direction of my bedroom, feeling bad for having let down my team.

I wrote to my mother to tell her about it, suggesting it might be rheumatism. She responded by sending me some homoeopathic arnica pills, which I took. Over three weeks went by before the pain finally went away. Having lived in dry Provence all my life, my body was not used to this extreme dampness. In fact, in the late autumn and through the winter, my bed every night was so damp that at times I could have extracted water out of my sheets had I wrung them hard enough! I decided to spend my pocket money on a small paraffin stove, and after that I was able to keep my room warm in the evenings.

Before I could master enough English to join in the conversation with friends, feeling lonely in the evenings was usual, and I would walk around to see what was going on in the other parts of the school. I realised that there was nowhere really cosy and warm in the school. The only place that could have been made cosy was in the children's sitting room if someone bothered to light a fire in its fireplace. We were allowed to use the coke from the school reserves at the back of the kitchen. The grim room possessed a large sofa with a broken frame and some of the springs coming through its cover, but it didn't matter, it was roomy enough to find a cosy corner somewhere. I enjoyed lighting fires, it was a pleasure for me to do it, and once it was glowing with warmth the children's sitting room would slowly fill up, usually with the younger kids who came in to warm up. At times, I would toast a slice of bread that I had kept from lunchtime.

It was in that room that I had my first puff on a fag end that I found on the floor with quite a bit of tobacco left in it. One part of the stub had been put out and flattened by someone's shoe, and squeezing either side of its flatness in between my thumb and index finger, I brought it back roughly to its original shape. I lit it from a lump of coal that I held with a pair scissors shaped tweezers that always stood by the corner of the fireplace. I was by myself in the room. Had there been other children present, I could not have tried it… I would have felt too embarrassed. As I pulled on the fag end, it glowed, then, not knowing what to do with the smoke in my mouth, I blew it out immediately. I repeated this action several times until I felt a prickle at the end of my tongue together with a bittersweet taste. It became too short to hold and I threw it in the glowing embers, while thinking how strange it was that there was such a difference of smells between a freshly opened packet of cigarettes, the smoke that came out of them when lit, and the unpleasant bitter taste in one's mouth and the smell of the old stub. Each time I found a cigarette end long enough,

CHAPTER 5

I repeated the experiment. Once I found in the grounds an old cream-coloured packet of 'Weights' and to my surprise there was still one of the skinny cigarettes inside it. I put the box in the depth of my pocket, with the intention of trying it out later.

In the 50's, 'Weights' and 'Woodbines' were the cigarettes of the poor. I had observed the older pupils doing their rituals when opening a packet of cigarettes. After rapidly removing the cellophane wrapping, pulling out the first cover of thin silver paper and with the fingernails pulling out the first cigarette. Then, some tapped it energetically on the closed packet before offering the compressed end to their lips. The lighter or match act was next; each had his or her own way of lighting their fag, and some never had a light themselves, so they chased the glowing cigarettes of others and by end to end contact, while puffing their cigarettes, the glow was transferred. Then came the real first puff, usually the one that received the longest pull, and when the maximum smoke was taken, it was deeply inhaled. I had watched this action many times and noticed how their eyes looked absent while their eyelids slightly closed just before the smoke was expelled. The smoker looked semiconscious in that brief instant. All this inspired me to try it myself, but in peace. So, that evening, I went to my bedroom earlier than usual. I lit the paraffin stove, sat on the edge of my bed and pulled out of my pocket the packet of the so desired fruit. First, I smelt its honeyed spiced bread scent and examined its small narrow thin tubular shape, then put it in between my lips. I struck the Swan match, waited for the sulphur smoke to escape and gave three short pulls to start it off. I thought to try to inhale the smoke as I had seen the others do. Once my mouth felt full of smoke, I opened it slightly and took a big breath into my lungs. The doing of this act of smoking, was very different from seeing others do it. As the smoke went down, a slight tickle irritated my throat, then it invaded my lungs and made me feel like coughing and at the same time I felt dizzy, with a certain pleasant numbness that took over my body… I needed fresh air, so I expelled as much smoke as I could and noticed that it came out a different colour, more faded.

I went on expelling it until I could go no further, yet I still felt some smoke was left inside, and started coughing it out. The pleasant feeling of numbness dissipated slowly; I wiped dry my watery eyes, looked at the smoking cigarette between my fingers and took another smaller puff. Again I felt as if my body had been taken over by an ephemeral being disconnecting my normal consciousness with a different foggier one, not so sharp, that gave me an imprecise awareness. Deciding after the third or fourth puff that I had enough, I put out the cigarette, blew the smoke out of it and put it on my shelf for another experiment. I lay on my bed now feeling slightly sick; I did not realise then that I had unconsciously started a long partnership with the tobacco plant that was taking root in the depth of my emotional and physical being.

Before I could express myself coherently in English, I tended to feel rather lonely in the evenings. After supper the children disappeared to their bedrooms with friends, to listen to music or to play games, such as poker, which was in vogue. Others did their homework or went into their rooms to read. I had finished the three books I had brought with me from France, and wished I had access to others, but it wasn't the case and reading in English was still too difficult. Not without some envy, I saw how the children exchanged books and recommended them to each other, and some had radios and listened to jazz programmes. The younger ones played outside or in the assembly room, shouting and chasing each other endlessly. At times, I went into the old library where there was a piano. I liked that peaceful room at the back of the main building, with much light coming in from the north and west sides. For some strange reason it was always quiet in there, except of course when someone was playing the piano. Quite a few of the older children played it, boogie-woogie and blues was the thing, but also classical music, which was played by a teenager called Michael Proudlock. He spent much time practicing Beethoven's most vibrant piano concertos and I would often go in to watch him play. Michael was tall, lanky with extra-long hands, his flat chest curved in like a bent wooden plank when he leaned over the keyboard; his acned red face held a prominent nose; his thin lips and sunken eyes were often closed when lost in his musical fervour. A lock of dark curly hair fell neatly to the side of his head, except when he played the piano... then his whole body shook violently, taken by the turbulence of his music. Michael was probably the only one in the school who wore a white shirt with a tie and a dark blue jacket every day, always dressed in charcoal grey flannel trousers and highly polished black shoes. I noticed that he had a problem with girls and was often teased by the older children. We never exchanged a word together and sometimes he would smile to me in the rare times when he was not in a bad mood.

Dealing with my hunter's instinct

Using my sharp Opinel knife, I made myself a catapult. I bought from the ironmongers shop in town some waxed linen thread and a strong square rubber band. Out of an old pair of shoes I cut a wide strip to form the pouch to hold my projectile. This catapult was a powerful weapon: when I held the loaded leather part with my right thumb and index finger and stretched out the rubber fully, my whole body felt the destructive force of the instrument. One Sunday morning, I let my hunting instinct freely take over and went off to investigate the local woods. The sky was clear, the air sharp, the ground frosted. Looking up into the higher branches and placing my feet carefully on the ground so as to be as silent as a Red Indian, I searched for a prey. I heard pigeons cooing, and spotted them on the highest branch of a large oak tree. I prepared a few round stones that I placed in my pocket, and loaded my catapult with one; as I came closer to my prey, my heart started thumping with excitement. Now I stretched the rubber, aiming at the underbelly of the larger of the two birds, and released the leather pouch. Like a rocket the projectile went up through the air tearing off an oak leaf on the way... a loud thump followed. I had hit the branch on which the birds were resting! The couple flew off, but I felt pleased with the accuracy of my shot. I searched in my pocket for another round pebble, loaded the catapult and went on my search for the next prey.

It was to be a starling and this time I did not miss! In an explosion of feathers, the poor bird came tumbling down through the branches and landed at my feet. The stone had partly torn off its wing, its half open beak was squeaking out in agony, while it stared at me angrily with its shiny black eye. A loathsome quiver went down my spine, what had I done? I felt terrible, the damage was not repairable and I had to find a way to quickly end this poor bird's suffering. By now my whole body was shaking, I felt nausea and shame, my lips were dry. My eyes became wet with tears while desperately looking for a stone heavy enough to finish off the bird. At last I found one, lifted it up over my head and smashed it down, unfortunately missing the head thus prolonging the messy agony. I picked up the same stone and concentrated to make sure that this time I would not miss. The stone came down crushing the head into the ground! To be absolutely certain that the bird had entered the kingdom of birds, I stood on it. I stood on the rock of death in silence in the middle of the small wood. Now feeling quieter but still standing on the rock with a heavy heart, I became aware of a very fine vibration that was rising up from under my feet, legs, body and finally escaping through my head. I heard a sudden rustle of air going through the leaves over my head, and felt that it was connected somehow to the invisible part of the bird being freed... I never used a catapult again.

One cold, damp and foggy late November evening, I saw Tony by the dilapidated building walking slowly towards the huts. I ran to him to say hello and asked if he would play a game of table tennis with me; I knew he liked the game. "Yes, let's go!" he answered as he turned on his heels and rushed up the wooden staircase. He had shown me many tricks already and I was now able to send the ball back with more precision, faster, with some spins and even, at times, make him believe that I would send the ball to one corner, when indeed the ball would shoot off to the other. We had great fun; I could not yet beat him but was able to give him a jolly good game.

CHAPTER 5

Finding a new friend

"Have you been to Ivor Cutler's hut yet?" He asked me as we walked down the staircase. "No," I replied not really knowing who Ivor Cutler was. We walked to the light of the window next to the science lab. We could not see in as the curtains were drawn. Tony knocked at the door and a low rumbling deep voice with a strange accent was heard coming from inside. I learned later that it was from Glasgow, "Who's there?" "It's Tony… with a friend…" The door opened slightly, one protruding light blue eye looked at us inquisitively, a round nose followed and a small mouth that slowly stretched into a huge smile, "Come in… ah! The French boy." He invited us in as he opened the door wider. We stepped down into a small, poorly lit room, which felt instantly familiar. Like mine, it smelt of paraffin and burnt orange peel. Strange drawings were pinned everywhere on the boarded walls, odd bits of sculpture made with twigs or branches, interesting pebbles lined his windowsill, a mobile made of cut bits of cardboard hung from the ceiling, and on an old armchair covered with a worn out Scottish blanket rested a guitar. "Sit down," he ordered pointing to his small divan bed in the north corner of the room. "Tea? I have just made the water hot."

Ivor was a short man who wore a worn-out camel colour duffel coat and a grey speckled hand knitted bonnet that rested on bunches of curly, bushy hair that stuck out on either side of his large head. My mother had told me that Scottish people were close to their pennies and I thought that was probably the reason why it was so cold in his room. While he made the tea he talked with Tony; what he was saying was obviously funny as Tony kept giving little bursts of laughter, but I found his accent too difficult to understand to join in. I greatly enjoyed his humoristic, clown like presence. I liked his originality, also his hands that were very white, powerful but soft and generous. "Do you like songs?" He questioned, offering me the mug of hot tea. "Yes I do," I managed to answer and confirmed it with an up and down movement of the head. I was longing to hear him play his guitar and felt so happy when he respectfully picked it up. After having removed his bonnet and his duffel coat revealing a thick white knitted jersey, he sat down, ceremoniously rested the instrument across his knee and announced solemnly, "The boo-boo bird." I had never heard such an unusual song! It was very melodious and the words went something like… "I am the boo-boo bird, and when people see me, high in the sky; I say, I am the boo-boo bird! And I go booboo booboo… I am the most absurd…" etc. I was attracted by the offbeat rhythms of his playing and watched with amused admiration. Absurdity rang a bell with me, as I liked oblique humour myself; I felt that I'd found a pal who understood me and would not rebuff my own unusual wit.

Ivor became more of a friend than a teacher; with him I could be entirely myself letting my humour out freely each time it came up. We would laugh together and later, when my English improved, I took much pleasure in sharing with him the beauty of the Ile du Levant, of my fishing exploits and long walks on the rocks. Aware of my interest in sound and music, he let me play my mouth organ while he strummed his guitar or played the piano. He was not so keen though to hear my repertoire of French popular songs, but kindly took me over to the piano room to show me the basis of boogie-woogie. He was equally good at playing the piano, as he was the accordion or the guitar, but apparently preferred the organ above all. He taught the younger children, who adored him.

When I felt lonely in the evenings I often visited him, like one goes to visit a close friend who you know will always keep their door open. Knowing this, I'd put out all my feelers to make sure that I was not intruding on his privacy. His face was discreetly expressive and I was able to detect what was going on inside him just by reading the movements on either side of his mouth or the wrinkles around his eyes. He liked to appear as if he was hurt sometimes and stayed silent for a while looking at his feet, or hunched his shoulders and said nothing, but suddenly exploded in laughter showing the gaps between his small front teeth. He encouraged me with my art and enjoyed looking at my caricatures in my sketchbook; they made him chuckle. He himself was very creative, using pastels and crayons. I loved looking through his ghoulish and surrealistic drawings, some really weird and totally unique. Actually, they were almost frightening, and showed a world of deformed beings, of unfinished bodies, of desert land with leafless trees, of weird faces with one eye or no nose; they displayed unashamedly an inner hidden agony.

Schooling at Summerhill

I had come to Summerhill from the Beauvallon School, which was highly structured, everything in its slot, everything absolutely rigid. As pupils we simply had to fit the organisation; there were no negotiations, no space for the expression of how one felt. All we had to do was to follow the rules, whether we liked them or not.

During the first few days at Neill's school, I did wander about like a cork floating on the sea. I did not like this situation, as I wanted to learn and was not at all keen to stay out by myself, when others were learning in the classrooms. So I went to see Jimmy East whom I knew spoke some French and thought he would help me to sort out a programme. I knocked at his door, "So, you want to come to lessons, do you?" He questioned, while removing from his thin lips the old, silver ringed, swan neck briar pipe that lived almost continuously in his mouth, and gave a short chuckle. He looked at me with his powerful blue eyes and opened the door wider to let me in. Not waiting for my answer, he carried on, "Good, come in, find yourself a seat in all this mess!"

The room where he lived was actually the classroom where he taught. It was part of a row of three lean-to huts, set against a brick wall that demarcated the south side of the grounds of Summerhill. His hut, the largest of the three, was centred by a rectangular cast-iron wood stove from which a long iron flue, held together with bits of wires, went out through the brick wall of the south side. A kettle, obviously happy to be on the fire, purred and sang gently.

275

WALNUTS & GOAT CHEESE

When I came in, two distinctive smells invaded my nostrils, the acid aroma of the pipe tobacco and the sweet sweaty doggie smell of Vladimir who was spread out on a grey, worn-out sofa. The dog was following all my movements quietly with his worried looking eyes and seemed to be smiling. As I passed near the sofa, I heard his tail tapping the fabric, a gesture of welcome I thought. Behind his sofa, the setting sun was trying to come through old dusty cotton curtains giving the room an ochre tint. There were many bookshelves on the cream painted brick walls displaying all kinds of books, a small kitchenette in the corner, and a record player with a pile of 78 records. "Tea?" His blunt offer brought me back into reality and the reason for my presence.

Drinking the tea, we talked about how to organise a programme especially for me, that would fit what I wanted to learn with all the subjects available at Summerhill. Behind his unemotional appearance, I could feel that he was very kind and caring but did not want to appear so. I also felt that he was probably a very quick-tempered man. At times, when his pipe became blocked with saliva and made gurgling noises, he would unexpectedly shake it in one energetic strike towards the stove, the projected bits of liquid nicotine would splash onto the hot cast iron, thus creating a minute explosion, followed by a tiny cloud of steam. The uneven brick floor was covered in old rugs; a few framed drawings decorated the walls and gave the room a friendly feeling.

As I walked back to the main building, the sun had settled down behind the tall trees, I felt peaceful and reassured by Jimmy's care and attention. From now on, I would know where to go and join the classes with my friends. Jimmy taught me English, French and history. Mr Corkhill took science, physics and botany. Neill taught, mathematics, algebra and geography. I enjoyed going to Neill's classes as he always made us laugh. Doing riddles with us was one of his ways to teach us maths; if we became too serious or too studious, he cracked a joke. His classroom was in the same block as Jimmy's; the room was smaller and absolutely bleak. A few metal tables and uncomfortable chairs, a blackboard and some chalk were about all it contained. I had to re-learn everything: it was difficult, my brain just did not understand inches, feet, yards, miles, ounces and pounds, even a ton weighed differently from a French one. Liquids too were measured differently and made no sense to a brain that was set on metric. I could not grasp why there were 12 inches in a foot, or 3 feet in a yard. The Britons did make it hard for themselves when dealing with money in the shops; there seemed to be no logic in their pounds, shillings and pence!

Neill's broad Scottish accent did not simplify things for me either… even the way to work out a division was different! Neill was always amazed and puzzled by the way I arrived at the same final results as the others and concluded, "I don't get how you work it out François, but the result is fine, and that what's matters." I still do not understand the English way of working out a division, but never mind. He was extremely patient with me, and for the first three months gave me simpler work than to the others. Working with Corky I found similar problems. We had to measure weights and liquids, pints and gallons; I could not get why the English people, who seemed so nice and intelligent, would be so crazy as to complicate their life to such an extent! I thought that Napoléon was really brilliant in arranging things so that the whole of France used the metric system; it had certainly simplified the children's learning at school.

Mr Corkhill smoked a pipe too, like Jimmy East, but his was straight, not bent and so worn, the crater was charred out and so was the tip of his thumb, crackled and black. He talked to us keeping his pipe between his teeth and only took it out to release its burnt contents by tapping its head on the sole of his shoe. Working in the lab, doing all kinds of experiments delighted me; making plastics with crude oil, working with different acids on zinc, copper iron or lead and learning about their interactions. It was cold in the lab in the winters, so we kept the gas burners alight on the workbench to warm the room and often used them to melt glass tubes and shape them into different abstract forms or animals and birds. I looked forward to the days spent in the science lab. Mr Corkhill took pleasure in explaining the reactions of different materials to acids, to gasses, to heat and to cold; his enthusiasm was equal to ours when the materials reacted by creating a new mix. The process of learning became a joy.

Once, he asked us to find a small tin with a lid, which we did and gathered around him. He took out his multi-blade pocketknife and pulling out the bodkin, pierced the top and the bottom of the tin; the holes were the size of two matchsticks. Then he explained by going to the gas burners: "You fill the tin with gas like this through the bottom hole, until you can smell it coming out of the top." After a short while, he directed his long, sausage-like nose over the top of the tin, sniffed the gas and said, "Now I block the two holes with my fingers and we take it outside... by the way turn off the gas for me, will you? Thanks!" Highly intrigued, we followed him out of the lab into the courtyard and he asked us to stand some distance away from him. Bending down with some difficulty, he deposited the tin while keeping his index finger on the top hole. Then striking his lighter he removed his finger and lit the gas that was coming out. He then moved away swiftly... we all looked at the flame burning... truly wondering what he was up to? When suddenly there was a large bang! And the tin shot up in the air higher than the table tennis building. We were all amazed of course and interested to know how what we had just seen was possible.

He explained that the gas burning away created a vacuum in the tin and when the air suddenly came back into it, it created an explosion that sent it up high in the air. Of course Clive Horsefield, Tony, Andrew and myself had much bigger ideas and when the class had ended, we started looking around the school for a larger tin. Tony found a half-gallon drum and without telling Corky what we were about to do, we borrowed the keys of the labs from him and he said trustingly, "Make sure that you bring them back to me when you've finished, I don't want to lose them you know!" In the lab we found a hammer and a big nail, we made our holes and filled the large drum with gas as we had been shown. Clive held the tin with his two index fingers as I turned off the gas, and we followed him outside. Carefully Clive deposited the drum in the middle of the courtyard. Keeping his finger on the top hole, he turned to me and said in a controlled calm whisper, "You've got the matches?" I took them out of my pocket, struck one and brought its flame up to the hole as Clive's finger slid to the side. Immediately the match lit the gas and a beautiful blue flame came straight out like a blowtorch. We all stood back and watched in anticipation… it seemed to take an awfully long time, no one spoke as we waited… the tension lessened as we felt that our experiment had probably failed. "Has the flame gone out?" someone asked, "No, I can still see it flickering a little," Clive answered.

The flame was now going up and down as if resisting the vacuum pulling from inside. Unexpectedly, an almighty explosion occurred 20 times louder than the first trial supervised by Corky. I felt my heartbeat change its rhythm caused by the excitement and I watched the tin rise so, so high… until it looked like a small brown rusty speck in the sky. We were by now having fits of laughter, feeling great from our success. Aware of the possible danger of the drum's return, I shouted, "Watch the drum!" We had all lost sight of its whereabouts and for a moment a tense silence pervaded. Suddenly a crashing sound was heard by the back door of the school, as the deformed drum hit the ground, inches from Storm, a younger lad who ran to see what the loud bang was about. We examined the metal container; its shape had changed to more like a football and it was not really re-usable. We had other tries and finally decided to stop when a smaller tin we had used several times and which also became an odd shape, shot off unpredictably at a low angle and hit the brick wall of the school, just next to the dining-room window! We took the keys back to Corky and did not continue our somewhat dangerous experiments.

Clive wanted to become a dentist; he was very practical and when we were together we did not talk much but did things like making cider, making kites, making bows and arrows. We exchanged our knowledge through doing. He knew how to make cider, I knew how to make arrowheads. He knew how to make large kites; I showed him how to make bows and arrows out of hazelnut wood and chicken feathers, just as I had done with my friend Jacques in France. From the Bramley orchards, near Daphne's house, we gathered several baskets full of the large green apples and put them into a tall cooking oil drum that we had cleaned. We set ourselves up near the entrance steps of the carriages with the intention of storing the cider bottles in some dark corner upstairs under the roof, next to the bathroom. From the branches of a nearby ash tree, we made long African type pestles to smash the apples and we set to work. Wonderful smells from the crushed apples vapours soon came out of the drum filling our heads and lungs, bringing joyful giggles as we accelerated the pulping. Satisfied with our work, we decided to leave it for the night to ferment; we covered the top with planks and went back to the main building for suppertime.

After breakfast on Sunday morning, we both rushed back to the carriages to inspect our brew. It was already turning alcoholic and gave a delicious scent. Clive and I spent most of the day getting the juice out of the brown pulp and we managed to fill some 20 dark brown empty beer bottles using a cloth filter and a funnel. A few had screw tops and with most of the others we used ordinary corks. We took them upstairs and hid them in the chosen dark corner, although we felt like drinking it right away, we knew we had to be patient and wait... at least a few weeks. We forgot about our bottles, until one day Philip rushed to up to us saying, "I've heard some explosions when I was in the carriages, I think it's your cider bottles!"

As we ran down to inspect our bottles, I was thinking, what on earth was doing Philip in the carriages? To our great sadness, we found out that all the corks had blown away. The cider had bubbled out and what was left in the bottle smelt of vinegar! However, we did enjoy drinking the four screw tops that had held fast during the fermentation.

Neill was accessible to us and we could ask his permission to use his workshop, "What do you want to use my workshop for?" He would always ask, "Why can't you use your own?" Indeed, Summerhill provided us with our own workshop, but all the tools were blunt, many were missing or hadn't been put back in their proper places; there were no more nails or screws, and if there were some, they would be bent or unusable. So we'd explain in some details what our project was, he would then look up and down at us while searching in his pockets for the precious key to his so desired workshop, "… and make sure you don't blunt my chisels, and bring me back the keys as soon as you've finished," we'd hear him say as we ran off impatiently, bubbling with our desire to start. Neill's workshop was well provided; he always went there after our visit to check that all was in order and re-sharpen the tools if necessary. Sometimes, as we brought the keys back to him, he would ask, "How did it go? Tell me." If I had encountered a problem he would listen, but rarely go back with me to show me how to solve it.

The art room reveals my hidden pains

I was regularly drawn to the art room that was always open, and spent much of my time in its quiet creative atmosphere. Waiting there were piles of paper, brushes and powder colours, always available for the creative person. Most time empty, the art room satisfied my need for solitude.

Through Ivor's drawings, I saw that residing inside him was an unspoken suffering, which I immediately recognised in myself. Almost every night, I cried about my father before I slept. Often in the night I lived through nightmares that were to do with the war, with soldiers running after me to do me harm. Fonsou going to prison had had a deep impact on my fragile emotions, as faces of fierce looking men behind bars, wearing striped outfits, would suddenly appear in my sleep. Nights were often dark and turbulent, but I kept it all to myself. However, in the day I always showed happiness and good humour. My paintings were not surrealistic like Ivor's, they were on the contrary very realistic and I felt soothed as I painted them. I had no problem showing them to anyone who cared to look at them, but the darkness and insecurity I had been secretly hiding was being unconsciously exposed.

The sheets of paper were the large A1 size and the powdered colours bright and easy to use just by adding a little water; the brushes were diverse in their shapes and sizes. I used violent contrasted colours to express my inner pains: Men's faces lit by torchlight, appeared on a black background, unshaven prisoners holding the prison bars with blood covered hands and expressing, through their sunken pale blue eyes, frozen empty spaces. Another painting with myself crying, sitting on a bare gravestone in some lost graveyard, or a freshly cut hand, wriggling in agony by a bloody axe, the blade jammed on a wooden block. I also painted abstract forms with geometric shapes in bright colours. Harry was the German art teacher who kept the place extra clean and enjoyed keeping an eye on the development of my work, never interfering. At times I'd ask him a question about what I was doing and his remarks were pertinent, sharing his appreciation and always giving me encouragement. One day he asked me to pose for him while he painted me sitting on a chair; a few times he painted with me in the room to keep me company.

There wasn't a day when I did not go into the art room. It possessed a special kind of smell that I liked: the rabbit skin glue of the powdered paints, mixed with a definite odour of the cheap paper and of the Pears brown translucent soap that stood by the side of the deep washbasins. The room was clearly in two parts, one for painting, the other for clay work, but to obtain some clay, we had to ask Peter Wood, Ena's son. He was himself a potter but he was difficult to find and not always agreeable or willing to help, so one didn't bother to use this facility. I saw Peter once in the pottery turning pots on the wheel, and only once did he fire the gas kiln. He was short and thick set, with jet-black hair, round black eyes and a Hitler type moustache. I always knew where he was, as he was very keen on Jane and spent much time in her bedroom, which incidentally overlooked the pottery.

Awakening of my bodily senses

I liked Jane very much. She was tall and thin with shoulder length fine light chestnut hair. Her almond shaped, ochre green eyes, showed a distant kindness, her straight nose and well-defined thin lips attracted me, especially when she laughed, as they revealed a neat row of teeth. But for only an instant, as her hand shyly rapidly covered her mouth. There was something peaceful and dignified about her. Of course she was completely out of my range age wise, but when I could, either in the queue, or sitting at lunch, or at a meeting, I would quietly come close to her to savour the presence of her femininity.

Being aware of my body was for me a natural thing; climbing trees, jumping from heights, running fast, peddling wildly on my bicycle all made me feel at home in myself. These were moments when I did not think, but just allowed the mechanics of my body to take over. Feeling the regular rhythm of my breathing while my body was under effort pleased me, and I never missed an opportunity to exert myself in some physical activity.

I longed to dance on Saturday evenings, but being too shy to ask a girl, I just stood there and let the jazz rhythm move my body discreetly, while looking at the dancers. Once, I took all my courage and went up to Jane to ask her for a dance. She was older and I did not mind if I looked ridiculous dancing with her; I had been observing the dancers for weeks and was now ready to launch myself onto the floor!

Well… I have to say that I did not expect that the physical contact of my left hand meeting her soft, warm long fingered right and that my right hand, resting lightly on her rounded hip, would have such an effect on my emotions. I suddenly felt myself as a sea captain in command of a large ship, feeling responsible for its good navigation. Pulling in a little with my left hand or releasing it and indicating gently to the hip, one way, or the other made the liner respond instantly! It was exhilarating, I didn't dare to look at her, nor at any one else, I simply stared into the distance, letting the music guide me and hoping that I would not trip over her feet. I was already feeling more confident, my right hand now rose to surround the agreeable part of her waist, feeling the counter movements of her hips as we turned and intertwined the other dancers. Feeling more at ease now, I dared look at her face: her large hazelnut eyes smiling, the slight smile on her Mona Lisa mouth reassured me that all was ok. I felt her presence as her light perfume encircled me; her measured sensitivity made me feel that I was driving the dance, when in truth she was discreetly showing me the way through the imperceptible responses of her hands and body. This was absolutely tremendous, colossal… I thought of my mother, 'She would be pleased if she'd seen me dancing with Jane, as dancing was to her what singing is to a nightingale.' This thought made me smile.

The music stopped. Now I noticed that my whole body was trembling deep inside, I looked at Jane with a questioning smile, "Was it okay?" She laughed, "Yes, very good François, you're a fine dancer." And she walked away in the direction of the large staircase. I went back by the music box and leant against the wall to savour this very first dance. The trembling was still there and took some time to dissipate. Now I would feel more confident to ask Mary, Jill, Tessa or any other girl for a dance.

Sylvette in her own world

I had not seen my sister for quite some time, and I found all the older boys were always around her, especially Toby, and she was never alone. It seemed to me that all they said and all they did was to get her attention; my presence would have disturbed them as we would have talked in French, and I did not feel like being with them because of this. I missed not being just with her, yes, by myself, to talk in our language, to ask her many questions: the latest news from Maman? What she was doing all day with Toby? Had she received a letter from Mano? The time went by and I could not find this gap. I felt at times as if Sylvette had been kidnapped, and it irritated me somewhere inside.

One evening sitting on the back steps of the main house while waiting for the supper bell to ring, I saw Toby arriving from the direction of Jimmy East's classroom. He came towards me and gave me a slightly tense smile. Kneeling on the lower steps he said right away, "I have been wanting to talk to you, for some time..." He was looking into my eyes; his were very pale blue, almost pink, and I furtively read into them an expression of accusation. I could not bear his look, and turning my eyes to the ground, I answered, "Yes?" I felt my heart pounding inside my chest, indicating that all was by no means clear between us, and that I was more disturbed by our relationship than I wanted to admit. "It's about Sylvette and me... you know that I love her, don't you? And I care for her very much!" He went on, "You seem to avoid us, to avoid me specially and that's not fair, is it? What is the matter?"

Silence followed, I did not know what to answer. I swallowed my saliva; it felt as if it had became solid, tumbling down my throat like a fair sized stone, rumbling down into a deep gorge. I wondered whether he'd heard it? "It's not fair, is it? I am with your sister because I love her! But I have no bad feelings towards you. In fact I would very much like to make friends with you." I knew Toby was right; what he was saying made sense, but how could he be aware of how I was feeling? He did not have a three-years-older sister like Sylvette. In truth, I secretly missed her but I do not think she was aware of it; everyone lives in his/her own world, a bit like astronauts in their spacesuits.

Toby was waiting; I had to come up with something, for his courage and sincerity touched me. I suddenly felt waves of love flowing towards him that instantly healed my inner tensions. I lifted my head, looked at him with a shy but happy smile and managed to say in my poor English, "Thank you, talking to me, yes, let's be friends." We shook hands, and I was able to look into his eyes, which had become tender and slightly watery. The dinner bell rang; we moved into the building to join the queue.

Toby became very caring towards me, always helping me when I needed him to clarify problems I had with mathematics, or English grammar. He was very gifted in all sorts of ways; he was at the time preparing his A-levels with a few of the other older boys. Toby was good with his hands and made for Sylvette, with two tiny Victorian silver sixpence coins, a most beautiful small ring in the shape of a fish.

English culture becomes part of my world

One late Sunday morning, in the winter of 1951, on my way to play a game of ping-pong with my friend John B, I was walking by the back of the main house, when I felt attracted by the speaking voice on a radio that came from Ulla's bedroom, just above my head. I looked up, and noticed that her sash window was slightly opened, just enough for me to hear a man's voice giving the world news. I was surprised to find that I could understand every word he was pronouncing and suddenly felt a great joy. Inadvertently I had joined the vast pool of the English-speaking people! I was at that instant actually in it, as if swimming in words. I relished, as I let each one of them penetrate the emotional impact and feelings they carried into my being. My brain opened wide its doors to English culture.

I had not heard the news since I left France. This time it came from England; it was different: there was nothing much about my country, but English politicians, who I knew nothing about. Then the sports news came on reminding me that my friend was waiting for me in the table tennis room. Filled with the excitement produced by the realisation that I now had access to the culture of a large portion of my ancestry, I rushed up the rickety stairs and burst into the table tennis room saying from the top of my voice, "I just heard the BBC news! And I understood what the speaker was saying! Isn't that smashing?" John, who had been patiently waiting for me for some time, would have normally been reprimanding and would have remarked, "You're late!" But instead he looked amused by my excitement and answered, as he served, "Really? That's good... come on, let's play to warm up, it's cold in here!" Realising that I could now comprehend the BBC, I could not stop talking and as we started playing, words were pouring out of my mouth like an unblocked spring. I wanted to share all that went on inside me, to share my French culture, my Provencal jokes, talk about girls etc. In my French school with my friends I had been communicative, but since I'd arrived in England, I had found it too difficult to say anything, as I thought that I could not speak the language.

When I played table tennis with my other friend Tony, we were more serious; he was more like a sports teacher, keen to show me better ways of doing things. It was hard to make him laugh and when I managed to pull a smile out of him, I felt relieved as if I had won the game. With John it was different, his body movements were very amusing; springy on his bent knees, standing far away from the table, he would jump up every time he served and at the same time lifted his shoulders up, making his neck disappear into his body, giving the impression that this large head was resting on his chest! We would do a lot of clowning together, playing as if we were two orang-utans or as if we were simple-minded people. John was much better at it than me and could keep a straight face while mimicking. We felt comfortable with each other and rapidly developed a strong friendship. As my English improved we enjoyed talking together, exchanging opinions, our thoughts and feelings, and we no longer had any problems communicating with each other.

Lip to lip contact brings a new dimension

John, I knew, was ahead of me on the girlfriend front; he would tell me of his amorous adventures and it was he who introduced me to the enjoyable rituals of the girls kissing goodnight sessions. We soon discovered that we were attracted to similar types of girls - witty and vivacious. The ritual consisted of entering into the girls' bedroom, once they had all gone to bed, and going to one after the other to kiss them goodnight. We waited outside their bedroom until we felt they were ready, then knocked on the door and listened with attention for the, "come in!" Or the, "no, not yet!" or a simple "OK!" There were five beds in the room, but a Danish girl called Anne had left the previous term so now there were four. The first bed I came to was surrounded by bay windows. I had never played this unusual game before, and for me it was quite a heart stirring moment. It was one thing to be talking and teasing and joking with girls, but when it came to be actually lying on their beds, specially that first day and above all with the girl I had been day-dreaming about so many times, it was something totally overwhelming.

As I lay down next to Mary, I recognised the scent of the Pears soap she had just used and immediately heard my heart thump. My face came so close to hers that I felt her gentle warmth; my eyes were closed but I knew that she was observing me. When my lips met hesitantly and delicately the extreme softness of hers, when I breathed the damp vapours of her breath, I went into an inner space of extreme finesse. Meeting her witty black eyes connected me further with her feminine world. I was not just entering into a new physical ground, where my flesh communicated shyly and tentatively with the feminine kind, but I also became aware that I connected an invisible part of myself where my fine inner feelings awoke to a new awareness of extreme gentleness. I felt my consciousness wide, enrobing, peaceful, as if this non-physical part of myself had grown to a much larger dimension than my actual body. Suddenly, I was brought back to earthly reality by a short restrained giggle and a slight tense tremor through Mary's body, and as she gently pushed me away, she murmured musically, "Goodnight!" At that moment I would have preferred to go straight back to my bedroom to savour this tender but powerful moment and to let it dissipate naturally, like when the morning fog finally vanishes under the rays of the rising sun... but that was not part of this game... the next bed was waiting for me.

I came to Tessa's with hesitation in a slightly darker corner of the room between two windows. I could see her smiling, showing the attractive gap between her teeth, her arms stretched out inviting me to come closer, her dark brown eyes looked at me reassuringly indicating that she found much enjoyment in this game. I knelt on the floor, half present, the invisible part still not wanting to leave the magic of the first contact with Mary, I felt Tessa's arms gently surrounding my neck, pulling me down with a slight insistence as if to bring to my attention that there were yet two more girls to kiss. As I came close, the smell of cold tobacco reminding me that she was a smoker, this brought me back completely into a crude reality. I kissed her as one kisses the head of a cat one likes; the lip contact was gentle but disconnected. "Goodnight." She said giving me again her generous smile.

Jill was next, waiting in her bed in the darkest corner of the bedroom. Our eyes met briefly, I saw them large, wide open, and I noticed in them the flicker of a passionate pale blue flame; I understood right away that she wanted me to know how she felt about me. I lay down coolly alongside her round body, resting on one elbow, looking at her keen mouth; the lips were red, slightly open showing her large, white front teeth. I felt the heat of her breath; her nose was blocked due to what seemed to be a permanent cold. While I hesitated, I felt her narrow, long fingers enveloping the back of my head, pressing and holding it there firmly... there was no escape, she was taking me into her world. Our lips came into contact more rapidly than I expected. I opened my eyes, to find her eyelids slightly closed, just as if a tissue paper curtain had been drawn; behind it she could not be distracted from her own amorous world. Something slippery furtively caressed the inside of my upper lip. I immediately became very self-conscious, also by the fact that we were not alone. Her need to breathe through her mouth allowed me to pull back and move off the bed. She gave me a triumphant smile; I felt her looking at me as I turned my back and moved in the direction of the last call.

I went round the fourth bed and felt relieved that this first round of kissing the girls goodnight was coming to an end. It was something so totally new to me, I was dispersed in myself, somehow floating and needed to have time to digest it all, to put these fresh experiences in my own perspective. I was longing to go outside and be on my own.

I moved rapidly to Jacquie's corner, and noticed that John was finishing his round with Mary. As I knelt down, I could hear a light feminine giggle. John was mumbling something to Mary in a low voice. Gathering myself back to where I was, I gave an overall look at Jacquie. She was tall compared to the other girls, her very thick black curly hair contrasted with her very white skin. Wide eyebrows and dense eyelashes almost hid her gentle deep blue eyes…

"Get off!" "Scram!" I heard coming from the lighter part of the room. It was Mary pushing off my probably too keen friend. Deep inside, I felt a little satisfaction, pleased at the thought that she was refusing John's eagerness; but I knew deep down that she liked him more than she liked to show. I heard him grunt and leave the room. I was back to Jacquie who was smiling timidly, waiting for my kiss. I did like Jackie, she was kind and understanding but I was conscious that she was rather left aside by the boys and I felt a kind of compassion towards her. I kissed the waiting lips similarly to when a butterfly lands on a flower and realises that it is not quite the one to its taste. "Goodnight," I said kindly.

As I came out and turned off the centre light and closed the door behind me, I heard the muted sound of the girls chatter. John had been waiting in the lounge and looking straight at me inquisitively, queried, "So, how was it?" Leaving a little time to answer, I replied, "Yes, okay!… Good!" I did not feel like talking about the experience, which John sensed, and as he walked off he uttered a light, "See you. Goodnight!" I returned his good wishes as I took the direction of the carriages.

I hurried along as if carrying a precious parcel that I did not want to open before making sure that I was in an undisturbed place. I felt good, and was letting no other thoughts come to disturb the exciting anticipation of reliving these latest moments passed in the girls' bedroom. I lit the paraffin stove in my room without hurry, still holding back the flow of all the feelings that were longing to become alive again, almost enjoying the restraint, I was moving slowly, taking my shoes off and going under my blanket to find a position that I would not have to change for a while. Lying on my back, bringing the blanket under my chin, and putting my hands on the nape of my neck, I closed my eyes and waited for my body to create its own warmth. Now, in full comfort, I allowed myself to slip back into the blissful sensations that had brought me to the new perception of the delicate and tender contacts with the feminine world I had just discovered, especially in the first bed of this first round.

The influence of Summerhill changes my behaviour

Around six o'clock one morning, I was woken up by a creaking noise that came from my carriage door. Dawn lit the carriage; intrigued by the thought of who would visit me at such an early time, I half-opened my eyes to see a shaky feminine and fragile hand reaching out in the direction of my jacket that hung by the side of the entrance door. The arm was not quite long enough and couldn't reach it. 'A body has to follow…' I thought rightly, as a shoulder and slowly a lock of fair hair appeared. I immediately recognized Philip, who did not look at me, thinking I was asleep.

With agility the delicate hand flicked my jacket open and pulled out my wallet from the inside pocket. I knew that in it was one pound, ten shillings for these were all my savings. I felt in myself the wild animal ready to pounce to blindly protect its territory, but the feeling that I should tackle this situation another way held me back and I kept silent. Like in a slow motion film, the lock of hair, the body, the arm and the hand left the room to reappear shortly afterwards with the wallet, to drop it back into the inside pocket. The door closed, this time without a squeak, and I waited for quite some time before getting up to check what was left in my wallet. I felt touched when I saw that the 10 shillings note was still there. I knew that Philip was fond of me but I knew also that he was very sharp and clever. Had I not seen him in the act, when finding the 10-shilling note in its place, I might have thought… 'How strange, didn't I have one pound ten shillings left in my wallet?' I might have blamed myself for having lost it, as I had not before encountered any situation of stealing in the school. This incident bothered me the whole day. I wondered how to tackle it… could I try to forget about it? But I knew I never would. I myself did not have much money and realised that Philip probably had none whatsoever. Finally I thought that I could lend it to him, he could pay me back in bits. I decided to find him and talk with him about the incident.

I found Philip at the back of the main building, near the dustbins; he was lighting a cigarette. "Oh! Hello Philip, I've been looking for you… I'd like a chat." I said feeling happy to have found him in an isolated place. I was surprised to find him so cool, he gave me a nice pointed smile, his dark blue eyes not showing any anticipation of what was to follow. I suggested, "Come, let's have a little walk." He pulled out of his pocket a packet of John Player cigarettes together with a box of Swan matches. "Would you like a fag?" He offered sweetly presenting me with the packet drawn open with a cigarette already half pulled out. I hesitated for a fraction of an instant, but took it and lit it from his offering steady hand; I noticed rings of dirt on his fingers. I drew out a big puff that instantly made me feel dizzy; I had not been smoking for that long, and only the milder Woodbine's. As we left the dustbins and walked slowly towards the carriages, I could not help saying: "I don't often see you with a packet of cigarettes?" There was silence… then he drew on his cigarette and while he blew the blue smoke out, answered in a monotone voice with the smoke coming out synchronically, "Yes true, but I got some money from my grandmother by post this morning." Stupid me,

CHAPTER 5

I thought, why did I ask him that question? I somehow wished that I had not pushed him into lying, as I had just made my task more complicated. I decided not to let any more lie take root, and went straight to the point, "You know Philip, I'm sorry I made you lie about the money for the cigarettes. You don't realise but I was awake when you came into my bedroom early this morning and took out of my jacket my wallet and my money." I did not let him reply and went on, "Thanks for leaving the ten shilling note, but you know, with that pound note I was going to buy paraffin to heat my bedroom."

I could see that this sudden direct approach put him into a profound turmoil; his thin lips were now tight and he was looking at the ground. I felt sorry for him, at the same time a feeling of love came up from deep inside myself, I wanted to protect him from too much suffering. I continued, "You know what? I suppose that you couldn't have spent all that money since this morning? I suggest that you give me back 10 shillings from it now, and then I can lend you the rest; you can pay me some back at your speed, when you receive your pocket money on Saturdays, how about that?" I looked at him and saw that he was crying quietly; he looked distraught and I put my arm around him. He gave me the 10-shilling note left without looking at me and replied feebly, "I'll try." And in an attempt to make him laugh, I said jokingly, "You know, when I saw your hand and arm stretched towards my jacket, I wished then that I'd had a long feather and tickled your hand with it, that would have been very funny! He laughed timidly and looked at me feeling relieved that he hadn't lost my friendship.

The 10 shillings never came back and it was never mentioned again. This incident brought us closer together and on several occasions Philip opened his heart to me. His parents lived somewhere in Suffolk; they were unemployed and alcoholics. His father regularly hit his mum and she was very cruel towards her son, often beating him. Living in his messy house was a nightmare, and he told me that when he went there, he only stayed in to sleep; the rest of the day he would walk endlessly in the streets of the town, frightened to come home to his drunken parents. He fed himself from the fridge so as to avoid any confrontation with them. I remember once on the Leiston railway station platform, when it was time to go home for the summer holidays, he refused to get up on the train and screamed while holding tightly onto a lamppost, "Leave me alone, I don't want to go home, please, I want to stay at school!" He had not been forced to leave, as Neill decided to keep him in Summerhill during the holidays.

The unique, self-educating School...

One late evening, in the early spring of 1952, we lit a fire in the carriages with the intention of making toast, as one boy had half a packet of salty New Zealand butter. "Who's going to get the bread?" He asked defiantly. Two boys volunteered, I offered to go with them wondering – where we would find bread at this time of night? They walked straight to the back of the kitchen and stopped by a small window of which the latch had been set to let a little air flow into the kitchen. The older boy pulled out of his pocket a long bladed school knife that he must have taken from the dining room, and proceeded with much concentration to free the latch. "But, what are you doing? That's stealing!" I exclaimed keeping my voice as much down as possible. He turned his head giving me a crooked grin, and said in a whisper, "You have a problem with stealing?" He then carried on attentively. I did not know how to respond to his question, I was taken by surprise. I had never really thought about nor done any stealing, except... maybe when in Dieulefit I had pinched a few ripe cherries from the farmer's cherry tree. But this was breaking in! Should I take part in this? I began to feel uneasy. Should I stay with them? After all they were my friends - or should I go and leave them to it? This put me into a complete quandary; I hesitated not knowing what to do. The window was now open, "Come on, give us a hand!" I heard him say as I walked off, not being able to follow through with this new type of adventure. I went into the big house feeling very alone; it wasn't fear or morality that stopped me from stealing, it was just that I was not interested. Certainly my mother had never told me that it was bad to steal and Christian morality, from what I'd heard, was taught in the church and had not been drummed into my head. It would not make a difference in my friendships whether my friends were stealing or not, I just did not feel like taking part and felt no great need to have the bread that was locked up in the kitchen. I felt terribly low, was I disillusioned? Disillusioned by the fact that I had placed Summerhill too high? Had I idealised it into something too perfect?

Actually, this experience made me realise that Summerhill was similar to the real world, where each one of us in the school was allowed to be who he or she really was, able to live according to our true nature, be where we were at in the present moment of our personal development. In my last school, in Beauvallon, we were all asked to perform according to what was called being a 'good pupil', we were formatted into a shape that pleased the school organisation and we had no chance of growing into or of expressing who we were as individuals. By breaking into the kitchen, my friends were living exactly where they were at; there was no ideal set between their own 'consciousness' and 'conscience'. I was living my life as I was, where I was at, and I felt that I should not feel bad about having walked away. I wondered what they would say when I returned, and, finding no one to be with in the main building, I slowly walked back towards the carriages. The smell of toast greeted me as I entered the room where my companions were sitting round the coal fire, "Hey! François come and have some buttered toast with us. We also found in the kitchen a tin of golden syrup!" They all laughed. I stood behind the stove warming my hands around the hot flue, "No thanks, I don't feel like any just now." I replied without much conviction. "You know François, normally every pupil that comes to Summerhill steals, especially at the beginning…" Clive said and continued after a short pause, "There must be something wrong with you for not joining in with us." Then another boy took over, "Neill apparently says that what pushes people to steal, is a lack of parental love, and that we take back the love we were deprived of by stealing." I noticed that there had been no judgement on my walking away from the kitchen, as if they respected my behaviour as it was. What they were saying made sense to me; I felt relaxed and at home with them now. "Yes, my mother gave me an enormous amount of love, more than I would want at times; she always gave me her support in any circumstances, without judgement, without criticism. Even when I do something stupid, she does not reprimand me. She just loves me whatever I do!" I replied feeling thankful for having such a Mum.

The conversation seemed to interest all of us. A Swedish boy who had been silent up to now, commented, "You are lucky François, to have such a nice and understanding mum; mine is, on the contrary to yours, after me all the time: Why don't you do it that way? You shouldn't do that! Come here! Go there! Eat this! Don't drink that!" And he continued, "In fact, to tell you the truth, I much prefer to be here than at home with her!" The conversation went late into the night. Each boy had his say about his parents, about their relationships, the arguments that went on at home, the father who was never there, or who was too authoritative or alcoholic. I realised how lucky I was to have such an understanding mother; a hidden wave of love flew towards her. I was not able to talk about the masculine presence in my home. I told them that my father had died in the war, but I was not clear enough inside myself about Fonsou to talk about him. I did not really give my friends a true picture of where I was in the mum/dad relationship in myself. I still missed Marcel Lassalle very much. He was my father figure and I had placed him so high that no one else could replace him, and certainly not my mother's partner.

Although I easily adapted myself to the free Summerhillian life, most nights, I cried about my dad; the tears were probably my way of keeping close to him. It never came to me that I could have talked about these tears with someone; that part of my life was entirely kept to myself and not even my sister knew about it. I'm sure she had no idea that her little brother missed his dad so much. Maman did not know; she would have been the last one to tell, as I would not have wanted her to witness my suffering. I wanted to paint; not questioning it, I just went into the art room and painted passionately. I felt relieved for a short while, after each one and was then able to get on with other things.

Meeting with A.S. Neill

"François, François!" I heard Philip's voice calling excitedly one day while I was in the art room, "Neill wants to see you, up there… in his office." I was surprised; Neill had never called for me before. I wondered what it was all about while washing the paint off my brushes and putting safely away my wet painting for it to dry. Had something happened to my mother? Was it a phone call from her? Was it a phone call about my grandmother? The questions were coming one after the other as I climbed up the great staircase two by two. Philip, as curious as ever, was following close behind.

Coming up to the big oak door of the Head Master's office, I waited for a few seconds and glanced coolly at my clinging and inquisitive young friend, wishing that he would mind his own business. I then knocked timidly. "Come in!" said a croaky voice as he cleared his throat. I opened the door slowly and put my head in, smiling shyly, "Come, come in," Neill said invitingly; I closed the door behind me. "Take a seat." He offered, pointing to the comfortable leather armchair opposite his desk. I sat down quietly and looked around… Neill was sitting at his large leather top desk with his back to the window and a tall filing cabinet projected a dark shadow onto the ancient Olivetti machine he was typing on. An angle poise lamp was trying to eliminate this shadow, making it difficult for me to see him. The room was panelled, bookshelves on two of the walls were loaded with books; without looking at me he went on typing, obviously finishing what he had on his mind. A few minutes later the typing stopped, the desk light was turned off, he pushed himself away from the desk to liberate his long legs, which he then crossed and, to my complete surprise, he commented: "So, I hear from the teachers, that you are the happiest pupil in the school? Always laughing… Is that so?" "Yes, Neill, I am happy in Summerhill." I replied joyfully. And after a slight pause, Neill continued, "Tell me, how is it then that every night you cry in your bed?" I was flabbergasted! My mouth dropped open. How on earth did he know that I cried at night in my bed? How did he know my most profound secret, which I had not even told my mother or my sister? I tried to hold back my tears as I felt them flooding up, and managed to say emotionally, "How do you know this Neill?" "Well, it's easy François, I just look at your paintings and they tell me how you're feeling deep down inside yourself." His answer triggered off the flood of tears I had been holding and I did not resist their flow. I felt then that I could be completely myself with Neill, who had suddenly become a second father, in fact more than that, as he was the first man who really understood the suffering deep inside me. I was able to share with him how Marcel Lassalle had left the island to go to join the French army in 1940 and how he had died apparently electrocuted in early 1943 in Germany. I told Neill of the difficulties that I had in communicating with Fonsou, but he suddenly changed the subject, "You're a lucky boy you know, you have a wonderful mum. We talked a lot together, she's a fine and interesting woman and she is so open to new ideas in education."

I felt happy that Neill said he liked my Maman, and became so full of joy that I felt like dancing and singing just there in his office! Something changed, shifted inside me, and I discovered an unexpected peaceful space inside my chest. He then said with affirmation, "You can go now." Although I would have liked to stay longer with him, I rose to my feet, smiling to my ears and, as I went out of the room, I said, "Thank you Neill."

Once on the landing, to my delight Philip had gone. My whole body was feeling weightless, explosive, as if I had drunk a mysterious magic potion. I flew down the stairs hardly touching the steps, into the main hall and darted through the porch, into the open air where I felt my being expanding into pure joy. There seemed to be no limits around me, not even the sky. An immense feeling of love for Neill overtook my being, and I became aware that it would be with me forever. I did not cry at night any more; after that visit my life had opened up into a new dimension.

Discovering the subtleties of English

No barber came to Summerhill to cut the children's hair. Either the pupils had it cut when they went back home on holiday, or the girls cut it between themselves and when a boy trusted the teasing girls, he let them do it. But some of us used our own pocket money to have it done by a professional in Leiston. Once Tony and I were in the village together and he pointed to a barber's shop in the High Street, saying, "That's where my mum takes me."

My hair was much too long for my taste, so I decided, on an early crisp Saturday morning, to ride to the village on my bike. I came to the barber's shop, leaned the bike against the wall under its front window, and pushed the door open. An overwhelming smell of eau de Cologne, mixed with a powerful smell of English tobacco, hit me as I walked in. At the same moment, I heard a bronze bell ringing over my head activated by the opening of the door, as I discovered when looking up.

The noisy conversation stopped; in the silence all eyes were staring in my direction. The barber, his hands and scissors completely mingled in his client's hair, said with a heavy Suffolk accent, "Good morning Sir, take a seat, won't be long now!" The client sitting in the chair was a red-faced man resembling a statue carved out of a pink marble; he was absolutely still, lifeless. Three elderly guys waiting on the only bench had not stopped staring at me, making me feel as 'the stranger'. "Good morning, can I have my hairs cut please?"

I said with confidence. After a hesitant instant, there was an explosion of laughter from all the men in the shop! Even the one sitting in the barber's chair! The barber, who had lowered his arms, said once he had stopped laughing, "Sure, I'll cut your 'hairs' all right, if you so desire!" Another explosion of laughter came from the men. Self-consciously, I sat down at the end of the queue now red in the face, feeling hot and sweaty and wondering what was so funny about having one's hairs cut.

Two more men arrived, we squeezed up, they were not very talkative, and the little they said I could not follow due to their broad local accent. Finally my turn came to sit in the old swivel armchair. A white nylon sheet was thrown over my shoulders and tightly tucked inside the collar of my shirt. The barber leaning slightly forward and turning his head to look into my eyes, said in a questioning manner, "So, we want some hairs cut off, do we?" "Yes!" I confirmed. Another explosion of laughter filled the room. I felt the blood shooting up into my head, and my ears started to throb. What the hell is so funny about that! I thought to myself. "But there ain't no hairs!" The barber managed to utter as he scrutinized my face and triggering another wave of laughter. I pointed to my head uttering through my tight lips, "Cut!"

"Oh, so we want our hair cut then?" He said, as if he had just understood, and laughed again, "Yes!" I retorted sharply feeling irritated by their games. "Anything else Sir?" the barber asked as he swivelled my chair towards the large wall mirror, placing another mirror behind me to show me the result of his work. I wasn't too impressed, I must say, it was way too short; I didn't like the manner in which he used his brand new Electric cutter instead of scissors. "Thank you!" I replied quickly, longing to get out of the place. I freed myself from the white nylon sheet and left the swivel chair, paid him the sixpence due, said goodbye and left. I felt immediately relieved by the cool air outside gripping my ears and round my head; it was nice as I had been much too hot in the barber's shop, and I jumped on my bicycle to ride back to school.

When I arrived on the large forecourt of the school, I noticed Brum walking towards the porch. As he saw me arriving he smiled, "You look like an American GI with your awful crew-cut," he remarked, amused. I did not reply to his remark, too intrigued by what had happened at the barber's shop. "John? Tell me: why did all the men in the barber's shop laugh when I said that I wanted my hairs cut?" Brum started laughing too and making a funny face he pointed to his pubic, then to his armpits, then to his arms and legs saying, "Hairs, hairs, hairs." Then pointing to his curly hair he explained, "All this is hair, no 's', one hair, two hair!" I now understood why all the men had laughed and thought that I would never put my feet in this barbershop again. Then John and I had a big laugh together about it, as I gave him more funny details of the event.

I liked it when people laughed at what I said, or due to my funny behaviour, but it was awfully unpleasant when people laughed at me when I had not specially meant to provoke laughter.

The first time I played cricket was another occasion when I felt much embarrassment. We, the Summerhillian boys, had organised with the sport teachers of the village school, a cricket match on the village grounds. The large field was outside Leiston and I was waiting for my turn to bat along one side in a shelter. I had never played cricket before, so I had not been placed as the first batter, but the third or fourth, giving me time to study the game to see what was needed of me. After some time into the game, the referee, who was native of the village, called on the top of his voice, "Arsehole?"… A long silence followed while everybody looked round to see who this person could be? The voice repeated the call but this time louder, "Arsehole!" A tremor of restrained laughter went round the field. Clive, who was to bat after me, knocked my arm with his elbow to get my attention and said quietly into my ear, "I think it's your turn to bat now."

Not understanding why my name had not been said out clearly, like it had been with all the previous players, dragging my bat behind me I walked courageously yet nervously, to the centre of the pitch. As I advanced, I could hear some people laughing, not the Summerhillians, but all the locals, and they were now shouting excitedly,

"Arsehole, Arsehole…" Now feeling very self-conscious, I stood by the wicket, adjusted my bat into position and waited for the hard leather covered, wooden ball to arrive. And it did at a tremendous speed! Hitting the three stumps violently, sending flying into the air the two bails, before I could even lift up my bat! I was out and heard another roar of laughter and a few claps of hands as I walked away to my seat confused. "Orefield next!" The referee shouted. I leaned towards Tony, who was next to me, "Why did the referee call me Arsehole?" Tony smiled and explained kindly, "He didn't really call you Arsehole, but with the broad local accent, Lassalle, sounds like 'assalle', which can be heard as 'arsehole'." I was learning slowly, sometimes painfully, the subtleties of the local accents!

Fonsou told many rude Provençal jokes, and I had been longing to share them with my Summerhill friends, but had not felt sure enough of my English to attempt to tell them.

Now, that I was more confident with the language, my talking moved at the same speed as my thoughts, making me practically fluent. I did not have to search for my words any more. One day, I was standing with a group of four boys in the forecourt; they were telling English jokes, each one hoping that his would be better than the previous one. I enjoyed English humour, it wasn't so direct as the French, it was more devious and subtle, one laughed, but not right away; one waited in jubilation for the cherry to be put on the cake, then according to its finesse, one would comment: "that's a good one!" Or "brilliant!" Then one allowed a measured laugh out; when the joke was good the laugh lasted longer and was more generous.

After some hesitation, I finally decided to take a plunge into the space created by a joke that had not been so funny and now was my time! In the hope of getting a good response, I chose a rather crude one about 'Fannie and Marius' of Marseilles. It went something like this…

'One day, the very blonde Fannie in her mini skirt was getting her legs browned by the morning sun and was standing on the wall that overlooked the famous fisherman's harbour. She was watching the fishing boats coming in with their latest catch. Marius, a long time friend of Fannie's, was gathering fishing nets down below on the wooden quay and upon seeing her, he looked up and exclaimed with a large smile, "Hey Fannie! I always thought that you were a blonde!" And waving her hands rapidly over the upper parts of her legs, she replied, "Oh yes I am, it's only these blooming flies!" I had a job to put in that last phrase, as jerks of laughter had already invaded my chest and I was expecting my friends to follow suit! But there prevailed a deadly silence, followed by a heavily expressed response, "Disgusting!!!" Disarmed by the effect of my joke, I looked round at my friends for some kind of support, a bit of help, even just a little sign of amusement, but nothing except other reprimanding words. One of the boys said, "Filthy French jokes!" Feeling completely abandoned with my 'filthy French joke', there was no way I could have told the other jokes that were queuing at the back of my mind. Some were really good ones too! The one about Fannie dreaming that she was serving at the petrol station… and especially the one about the director, who, at a board meeting, after a good meal was standing on his chair was about to deliver his speech… but I now realised that the differences in cultures were too great and that there was no way these jokes could make my English friends laugh; I would only deteriorate further my own image together with that of my compatriots.

I learnt that day, that it was preferable not to share some parts of my original culture, if I wanted to fit in with the British. As much as it was possible I put away my own culture, as if I had changed my jacket for another, a tweedier one, or a Viyella shirt from Marks & Spencer's, and I tried to wear them phlegmatically like an Englishman. After this painful experience, I kept my French jokes to myself, opened my ears fully to English humour and learned to appreciate it, to cultivate it and to become one with it.

I was feeling part of the school now, I belonged to it somehow, I found harmony with it and would have defended it to anybody who tried to discredit it. Summerhill had become my town, my city, actually my culture. I liked the social aspect of the school, taking part in it broadened my understanding of the psychological interplay between people and myself. Yes, there was no hierarchic difference between pupils-teachers-headmaster as each individual had the same importance. Each was free to be who he or she was, and carried fully the consequences of his or her behaviour.

Now that I could follow all the discussions at the Saturday afternoon meetings, I took an interest in what was being said, sometimes coming in with a suggestion or an idea on how to solve a problem. They were called propositions, and once one was put forward, the chair of the meeting asked: "Proposition accepted?" Then a show of hands followed, and after careful counting, the chairperson announced, "Proposition accepted or proposition refused." These meetings ran the school, rules of behaviour were done and undone, and it was important that the majority felt happy about the decisions taken. Not all matters were resolved at the Saturday assemblies and often the children themselves resolved their problems with each other soon after the events. Like when I hit the American boy Jimmy: it was never mentioned at meetings. Nor did I mention the incident when Philip stole the one-pound note from my wallet.

Neill's wife Ena looked after the organisation of the kitchen and she regularly reported, with some anger and agitation that the kitchen had been broken into again. She did not realise how much fun it was to break into the kitchen, and how the older children who took part gradually became more and more expert at this game. One day Ena complained at a meeting that for several weeks she had noticed that tins of fruit in syrup, butter, biscuits, cheddar cheese and other expensive food had gone missing, and she authoritatively added, "I have no idea how the little devils get in there, but they must stop doing this as they are robbing the community!" Well, a few of us knew the secret of how to penetrate the larder. It might have been Clive who, with another boy, found the clever trick of introducing a piece of cardboard in the female part of the Yale lock, so that the latch was unable fall completely into its socket. That was done while the kitchen staff were deep inside the larder, facing the shelves... afterwards, by pushing hard with one's shoulder, the door would fly open, giving free access to the Aladdin's cave. This activity went on for quite some time until eventually the boys decided to stop doing it. The staff never discovered the mystery of the piece of cardboard blocking the lock. Of course there had been also other occasions that preceded this one, when for instance, Toby, John and Michael Proudlock managed to pinch the key of the larder without the staff noticing. The art of these exercises of course, was to be undetected. When it came up at the meetings Ena gesticulated to manifest her anger; but I never heard Neill mention anything on the subject; rather he played it down as an unimportant matter. He certainly was not for punishment, and considered stealing as a process some children had to go through before the need to steal would dissipate.

Finding more confidence with the girls

We enjoyed Saturday evenings as the only moment in the week when together we listened to jazz and danced. We exchanged and discussed our latest discoveries, such as Negro Spirituals or New Orleans jazz records. Sharing them was an important part of our getting to know each other. Dancing with different girls each time brought a new sensation. With Tessa it was chatty: she talked loudly to override the sound of the music; maybe the reason was that being small, she was far from my ear? She danced well, moving so lightly that I hardly felt her in my hands. Of course, deep down my heart was with Mary, and my attention was discreetly on the lookout for her. It was not the first time that I had fallen in love; in Dieulefit with Roseline, when my shyness turned into a faraway dream that I enjoyed living – just by looking at her I felt my heart swell. And on the island, when I was very young, it was Didi, with her curly fair hair and her contagious laughter, who also made my heart swell...

With Mary I had to hold back my passionate horses that wanted to run off in a wild gallop with her; I played it cool, so that she would not notice my true feelings. I was happy when she was laughing, and wanted to comfort her when she was sad or seemed distant. So, I chose very carefully the moment to propose a dance. Before catching her attention, I first felt whether she was in a space where she would be available. If I saw the space, I offered her the dance, and, as I led her into it, my feelings expanded discreetly and invisibly enrobed her presence. As if she had entered into my own garden, I felt peaceful and happy yet fully aware of her lively firm body responding beautifully to the rhythms of the New Orleans jazz. Sometimes, in the turbulence of the jive, the prominent parts of our bodies touched inadvertently, bringing closer the delicate bouquet of her aroma and unexpectedly taking me, for a brief instant, into the sensuous world of oneness. But the meeting with my partner's smiling witty eyes would rapidly draw my presence back into the more earthy reality of our dance.

With Jill it was quite different. I knew she liked me and it would usually be her who came up to me for a dance. I was aware that she mostly chose slow blues, she was not so sporty as the others and this kind of music suited her physique and character better. With her questioning prominent blue eyes and a slight smile on her face, she'd come up to me quietly and, without saying anything, would take my hand and lead me to the dance floor. I always accepted her offer without resistance, bodily contact was almost immediate, the warm long fingers would take mine with great gentleness drawing me close, the other hand splayed wide on my back, applying a slight pressure. I felt embraced by womankind, enjoyed the effect and fully allowed to pervade me the feeling of being cradled by the feminine. At times the length of her thigh met mine and it felt good. We did not talk much, but allowed the rhythms of the music to unite with our bodies.

One Saturday night, Jill whispered close into my ear during one of the last dances before the end of term, "Is it okay if I come to your bedroom tonight?" She had been particularly affectionate that evening, almost to the point where I felt embarrassed at the thought of others noticing her passionate behaviour. I looked around to see that the room was almost empty except for a group of lads up by the music box. The part in me that was so attracted to Mary did not want to follow this hot request, but my whole body was lit by an unknown desire to discover Woman and merge blindly with the as yet un-tasted waters of the feminine. We walked down to the carriages; her arm was around my waist and mine around hers. We were silent, both allowing what was to come. There were no images in my mind, which felt at rest: my attention was all in my perception. I could hear her breathing, smell her feminine presence and feel her soft round body moving as we walked down the concrete slab path. The grating sound of my carriage door seemed to be louder than usual. I noticed in myself a hyper awareness and a change in my breathing; also my thinking was not active, yet my being was completely present.

When we were in my bedroom the atmosphere changed. The room became my ship and we were going together towards some unknown horizon. I closed the door behind me and went up to the head of the bed to switch on the small light that was clipped on the shelf. I did not see Jill undress, as I turned around, she had slipped quietly behind me and was already between the sheets. I took off my clothes rapidly and laid them neatly onto the chair. My breathing quietened down again, and I felt as if I was on the top of a rock by some vast ocean, about to dive into something that possessed all the attention of my senses. I stood there naked for a moment, in between the two worlds, one that I knew well and in which I began to feel the sharp cold creeping up into my body from the floor, the other, a world I knew of but I had not yet explored. "You're getting cold! Come!" She said with concern, revealing the vibes that were moving her heart, her eyes looking at me invitingly. I jumped over her, on the wall side, and crept in, trying not to disturb the bedding. The sheets were freezing damp as usual... Giving me no time to create my own bubble of heat, she turned towards me and murmured gently, "Come." I knew that once our bodies touched, I would be completely taken into the powerful hands of nature.

The sensation was not comparable to what I had expected at moments of sexual daydreaming. Coming into contact with the softness and the delicate warmth of her skin, was beyond expectation. A moment of stillness took over my awareness and, as if perpetuity descending, my senses became totally absorbed, savouring the timeless moment. We must have stayed like this for a very long time, neither one of us wanting to alter the peace; it was as if we had created another living entity. A cosmic wind of love blew a little harder into Jill's sails, and she totally surrendered to it and responded by deepening the experience further, directing her eager burning lips to mine. An almost violent tremor occurred when they fused, our tongues met and intertwined clumsily, sending me further into the depth of my being. It created a space into a dimension I had not known before, where the other extra sensitive parts of my body took over, guided by a primeval instinct that took us into the waters of the most refined feelings. Our intimate embarkation was sailing harmoniously when it suddenly accelerated, as if pulled by some fast rapids. We found ourselves taken by a divine current, the intensity of which somehow brought me back to an earthly sense of responsibility, "We don't want a child, do…" I managed to whisper but before I could finish, she said in a reassuring short breath, "It's okay! I've taken care." We were then propelled together onto an immaculate sandy beach where, enlaced in each other, we found a deep tranquillity. The feeling had become so fine, that I felt weightless and allowed my being to float into space.

When I woke up at dawn, feeling cold, I searched with my hand looking for my night companion… she'd gone. I curled into a little ball and tried to find back the peaceful space we had been in.

That morning, I came into the breakfast room and saw her sitting with the other girls as usual. She gave me a long look as if we were accomplices, but I didn't want to encourage this, and smiled back furtively looking for another table. I wondered whether she had shared her night's experience with her close friends, and I wished this night to be our secret, that we would both keep entirely to ourselves. These moments of natural sexual blossoming spent with Jill were precious. No feeling of guilt was present; together we were just discovering who we were, in the most sensitive parts of our physical and emotional beings. We were both fully aware of the possible fecundity situation that might arise out of our sensuous pleasures, but, as neither of us wanted conception to take place, we took appropriate precautions.

I was surprised to find that there could be a separation between sex and love. Being worried that, after that first night with Jill, my loving feelings towards Mary might be disturbed, I found them untouched, as if they were two completely different worlds. She was still the irresistible fruit to pick and taste, and she certainly knew how to make herself rare and desirable, without going much further than the evening kissing rituals. John and I still enjoyed the agreeable habit of the girls' bedtime rounds that we had made a habit of. When discussing this subject with other pupils, I learnt that up until 1952, only one case of pregnancy had occurred, and that had taken place outside Summerhill School.

End of the first year

Ivor Cutler left the school after the second term of my arrival. I had had time to become close to him but I did not miss his departure, for I was already well integrated into the school's life. Sylvette and Toby and many of the older pupils left the school at the end of the summer term of 1952. The end of term party of the year was always more important than the others; many would not return after the summer and a nostalgic feeling pervaded the festive atmosphere. Decorations were put up in the assembly hall; in the last few weeks the theatre became alive, as we had prepared several plays for the occasion. The older children who could afford it bought drinks, and some of the parents attended the festivities. The weather was warm and pleasant, and everybody seemed very relaxed, although there were some tears when couples had to separate from the shelter of the school to face their unknown futures. My sister was crying, for she did not want to leave Toby, who was consoling her but nothing seemed to stop her tears. It was arranged, between the respective mothers, that he would come and join our family in Vallauris, near Cannes. Once on the Ile du Levant during that summer holiday, Sylvette plucked up her courage and informed Mano about her boyfriend. His reaction was immediate and positive, and he said that he was keen to meet Toby one day. This greatly reassured her.

Our relationship had dramatically changed since the previous year. We had become independent of each other, and, although still close to me, she had now become a woman. Toby took the whole space of her heart, inspiring her to write lengthy letters every day. He wrote frequently, calling her intimately Bira, probably to make him feel that she was really his own. He wrote to our mother as well, who enjoyed reading his letters and thought highly of him.

My first year at the school had brought out positive changes in my self. I did not cry at night any more, I felt more at ease, I could express my feelings more clearly and my understanding about people and myself had broadened. I enjoyed talking about the psychological aspects of things, such as what makes people act like they do, and I understood my brother better too. Mano noticed the changes in both of us and mentioned it to our Maman one day while she was cooking in the kitchen, "The children's stay in your English school has done them a lot of good!" Hearing this was like spreading a soothing, precious balm onto the scars of my heart painfully accumulated from the previous years. This summer holiday was very different, as Sylvette became less irritable and more centred. I was now able to be undisturbed by Mano and Philippe's remarks, and I saw them in a different perspective and allowed them to be who they were, as they were, without being affected by what they thought. I also became less self-conscious with adult women and that was nice! I do not mean sexually, but simply by absorbing their presence into myself; whether they were aware of it or not did not matter. I understood that there was one large invisible feminine part of myself that resided somewhere in the innermost of my whole; I now felt more unity to my being.

During our first year in Summerhill, Maman and Fonsou moved south from Dieulefit to a place called Vallauris, two miles from the sea between Cannes and Antibes. She rented a small one-bedroom flat on the first floor of an old building in the small pottery village. Fonsou found a poorly paid job in one of the nearby potteries and our Mum started a small business making raffia lampshades. One hundred and twenty potters worked in the busy little town, with most of them lining up on the high street with their shop fronts of brightly coloured pottery displayed onto half the pavement. Our mother rightly felt that there would be a demand if she started a small lampshade enterprise. Sylvette and I never went back to Dieulefit after the move. Ten years had elapsed since we'd left the Ile du Levant and arrived in Dieulefit in that freezing cold winter of 1942. Not having taken part in the move made it an abrupt change for us. Maison Martin, the view of the majestic mountains and our animals, vanished suddenly and became stored in the invisible book of experience. We just turned the page, and for me it was easy: the Dieulefit part of our lives was over.

Mum had warned us how small the flat was, explaining that there were two bedrooms beside a small kitchen, but neither Sylvette nor myself had imagined anything close to the reality that we discovered as we entered the old four-storey building Number 3, Rue Sicard. A thin elegant but wobbly metallic balustrade greeted us as we entered the hallway; to its right a hexagonal-tiled stairs each held by an oak threshold, led us up to the first landing. A tall window gave light to Maman who was searching for the key; I saw that a few of the red hexagonal tiles of the floor were missing. The walls were painted pale grey, and under the black dado line, a deep Venetian red. The space in the stairwell echoed to the sound of the key as our mother activated the lock to open the door.

"You'll see, it's a bit small but we are really lucky to have found it!" She said positively as we entered into a tiny kitchen. To the right was a butane gas cooker resting on an ancient walnut bedside table, set inside the original tiled fireplace. I recognized the pine kitchen table covered by the same oilcloth, bringing to my mind many memories of Maison Martin. Wooden boxes with chequered red and white cloth curtains were the storage spaces. One low voltage light bulb hung from the ceiling. We stood there silently... "By the way, to the right is the loo. It's the Turkish type you know... any way, better than the outside one in Dieulefit!" While she talked her nose was in her shopping basket looking for the vegetables to prepare lunch, obviously fully aware of our lack of enthusiasm. Opposite the front door was another that Sylvette opened with curiosity. I followed her into a small corner room with blinding luminosity, due to the sun pouring in through wide-open windows and bouncing off a white partition wall. The only furniture was a single bed and a Provençal straw seat chair. We heard Mum's voice from the kitchen, "This room will be for you and Toby, it gives on Rue Sicard and is a much quieter one than ours!" My sister did not answer, lost in her thoughts, trying to imagine herself with Toby in the small irregular space.

 Wondering where my resting corner would be, I pushed the grey door on my right and stood at the threshold of a dark space; the contrast from the extreme light dampened my vision. When my eyes finally became used to the sun-starved room, I saw that it was much larger. To the left were two windows that gave onto a noisy narrow street; the block opposite was taller and was the main cause for obliterating the daylight. Immediately to my left was a small bed, which I presumed would be mine. At the end of the room, to my right, I could just determine in the obscurity an alcove in which was a double bed filling the whole space. I looked opposite to see a plain black marbled fireplace on which stood an 1870, moulded silver framed, bevelled mirror. Immediately to the right was a tall wardrobe flanked by two chairs. In the middle of the room was an extendable dark oak dining table over which hung a raffia lampshade, probably made by my mother I thought. The dark grey wallpaper was sparsely covered with green and red flowers, which contributed to making the room look weird. The loud strident sound of a siren took me by surprise echoing through the streets of the town as if to make sure that no one would be forgotten. I looked at my watch - it was noon. I heard Sylvette behind me say, "is it where you're going to sleep? Where will Maman and Fonsou sleep then?" "I suppose I'll sleep in this small bed, Maman and Fonsou… I guess, in the cave over there!" I replied sarcastically pointing to the dark hole; there was a short silence then she sighed, "Oh well!" And she walked back towards the kitchen. I threw my bag on my bed and followed her.

I knew that our Maman had practically no money and that Fonsou did not give her much out of the little he earned; she lived mostly on the 300 Francs that Mano kept sending monthly. Yet, as usual, she was positive and said, "You'll see it's going to be fine, this is a lovely town. We'll find some work - Fonsou has! And the blue sea is only 2 kilometres down the road!" My sister's cheeks were now wet with tears and in between two sobs, she said with desperation, "It's not fair, we never have any money, and what if Toby left me because of all this?" Maman did not have time to reply as the door of the kitchen opened and Fonsou appeared. He stood there in the doorway wearing his sleeveless vest and usual grey dusty shorts, smiling hesitantly. "Bonjour Fonsou!" We both said monotonously and in unison, as we went up to kiss him. His presence and body odour brought me back to Dieulefit, when he used to take me to the town's football club where he'd disappear to the bar to drink Pastis while I watched the game. "Bonjour!" He replied, his smile now more relaxed expressing happiness to see us. After having kissed Maman from the extremity of his lips, he sat down just as he always had, ready for his meal. In a short time she had prepared a delicious lunch, we helped her to lay the table and I fetched the two extra chairs from the bedroom.

Knowing that I would soon go back to Summerhill School, and that my stay in Rue Sicard would be short, I felt deeply for my sister who was feeling quite distraught. There would be no privacy in her room, it was really only a passage into the other, and she was anticipating Toby's reaction. During the meal, no feelings were expressed about the situation. I asked Fonsou a few questions about his work in the pottery and they were answered by a yes or no, as he found it difficult to find the words to express his feelings. Our mother often tried to lead him into a conversation, "He does like his work at the pottery... don't you? It's better paid than in Dieulefit, isn't it?" But he would rarely reply more than a short sentence. At quarter to two precisely, he said, "Bon! It's time to go to work." He would then wipe his mouth with his serviette, push back his chair, kiss our mother and repeat always in the same tone of voice, "See you later." As soon as he had left, the three of us came back into what I felt was the family, where we could laugh, cry and express whatever we felt freely.

The time came for me to go back to England, this time by myself without my sister who was now waiting for her beloved Toby to arrive. Her love for him took over everything, it was her priority and his love for her gave her security. I helped her to arrange their bedroom and make it as pleasant as was possible. In the late afternoon we took the bus to Cannes railway station. Maman and Sylvette sat and I stood, looking out empty minded at the passing landscape: how beautiful this part of the world was, with its ultramarine sea, the red ragged coast, the palm trees, the hills with the Alps beyond. I breathed in deeply, feeling happy that my family had moved to the prosperous Côte d'Azur.

In a bustling cloud of vapour and smoke the train appeared on the platform. After finding the appropriate carriage, I gave my sister a long hug, then I turned to my mother and in her tender embrace, I felt the loving bond that we had for each other. Letting go of her François onto the large ocean of life, was not an easy matter for her. As I pulled myself away to climb the tall steps into the carriage, she said with some emotions and watery eyes, "You will take care of yourself, won't you?" "Yes, I will Maman!" The whistle blew, the train moved, we waved to each other until I had to close the door of the carriage as we were picking up speed and entering the first tunnel. This train coming from Nice was practically empty; I found my compartment and a seat by the window, threw my sailor's bag into the net above my place and sat down. A middle-aged woman who was sitting opposite me, smiled kindly. On the extreme end of her bench seat was a large man sleeping with his mouth open and his fingers crossed, hands resting over his prominent belly.

Suddenly I felt an infinite space around me, I was on my way back to England, just with myself. Any decisions I took from now on, I would carry the consequences. For the first time I felt responsibility for my person. 'I'll have to look after this guy François now,' I thought, and it felt good. I'd become the driver, alone in my world facing the immensity of what surrounded me. I closed my eyes, into nothingness... just hearing the regular knocks of the metallic wheels hitting the intervals between the rails. The loud puffing of the steam engine echoed against the cliff, and the whistle blew announcing another forthcoming tunnel. Across the corridor window, I observed the normally deep blue sea, turned golden in the sunset. In my mind and feelings I pictured Sylvette and Maman on the bus, chatting and preparing for the coming of Toby who was due in a few days. I understood my departure would create a different dynamic between them, the joyful complicities of the mixing of feminine energies. That evening they would probably go to the cinema, just by themselves.

The second year at this wonderful school

The next day from Liverpool Street I took the train to Leiston, and noticed how arriving at Summerhill on my own was different. I felt changed, not quite the same person as I had been before the summer, feeling now more aware and fully responsible for myself.

Was it due to my roots being pulled out of Dieulefit? Or that I did not feel my mother's flat at n°3 rue Sicard was a place where I would ever live? Now my roots will have to be in a place somewhere deep inside myself, where I was beginning to feel comfortable. Also, the fact that the older pupils had left meant Brum, Clive, Mary, Jill and the others of our age group now became 'the older ones'.

It felt like coming home when I walked back to my carriage room, and life in Summerhill continued as if I'd never left it. We socialised more and enjoyed developing our thoughts together, about all kinds of subjects: about the well-being of the school, politics, nuclear threat and the cold war, standard education as opposed to Neill's ideas, about the conscious and the unconscious, about nonviolence and the thoughts of becoming a conscientious objector, about films we had seen, or our latest discoveries in music. There was no competition to take command of the conversation, but it was more of an exchange; a feeling of togetherness pervaded the discussions. Of course, it did not mean that we agreed on all subjects, but there was a respect for each other's opinion.

John and I, with playmate simplicity, did not wait to re-ignite our insatiable pleasures of the kissing rounds. Re-uniting with our feminine friends after the two months of summer was indeed something to look forward to, it contributed greatly in developing my maturity, bringing me closer to the fuller person I was discovering in myself. That first evening of our return from the holidays, I sat down on Mary's bed first and was surprised to notice how my attraction towards her had not diminished but had actually increased. Discreetly, I tried to keep my feelings to myself and show reserve, as I suspected that she might not feel the same way towards me; the last thing I wanted to do, was to trespass on her feelings, or upset her. I therefore moved on quickly to Tessa, then to Jill who too played it cool; we both secretly knew that sometime later, alone in intimacy, we would let our bodies follow their natural instinctive paths. Jackie was next, she asked me if I'd had a good holiday and we chatted a few minutes before I left the room.

Our bicycles played an important part in contributing to our feeling of freedom. They allowed us to leave the school and go as far as the North Sea coast and its beautiful dunes; also we often visited Aldeburgh, a small coastal town, where we went to see films in the spacious cinema. Sometimes we cycled north to Dunwich Heath, where we played in an abandoned military airport overtaken by heather-covered sand dunes in colourful mauve patterns. Dunwich had been a village that was now partly falling off the cliffs into the sea.

Swimming in the yellow-grey North Sea with its constant wind and shallow waters going into sudden depth and coming up again into sandbanks, was very different from swimming in the Mediterranean. Not only was the water cold, but it was sticky; the very fine sand, stirred up by the constantly moving waters, stuck to your body, to your clothes, socks and into your shoes. Of course my English mates were not able to compare this sea to the Med, which they might only have seen on postcards; so these conditions did not disturb them. It took me some time to get used to this new situation and I later found that there was actually something pleasant when the freezing waters stung my skin; at times it could even feel warmer in than out when the cold wind was blowing. Shivering, we would dry ourselves and jump back onto our bicycles feeling revived, as if we had absorbed new energies from the sea.

My bicycle was a good bargain; Uncle Ralph together with GG had given me the money to buy it second hand. It was tall, black, with wide chromed handlebars garnished with a bell and two powerful brakes. The general condition was good although it had no gears, but the ratio seemed to be perfect for the flat roads of the region. The seat was wide and comfortable and it was a pleasure to ride, especially after having ridden my horrible little pale mauve bike in Dieulefit. I enjoyed cleaning it, tying a piece of string on the hubs of the wheels so as to keep them constantly shiny, fixing lights on to it, and a luggage carrier which I discovered to be most practical to carry my swimming gear. For some reason, the girls did not seem to be as bike-minded as we were; sometimes they came to the beach with us, but in the cinema, they preferred to be amongst themselves.

Once I had gone with two friends to see a film in Aldeburgh; the cycling had been a struggle for the 6 miles as there was a violent wind coming in from the sea. When we arrived in the small town we could hear the tremendous roar of the waves breaking on the beach beyond the high street. In fact, after parking our bikes, we saw slight flooding further down the high street. We had cycled the long distance to the cinema and needed to rest from the exhausting ride against the wind, so we did appreciate falling into the comfortable red velvet seats and, with no resistance, allowed ourselves to be completely absorbed by the exciting pictures of the film. At about halfway through the film, we heard a kerfuffle behind us by the exit; people were getting up and going out in a hurry. The film was stopped, lights were put on and we saw that in there was water in the well of the room! We heard people cry out, "The sea is invading the town!" "Quick, everybody out of the cinema!" Clive, Tony and I left our seats, paddled through a few inches of water and came outside to realise that our bicycles were already in a foot of water. It was an incredible scene; all the lights went out and the howling wind together with the breaking of the waves made it difficult to hear one another. "We'd better get on our bikes quick and get out of here!" shouted Tony, his voice rising high with adrenalin. Wet up to well over our ankles, we pushed our bikes through the flooded streets until we came to the beginning of the slow hill that took us back on the road to Leiston.

The next day we decided to go back and see what had happened as we heard on the news that it was probably the biggest flood of the century on the east coast of England.

This time we wore wellington boots and left our bikes in a thick bush at the bottom of the hill. Seagulls were crying aloud all at once as if they were desperate to tell us what they were seeing. We were amazed to discover that heaps of pebbles had been rolled into the streets by the furious waters at high tide. The shoreline had changed: it seemed as if half the beach had been removed and the sea had taken its place. It was still very rough although the tide was on its way out. The powerful wind loaded with sea spray challenged our curiosity to investigate the beaches. It was difficult for us to walk straight on the heaps of wet pebbles mingled with seaweeds, driftwood and all kinds of man-made rejects. Soaked by the seawater, we finally reached the bottom of the town where the river Alde that normally flowed sharp right at Slaughden, stopped by the 'Orford ness' (a 20 mile long sandbank), forcing it to flow south before it reaches the sea. Well, the Equinoctial tide, together with the strong winds and the rain, had forced the swollen river to come over its bank, thus creating a gigantic lake. There were many men with water up to their knees frantically placing sandbags with the help of a bulldozer, trying to stop the flow of the water going into the village and divert the Alder back to its original course. But there was a hopeless disproportion between the power of the elements and the few men bravely trying to save their homes. Eventually the wind stopped, the sea drew back, Aldeburgh dried out and all that was left of it was in the memory of its inhabitants.

GG, my beloved grandmother, came to visit me some months later and stayed in a delightful old cottage turned into a bed and breakfast on the heights just behind the small town. For some reason she did not come to Summerhill this time, but thought it better to spend a few days at the sea resort. Riding my bike I went to visit her on the Saturday for a meal, and on Sunday for tea. It was out of season and we searched for a place to eat, finally finding only one place open, where they served us greasy fish and chips with tomato ketchup and a strong cup of tea. It wasn't to my grandmother's taste, or mine, but we enjoyed each other's company so much it didn't matter.

I knew that she had been brought up in a public school where punishment was the rule, and realised that A.S. Neill's educational ideas were well beyond her comprehension. She did not ask me any questions about how the school was run, but preferred to answer my questions about my grandfather and her, where they had been, what they had done in their lives together. She always carried a Bible with her and certainly delighted herself in telling me about Jesus, but without trying to convince me one way or another. She was impressed by my apparent maturity, by the fluidity of my English, although I loved talking French to her just to incite her to follow suit, so that I could hear her exquisite soft English accent. She was always dressed in blue, a royal blue, always wore a hat the same colour when she went out; her tiny feet were tightly fitted in top-quality navy blue shoes. I enjoyed making her laugh, putting her hands between her knees, she'd throw her head back and reveal the inside of her bright pink coloured palate and creamy-white false teeth. Sometimes, if what I said had been extremely funny, the brace would start to wobble about in her mouth, and the naughty boy that I was thought that it was hilarious.

Grandfather Edward had died the previous year, after being in a wheelchair for 12 years, half paralysed with poliomyelitis. She had nursed him and looked after him all that time and was now re-adapting herself to a new life on her own.

Uncle Ralph and Kay came to visit us twice in his sumptuous Jaguar when Sylvette was still at Summerhill. He and Kay only had sons and this was probably the reason why he adored my sister as if she was his own daughter. We appreciated these visits, taking us out to posh restaurants serving us red wine and roast beef and Yorkshire pudding; it was a real treat after the boring and monotonous meals at the school. Ralph and Kay were interested in the educational ways of Summerhill School and at the table they would ask us many questions about how it was run. Some time later, they decided to send their own boys, Brian, Philip and Tim, to Dartington Hall, in Devonshire. The complete freedom offered by Summerhill was for them too much to grasp, and they felt Dartington Hall would be better suited to their sons. Dartington was not as free as Summerhill but it was a mixed school that believed in self-discipline, although I learned later that my cousin Tim, when found in bed with a girl, was thrown out of the school!

That second year in Summerhill helped me to build up my self-confidence. Since my visit to Neill's office, the heavy burden I had been carrying relating to my father had gone, and I was now much happier in myself. With my improved English, I was able now to follow the lessons and enjoyed them thoroughly, especially classes with Neill, although mathematics was not really my strength. Jimmy East was most direct and demanding. He did not accept rubbishy answers to his precise questions, and I liked the atmosphere in his comfortable room and discovered with delight the finesses of English prose and poetry that has no equivalent in the French, Latin-based language.

The year went by terribly quickly and there was no time to be bored. Every day was filled with living in the moment, whether in the art room painting, in the classroom studying, sitting in the sun with other pupils chatting, writing letters to my mum, playing the piano or doing some sports outside, dancing and listening to music… all these activities kept me fully occupied. I felt able to grow at my own rhythm and speed without interference or conditioning from outside. Summer was already arriving and we were preparing for the end of term festivities. The nostalgic feelings that I'd felt the previous year and described earlier in the chapter, started to take a grip on my heart. It was hard to come to terms with the fact that my stay at Summerhill was coming to an end. I felt inwardly so thankful for having been there, knowing that the two years had helped me to liberate myself from the invisible chains restraining me. I had now grown out of my Summerhillian frame and needed a different space to develop further into who I was.

I realised that my academic training had been inconsistent, both in French and in English, and that made me feel slightly nervous when having to face the outside world. But I knew that somehow I would manage, and that my passionate interest in the arts was to be the road I'd choose to walk on. This end of term party was for me a particularly vivid moment; it was a bit like putting a full stop at the end of a sentence, or like coming to the last page of the book that you've been captivated reading. It was difficult to close it but I knew that it was unavoidable. Talking to my close friends, wondering where and when we would see each other again, not knowing what the future would bring, created a kind of floating atmosphere in each one of us. A small part of me had already left, yet I was still relishing each instant with a kind of gluttony, as if finishing a delicious dish. I took a few addresses knowing too well that I would not contact most of them for a long time, if ever? Clive said he wanted to study dentistry; John was going to try to be a conscientious objector, so as not to do the British military service. Tony had already gone back to Ipswich where his mother had moved, and was talking about going into the air force. Mary was going back to finish her schooling in Canada where her father was a diplomat, and Tessa, Gill, and Jackie were going on with their studies in England.

We danced and feasted till late, everyone wanting to enjoy the last moments. Only the younger pupils had gone to bed, not yet finished living their own Summerhill book. There had been no round of kisses in the girl's bedroom that last Saturday; the agreeable routine had already been stored somewhere in the depths of my positive experiences.

I danced with all the girls who were leaving, and with each one the feeling was different, the character of each made my behaviour change, adapting myself the best I could to the nature of each. With Mary I knew there was a strong link that would stay on, although I had no idea when I'd see her again. While dancing I felt free and light, living fully these last moments together; attentively feeling the movements of her body and almost happy to know that the attractive fruit would not be around any more to test my composure.

The last girl I danced with was Jill. We both knew that after the dance we'd leave the ballroom together, first side-by-side, then, as we came away from the hub of the evening, our bodies came closer my arms round her waist, hers round mine. There was no passionate desire in me to spend a hot last night with her! No, it was not like that, sex had not yet taken a space in my thinking. It was just a natural thing to follow, as if we were obeying some powerful hidden law that came from a world we were just beginning to discover. Delicately, almost slowly, we climbed the ladder of feelings and as they became finer and finer we arrived at a point when there was no more ladder and we just dissolved in unison.

I woke up the next morning feeling extremely happy and light. Jill, following her character, liked to wake up in her own bed and had left at an early hour. There was much to do that morning and after a quick breakfast I had returned to my bedroom to pack and tidy up the room. I went round to the hut behind the theatre, to say goodbye to Harry. I was very fond of him and we had spent some good times together in the art room. He appreciated my visit and we chatted; he encouraged me to pursue my art and asked me if I knew what I was going to do next? "You'll keep me informed of your whereabouts, won't you?" were his last words as we parted.

Then I went to kiss Ulla goodbye, my dear housemother. I felt close to her although I had not seen much of her. Her presence and attention was constant and as I left she said lovingly, "Take care of yourself, and give all my love to your mother, Sylvette… and don't forget Toby." "Yes I will Ulla, I promise!" I answered as I left her bedroom. In the forecourt I met Ena. She looked at me and smiled: "You're going back to France aren't you? We'll miss you at the school, it's been good to have you here," she said kindly. Ena could be very kind to the pupils she liked, but she could be pretty hard and awful to the ones she did not get on with. My French habits must have been creeping back into me, as I responded by leaning forward to give her a kiss. Unaccustomed to this "frog" habit, and taken by surprise, she turned her head when I was about to kiss her cheek, which resulted in a clash of noses creating a short confusion. She tensed up, letting out a dry embarrassed giggle and tapped my shoulder gently as she pushed me away,

"Have a good journey home, my love to Honor!" She said as she turned away in the direction of the main building. Zoe, their daughter who must have been 4 or 5 at the time, was standing there watching us. She was wearing a short sleeved, round collared, pale pink chequered dress; her long thin legs in white socks and dark leather sandals gave her a fairy tale appearance. Her lively black eyes had been amused by the incident, her open mouth revealed the large gap of her missing front teeth. She looked up at me shyly for an instant longer and smiled; then suddenly, she departed after her mother.

Many of the older pupils had already left by car with their parents or relatives, and there were not so many of us left to take the train at Leiston railway station. A small group was waiting on the platform. Neill arrived to see us off and came up to me slowly in his usual way, with his large black shoes pointing in, his brown corduroy trousers, his chequered Canadian jacket, "So, you're going home, hey?… It's been good to have you here. Give my fondest regards to your mother." He said this softly, his thin lips hardly moving while the strong Scottish accent pushed the words out. "Thank you Neill, yes, I will!" This was all I could say, while giving him the biggest of my smiles.

Summerhill School

CHAPTER 5

Tony, John & François

Neill, Zoe and Inal

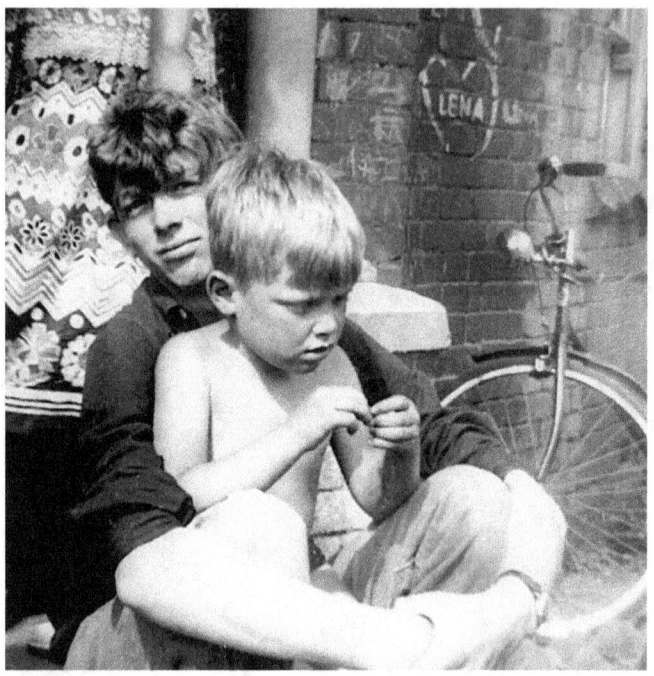
François and Storm sitting at the entrance of the school

Jill and Mary

CHAPTER 6

Chapter 6

Vallauris 1953 and Student life in Paris 1954-1956

The time spent in Summerhill changed many things in me, and one of them was that I felt fully independent and responsible for my own decisions. I did not need to refer to mother or Sylvette to make up my mind any more. On the whole, my stay in England had been extremely positive, but for my French school academic level, it had been pretty disastrous. I had stopped my French education at the age of 12, and although my reading was acceptable, my French expression and writing was poor. I decided to try and complete my Baccalaureate at the Lycée Carnot in Cannes, and registered my name for the coming September term. Something in me wanted to prove that I was able to obtain it. In those days in France you were not considered anything if you didn't have at least a Baccalaureate; but I did not quite realise what it involved!

The living conditions at n°3, rue Sicard were not easy. This flat was really tiny and having to sleep in the same bedroom as Fonsou and my mother was challenging for all of us especially after having first to go through Sylvette and Toby's bedroom!

However, the warm sunny weather of the summer, the beauty of the Cote d'Azur and its wonderful sea, together with Mum's delicious food helped to overcome these difficult conditions. Toby,

Sylvette and I picnicked every day, swam, and fished with harpoon guns off the harbour of Golf Juan. I was pleased to share my fishing experience with Toby and he soon caught the bug.

The time came to start school again and early one morning in mid-September, I took the bus to Cannes for my first day at the Lycée Carnot. I had not realised how busy buses were early in the morning with people going to school or to work. I stood all the way, hanging onto the chrome railing and finding the correct position with my feet to counterbalance the bus braking and accelerating as it manoeuvred the busy road. Everybody seemed to be smoking, creating a dense atmosphere.

The Lycée Carnot was a huge, 1925 building with wide steps leading up to tall metal-framed glass doors, where hundreds of students gathered, and slowly entered the building. My whole body was shaking; I was nervous to be going into a world I had no connection with, one I did not know and, in fact, one I did not really want to know. I wanted to turn round and run towards the sea, to breathe its fresh air and let my emotions quieten down. Not being free enough to follow this impulse, I stood some distance away, lit a Gauloise and deeply inhaled the blue smoke, which created a vague numbness throughout my body. Soothed by the tobacco, the shaking gradually lessened and, as I came to the entrance, I put out my cigarette and walked in.

After searching and making a few enquiries I finally found my classroom. It was an unfriendly space with a very high ceiling, the room long and narrow, and the north light poor. Rows of old wooden desks faced a platform and a huge blackboard. Feeling shy and uneasy, I sat right at the back, next to an attractive girl with glasses. A tall, lanky maths teacher entered, and everyone welcomed him in unison, "Bonjour Monsieur Lambert." He put down the pile of books he was carrying on the pale green Formica table and looked at us absently with a slight smile. He explained what he was about to teach us that morning and turned to the blackboard. It seemed that most of the students could follow what he was saying, taking the information down in their notebooks.

I found it all incomprehensible and finally opened the maths book I had been given, to look for the appropriate page. Feeling stupid and incapable, I just stared at it.

Noticing that I was struggling, my desk companion leaned close to me and offered to help; I instantly smelt the delicate scent of her shampoo. I felt enveloped by her feminine aura and studied her silky auburn hair while she was finding the desired page.

"Here it is, page 9, that's what we are on." She whispered in a strawberry flavoured breath, as she pulled back to her initial position.

I tried to concentrate, forcing myself away from the feminine attraction, and managed to recognize some of the symbols; this brought my attention back to the teacher. He seemed lost in his mathematical world, greatly enjoying explaining his beloved subject, obviously not aware that some of his students were not able to come even close to his reality. I floated on through the morning, my mind not able to focus on the subject. It was like trying to force a horse to drink when all he wanted to do was to run in the fields. An alarm went off and the teacher said in a surprised voice, "Dear me! It's already morning break. Time flies!" For me these two hours had been an eternity, and I was greatly relieved when it was time to leave his class. He indicated which pages of the book we should study for our homework and disappeared.

Behind the Lycée was a large playground with only two rusty basketball posts and rings without basket nets. The whole place was paved, surrounded by 3 metre high, old wire netting. I noticed the girls gathered in small groups all talking at once, perhaps because they had not seen each other during the long summer holiday month. I stood there wondering where to go when, in fact, I wanted to be by myself. But also I did not want to be considered shy or unfriendly, so I walked towards a group of lads who were talking loudly.

Not wanting to intrude, and hoping they would welcome me into their group, I came close and listened to their conversation. No one took any notice of me – it was as if they had not noticed my presence. Although they had adult voices and gave the appearance of being men, what I heard were things like whose dad had the biggest car, which of them had the best holiday… each person was trying to amaze and surpass the others. They were emotionally trampling on each other, not missing an occasion to create anguish, or to diminish the person who hadn't come up with something impressive. Their laughter was mocking and they seemed to take pleasure in embarrassing each other. I could not help noticing the difference from my experiences at Summerhill. I realised how privileged I had been to have gone to this unique school where I had been able to be who I was in my own right, without having to compensate with artifice. They didn't listen to each other properly and each one raised his voice wanting to be on top… on top of what? I wondered. I felt I did not want to take part in this aimless conversation, and I walked some distance away to sit on the low wall facing the sun. With my eyes closed, I allowed its heat to veil my face and calm my disturbed feelings.

I returned to the Lycée Carnot day after day, trying to fit in, but the courses were difficult for me, except for English, where I was far ahead of the others in the class. Individually I found these guys were okay: I could have a normal conversation with them; but I did not stay long enough to establish a real link with any of them. When they were together they were a bit like a pack of dogs. Actually no, a pack of dogs would not have behaved like that, boasting about their sexual exploits, or making dirty remarks about the girl over there, or teasing the one that was a little plump, or the one whose bum was too round or too flat or whatever. My sexual encounters with the feminine had been too precious, too special, too inspiring, too divine to even attempt to share them with anyone, yet alone this rough lot of guys at the college.

This awkward situation lasted a few weeks and then I finally decided to stop going to the Lycée. After all, didn't I desire to be a painter? Or to study art and advertising as a way to make money as

CHAPTER 6

Mano had advised me? Why should I waste precious years to get something I did not particularly want or feel I needed for my future? I talked about it with my mother, Sylvette and Toby, and they understood that I would not get anywhere if I continued to go to the Lycée. My mother thought "L'Ecole Universelle", an affordable correspondence school, might suit me better. So I started to work at home, regularly receiving large brown envelopes, studying the books they suggested, writing, filling in forms, reading, doing maths and all possible subjects. When I got stuck on a subject, Toby patiently helped me to understand the problem. It demanded effort and self-motivation, but I ploughed on aimlessly, knowing jolly well inside myself that I could not keep it up for too long.

During the Easter holidays while I was in my last year at Summerhill, I had come down from England by train with my grandmother GG who stayed with us for 10 days. We were very happy to have her with us since this was the first time she'd visited us! Her spirit was high for she had not been to France for 20 years, and her return created great excitement in her heart. It also gave me an opportunity to talk with her about my future plans. She knew my wish was to study painting, and that Mano strongly recommended that I should first study advertising. She told me in a low whispering voice that she had put a little money aside for my studies. There was not much, but probably enough if I was careful. I felt comforted by her kind offer but at that time I still wanted to obtain the Baccalaureate. On her way back to England, she stopped in Camaret to pay a visit to her old friend Mme David, my sister's paternal grandmother. Then she went on to Paris to meet Mano and Philippe, whom she loved very much, and I suspect she shared with them her idea to help me with further studies.

Toby was now working in his own small business. For a very low rent he took a large room in an old disused pottery, opposite a famous potter called Gilbert Portanier. Tob, as we called him, bought himself welding equipment which consisted of two extremely heavy metal cylinders, one filled with liquid oxygen, the other with acetylene gas.

A blowtorch mixed the two gases to create a very hot blue flame. With this equipment he began making wrought iron articles to go with the local pottery, such as lamp stands, plate holders, tray holders, small tables for tiles etc. He was very creative and inventive and soon became very popular among the pottery crowd of Vallauris. Whenever I had free time, I walked down to his workshop and joyfully gave him a hand. Using my hands and brain together made me feel good; I could not work for long with total abstraction and needed something physical to do.

Living at n°3, rue Sicard, I began to fall into a rhythm. We were five people confined to a small space that gave us practically no privacy. In early December 1953, something totally unexpected happened... I heard the village siren reminding me that it was time to finish my morning study. I came out of my corner and helped lay the kitchen table while Sylvette went out to fetch Toby from his workshop. The kitchen was filled with the delicious smells of Maman's cooking. I began singing quietly to relax my body. Sylvette and Toby arrived, and mother asked her usual question to her future son-in-law,

"How did it go this morning? Tell me..." She always took great interest in our creative activities, she was very fond of Toby and wanted to know everything about what he was doing. Toby knew this and enjoyed talking with her; after all they both spoke in their own mother tongue and it was pleasant for me to see my mother enjoying her original culture so much. Also they were both great readers; they liked sharing the content of their last books...

The door of the kitchen opened, we all knew who was coming and in unison said... "Bonjour Fonsou!" He stood by the door holding a large bag, sending us all a beaming smile. Behind him stood an awkward young man of about my age – I recognized his eldest son Gilbert. I'd met him and his four brothers and sisters on a few occasions in Dieulefit, but had not developed any kind of connection with them. We didn't have much in common, due no doubt to our very different heredities, to the different ways our mothers had brought us up, to our different schools, different accents, etc.

"Bonjour Gilbert!" I welcomed him with a light smile and leaned forward to shake his hand, soft and lifeless hanging from his forearm. "You're well?" To which he replied without any enthusiasm, "Wouais." Meaning a non-committal ok.

Gilbert was introduced to Toby, who politely said, "Bonjour". While shaking the hanging hand, Toby turned discreetly towards me and raised one eyebrow imperceptibly, as if to say, "What's all this?" I looked back blankly at him, not responding to his embarrassing curiosity nor showing him my unhappy feelings about Gilbert's arrival. Our mum quickly laid another place and was looking for the missing chair, which Sylvette found in the adjacent bedroom. "Did you have a good journey?" Mother said while starting serving the soup. "Wouais." He replied timidly.

This was not the holidays, so why was he visiting us now? Where was he going to stay and for how long? These questions came up in my head and, although I already had the answers, I hoped my assumptions were not correct. Did mother know about this before? If she did, why had she not told us? At times, she really behaved strangely, 'funny Mum!' I thought. Sylvette, in her usual direct manner, questioned, "Gilbert, where are you staying?" It was obvious that Gilbert expected to stay with us and he felt most awkward at having to answer her. For the first time Fonsou spoke up and said without conviction, "We are going to look for some kind of work for him, probably in a pottery." He had not answered my sister's question, but mother quickly took over and said in a clear positive voice, "We'll make room for him… in the big bedroom. We'll find the space…you'll see! I know… both boys behind the folding screen, on the other military camp bed, alongside yours François?" I looked at Gilbert and saw his embarrassment. After all he had probably not been told about our living conditions, and he had not seen our tiny apartment. I felt sorry for him for he too was caught in a situation he had not imagined. Fonsou drank his usual cup of coffee before leaving, wiped his mouth with his table napkin in his habitual 'one swipe' manner. He rose up and kissed the air on either side of our mother cheeks, his eyes absent, and said mechanically as he departed, "See you later this evening." We cleared the table, as Mother was already at the sink washing the dishes. Gilbert gazed absently through the window, discreetly whistling to himself.

It was hard to for me to study that afternoon. I kept losing my focus and could not stop thinking about the conversation with my mother and GG, on her Easter visit earlier that year. Maman had told me about her Parisian life before the war and about the friend she had shared her painting studio with - Line Viala. Line was a renowned singer, accordionist and pianist, who had introduced Honor to her boyfriend, an artist who designed large posters to publicise her performances. His name was Paul Colin and his posters covered the walls of Paris before and after the war. He ran a small Art School in his large studios.

That evening I helped my mother arrange the separation of the bedroom, placing the folding screen as she had suggested, and placing the extra camp bed one metre away from my own. "There you are!" Mum said joyfully and appearingly satisfied with the arrangement. Her great generosity often fogged her awareness of how others felt, even her own children. Gilbert moved in, pushed his bag under his bed, took off his old tennis shoes, lay on his back with his hands behind his head and looked at the ceiling, whistling. I instantly picked up the disagreeable scent of sweaty feet. I tried to divert my attention away from the odour by trying to create a conversation with him, but his offhand "wouais" answers led nowhere. I finally let him get on with his whistling and left the apartment. I walked down to Toby's workshop and the cool evening air helped me to dissipate my troubles; I was pleased to see that Tob & Sylvette were still there. They certainly understood how I was feeling, for they were also not happy about the unexpected changes in our family situation.

As the days went by, it became more and more difficult for me to live and study at n°3, rue Sicard. I found Gilbert's continuous whistling, regardless of who was around, his habit of hanging smelly socks over the screen, leaving his clothes on the floor blocking access to my tiny space and never helping in the kitchen, accelerated the process of my wanting to leave Vallauris. The conjunction of all these factors became a source of irritation and I decided to go.

Around Christmas 1953, I wrote to my grandmother to ask if she would confirm her offer to help me with my art studies and arrange the finances. I planned to study in Paris at Paul Colin's Atelier and would like to start in the New Year. I explained that I felt I was wasting my time trying to study with the Ecole Universelle system. I showed the letter to my mother who was aware that my situation was distressing for me and approved my decision. She wrote at once to Paul Colin and at the same time let her friend Line Viala know of my intention. She also sent a letter to her other close friend, Lena Münz, to see whether I could stay with them, at least for my first term. All the responses came back favourable. Paul Colin's Atelier at this time of the year was normally full, but a student had unexpectedly left and I could take his place.

Life in Paris 1954 - 1956

The Münz tiny flat was in Porte de Versailles, n°15, rue Firmin-Gillot, five minute's walk from the underground station. At 7:30 a.m. I walked down to the Métro station to catch the tube to Place Péreire.

What an enormous challenge it was to find myself in Paris at the age of just 16! Everything was so different from what I had been used to, yet I was excited by the challenge of having to find ways of adapting myself to this large city. As I walked down the steps of the tube station on that first morning, it felt as if I was going into an ant hill where a million people, each with their individual intentions and thoughts, crisscrossed each other to go their different ways. The city had its own life rhythm, and I felt that these underground tubes were breathing, as if they were the lungs of a huge monster, pushing its millions of users to follow its powerful rhythm. I did not find the one and a half hours spent on the underground boring, as there was always so much around to entertain me. When we reached a station, I looked out of the windows to spot the interesting posters covering the glazed tiled walls. While in the tunnels, my eyes meandered through the dense crowd, looking for an attractive girl or an interesting face or body shape. I loved drawing caricatures, and I found much inspiration on these early morning trips.

I got off the Métro at Place Péreire, which was a quiet residential area of Paris. I liked its vast circular Place where all the avenues met like spokes in the hub of a gigantic wheel. At each intersection was a café-restaurant and we generally went to Café Péreire closest to n°17, Blvd Péreire, Paul Colin's lively two storey atelier. The two lanes of the Boulevard were separated by a deep gulley where trains could be faintly heard going to the Gare St Lazare. Protective black cast iron railings ran from Place Péreire way up to Porte Maillot, accentuating the perspective.

I was nervous on that first day when, carrying an empty folder under my arm, I rang the bell and heard the buzzer respond. I pushed the door open and entered a narrow dark corridor with a steep wooden staircase on the right, and a glazed door straight ahead of me. I saw a young man sitting lazily in the office with his feet up on the desk. He was reading l'Equipe, the French sports newspaper.

"You must be the new student who is replacing the guy who left in December…François Lassalle, is that right? I am Jean Paul, how do you do?" His pointed smile revealed a broken incisor and he put out his hand. I noticed his good looks and fair complexion; his aquiline nose forming a continuous line with his forehead, and his wide, round nostrils. Witty deep blue eyes under a continuous black eyebrow, looked at me with amusement. I firmly shook his warm hand and smiled. "The boss told me you were coming, and asked me to show you round and take you to your place."

As I followed Jean Paul into the corridor all my senses were on alert. I could smell the worn and recently washed wooden floors; the place seemed to be silent. The walls were painted pale grey with natural bright light pouring down from the glazed ceiling, reminding

CHAPTER 6

me of a greenhouse. Thin wooden partitions created spaces where the students worked. An opening immediately to the left led to a small room where two students were working on a large poster project. Jean Paul turned into an adjacent workspace.

"Here you are! This is your place, you can leave your folder here and follow me and I'll show you the rest!" Without any time to look around, I followed him back into the corridor that led to a large room with one wall made of opaque glass panels. The general Art Room was full of easels, an old velvet couch stood on a low platform in one corner, behind which hung tall, red-brown, dusty curtains. Straight opposite the entrance of the studio, a narrow wooden staircase led up to a mezzanine. Under the staircase was a private space for the model to undress. A large, dirty, square enamel sink and a row of brown pine cupboards completed the room. Jean Paul announced, "Every morning we have life classes here… the model will soon be arriving." We heard the doorbell ring and Jean Paul ran off to the office.

I went back to my corner to arrange my equipment and claim my space. Our working tables were large wooden boards resting on tall trestles and we sat on high wooden stools. In one corner of our room a still life had been arranged: a tall watering can, an old cast iron caldron, a pair of antique andirons and ochre coloured overalls hung from a rusty nail.

A young woman carrying a bulging shopping basket entered the room. She was tall, a little plump, and had a round face and short dark ginger hair that framed the upper part of her head like a 1925 bell-shaped hat. Her large sensuous mouth was thickly painted with shiny pink lipstick, and she smiled revealing a perfect row of large white teeth.

"Hello! I am Nicole. You're the new student?" As she leaned towards me she presented me with a firm, round and richly powdered cheek. I detected a sweet tropical scent as I kissed her. "Yes, I am François."

I felt immediately that I would get on with Nicole. Her large brown

337

eyes were honest and open, and I was happy to be sharing the working space with her. She told me Jean Paul and Pierre worked at the other table in our room. Nicole unpacked her shopping basket, arranged her art materials and talked without looking at me.

"I was in another art school before coming here, Les Beaux Arts where they only use lead pencils for drawing! Here, the Boss only wants us to use charcoal! He says, quite rightly, that with charcoal you cannot fiddle, it's more basic, sculptural, and more direct. By the way, do you have any?" "No." I replied flatly. I knew all about charcoal as I had seen my mother use it, and I had used it in Summerhill. "You actually can buy different grades in the office; I like the softest one. You can also get Ingres drawing paper there - Jean Paul will sell you some, I am sure."

Equipped with my paper, charcoal and a drawing board to clip the Ingres paper onto, I entered the art room, found an easel and arranged myself. Nicole grabbed an easel and put it to my right, slightly behind me. The room slowly filled with the 10-12 students. I noticed they were older than me with ages anywhere from 19 to 35. The model, in her early 40's and wearing a worn, pale grey, chequered suit that was too tight for her, arrived and said: "Sorry I'm late! Never mind... sorry!" She let out a high pitch giggle and disappeared behind the screen under the stairs.

I felt uneasy not knowing how my drawing would turn out, frightened of revealing myself to this unknown crowd of artists. On the other hand I felt extremely happy to be doing what I always wanted to do – working in the arts. The model came out of her hiding place in a white towelling dressing gown, took it off and threw it on the back of a nearby chair.

Her body, stark white, 'has probably never seen the sunshine', I thought. Its rounded forms were pleasant and well proportioned. Her forearms and large hands were crimson and I realized that besides modelling, she must also do hard manual labour. "Good morning Mary!" said some of the students gaily. "Good morning everybody!" Her voice was monotone and raucous. Mary threw herself into a standing pose with her arms on her hips and one leg forward, "Okay like this?" A few grunts of appreciation came from the floor.

An intense silence descended in the room as we started drawing, soon broken by the musical sounds of the charcoal sticks scratching on the white paper. Everyone stood by their easels in deep concentration, passionately involved in their work. Every so often one could hear a deep sigh, a sign of the decompression of some accumulated tensions. Standing in front of my white Ingres paper observing the live model took me into an unknown space. My mind was no longer enveloped in thought, but actively observing, perceiving, and concentrating on guiding my disobedient hand to follow the graceful forms of Mary's body. When in intense concentration, I found my breathing stopped until my hand finished creating the line. Then I moved away to see if the proportions of my first drawing were correct...

"Oh no! How awful – they're not! The legs are too short in proportion to the rib cage, and my drawing is not well placed on the page." I was now standing near Nicole and could not resist looking at her drawing. Her lines had a lively swing to them, somehow she stylised the reality and produced a powerful, easy to read drawing. I leaned towards her, "Do you have, by any chance, a putty rubber?" She immediately replied in a whisper, "The Boss doesn't like us using them." I went back to my easel, looked at my drawing again and saw how terrible it was, 'I have a long way to go,' I thought...

"Time's up!" An older female student said, as she went on drawing; half an hour had already gone by.

Mary slowly unlocked her pose, her face grimacing as the blood started to flow again, and stretched. She slipped on her gown, sat on the chair and lit a cigarette. Some students went on drawing as if to clear their minds of the last information they had accumulated. Others walked round, curious to see how their fellow students had captured the pose. I felt rather self-conscious and embarrassed by the rigid and awkward drawing I had produced. I left it there for it would have been more embarrassing to hide it away.

I walked round to see what the others had done. There were certainly a great variety of talents, and I was surprised to see that by comparison to some of the others, my drawing wasn't so terrible after all. It was interesting for me to realise that the lines each student produced were different and reflected their individual characters. Jean Paul's lines where thick, black - almost messy - with straight strokes as if his hand could not follow the gentle curves of the model. I liked the delicate drawing of Eric, clear and precise, as if his charcoal hardly touched the paper, leaving light, accurate lines, and I thought to myself, 'I am pressing too hard with my charcoal, for a start, and my figure is too small…. I must correct that.' Mary went back to her platform, knelt on one knee and with both forearms crossed on the seat of a high stool, rested her head delicately on them. I saw her back now, her leg, forearms and head directed away from me. I pinned another Ingres sheet on my board and glanced at the pose wondering how to tackle it. As soon as the charcoal was in my hand, I felt pushed to hurry into it as if I had a train to catch. My rational nature was put aside, giving room for my impatience to obtain quick results. A while later, Nicole warned me, keeping her voice down, "The Boss is coming!" Instantly the atmosphere altered, the sound of the charcoal dancing on the paper suddenly lessened, reminding me of the Island when the cicadas stop singing as one approaches them.

The Boss was short, round and baggy eyed, with a heavy hooked nose that hung over a thin mouth. His large forehead was encircled by long whitish yellow hair resting on the collar of his camel coat.

"Bonjour Monsieur!" said in unison the students. "Bonjour." He replied and started his round with Nicole's drawing, while everyone gathered behind him to listen to his criticism and advice. We all were great admirers of his artistic talent, his way of catching just the right line, and adjusting its thickness just in the right places to reveal the form. It was fascinating to watch him correct our drawings. After having looked at her drawing for some time he said, "It's good, you're making progress Nicole, continue."

Then he came to my easel. I moved out of the way, leaving him space, but he didn't look at my drawing right away. His piercing pale blue eyes looked up at me instead and carried a touch of nostalgia, his mouth in a faint smile, "So, you're Honor's youngest son, hey? It's a long time since I've seen your mother... how is she?" All eyes were on me now, making me feel self-conscious... "Fine, thank you."

He turned round to the small gathering and explained, "Before the war, I designed several large posters of Honor's friend, Line Viala, who is a great pianist, accordionist and used to sing in the cabarets of Paris. You've probably seen one of the posters on the wall of my studio." As his hand pointed up above his head, I smelt a strong odour of Eau de Cologne. Becoming serious again, he scrutinised my drawing and demanded my charcoal holder. As he concentrated all his attention on my poor sketch, he said emphasising each word, "Look! Proportions, proportions, proportions, get them right!" Using the charcoal holder as a measure-stick, his thumbnail as an adjustable marker, he stretched out his short arm towards the model, closed one of his heavy eyelids and said,

"Always keep that arm absolutely straight! It will always be constant and gives you the information you need. Not like this, but like that!" He bent his arm forward and jerked it out again violently to emphasise his point. During the morning most of the students used that same technique. He proceeded to demonstrate, "Imagine her in a rectangular box, take the head... measure it on our stick and mark with your thumb... exactly 3 heads make up the height of your box. Now, how many in the length? 4 and ½; here you are, the correct proportions are revealing themselves!" Taken up by his own lively drawing, he went on in silence. Watching him draw was fascinating and very instructive. He went round to the others, giving his comments to some, compliments on progress to others. He obviously enjoyed being the master amongst his pupils. He then left the art room as suddenly as he had entered it.

The morning flew by and it was already 12 o'clock. During the two-hour lunch a small group of students went down to the Café Péreire for a sandwich and a beer. Nicole and I followed them.

341

Walking down the long boulevard, Nicole told me she was studying fashion drawing and costume design. The students studied different arts: poster design and lettering, fashion, costume and theatre design, murals, interior design; and two were simply painters. "Paul Colin is brilliant at all these arts. But he says drawing is the key!"

It was winter and the sky was grey, the air damp and cold. We opened the large glass doors of the cafe and entered into a dense, hot, smoky, noisy atmosphere. Some students were already sitting on the long, oilcloth covered bench resting against a tall, mirrored wall, while others sat on chairs on the sides of two white marble top tables.

I suddenly realized – here I was, in the middle of Paris sitting in a cafe with artist companions I hardly knew! This was amazing and exciting and my whole being absorbed all the new impressions with curiosity. The cacophonous mix of sounds and voices were interlaced with the faint tones of a distant singer. The air was rich with the smell of beer, wine, Gauloises, ham, fresh baguettes and the scent of a lady's rich perfume. My eyes wandered avidly looking for beauty, searching for the new treasures I was discovering.

In the reflection of the immense mirror was a bouquet of white Arum lilies standing erect in a tall, fluted glass vase. The backlighting gave it a strange dramatic effect. The harmony between the few colours touched me with their orange/yellow pistils poking out of the white and pale green funnel shaped flowers. The dark green stems plunging into the vase reflected pale mauve, pink and dark violet shadows. The whole picture was so attractive and made me think of my mother, who used to love painting these flowers when she lived in Paris. I felt I was secretly sharing a hidden beauty with her.

Feeling as if I was being watched, my attention drifted to a pair of captivating sky blue eyes scrutinising me in the mirror. Large, thick, black eyelashes framed their perfect almond shapes. My shy self was not able to keep up their intensity. Her prominent cheekbones were very white, her nose short and straight and her lips emotionless and covered with perfectly applied, dark red lipstick. I now noticed a slight tremor on their surface as the mouth slowly, like a cat stretching after its sleep, took a different shape and lifted at the corners revealing two large white teeth with a tiny gap between them.

I now focussed on the whole face... and saw that nature had arranged the delicate features in a harmonious display. The captivating head rested on a long swan neck, with a large beauty spot where it met her wide square shoulders. Her thick black hair was short, well arranged in attractive locks that came forward. I dared to glance back into the eyes, and they were smiling; I felt my heart swell and became aware that a relationship had begun. This unexpected eye contact made me feel nervous, as I did not know what the outcome would be. A voice tore me out of my artistic and amorous emotions... "And what would Monsieur like?" It was the waiter reminding me that it was lunchtime. "A Gruyere sandwich and a beer, please." I ordered without thinking, still trying to deal with the throbbing of my heart. The sandwich helped to unblock my jaws, the beer helped to relax my throat. I realised the one who had made my heart throb was from the art school, and shared the room next to ours with the tall German and the older, short Turkish student.

After our brief lunch, walking back to the studios I caught up with her. She was tall and wore a black raincoat tied firmly round her narrow waist, emphasising the curves of her hips. Her gait attracted me. "Hello! What's your name?" "Laura, and what's yours?" Our eyes met again and I felt like jumping into the blue of their sky. "François."

Hearing the emotion in my voice, I wished it would go away. As we talked I could hear her French was not fluent. I switched from French to English and picked up a slight German accent. She had come from Cologne to Paris to study fashion design. Her father had been killed during the war and under great financial stress her mother had raised her three daughters in the bombed city. I was delighted to know that Laura was working in the room next to mine, the one overlooking the boulevard. Occasionally from where I was sitting, I could see her silhouette against the light as she moved across the room.

That afternoon an older student sent by the Boss instructed me on my next steps and gave me a list of the basic materials I would need. He told me that Paul Colin usually visited us on Tuesdays and Thursdays. My courses were life drawing every morning, still life and composition, and lettering and poster design in the afternoon. I left an hour early that first day, and looked for an art shop where I could buy art materials. Pierre drove a Vespa scooter and kindly offered to take me to a shop he knew, some distance away. He wore a grey casquette and duffle coat that he often kept on during the day, and a pair of stylish, square, rimless glasses that hid his gentle green eyes.

I was tired by the end of the first long day and stood in the overcrowded underground on my way to Porte de Versailles. Meeting so many new people, each bringing a different experience and carrying different emotions, drained me. Certainly the most pleasant but disturbing was the brief contact with Laura, who returned to my mind. The intensity with which she looked at me, together with her beauty, instantly started my heart beating again. How was I going to handle this shyness of mine? I had no idea and decided to switch to a different space in myself. Yes! The drawing class… that was great! But it showed me how much I had to practice to improve my drawings. I admired Paul Colin for his expertise and talent; no doubt he was a master and I felt privileged to be in his Art School. On the other hand, as a person I found him complex and arrogant. I felt that it would be better to keep on the good side of him.

Nicole… she was nice, just thinking of her made me feel peaceful. I smiled thinking how lucky I was to have her working at the same table. Had Laura been next to me…. gee! That might have made concentrating on my work very, very difficult! Pierre was a nice guy and always ready to do something for you. The trip on the Vespa had been fun. His glasses protected his eyes from the cold air and I remembered how they kept sliding down the sharp upper curve of his nose, and how he instantly pushed them back up into place with his tobacco stained finger. He talked a lot, even while driving the Vespa and on the first ride had told me from the corner of his mouth, "My father bought the scooter for my 19th birthday. You must come and meet my parents one day… you'll see, they're nice."

I finally arrived and felt apprehensive about going into the Münz's flat. This was not because I didn't like them, but because I felt like being alone. I knew they would be keen to know all about my day. I rang the bell of the brown door for the top floor flat. Lena opened it, and greeted me with a radiant smile. I gave her the customary Parisian greeting, four alternate kisses on her cheeks. My nose picked up a wonderful smell of cooking, and I heard the vibrant sound of classical music coming from their sitting room.

"You're hungry?" "Yes, I'm starving!" As I took off my coat, Mr Münz, and their son Pierre joined us in the minuscule kitchen. "It's a Russian Borsch. The bright red colour comes from red beetroot and red cabbage… would you like a little sour cream in it?" I nodded in agreement as she served me a steaming bowl of the dark red soup.

During supper I told them the events of my day, leaving out the personal, more emotional parts. Throughout the meal, the sound of the classical music was not lowered and I had to talk loudly to be heard. Every so often, Mr Münz would interrupt me by putting his index finger across his mouth and saying in his broad Jewish Austrian accent, "Shush, listen… this is a very special part. Did you hear the way that cello came in?" With his head slightly to one side, and his eyes half closed, we'd all stop eating, even swallowing, and waited for the 'special' part to pass. "Ah! That was superb!"

And he noisily went back into eating the deep red soup. Pierre must have been in his early 20s and kindly shared his room with me. The flat was very small and the rooms tiny. I realised that my presence was not easy for them due to the lack of space, and I did my best to be there as little as possible. I stayed with them for two and a half months until the Easter holidays came.

A stroke of artistic good fortune touches the family

The first three months of 1954 was a time of positive changes for all of us at home. It was as if a ray of light had descended onto the family, bringing good fortune. Mother, Fonsou, Sylvette and Toby moved just outside Vallauris to a new property with a large garden that gave onto the Route du Cannet. Gilbert finally returned to Dieulefit; he had not found the work he had expected and was missing his friends. I was pleased to see that the house was big enough for the five of us with three bedrooms, kitchen, bathroom, dining room/sitting room. From the large terrace we could see a little blue triangle of the blue Mediterranean. This was the first time we had a 'proper' house and it felt good.

I found it so enjoyable to be coming down from Paris with stories to share about my new friends, and showing the family my latest work. My Parisian adventures amused them as I emphasised some anecdotes here and there, just to highlight the realities and make everybody laugh. But I did not tell them of my feelings for Laura, as they were too fresh to share.

In the High Street, mother had rented a small shop she called 'Isis Lampshades'. The business was keeping her busy making raffia lampshades, pottery lamp bases, necklaces out of seeds and seashells, silk scarves and many other decorative objects. Sylvette helped make the lampshades and necklaces. Toby's business had grown rapidly and he had lots of orders, so he had moved his workshop to the first floor of another old disused pottery, with an extensive terrace where the potters used to sun dry the freshly turned pots. Fonsou had found a better job and earned a little more. I was in a good place in myself. The contrast of being in grey noisy Paris and the dark flat of rue Firmin-Gillot and arriving on the Cote d'Azur with olive trees, blue sky and my mother's cooking, was enormous. It filled me with a light positive energy.

Sylvette and Toby had stories to tell too. While I was discovering Parisian art life, Toby had designed and created a very beautiful 'modern' wrought iron armchair. Its elegant frame was painted black, the seat and back were webbed with a thick white cotton rope. He'd sewed bright red felt cushions – a triangular one for the headrest, and a square one for the seat. The armrests ended in large, perfectly round, beech wooden balls. It was impressive and was exhibited in the Madoura Pottery's exhibition room. Picasso often worked at the Madoura pottery; he fell for the armchair, and bought it. At the time Picasso was living with Françoise Gilot in a modest villa on the hill overlooking Vallauris. Sylvette and Toby walked the long distance to deliver the armchair. The master was kind, paid them cash and invited them in for tea. They met Françoise and their two young children, Claude and Paloma.

It was a pleasure for me to be in Toby's company and I helped him with his work during my short holiday. Across the road from the first floor aerated terrace of a disused pottery, that he sometime used for painting his metal-work, was a small grassy hill with on its crest, an ancient stone barn called 'The Bergerie'; at that time it was Pablo Picasso's atelier. A high stonewall surrounded the property, a green wooden door was its only access. One sunny morning, while we were painting in black cellulose paint some of his latest wrought iron pieces on the tiled floor of the large terrace, we heard a voice calling... "Toby, Toby!"

It seemed to be coming from the direction of the Bergerie. We looked across and saw no one at first... but suddenly, to our great surprise, from behind the wall slowly rose a huge white canvas with a hurriedly sketched profile of Sylvette with her ponytail tied up high with a ribbon. Then the canvas disappeared behind the wall... A few seconds later, Picasso appeared further up on the grassy hill, and turning around, he waved his arms inviting us to come over. As I recall, We rushed down into the courtyard of the old pottery, across and up to the road to the green door as it opened.

Picasso was standing there smiling, his large dark brown eyes sparkling. Addressing himself to Toby he said with excitement in a soft voice that carried a Spanish accent, "Could you ask Sylvette if she'd sit for me? I would very much like to paint her!" He then showed us the fresh canvas sketch that was resting against the wall. "You like it?"

He said without expecting an answer. Toby wisely replied that he could not decide for her and he could not guarantee anything, but he would certainly ask her and come back the next day with an answer.

We bought the news back home with excitement, and Maman, who was cooking in the kitchen, came into the dining room with her apron on and said with much admiration, "That's wonderful news!" But my sister was not the type to be impressed by such an offer. She did not want to rush into things and her lack of self-confidence made her extremely careful about taking any decisions. "I don't want to… anyhow I am not a model, so… I don't want to undress in the front of anyone, not even Toby, so? How terrible it is that you think I should want to undress in front of an old man!" She frowned and there were traces of anger in her voice. Toby looking amused shook his head in agreement and said, "Unfortunately, I must admit that it's true, not even in front of me!" How could anyone dare to think she would? How could Toby or her brother imagine or think of such a terrible thing? We were sitting round the dining table and about to start our lunch, when mother broke the silence, "After all, it is Picasso, not just any old painter!" Sylvette instantly sent back a stinging reply, "Oh you, you would sit naked for any passers-by, you love showing your naked body!" I took over and tried to reassure her, "It is an amazing opportunity Sylvette! Picasso is the greatest and most famous living painter of our times." "I don't care! I know you all want me to sit for him, but I won't, so there!" Toby wisely proposed, "I suggest that we stop talking about it. I said I would give Picasso a reply tomorrow morning."

Of course we all stopped talking about it, but the subject did go on in our heads for the rest of the day. The next morning Sylvette, Toby and I were starting breakfast and I was curious and impatient to know what they had decided, "What's the outcome then? Did you sleep on it?" Sylvette answered positively, adding a short laugh, "Yes! We have." "So… what's the outcome then?" "Well, if he wants to paint me, he can, but I'll keep my coat on, he will have to paint my head only or whatever, that's all!" She exclaimed as she burst into laughter.

With the help of our mother, Toby had made Sylvette a large raglan, lavender grey wool coat with a wide round collar and enormous round flat buttons. The material was made of such heavy wool, the collar stayed up by itself. Sylvette loved this coat for it hid the shape of her body, which she did not like. She felt protected in it and would wear it right up into the early summer. It was in that coat that she and Toby went to give her reply. On their return they said that their meeting had been extremely pleasant and they came back feeling bubbly and positive. "You see… he is going to paint me and I won't have to take my coat off! I said that I did not want to be paid, because I am not a professional model!" She laughed triumphantly, "He was very nice and showed us round his atelier – it was great!"

Sylvette sat every day of the working week for Picasso for over three months. He painted 46 portraits of her, many drawings and created large sculptures. She became known later as 'the girl with a pony tail.'

This is, by the way, my own experience of this story; I have heard from my sister slightly different versions…

The 1954 Easter holidays were extremely productive, not only in meeting Picasso, but also because my sister, mother and I had been able to take part in a 'Picasso and local painters' exhibition that was held in Vallauris Mairie. I exhibited two large, colourful gouaches of clowns performing in a circus. A wealthy American couple, who owned two circuses in California, bought them and invited me to deliver the paintings to their hotel in Nice. These were my first art sales and I felt very chuffed!

Pablo Picasso was already a renowned painter in 1954 and it was impressive for a 16 year old like me to meet such an important artist. He was obviously very fond of Sylvette and Toby, and somehow I fitted into the family picture. For some reason he gave me a nickname and called me the goat. I suppose my long, skinny body, and my freshly grown moustache and short fluffy goatee reminded him of the animal. I did not mind, and I felt it was a privilege to be called the goat by such a famous man.

His studio was a fascinating place – an artist's Aladdin's cave. Looking around, I saw how this artist oozed with creative originality, for everywhere were objects he had collected and transformed into his own artistic expression. The Bergerie was entirely lime-washed with old, warped, wooden shelves haphazardly placed on the walls, holding some of his decorated pottery, small sculptures and all kinds of captivating things: an antique oil lamp, books, several straw and other hats, masks of all sorts, some given to him by fans from all over the world, unusual pieces of rusty wrought iron. All these contributed to the originality of his working space. "They send me presents from all over the world!" He said with a giggle pointing to the masks and hats. Against the walls piles of paintings rested, some with dates written on the backs of the canvases. When I entered the studio for the first time, what surprised me most was a pyramid, two-metre at the base, made of empty cigarette packets. "Why such a pile of Gitanes packets in the middle of your studio?" I asked with curiosity, and he replied with a short laugh, "When I have finished a pack, I throw it on the pile and each time I look at it, it reminds me of how much I smoke! That helps me to smoke less." Becoming serious again, he glanced through a small window looking onto Vallauris' ancient cemetery behind the village and, taking on a frightened expression he turned his head away from the view, saying gravely, "One day, I'll finish up there!" After a short silence, he suddenly changed the conversation to happier matters.

The floor of his studio was covered with fine, well-worn Persian carpets thrown about haphazardly; saucers used as ashtrays were everywhere, some on the floor with half empty tubes of paints mixed with ashes and fag ends. Receptacles with paint or brushes sitting in turpentine lay scattered around the wooden garden chair he sat in.

When looking at him, it was difficult not to be caught up by the dark lively intensity of his brown eyes that demanded all your attention and awareness. There was much power and integrity in the man. When standing next to him, I felt as if I was next to a radiating part of the sun. I felt love and respect towards him and gradually became more at ease in his presence.

Moving closer to the centre of Paris

I told my mother how the lack of space at n°15, rue Firmin-Gillot was difficult for all of us. So she wrote to an old friend called Myrette Dewèvre who lived right in the centre of Les Halles, the enormous wholesale food market in the centre of the city that was open all night; the equivalent of what use to be Covent Garden in London. So it was arranged that I would go back directly to Myrette's flat when I returned to Paris. I felt much happier about leaving my family in Vallauris now with their different interests and occupations. It was reassuring to know that their material situation had greatly improved.

When I arrived in the late evening, Les Halles was already coming alive with preparations for the night's commercial activities. On every section of pavement, at every corner and by every porch, lorries were starting to unload their merchandise. I crossed over to n°11 rue des Halles, towards a parked lorry unloading gigantic Gruyere cheeses. Perfectly round, each was carefully rolled down a gangplank beside the filthy gutters. Their dark yellow skin was stamped all over with large, bright red marks and when they hit the ground they bounced as if they were made of rubber. They seemed extremely heavy and were as tall as me and their strong scent reminded me that I had not eaten since the morning... 'next time I eat Gruyere cheese, I must take off the rind!' I thought. Myrette had told me to simply walk into the flat for she would be late that day and she had left the door open. She lived with her husband on the second floor of the late 18th century building. It was a busy junction, three noisy streets surrounded the block, and each floor carried a wrought iron balcony that overlooked a multitude of small stores.

Entering the flat was like going on a film set of an 1870 bourgeois interior. The first thing I noticed in the darkened hallway was a hollowed-out elephant's foot filled with umbrellas and walking sticks, each one more interesting than the next. An old bentwood stand held black felt hats and a lady's straw summer hat. Through two thick curtains I came into a large sitting room where many fabrics and cushions smelled of musty camphor mothballs. Dusty books and magazines covered every available flat surface, a glass cabinet contained fine porcelain, and half opened cardboard boxes were scattered across the floor covering the Persian carpets.

I was suddenly brought out of my investigation by a razor thin man's voice, "Good journey? But excuse me, I have to go back to my boiled egg. I mustn't miss it – it has to boil for exactly 3 minutes!" A very skinny man with a black hairline moustache appeared for an instant from behind a thick bottle green velvet curtain, and then disappeared again. 'That's got to be her husband Jules,' I thought… I heard the voice again, but this time it was muted by the curtain. "Myrette will be back shortly; she went to one of her book reading meetings."

Removing a pile of newspapers from the sofa, I made myself a small space to sit and waited. The first time I'd met her was in Vallauris when she visited us briefly, and I had liked her instantly. She was tall and frail with fine features; her white hair, which at one time must have been blonde, was untidily tied into a bun. Her spirit was light and she laughed easily, specially about herself. She came from the Alsace region and her husband Jules, a lawyer who rarely gave a smile, came originally from Lyon.

After some time, the sound of keys took me out of my reveries and Myrette walked in with heavy bags. She noticed me through her pair of dusty old glasses; her intelligent blue eyes were lively, witty and expressed joy. She questioned, as if to reassure herself, "Are you there? Is that you François? Have you arrived already?"

CHAPTER 6

"Yes Myrette, I am here." I walked in her direction to give her a hug. "Have you eaten?" She murmured trying to recover her breath while she put down her heavy bags. "No, I haven't" I replied, feeling my empty stomach.

From birth Myrette had had a problem with her right leg, which was not as long nor as strong as her left, and this made her limp. She used a walking stick to keep her balance.

"Sorry about the mess!" She started clearing a corner of the large mahogany dining table, "You know, next week we are moving out of here! I have bought a first-floor flat in Rue des Martyrs in Pigale. I'll tell you all about it later."

I helped to clear the dusty table while she went to the kitchen. She soon came back, carrying a tray with a small piece of bread, a lump of Gruyere cheese, a few lettuce leaves, half a bottle of wine, 2 glasses, 2 plates and cutlery for two. While we ate the meagre meal, Myrette explained that Jules was going back to live in Lyon. They were selling the flat and from now on would live apart from each other. Leaning over to me, she said quietly, "You know, he's so obsessive! You have no idea! We shall be happier away from each other, no doubt!" And she laughed.

My bedroom was like a temporary cupboard piled with books and boxes – there was just enough space for the bed. Before going to bed, I stood by the window to watch the human ant-like activities going on down below in the street. The large stomach of Paris was waking up, noisy metallic shutters were rolled up revealing different wholesale food stores; strong men pushed out handcarts full to the brim with fruit and vegetables; lorries were arriving to unload or load up. Grocers, bakers, butchers, cheesemongers, greengrocers, delicatessen and fishmongers… in fact anything to do with feeding people was present. Then, to my surprise and fascination, I noticed another type of commerce. On the opposite pavement, under a doorway next to the café, six overly decorated, glittering females were displaying the fruit of their bodies to whoever might be interested.

This scene intrigued me. I had never seen prostitution in action before and I searched for the one I found most attractive. I focused my attention on an ash blonde with long legs that finally reached a narrow waist dominated by a protruding bosom. She wore a very short, white leather skirt, white boots and a very low-necked, short-sleeved, golden sparkly top. Down below was surely a man's world! Everyone seemed to be concentrating on his individual work either carrying or pushing, selling or buying. The only women in the vicinity were the brightly coloured girls across the street. There was so much noise that everyone had to shout to be heard. A fine rain started to fall, adding more glitter to the scene.

'Ah! A client in need' I thought, amused, as a short man, wearing a dark oversized coat and a felt hat arrived in the picture, he stopped close to my selected blonde. The girl had to bend down to hear what he was saying due to the hullabaloo of the street; they seemed to negotiate... he raised his felt hat briefly in agreement and took his freshly hired lady by the arm, and they disappeared into the dark shade of the doorway. 'How long would it be before my blonde returned? Who would be the first one to choose the overweight black girl?' These were the questions occupying my mind...

Fortunately, once I was in bed I could not see the street down below, but only the orange and black cloudy sky of Paris. My thoughts went to Mary and I remembered the kissing rounds at Summerhill. But this fantasy didn't last long as it was rapidly superimposed by the captivating face and presence of blue-eyed Laura. I remembered the long stare she had given me in the Café Péreire that had changed the rhythm of my heartbeat. It was actually slightly unnerving but pleasing to be caught in the net of such an attractive woman. I felt excited about seeing her again, yet somehow apprehensive. My experience with Jill had been tender and innocent, but if Laura changed my heartbeat just by looking at me, how would I react if we were actually in direct physical contact with each other? This thought made me feel vulnerable and I put it aside and tried get some much-needed sleep.

The underground journeys were now shorter, and being in the hub of Paris was much more interesting. Returning to Paul Colin's studios after the eventful holidays in Vallauris was exciting. I so enjoyed the work I was doing there, not only the life class, but also Paul Colin's challenges when he asked us to design a poster on a specific subject. For instance, the colossal exhibition called 'The Art Ménagers' (a yearly international household show), or a poster for an important horse race, or for the fizzy orange drink called Orangina. Each student worked on the same poster design and this created an interesting interplay between us. First, we had to understand clearly what the subject was about. Second, we had to come up with an original idea. I took pleasure searching for it in my brain throughout the day and sometimes in the night. Once I felt an idea budding, I took a piece of paper and a pencil and I scribbled down all the information my mind produced. When I felt I had completely tapped my imagination, I went through the scribbles and choose the most appropriate one. Nicole, who had a good critical mind, often gave me her valuable opinion. Next, we drew the chosen subject in correct small scale proportions, without too much detail, in order to create a maximum impact. Paul Colin used to say: "The first thing for a poster is to have punch!" So we drew tens of little rectangles and in these we placed all the possible ways the ideas and lettering could be displayed. Once the final choice was made, we designed the lettering of the title, to be in harmony with the whole. The next step was to stretch a wet sheet of white Canson paper onto a wooden frame using gummed brown tape and, while it was drying, we made a grid on the chosen sketch and enlarged it onto tracing paper the same size as the poster. When the paper was dry and taunt like a drum, we transferred the design. Only then did we paint the colours and text. Each finished poster represented days, sometime weeks, of work.

The "Open Criticism Day" was usually an enriching moment. All the posters were displayed in one studio, ready to be inspected by the master. Entering the room as if he was Louis XIVth, Paul Colin paused with legs slightly apart and took a long sweeping look at all the posters. Then, choosing the one that called him the most, he went up to it and intensively scrutinised the minor details. The students bunched around him like a swarm of bees and waited for his comments and criticisms. A blanket of silence descended while our attention sharpened in expectation. The Master briefly gave his first impression of the poster and only then did he go into the details… impact, composition, colours and execution of work. He could be very hard in what I thought was not always positive criticism; he rarely gave a compliment.

On another occasion Paul Colin burst into the room seemingly in a bad temper, his eyebrows pulled down over his fiery eyes. He stood for a moment looking at our work, fuming. Feeling the thunder brewing in him, we were each apprehensive about becoming the chosen lamb. In truth I was not happy with the poster I presented, that announced the opening of the yearly Parisian household exhibition at the Grand Palais. The letter design did not fit with the character, an immaculately dressed butler lying down and resting on the title of the exhibition and waving about an old-fashioned feather duster. He seemed to have no more work to do, since the household exhibition made life so simple for him. I thought the idea was good, but for some reason I had not succeeded with the design and it looked terrible. I felt embarrassed having presented it.

Suddenly, pointing his finger at my poster, the Master exploded offensively, "This is a heap of shit! Who has done this crap?" His words pierced me as if by a spear, my throat froze… and all eyes in the room focused on me. Paul Colin ferreted me out with his finger and his flaming eyes met mine; I looked down. "Me…" "Your work?" He barked. "Yes, it is." I replied faintly, now looking straight at him. It seemed that my reply made him even angrier, "Who do you think you are? When you address me, you must show respect! And say: Yes sir! No sir! Good morning sir!" His angry behaviour became comical as he shouted on, "You know something? I NEVER kept pigs with you!" (This is a French expression meaning "you are not showing me due respect") My response was immediate, "I do agree with you Sir, as I have never kept pigs in my life!" I replied, seemingly serious and concerned, but inwardly feeling amused by the weird, almost ridiculous situation.

I felt an undercurrent of restrained giggles among the students. Now, letting loose his anger, he picked up my poster with his trembling hands, threw it across the room and stormed out! Pierre rushed across to pick up my miserable poster from the dusty corner, and brought it to me. As he wiped it gently, blowing on it to remove a spider's web he said softly, "It's okay, just a little dust, no harm done." Nicole followed compassionately, "Don't worry François, the Boss is often in a bad mood, your poster is not that bad really." Then Maurice joined in, "You were jolly witty to answer him tit for tat like that! 'As I've never kept pigs in my life!' It was actually terribly funny!" His contagious laughter revealed the neat row of white teeth under his thick, black moustache. Everyone joined in, while I stood there silently with a faint smile. I knew that it would take some time before the Boss would take notice of me again, and felt unhappy about that, but I was agreeably surprised that this strange event changed something in my relationship with the other students. From then on they took me more seriously and gave me their attention freely. By revealing my independent character through this incident, I'd established myself amongst the pack. It took the whole term before Paul Colin inspected my work again. I continued working, following the advertising programmes, and the kind Maurice never failed to bring me the latest directions from the Boss.

I enjoyed designing so much that I organised myself so I could work full-time. I was surprised to see how some of the other students mucked about for much of the day, seeming to work only when the Boss was in the building. Jean Paul spent most of his time teasing the girls, and would take great pleasure in putting his charcoal stained hands on Mary's generous bosom, leaving their grey marks on her white jerseys. Nature had given Mary attractive proportions and a doll-like face and she always wore tight clothes to underline her femininity. She stood on needle thin high heels that accentuated the curve of her back, thus emphasising her perfect round buttocks. With her good sense of humour she laughed a lot and enjoyed telling us stories of how she had been an orphan raised and educated in a convent, which she had left two years previously when she was 18. "… and we were not allowed to go out. Do you know that I had no idea what a naked man looked like! The nuns were so strict… when we had been naughty, they would force us to bend down, lift our skirts up over our heads and they'd beat us with a bunch of reeds or sometimes simply with their naked hands!!!" She enjoyed captivating our attention and the laughter that her stories created, "And do you know what was written in blue on the white tiles of the showers?" She waited a while, making sure she had caught everyone's attention. Then delivered her juicy answer pointing a finger authoritatively at her listeners, "God is watching you!" Everybody was now in fits, but inside I felt pain, and thought of all the suffering Mary must have gone through in that convent. Her tragi-comic stories helped me to understand why she was such an extrovert and I felt loving compassion towards her. Jean Paul once hid her high heels that had fallen off while she was sitting on her high stool. "Jean Paul! Give me back my shoes… please…" She begged. "Your shoes? What shoes?" he replied with a twisted smile. Feeling her distress Maurice said in his particular deep voice, "Come on, Jean Paul, give them back to her. You are a bore!" "Yes, please find them!" Mary was now feeling angry. "Get them yourself! They are over there, under the radiator!" Maurice kept his nose in his work as if he was concentrating. "But I can't walk without them," she replied distressingly. I was intrigued that her attractive 20-year-old body was deformed by the constant use of high-heeled shoes. Later she explained that the tendons in her calves had shrunk so much that it was painful for her to put her feet flat on the ground.

"But how do you manage when in the shower? Or to reach your bed?" I asked with some concern. "Oh! I stand on tiptoe while I wash, then I slip on a pair of high-heeled pink furry slippers that I always have with me in the flat." She was amused by my concern.

The art students came from all walks of life, each one so different from the other. I came to know the ones who worked on the ground floor best, especially in our studio with Pierre, Nicole and Jean Paul. In the adjacent room were Laura, Maurice, Ron (the Armenian who was brilliant at lettering), Eberhardt (a 6' 10" German), and Fikrett (the silent, hard-working 5' 4" Turk). The men were inclined to study advertising, while the women went into fashion, interiors and painting.

I became friends with Eric, the son of an army colonel, who was kind and attentive to me; with the tall and glamorous Laurence who came from a French aristocratic family; with Ron the powerful 26 year-old American with whom I spoke English; with Pierre who gave me lifts on his Vespa. Now well settled and at ease at Paul Colin art school, I did not mind that the Boss still ignored me. One-day I observed him looking at an almost finished still life drawing on my easel and the way he scrutinised it, showing his interest, greatly reassured me.

In the last week of May 1954, Myrette and I moved from the crowded and noisy district of Rue des Halles to the steep cobbled street of Rue des Martyrs, meandering up La Butte Montmartre. N°81 was half a block up from the Boulevard Clichy, just above a renowned gay nightclub called 'Madame Arthur'. This flat was lighter and more spacious, and Myrette got rid of a lot of her junk before the move.

"Now, I want everything to be Modern. You see how I have had all the walls painted white? The furniture must be simple and I want bookshelves for all my books... of course! We'll have a low coffee table here and a comfortable sofa over there. You will help me to make a nice interior, won't you?" She was joyful and happy to include me into all parts of her life. "As for the lighting, my electrician recommends the latest thing done in Paris today - neon strips of light over the windows; but hidden behind a narrow board, so that we are not blinded by the glare. And here, I'll need some sort of lamp stand for reading... what do you think?" She was obviously delighted to have an attentive ear. I enjoyed giving her my ideas and helping her to arrange the space we were going to share. She talked all the time, informing me of many aspects of her life, all kinds of stories about her whereabouts, how she had met my mother whom she adored, how she had an only son called Claude, who had just come back from the Indo-Chinese war. She usually started talking as soon as I entered the flat, and invariably I heard her voice coming from the sitting room, "Is that you François?" After my response she continued, "By the way, I've mislaid my glasses. I can't see to find them... could you possibly help me? Come on, let's hear what you've done today!" She took an interest in all my creative work, and, although she did not really know anything about art, her feminine intuition often led her to give positive criticism. After our short art discussion, I went into the kitchen to see if any shopping needed to be done to prepare our supper.

The nightclub of 'Madame Arthur' was a magnet to the many Parisian gay men who from 6 pm until 2 or 3 am continuously went in and out of the mysterious cellars. Its front panel was a shiny dark red with 'Madame Arthur' in gold letters over its arched entrance. A wooden board advertising the club hung on an unsophisticated wrought iron sign projected into the street, and a red light dimly lit the descending steps. I never investigated the Club. The dense atmosphere and the potent smells of alcohol, sweat and extravagant perfumes together with the loud music and the shrieks of laughter, was a barrier that curbed my curiosity.

As I came out of Number 81, there was no way I could avoid the group of guys always standing outside the entrance. I soon became aware of how it must feel to be a woman being devoured by sexually avid eyes, full of desires of ever-needy men. As I walked by, I'd hear things like, "Hey! Fancy him?" Or, "Hello darling!" Or, "Nice, nice!" This made me accelerate my steps away from the group, or, when I arrived back from work, I dived into my porch, unpleasantly conscious of the attraction I was causing. After some time I deduced to myself, 'I must not look at women with such sexual desires any more, for now I know how it feels and it's very disturbing and unpleasant!'

Living in Montmartre opened my eyes to the darker side of the big city. One sunny Saturday morning around 10 o'clock, I was looking down through the French windows at the passers-by in rue des Martyrs, when a plump North African man in a white shirt appeared on the doorstep of the porch opposite. The man took a big breath of the cool spring Parisian air and looked to his left, perhaps wondering which café to go for his breakfast. Suddenly a tall thin man coming down the street pulled out a large cooking knife from under his coat and violently planted it in the man's liver! Then he vanished...

The plump man looked horrified at the knife planted just under his chest, and his white shirt flooded with the vivid colour of his blood. He looked up to the sky as if to ask God why, and collapsed heavily onto the pavement. A few passers-by gathered around him and someone ran up to the nearest café to call an ambulance. A nauseous feeling came over me and I turned away from the scene thinking, 'and what can I do? A man has just been murdered, his life taken away just like that, in a few seconds. Why?' I concluded there was nothing I could do and I did not want to get involved as a possible witness, with all the complications that it would bring. I just did not understand why a man could be alive one minute and dead the next. I thought the tragic event was probably due to a squaring of accounts between the O.A.S. and the F.L.N. (the secret organisation for French Algeria and the National Liberation Front of the native Algerians). The waves of unrest and violence in the French colonies were now reaching the capital and the larger cities. The French had recently lost the war in Indo-China to the Communist Vietcong and, quite rightly I thought, the Algerian people also wanted their freedom.

On that particular day, Myrette had gone to a village in the country called Mézière where she owned a small property. She enjoyed retreating there to find absolute quietness. I never told her about the murder on the rue des Martyrs.

First steps towards a relationship

Although the big city had its dramas, on the whole I was happy living there. I created my own rhythm of life and I looked forward to going to the art school every morning, which took less than 30 minutes. It felt good arriving early and starting my work before everybody. Nicole was an early bird too and she chatted to me as I tried to concentrate on whatever I had decided to do that day.

I became aware of how much Laura had begun to take a place in my heart. There was not one morning I did not stretch my ears to listen for her voice among the tumult of the others students. Had she arrived? Usually she was late… yes, I could now hear her crystalline laugh, a warm feeling of reassurance would descend over me, allowing me to go back into my work. A short time after her arrival, similar to a cat needing loving attention, my passionate feelings came to the forefront and occupied my work space, temporarily obliterating what I was doing and demanding that I give them full attention.

Finally I gave in, searching for an excuse to justify my visit, like going to the loo, or boldly popping into the room where she worked to borrow a tube of gouache or a brush, or to ask a question of the student next to her. When luck was on my side, she turned round looking at me with her pale Nordic eyes questioning, and then giving me a faint, frolicking smile. I would beam back and feeling satisfied, go back to my desk with the pussycat in me purring in my heart, giving me back the space to get on with whatever I was doing.

'I must ask her out for a meal somewhere… but it must not be too expensive… where could that be? I know, the Brasserie Avenue des Ternes, where they served me once a wonderful plate of sauerkraut with juniper berries, Frankfurter sausages and plain boiled potatoes… and of course Alsatian beer! That will be perfect!' I thought smiling to myself while travelling home in the Métro. The idea of the Frankfurters and Alsatian beer amused me. Good! That was decided – the Brasserie it will be. Now, all I had to do was to find the appropriate moment when she was by herself and invite her…

Strangely enough, as if fate had been mysteriously aware of my intention, the following day Laura was alone standing in her classroom, completely absorbed in her work, her fingers blackened by the charcoal she was using to sketch a freely drawn fashion figure. I came up quietly behind her. The thumping of passions in my heart made my task difficult, but I let my legs carry me right up to her. I could smell her delicate perfume imperceptibly mixed with another rich earthy scent that awoke in me an awareness of maternal feminine potentials. I leaned over her shoulder to look at the freely drawn sketch. Feeling me close and being surprised by my sudden presence, she turned her head, "Oh! It's you François," she let out surprised; I did not dare look into her eyes, as my thumping heart would have exploded! So instead I looked down at her drawing and said quietly, as I felt my cheeks blushing, "That's a nice evening coat you've drawn here." She immediately replied, "Thank you, but I am not satisfied with it; I can't get the collar right somehow… what do you think?"

Looking intensely at her drawing was like a cool breeze on my burning heart, and I felt more together. "Bigger, make it much bigger like the wrapping paper one puts round a bouquet of flowers. It is a winter coat is it not?" "Yes it is!" She held the black charcoal firmly in her silky white fingers and in one skilful swoop, increased the size of the collar. Then she rapidly added texture by making light, fast circular movements within the collar to give it a fluffy appearance. "How is that now?" She smiled and looked into my eyes. The magic of art worked; the new collar brought perfect balance to the whole design. "Great! Most elegant, when will we see you in it?" I made her burst into laughter, so I continued, as the timing was perfect, "Laura, how would you like to come out for a meal with me tonight?" She paused and hesitated while looking up and down at me as if evaluating the pros and the cons… "… Yes, all right then, where and when shall we meet?" "How about at 8 p.m. on the Place Wagram, by Les Ternes underground station?" I really wondered what I was getting myself into when she accepted my invitation.

Later in the afternoon I left Paul Colin's studios feeling rather ethereal. I only had two hours… to go back to the flat, make myself some tea, have a quick shower, shave, brush my teeth, and put on clean clothes before diving back into the underground.

'Hey! You're taking Laura out for supper tonight… oh, oh! Come on François! Be more serious!' I said to my grinning face in the mirror as I shaved, trying to ground myself and get out of this euphoric state. Then came choosing a shirt… they were all rather worn, so I decided to wear a thin black polo neck jersey, which went well with my grey tweed jacket, dark charcoal trousers and my suede moccasins.

I arrived five minutes early, looked around and not seeing her, I rested my back against the Art Nouveau wrought iron railings, lit a Gauloise and waited, now feeling peaceful and quiet. But it was not for long… at 8 p.m. precisely, she walked across the Avenue Wagram, her elegant figure wearing a long white raglan raincoat and white high heeled shoes. I took her arm as we walked down Avenue des Ternes and felt her gentle strength, keeping my arm tight against her waist. I was in a not too familiar situation as all my previous close encounters with the feminine had been at Summerhill School. This was completely different; I did not know what the outcome would be and decided not to think about it but to enjoy every second in her presence. "Are your digs near here?" I asked wondering if I could take her back after our meal. "Yes, not too far…" She replied followed by a short laugh, "Actually, I share a flat with three other girls." 'Now I know that I will not be taking her home after our meal,' I remarked to myself.

Typical black and white dressed Parisian waiters were rushing to and fro from the kitchens to the tables in the rather full, smoky and noisy restaurant. We found a quiet corner upstairs by the large window overlooking the Avenue. Two other couples talking quietly contributed to an intimate atmosphere. While I helped Laura to take off her white coat, I was tempted to caress her pale blue angora jersey but I refrained. Wearing a tight, tubular, marine blue skirt that moulded her hips, she slid up to the large window on the shiny surface of the oilcloth bench. I sat down in turn and met her smiling eyes, with their lively, almost iridescent blue irises and deep black pupils – attractive openings into the black hole of her universe, which I did not dare enter. I might have lost my frail stability and disappeared altogether into confusion. At that instant, my throat stopped functioning and swallowing my accumulated saliva noisily, I took a menu pretending to look at it while I recuperated. "Shall we go for the sauerkraut and two half pints of Alsatian beer? You'll see, it's very good!" She agreed and the waiter took the order and disappeared as quickly as he had come.

I wanted to get to know her and asked many questions about her youth and life in Germany before and after the war. But I knew that her life during the war would be too painful for her to share and didn't ask. Her mother had been a costume designer for the theatre; her father, originally a musician, had been an officer in the Wehrmacht and had died on the Russian front in 1942 when she was 13. Life had been really difficult for them in Cologne without her father. Their home was bombed in 1944; all that was left standing in the city was the Cathedral. As she was recounting her story, a grey cloud of sadness descended on our table. I began to share some of my past with her, to show her how similar our backgrounds were and that, in the South of France, it had not been easy for our mother either. This didn't really lighten the atmosphere, but somehow brought a wider dimension to the realities of war and at the same time made us feel closer to each other. "Is it not strange, that you and I, whose parents were struggling to survive in opposite sides during this terrible war, are both now sitting comfortably opposite each other, in a cafe in Paris? Sharing the parts of our lives that have been so painful… due to the deaths of our respective fathers… and isn't it weird that we are about to devour an enormous plate of appetising sauerkraut and Frankfurt sausages?"

She had been listening intensely, but the end of my sentence made her explode into laughter, which, like a gust of warm wind, cleared the heavy cloud over our table. We stayed silent as we savoured the delicate mixture of the sauerkraut, smoked sausages, boiled potatoes, and the indefinable taste of juniper berries.

I was aware that Laura was eight years older than me and as I told her my stories, I took care not to reveal my age, since I thought she would not take me seriously if she knew. Now I was making her laugh, enjoying watching her mouth, her well drawn dark red lips and her beautiful teeth that attracted me so much. Satisfied by the meal, feeling full and slightly numbed by the effect of the beer, I pushed my chair away from the table to stretch my legs, pulled out a Gauloise from its blue packet and presented it to her, "Would you like a cigarette? A small coffee?" "Yes I would, but, if you don't mind, I'll have one of mine, I prefer American ones."

She searched in her white handbag and pulled out a packet of Lucky Strike, I smelt the honeyed, spice-bread scent of American tobacco. I then offered her a light from my primitive looking but efficient windproof lighter. As she drew a long puff, I noticed that her shiny dark lipstick had tinted the tip of her cigarette and I thought at that moment, 'I suppose that when I come to kiss her I will be covered in dark lipstick too.' Amused by my thought I looked at her. "Why are you smiling?" She queried, her eyes enlarging as she raised her dark eyebrows. "Oh! Upon seeing the quantity of lipstick on your cigarette, I was wondering how much of it you must eat when you're simply eating bread?"

"You are a funny man!" She remarked. I was much too shy to share what was in my mind and preferred to hide my lively desires. "What's the time?" She suddenly asked. I had stopped checking my watch, wanting these moments with her to last for as long as possible. How could we allow this thing, this avid monster called Time, to be the arbitrator, to rule over our time together? But I knew that the tic-tac of the mechanical ogre was ever more powerful than my vulnerable wishes. "10:45!" I reluctantly replied. "Oh, dear, I must leave, it's so late!" She exclaimed with surprise. At that instant I felt sadness, our evening was coming to an end.

    The waiter stood by while I glanced at the bill... Laura was struggling to put on her coat while still sitting down. An unexpected wave of panic took over me when I looked into my wallet... I could not believe it! How was it possible to be so stupid on such an occasion? Oh no! The reality was staring at me, there was not one bank note in my wallet, just nothing! A sudden change in my presence toppled over, from being the François taking the beautiful Laura out, being the "Man" who takes the girl out, to a poor, embarrassed, young man who had been in an instant stripped of his colourful feathers. Now I was sitting there hesitantly looking into my empty wallet... "Is there anything wrong?" Laura looked at me bleakly. "Yes, I have no money with me, I forgot to take some when I left... do you have some by any chance? I'll pay you back tomorrow morning." Looking straight into her eyes sincerely I wanted show that I wasn't trying to get a free meal out of her. "How much is it?" She questioned discreetly, searching in the depth of her white bag. "Err, 135 Francs, excluding the tip." I managed to reply in a thin voice. Laura pulled out a 200 Francs note and gave it without looking at me. Now feeling more relaxed I said, "How amusing, I invite you out and you pay the bill!" I let out a short hesitant laugh. "Is that funny?" She was not amused. "Lucky that you had money with you!" I replied, trying to turn the situation around and be more positive.

    It was raining as we came out of the Brasserie, I breathed in deeply the welcome fresh air, to clear the embarrassing murky feeling that had settled over me. This time, I did not take her arm and simply walked quietly beside her. She seemed to be lost in her thoughts, looking at the pavement as she walked. How was it that we had been so close during the few hours together in the restaurant and now were seemingly so far apart? Laura had retreated into her own universe – the one I had had a brief glimpse into while sitting at the table. I broke the silence as we reached Les Ternes tube station, "Where do you go?" "Trocadero, it's direct," she replied as she stepped down into the Métro.

    When I entered Laura's studio the next day, I felt more confident in myself. I now knew her a little better and was able to go up to her without my heart thumping as it had previously. "Thank you for pulling me out of trouble last night. Here are the 135 Francs I owe you, and all my apologies for the embarrassment I may have caused you." I said, as I put the exact amount on her work surface. "It was fine, really… are you sure you're ok though?" she said thoughtfully. "Yes, positive! You were my guest after all." "Thank you. I did enjoy the evening very much." She softly replied and looked at me kindly, almost tenderly. While talking with Laura, I noticed from the corner of my eye, that Eberhardt was listening to our conversation. As I left the room he turned his head slightly towards me and gave me a strange bitter smile. I felt his hard blue eyes follow me out of the room. Then I heard him questioning Laura in German, probably about our evening out. This left me with a feeling of unease. I wished he had never come to this art school and that I had never known of his existence. But I realised that I could not do anything about it, and that it would be best to let it be, and trust that I was the one closest to Laura's heart.

Tasting the flavours of wealth

Once a month, always in the late afternoon after I finished at Paul Colin's studios, I went to collect my regular cash payments from my grandmother at the Drouant-David Art Gallery. The gallery was partly owned by my mother's first husband, Emmanuel David and had been open since 1942. Its entrance was situated almost opposite the Elysée Palace, at n°52, Faubourg Saint Honoré. To access, it I went under a large building, through a wide corridor between two classy fashion shops, into a large inner courtyard, and opposite was the entrance of the renowned Art Gallery. Its two display windows consisted of heavy velvet burgundy curtains and a sturdy oak easel displaying the work of a famous artist. I always stopped to look at the painting – one month it would be a Rouault, the other a Duffy, or a Vlaminck and at times a Cézanne.

CHAPTER 6

Stepping on the Gallery's doormat activated a buzzer that announced one's presence. At that moment a mixture of impressions always invaded me. First, I smelled the oil paint varnish, scented wax polish blended with dashes of expensive perfumes and cigar tobacco. I was aware of a heavy dense silence only broken at times by whispering voices. The gallery space was divided into three parts: the first was a permanent exhibition of renowned painters, each painting lit by a shaded, tubular light just above it. Then three wide steps took me into a large square of white marble, which in the daytime was lit by a glazed ceiling, with enormous back-to-back brown leather armchairs in the centre. This part of the gallery was reserved for the monthly one-man exhibitions. At the back of the Gallery were three steps that led up to an office on the left - Emmanuel David, Mr Drouant, who was rarely present, a secretary and my half brother Philippe. To the right of the office was a large stock of paintings stored behind a grey silk curtain.

One part of me enjoyed going there, observing the very rich in their world, surrounded by works of art, highly perfumed ladies, vast bouquets of flowers displayed on antique furniture, marble and bronze statues, fur coats and crocodile shoes. It was all very captivating and somehow opened my eyes to the existence of a totally different society from the one I knew.

Another part found it rather painful, l and that was my self-conscious ego. I was not in my element when surrounded by such wealth. I suddenly became much too aware that there were no sharp creases in my trousers, that my jacket looked scruffy by comparison to the immaculate jackets I saw in the Gallery, that my worn shirt collar was not perfectly ironed, and that my moccasins had done too much walking. The Parisian high society I came into contact with in the Gallery Drouant-David put much importance on appearance. When they met me I became aware of condescending glances trying to assess who I was, making me feel I was not worthy of being talked to. As the ladies walked by they often showed a trace of a smile on their highly painted faces.

Not wanting to disturb Philippe or Mano, I quietly looked round, silently enjoying one painting after the other, noticing the different expressions and styles of each artist. During these quiet moments, I felt in communication with them and entered into their world for a brief moment. Then I waited discreetly in an armchair and watched the life of the gallery. Mano was a great salesman and every part of his body became alive when he decided a customer was ready for a purchase. His passion for art lay particularly with the younger painters. His protégé was Bernard Buffet, who he discovered when the artist was only 19 and penniless and, moved by the originality of his art, Mano decided to take him on as a permanent artist. He had also many others like Carzou, Pricking, Kisling, Segovia, Guignebert, Rebeyrolles, Dany Lartigues to name a few... these artists were fortunate to be asked to produce so many paintings each month, as it assured their daily bread.

"Come! I'll show you something wonderful," Mano would say enthusiastically to a chosen customer. "Look! It hasn't been exhibited yet and the paint is still fresh! Come."

Taking his prey by the arm to the back of the Gallery, he energetically drew back the silk curtains that hid his treasures, pulled out the painting he had in mind and turning it round to the client exclaimed, "Has ever anybody painted a subject like this before?"

The collector looked perplexed: in full size, a sad looking young man stood with his trousers hanging below his knees, his private parts in evidence, behind him, a toilet without a seat, a grey pipe leading up to a water tank and a handless pull chain. This was painted in grey tones, its contours heavily emphasized by a thick harsh aggressive black line. "This artist is going to become a name, I tell you. Look at his drawing and how expressive is that line!" The surprised client asked, "How much is the painting?" "Oh! It practically costs nothing, compared to what it's going to be worth in a few years!" Mano always described the price as completely insignificant compared to the quality of the works he was selling. He made the client feel most fortunate and even privileged to be offered such a rare piece of work and they should absolutely not miss this unique opportunity to purchase it.

Observing the interactions of the very rich from my armchair, I waited for the correct moment to say hello to my brother, or Mano or to whomever I knew in the Gallery. Of course they were all busy in their own world, of which obviously I played a tiny part. Philippe walking around carrying paintings sometimes gave me a wink or a smile. At other times, he would come up to me, touch my face affectionately and say, "Okay?" And without waiting for an answer, he went on with his important doings. Once, he came up to me and said, "Oh, good you've come. Follow me and I'll show you something that might fit you." He took me round the back of the entrance where the hats, scarves and coats were hanging and pulled out a light beige, camel-hair coat.

"Try it on. I had it made specially but I find it much too big, and can't wear it." The expensive coat was lined with a pale creamy satin fabric that felt cool and smooth under my fingers. I slipped it on and it fitted me perfectly. I instantly felt at home. It had two large outside pockets with a wide flap, well-padded shoulders and an imposing belt with a leather buckle.

"Really? Are you sure? Can I really have it?" "Yes, you look good in it, it fits you like a glove, so it's yours!" His slightly forced smile, made me wonder if he suddenly regretted giving it to me. I wore this coat for many years for it was like having a protective friend, a magic carpet to lift me into the upper class Parisian society. When I wore it I felt respected by the wealthy, but as soon as I was in the presence of the poorer population, I became self-conscious. I looked like a rich young man, and I realised then how true the French saying was, "l'habit ne fait pas le moine"… appearances can be deceptive.

Once, on my monthly visit to the Drouant-David Gallery, I noticed my brother talking to a group of young, interesting looking people. Feeling confident in my beautiful camel coat, I walked nonchalantly towards them. As I approached Philippe exclaimed, "Hey! François, doesn't my coat look good on you?" A painful wave of embarrassment overtook me; suddenly I felt hot and sweaty as I stood there silently, finding it difficult to smile and not being quite sure what to answer. Philippe continued, "Yes... he is my half brother from Provence and he is studying advertising at Paul Colin's art school." Now I had become the focal point of attention for the group; the situation was hard to bear. My brother would not stop... "And how are you doing at the Art school?" "Very well, thank you..." I answered trying to put the pieces of my scattered self together again. Not giving me any space to say anything else, he turned to his friends and went on chatting... "Yes, as I was saying, I really find these Italian cars exquisite. I'm thinking of getting the little Giulietta, they're small, fast and nippy, good for the town..."

I walked away leaving them to their conversation that I could not possibly participate in and let myself fall into the farthest leather armchair at the back of the gallery. I did not feel connected to this display of wealth that surrounded me, and thought about our relationship. I knew it was far from clear by the condescending behaviour my brother showed towards me. In his view, our mother had abandoned her love for him and given it to me. Perhaps he felt that I'd taken his place. He was only 10 in 1936 when his father took him away from our mother and placed him in a Jesuit school in Avignon. Due to the war, he did not see his mother again for another 10 years, during which time he received no motherly affection. His grandmother Mamiche, Mano's mother, did care for him, but it was not the same kind of affection of course. His father was not affectionate and was always too busy with his work, and replaced this missing love by loading him up with toys and material comforts. Understanding this helped me to forgive him for his selfishness and insensitivity towards me.

He lived with his father, his stepmother Gany and her 4-year-old son Bernard in a luxurious flat at n°11 of the rue Vaneau. Gany had invited me there a few times and it was then that I really came into contact with Parisian bourgeois way of life. Comfortably relaxed in the large armchair, I recalled the first time I entered the impressive doors of n°11 and the elaborate black wrought-iron staircase and lift, oozing with imposing quality. Two floors up, I found myself in a spacious oak panelled, carpeted landing with a high ceiling to give the place a sense of importance. I rang the bell and waited… a shy, slender, country girl in a narrow black dress with a white lace apron, appeared through the massive door and said timidly, "Who should I announce?" "François." I replied.

I walked into a sombre hallway with no windows while she disappeared behind a door, leaving it slightly open. I peered through the gap and saw their spacious sitting room. I suddenly saw the slim, elegant figure of Gany walking towards me, on her face a large welcoming smile. It was difficult not to be taken by her beauty. She slowed down as she came close and offered me her shiny, taut cheekbone, which I kissed delicately, and she turned the other cheek. Two kisses on alternate cheeks was the Parisian way of greeting close family. I savoured the finesse of her perfume while my lips felt the extreme smoothness of her dark skin. I looked at her brown, almond-shaped eyes looking absently into nowhere and noticed that her smile stayed frozen. She now focussed on my camel coat and said in a soft low voice, "How are you? Here, give me your coat, make yourself comfortable, and in about half an hour, when you hear the bell, come into the dining room. It's over there." Without giving me time to answer, she turned away and I watched her feline body move in her tight, mauve, jersey skirt, emphasising her narrow waist and round buttocks that danced away into the shady parts of the apartment. I learned later that Mano had fallen in love with her when he saw her for the first time, dancing at a ballet performance at the Opera House. She was then 19.

I had never seen such a richly decorated interior before. The oak herringbone floor was covered in soft coloured Persian rugs, the walls were lined with dark green damask silk covered with many paintings in beautifully carved and gilded antique frames and lit by individual tubular shades. My attention was drawn to a small portrait of a lady and I recognized the brush strokes of Cézanne.

WALNUTS & GOAT CHEESE

'It must be the portrait of the artist's mother', I thought. Next to it was the head of a crucifixion by Rouault in wide, powerful pink and red strokes, each heightened by a thick black line. A Miro was hanging over an antique 18th century walnut desk. An immense black concert piano stood in the middle of the room. In a corner I admired a sculpture by Zadkine and on the coffee table was a small bronze nude of a reclining figure by Renoir. Everywhere I looked, fine art was glaring at me, so I walked to the tall windows to appease my artistic eagerness and looked down into a wooded private park. On the path below I watched an overly happy little dog gambolling about, then stopping, sniffing with excitement and lifting his leg to spray the cast iron leg of the park bench. Not far behind came a lady pushing a pram…

"Ha, ha! Who do I see here? When did you arrive?" The sudden voice of my brother made me jump out of my skin. "Oh, a little while ago… Gany welcomed me in." I replied as we gave each other a short hug.

"Come, I am in my room." He led me back into the hallway and through a door into a bright room, which also gave onto the park. "This is my grandmother's room, you know… Mamiche from Camaret?" I had not yet met Mamiche but he had told me about her once when we were on the island. This room was decorated in grey greens and old pinks and smelt of dusty face powder. Under the large gilded mirror standing on a Louis XVth overly carved marble fireplace, was a papier mâché wig stand. It was a delicately painted bust of a young woman and on it's head rested askew, a dusty reddish wig, the hair drawn back and set into a bun held together by rusty hairpins. "What's this wig?" I queried intrigued, "Don't laugh, its Mamiche's false hair, she'd be furious if she knew that you saw it!"

We went through a narrow door into what I thought was a walk-in cupboard with a tall window through which I could still see the park. Immediately to the right was a narrow single bed with an ancient Provencal bed cover and three large cushions. Behind it, a shelf displayed miniature metallic motorcars, a few sea urchin skeletons and a chrome base lamp with a dark green, glass shade. To the left a pretty, tall back chair, a small side table piled with books, magazines and cameras, and a large conch shell he had probably brought from the island. A photo of himself age six wearing a striped woollen bonnet stood amongst it all. In the corner was an elegant antique Spanish guitar. All the walls right up to the ceiling were covered by bookshelves filled with science fiction books, thrillers, and books about sailing. As I looked round I thought he must spend most of his free time reading!

We heard the distant sound of a hand bell, "Ah! We are called in for lunch. Shall we go to the bathroom? One must always wash one's hands before a meal, you know," Philip could not refrain from saying.

The long dining room stretched back to a wall on which hung a 17th century tapestry of a white bodied Diane with her bow and arrow, surrounded by greyhounds looking at her with admiration. Under it was an XVIIth century walnut dresser on which stood fine cut glass decanters, silver coffee pots and porcelain dishes. To my left was the door to the kitchens that I never investigated. Straight opposite were four tall windows with bottle green, cut-velvet curtains that fell heavily onto the oak parquet floor. The long dining table was covered with a fine white embroidered linen cloth and arranged with crystal, silver and porcelain tableware. Two highly polished copper jardinières overflowing with short white roses added to the impressive layout. And surrounding the luxurious table, erect like Buckingham Palace guards, stood eight bronze-studded, tapestry covered, tall back chairs. Touching my shoulder gently Gany murmured, "François, please sit opposite me, next to Mano's seat."

Her son Bernard came rushing in and his large black eyes looked around excitedly, quickly spotting me. They looked amused and a faint smile came on his dark violet lips. I had met this thin six year old with knobbly knees and long-fingered hands once or twice previously at the gallery. As he sat down on her right, she said to him, "Surely you know François? He is Philippe and Sylvette's other half brother, you know, Honor's youngest son… and what do we say?" Without looking at his mother, his eyes fixed on me he uttered shyly, "Hello!"

Philippe came in grabbing a slice of baguette out of the silver breadbasket and sat to the left of Mano, "Hmm, smells good, what are we eating?" He asked inquisitively as he sat down. No one replied. Then Mano came in and exclaimed as if surprised by my presence, "Hey, look at who is here?" Had he forgotten that he had invited me for lunch? Obviously not, my place had been laid, and then I thought it was probably Gany who had remembered the invitation. He walked round, I rose from my chair to greet him while he laid his hand heavily on my shoulder and we exchanged a light touch of cheeks. "Bonjour Mano!" With his hands still on my shoulder, he pulled me to and fro while looking straight into my eyes and said, "Okay at Paul Colin? You're working hard?" I nodded and without expecting more of an answer, he let go of my shoulder and sat down expressing a long-winded, "Good…"

I looked round the table and realised that the only person who was aware of how I felt was Bernard. He was still looking at me with the same faint smile. I read in his eyes that he understood my slight frustration and embarrassment at not being taken as a person, but only as a kind of thing, an object in the shape of a human, a boy from the South, who they had to appear interested in, but in truth, each one had other much more important things to do. I realised that Mano, Philippe and Gany were each sealed in their own world, each one not interested in the world of the other except when it had a direct impact on their lives.

Now all my senses were on alert as I was in a world loaded with manners and codes of behaviour that I knew were extremely important to them. Doing the 'wrong thing' would immediately label me as a country boy. I was not familiar with the table manners of wealthy Parisians and realised that I had much to learn. The arrangements of the cutlery, glasses, plates were different from what I knew and everything seemed more complicated, over done. I felt

CHAPTER 6

rather lost in the midst of all this material profusion. Which glass should I use to drink out of first? Which knife? Which spoon? Which side should I put down my bread? Which hand do I use to hold my knife?

My closest point of reference was several years before, when I visited my grandparents in England and we ate lunch in the posh rest home. I remembered that the first thing in table manners was to keep your hands under the table. So while waiting to be served, I consciously put my hands on my knees under the tablecloth. Gany grabbed the little bronze statuette of a lady with a large crinoline skirt and shook it… a beautiful high musical tinkle came from under the skirt. The object intrigued me and I wanted to turn it upside down and look under the skirt to see how it worked, but I refrained. The pretty young servant, who had led me into the flat, came out of the kitchen carrying a magnificent steaming porcelain soup tureen and stood next to me. "Good, you're on time Marie, leave it over here!" As she leaned forward to put down the heavy tureen, my eyes briefly escaped into the cradle of the soft curves of her attractive bosom. No one realised how much this furtive escape into the comfort of the feminine, comforted me.

I noticed that I was the only one with my hands on my knees. My brother's hands were busy nibbling the crust of the golden baguette, leaving behind a trail of soft white crumbs. Mano's hands were on the table, resting on either side of his plates, his fingers nervously pushing back the bits of skin around his nails. Gany was holding the ladle ready to serve the soup. My eyes rested on Bernard, with his little wrists tightly closed, the thumbs neatly holding his fingers, and he gave me a reassuring smile. I finally put my wrists on the table and decided that from now on, I would follow his table manners.

The meal was tasty, the Bordeaux wine excellent but I did not enjoy the tense atmosphere. In his usual manner Mano talked almost continuously about politics, about the world of art dealing, throwing in the names of famous politicians, rich businessmen, artists from the film and theatre world and of course the painters he met. Gany joined in at times with sarcastic remarks; her tongue was sharp with not a kind word for anyone, especially women. Aware of my presence, my brother would sometime calm the conversation by saying things like, "oh Daddy, it's not so bad." Or "don't be so radical Daddy!" Or "I don't think he means it like that."

I was relieved when the meal came to an end. We all stood up at the same time and, as I came out of the dining room, I felt a soft hand taking mine. It was Bernard leading me to his bedroom gently; he ordered, "Come and see my toys." We went to another part of the immense flat where Mano and Gany's quarters were, and Bernard took me straight to his room, which reminded me of a child's Aladdin's Cave. His bed in the corner was filled with soft toys, bears, lions, giraffes, rabbits, elephants and many others, some of them as big as himself! Some even talked when you touched them! All kinds of electric cars and trains littered the soft, carpeted floor. Many children's books were piled on his bedside table. We played together in silence for over an hour, each aware of the other and enjoying the harmony of our presence." You are already leaving?"

"Yes, I have to go now, it's been great being with you Bernard." I bent down and kissed him on his forehead as he went on playing, as if ignoring my departure. I found Gany in the sitting room lying on the sofa reading. "You're going already?" "Yes, I have some work to prepare for tomorrow. Thank you very much for inviting me for lunch." As she did not stand up, I bent down over the low sofa to kiss her. Holding her book with both hands so as not to lose her page, she stretched her neck out slightly and offered me her attractive cheeks.

Time passed quickly while I sat in the deep cosy armchair in the Gallery, reflecting on my first visit to the David's apartment. How they lived was so far away from how I was brought up, the contrast was immense. Their life appeared to focus mostly on the material, which to me seemed to take all the space away from human feelings. Love and the awareness of the each other's presence were practically non-existent. As I reflected on this, an enormous wave of love and

CHAPTER 6

admiration for my mother invaded my feelings. She had brought us up, Sylvette and me, without a bean in her pocket, yet we did not feel this as a lack. Seeing my brother's and Bernard's bedrooms filled with so many objects, made me wonder how they would have reacted on seeing ours – a bed, a chair, a cat, our drawings pinned on the walls, and one or two books was about all we possessed. It seemed to be enough for us though. I understood that our mother's love filled the place of our needs and wants.

The Gallery buzzer took me out of my daydream. Gany, elegantly dressed with a silver fox wrap round her neck, entered followed closely by two very distinguished gentlemen. Mano came out of his office and walked rapidly across to them, kissed Gany distantly and greeted the men with a welcoming smile, shaking their hands profusely. He then took one by each arm, talking to them confidently and led them towards a Goerg painting of a naked young woman surrounded by a profusion of flowers. Gany sat on the large sofa in the centre of the gallery and I felt obliged to greet her. Hesitantly I walked towards her not wanting to intrude. "Bonsoir you!" She said as if she had forgotten my name, and turned her face with closed eyes and presented her round cheekbones to me, "Bonsoir Gany." I lightly brushed the silky brown skin with my lips. Tonight there was no smile from Gany, not even a frozen one. She seemed to be in a bad mood, so I backed away awkwardly, turned round and reached my comfortable armchair in the corner of the Gallery, from where I could see the whole room. I felt safe in the unlit corner.

Two young men entered the Gallery, one plump and well-dressed who must have been around 26 years old, the other tall and thin, almost frail and looking unsure of himself; and probably not more than three years older than me. They walked into the Gallery straight towards Gany, "Bonsoir Bernard, bonsoir Simon," her voice was suave as she stood up to greet them. And I thought to myself that this must be Bernard Buffet, the painter Mano had recently taken under his wing. Bernard was swimming in his clothes and covered in oil paint, on his trousers, shirt and jacket, and under his long, dirty fingernails and hands. Some traces of paint even dotted his long narrow face, now smiling at Gany to show a pair of orange-grey incisors. I deduced that he must be a heavy smoker. They were a strange and unusual couple indeed. Their untroubled homosexuality appeared to unite them, like two dogs that had discovered friendship in spite of their different backgrounds. One could have come from the streets, looking battered and scruffy, while the other was well groomed, coming out of some wealthy apartment. They sat on either side of Gany on the large sofa and chatted.

Invariably at the end of every day when all clients had left the Gallery, Philippe and Eric the handy man took a ping-pong table out from behind the heavy silky curtains and quickly put it up. Eric did everything physical and practical for the art business, wrapping up the fragile frames and works of arts, and delivering them to clients throughout the city. He had the body of a gym master; his kind protruding blue eyes and his extra large mouth never failed to give me a generous, caring smile. It was their time to unwind - they let go of the day's tensions and frustrations through shouts, screams, laughter and gesturing at each end of the table.

Maurice Combe was the last person to arrive in the gallery before the door was finally locked, so as not to be disturbed by a late visitor. I'd never seen him with clothes on before. He looked out of place here in sophisticated Paris, with his muscular body about to burst out of its tweed suit. He smiled and greeted Gany and her small party, while taking off his jacket, rolling up his sleeves and already thinking of the wild ping-pong match he would give Mano. But seeing me in the corner of his eye, he came towards me, obviously pleased to see his young harpoon fisherman friend from the island. We exchanged a warm hug.

"Maurice! What are you doing? Are you coming?" Mano called, eager to start the game. Certainly they put a lot of energy into it, played well and soon became the centre of attention. Sometime they played doubles, my brother and Gany would join in. The games would last until 8.30 to 9, and by then Mano was completely exhausted. Maurice, soaked in sweat and laughing, would suddenly realise the time, "Oh dear, I must go back to Monette, she'll be furious!"

I came to the gallery to collect my monthly envelope, and always felt embarrassed to ask for it. I felt I bothered Mano's crowded schedule, so I waited until he mentioned it. Everyone was ready to leave and, as Mano put on his heavy navy-blue coat, his black felt hat and burgundy Kashmir scarf, his memory jogged upon seeing me, "Oh yes, your envelope! That reminds me that I must contact the Tooth Gallery in London tomorrow." Once reassured with my monthly money, I was the first one to leave, saying to anyone ready to hear my voice that regained its freedom, "Goodbye! See you and thanks again."

Over drinking leads me into a strange experience

In the 1950s, student life in Paris was a very full time occupation, for as much went on at night as during the day. The intensity of cerebral concentration of the studies in the day built up some kind of emotional steam that needed to be let out after sunset! Generally my friends preferred stronger drinks than wine or beer; white Martinis were popular with the girls, whisky or gin with the lads. For myself, after trying various drinks, I noticed that I felt better the next day if I drank only good red wine. Most of the students who organised these parties came from wealthy families, and held them in their homes while the parents were out.

My relationship with Laura was not progressing as I had hoped and I felt a great need to have a female partner. Once, Maïté invited me to a party at her parent's home in Neuilly, they were away on some world journey. When I arrived at the elegant villa, she greeted me under the white porch with a radiant smile and green eyes twinkling with excitement. Her bright red, curly hair framed her white oval face elegantly. "Make yourself at home! The kitchen is over here; there is a lot of food to eat! The party is in here and the loos are over there." It was only 9 pm and the party had already started. Seeing no girl to my taste, I poured myself a glass of red wine from the bottle I had brought and went into the kitchen. It was a spacious room with a wide pine table in the centre covered in all kinds of food: salads, cold chickens, cheeses, fruit and bread. A slim, tall figure stood by the table with long flowing black hair that hid her face. She attracted me instantly and intrigued, I walked round and stood opposite her. She did not look up at me, as she seemed too busy choosing her food. She was not drinking white Martini, but also had a glass of red wine. "You're a friend of Maïté?" A low, gentle voice answered from behind the black hair curtain and, lifting her head slightly, a pair of deep blue eyes looked at me. "Yes, we were at school together." "You mean when you were in the kindergarten?" I was trying to make her laugh and it worked. She exploded into a laugh that instantly revealed all her femininity and beauty, and exclaimed, "No! Not in the kindergarten... later." I was delighted to see that the attraction seemed to be reciprocal and we went straight into conversation, longing to know all about each other. I was pleased at the thought of spending the evening with her.

It became our party; time stopped and we drank, talked and explored each other's world. When we finally danced, I noticed how light and responsive her body was. I could hardly feel her; it was as if I was dancing with air that pre-empted all my moves, "Have you studied dance?"

"Oh yes, I did ballet until I was 18, then studied Fado in Portugal, and my parents wanted me to become a professional dancer, but I want to be a doctor, so I am now studying medicine." Absorbed by each other, we had not watched the clock and unconsciously consumed too much Bordeaux. Pushed by my burning desire to come into contact with her attractive lips, I gently danced her to the far corner of the room. She followed without resistance as if she shared a similar feeling. We found ourselves in the unlit hallway, I came closer and her small firm breasts gently rested against my lower chest. I was now under the powerful spell of her warm breath.

I noticed a slight hesitation in her body and she murmured, "I have to go, it's 12:30 and my parents are fetching me. They are probably waiting in the car by now."

I felt distraught, abandoned and just stood there, watching my night fairy getting ready to go. Throwing her coat over her narrow shoulders, she turned towards me and, sending me a regretful smile, disappeared into the night. The abrupt ending of our harmonious short relationship was for me a bit like savouring a wonderful meal, while anticipating a great final with a delicious sweet that never came! I walked back into the large sitting room where a few couples were interlaced dancing to a slow languishing blues. I did not feel like seeing anyone. There was some Bordeaux left in a bottle and I gluttonously finished it.

I could not find Maïté to thank her for the evening, so I put on my coat and toppled out into the brisk late autumn air. I decided to walk home as I was reasonably close to my rented home at number 6, rue Cardinet. When outside, I became conscious that I was completely drunk, and tried to get rid of the numbness in my legs by briskly swinging them to and fro. They finally obeyed and fell into a regular walking rhythm.

In my tipsy thoughts, images of her beautiful face came up, but my thoughts were vague, almost blurred. I wanted a clearer picture of her but it would not come, and I went back into my confused thoughts. 'That's right, she had lived in Portugal where she had learned Fado dancing. Ah! Dancing with her was like dancing with your own soul, so light and smooth were her steps.' In my left hand I could still feel the supple presence of her waist. I suddenly realised that I did not even know her name! How strange to have spent a whole evening with someone I felt so close too and not even to know her name. 'Did she know mine?' I wondered.

I walked through the classy Neuilly district, crossed the Boulevard périférique and headed in the direction of the Porte Maillot. Walking at night in Paris for a 16 year old was very entertaining. Beside the attractive, well-lit shop windows, the prostitutes were actually the most distracting. Walking close to them created in me some kind of thrilling emotions - a mixture of fear and curiosity, while my instinct knew that however sublime the appearances of the fruit was, it might contain a dangerous poison. I first spotted these girls a long distance away up the boulevard; then I hesitated whether I should cross to the other side or simply carry on walking. I also had to be on my guard in case of potential aggression from a group of rough lads, or a violent drunkard. Or even, as it happened once when I lived at rue des Martyrs, by desperate homosexuals on the hunt for young men.

As I walked on in the night, my thoughts developed the subject… Depending on which part of Paris I was in, I found that the parading prostitutes changed in silhouettes, hairdos, make-up, clothing and age. In and around Pigalle, Place Clichy and the Boulevard they were rather overly painted with bright lipstick, their hair or wigs too glittery, too much gold, their miniskirts too short. As I passed them they would come up to me and say things like, "How about a quickie darling?" Or "come, I'll make it special for you!" Further away near the Porte Saint Martin they actually looked pitiful, older, sad and destroyed by their disruptive life and probably by too much drugs and alcohol. Walking up or down the Champs Elysées it was more difficult to spot them in the crowd; I only discovered they worked there when once I stopped to light my cigarette near l'Etoile. Cupping my hands to protect the flame from the wind, I saw a few metres away, a tall and very attractive young lady observing me, not more than two-years older than myself. She stood in a small recess in the last block before Place de l'Etoile with a silk scarf tightly around her head, her makeup precise and discreet. She was dressed in a knee-length grey tailored suit, her long neck protected from the cold by a mink fur collar, and, the thing that was somehow out of place, white, much too high heeled shoes. Our eyes met for a brief instant and I saw a question, quickly followed by a total disinterest. I felt confused and sad and I did not want her to know that I realised she was working, so I looked down and walked on. The next day I mentioned it to Jean-Paul, "Oh yes! They are the most expensive ones in Paris; not for your wallet I am afraid!" he said with a laugh.

Lost in my reflections about Parisian nightlife, I finally arrived at the Porte Maillot, an immense junction where I looked round to find the Boulevard Péreire. As I entered the Boulevard past the café, I walked by three ladies standing close to the entrance of a scruffy looking hotel.

"Hello handsome! Come over here and talk to us... we are cold and bored!" I was surprised to notice that my legs changed direction and took me to them, as if attracted by an invisible magnet. The faint, lurid flickering neon hotel sign certainly was not ideal for seeing their faces. A strong odour of cheap perfume hung like an intriguing cloud around them. They were wearing shapeless old fur coats, making them look rather plump, and reminding me of sparrows fluffing up their feathers in a cold wind.

There I was caught in a situation I had never known before, hooked into the mysterious web of this trio of keenly available ladies, each one eager to add a few more francs to top up their evening's harvest. Pushed by a wind of unsatisfied desires and plain curiosity, yet vaguely aware somewhere deep inside that I was navigating in the dense fog of alcohol, I allowed my inexperienced ship to go full sail into the unknown.

"Come on darling, which of the little pussies do you fancy?" I found myself on the threshold of a world I knew nothing about, except through films, songs and books. Now this was the real thing, not fiction! Adjusting to the poor neon light, I looked at the girl furthest away from me, 'No, I couldn't!' I thought. Turning to the lady in the middle, she smiled at me revealing an unattractive set of grey teeth. Rapidly I moved on to the third who was standing closest to me, her thick red lips like a pair of well stuffed satin cushions thrown on a red sofa, their corners lifting up slightly, her blue eyes hard and vacant. "I am sorry to say, that you're all too old for me!" I said with a voice full of apology as I started to walk away. Their reaction was immediate and a growl of protest came from the first two, "Cheeky little bastard! Did you hear that!" I felt my arm being taken by the one next to me, she said affirmatively, "Oh no! Not me, I am just over 18 and that's roughly your age isn't it? Come, I'll show you…" She tightened her grip and pulled me through the door of the scruffy hotel. I felt like the fish at the end of a line that, after a short demonstration of struggle, suddenly gives up resisting the strong pull of the unknown. "First floor landing, second door on the left." She said mechanically, as she invited me to climb the narrow oak staircase first. I held onto the well-worn wooden handrail, resting on old rickety metal posts. The dark green paint on the walls was flaking off in many places. Each step creaked out what sounded like agonising memories. I could not help projecting in my mind all the different types of men who must have gone up those steps, each with his own fantasies, each with his different background. We were now on the small landing, and as she searched her handbag for her key, she moved under the light. I was now able to determine she must have been in her late 30s, early 40s.

The wallpaper in the bedroom was covered in bright red roses set against a pale green background; all the woodwork and the paint under the dado line was the same colour as in the staircase. Immediately to the right of the entrance was a large double bed, with several pillows the same colours as the bed cover - dark green, black and red triangular forms. Opposite the bed was a white washbasin with a frameless mirror above it and white towels on a towel rail. The transparent frilly green lampshade hanging from the middle of the ceiling gave the whole room a macabre light. A mirrored wardrobe stood in the darkest corner of the room. "For just a plain, it'll be 200 Francs, and I demand to be paid before. I've been burned too many times in the past!" And she continued to take off the little she had on under the fur coat,

"Put your clothes on the chair, and wash yourself. Use any of the towels…" I automatically followed the almost military orders, took out the only 200 Francs note that I possessed and gave it to her. I took off my clothes and went to the washbasin, mumbling quietly to myself, "I hope she's done the same!" As I mechanically went through the cleaning ritual, I dared to look at myself in the mirror. What I saw was a grim face, there were no smiles nor light in my inner horizon, I felt heavy. I was in a murky no man's land not knowing where I was going. I heard a faint call from somewhere inside me, 'Hey! Are you there? What on earth are you doing? Have you gone crazy?' But I was too weak and confused to react and it was easier just to let the events unfold.

"Come on sweetie, I haven't got all night," she said with a touch of irritation in her voice. I turned round displaying my nudity. She had pulled the bed cover to the other side and was now lying on her back on the bare sheet, resting on her elbows looking and smiling at me. She kept her stockings on held by a black lace garter belt that surrounded the doorway of the space she was offering; a black bra finished the provocative layout. Her thick jet-black curly hair fell on her shoulders; her white skin appeared to be pale green under the dim light. As I looked at her, I visualised the succession of men who had been there before, prostrating themselves over this offered body of flesh, each one depositing the loads of their passionate dreams. "Hey! What's that? Where's your erection? Come here!" She said in an authoritative voice as she sat up impatiently. I moved up to her, slightly amused by this extraordinary situation. She used all her finessed expertise to arouse life in the stubborn tool and, in a last desperate move, pulled me over to make contact, starting with lower body movements. I felt embarrassed and wondered how I could respectfully get out of this tragi-comical situation without upsetting her further. After some hesitation, I decided to bring this theatrical show to an end. "I am sorry, it's not your fault, it's me… let's stop, this will be just fine, I must go now." I said pulling myself energetically away from her clasp. Looking furtively into her eyes, I saw flames of anger, "You little brat! Shit! I have never known this before! Who do you take me for? You've humiliated me! Get out!" She was now in a rage, "Who do you think I am, your mother? Take your money back and fuck off! Or I'll call Freddie, he'll show you what a real man is like!" I had no intention of meeting her Freddie, and in no time I put my clothes back on and went for the door. "Take your bloody money!" She shouted as she handed me back the note. Although I didn't want to take it, after all I had taken up so much of her time, I knew it would be preferable as a way to restore some of her lost dignity. So I grabbed it, left the room, ran down the stairs and was out of the hotel in a flash.

My thoughts, revived by the cool air, became clearer and I felt reconnected to my whole being again. There was no one about and I started to walk fast down the Boulevard Péreire breathing deeply and regularly, hoping to erase what had just happened.

This brief Parisian nightlife encounter profoundly modified my self-esteem. I was changed and felt different. My mixed feelings, together with my confused mind, wanted to sort it all out, to be clear, but I did not know how to and I became angry with myself.

"How could I have done this? Allowing myself to be stamped with the indelible ink of these facts." I had been with a prostitute and this was irrevocable.

"Yes, but I was drunk, not really conscious of what was happening to me." I tried desperately to justify myself, but the sentencing of my deep inner self came down like a guillotine. "There is no going back, the truth remains that you followed that street woman into that hotel." "Yes, but I didn't make love, it was just a brief body contact." I argued, feeling again her soft, pale green body, the brief mixture of our body odours and her overly rich perfume. The slightly sticky contact of the moist flesh invaded me again, real in its most gruesome details.

I reflected back on powerful events of my life: when my Mum and Fonsou almost died from carbon monoxide poisoning and running through the snow to fetch a doctor hunted by the fear of losing my mother; when I hid under the dining table and Fonsou kicked me hard with the black leather boots he had taken from the body of a dead German soldier – I still could feel the anger carried by those blows; when I fought with the boys at the Beauvallon School in Dieulefit.

CHAPTER 6

As I walked across the Place du Maréchal Juin into Rue de Prony, I switched to more pleasant memories bubbling up from my inner depth. I was now beaming, sitting in happiness on the shoulders of my father, walking through the maquis, coming up from l'Aygade gently pushed by the sea breeze that carried the enchanting scent of the aromatic plants, the buzz of the cicadas in the pine trees, the gentle melodies of the returning waves gliding through the algae. Still fully absorbed by my thoughts and feelings, I suddenly found myself at n°6, rue Cardinet. Two by two I flew up the narrow oak staircase to the seventh floor, silently entering my small nest with great relief.

I looked at my watch, which read quarter to 5 a.m. and I suddenly felt drained. There was no bathroom in the tiny flat (the toilets were on the landing) but I felt like washing myself all over and went into the minuscule kitchen to warm up some water in the large aluminium kettle. While waiting for the water to bubble, I looked at myself in the large piece of broken mirror over the draining board, and found it difficult to look into my own eyes. I felt a deep shame, a feeling I had not experienced before. Gradually I raised my eyes again in an effort to meet myself with courage. Their whites were bloodshot, the iris normally of an azure grey blue, seemed to have become dark grey. I looked hesitantly into the dark pupils to find desolation, as if a hurricane had gone through my emotions leaving chaos behind. I questioned myself with tears rolling down my cheeks, "How will I be able to look into my mother's eyes now? Or anybody's at that?"

The singing kettle brought me back to my immediate reality. The warm water on my face was soothing, I methodically washed my whole body, as if to rid myself of the impressions of that strange night, then crept into bed and curled up into a foetus position giving a big sigh of relief as my exhausted body relaxed into much awaited and liberating sleep.

After some hesitation I decided to go to Paul Colin's the next morning although I was rather tired. There was a large gilded mirror over the fireplace of the sitting room, and before I left, I stood in the front of it looking at myself. My face did look a little rough, but I managed to smile realising that nothing could change what had happened during the night. I decided to let the disturbing experience slide into the muddy bottom of my deep inner self. After all, I thought with some irony, there is a positive side to this experience, I can no longer be judgemental towards the men who frequent street women! Having had a brief glimpse of that underworld; it was no longer a mystery and the taste of it was enough for me to know that I did not want to repeat it. I felt this experience brought maturity in my understanding and contributed to my leaving behind some of my youthful arrogance.

A taste of the commercial world

On one occasion Paul Colin gave us two posters to design, one for the soft drink Orangina, and the other for the Hippodrome de Longchamp, a horse race called 'Le Grand Prix de Paris'.

Although I thought that the soft drink was made with oranges, our Boss explained that it was made only with the pulp, and therefore we were not allowed to show the juicy part of the fruit. I promptly went out to buy three beautiful oranges and returning to my worktable, I took out my pocketknife and proceeded to peel them in three different ways. The first one I peeled into haphazardly shaped pieces, the second one I divided into quarters and pulled the skin carefully off the fruit to keep it all together in the shape of a star. The last one I peeled continuously from top to bottom into a long serpentine coil. Then, displaying the parts on my worktable, I looked at them to see if they would unlatch my inspiration. The long serpentine peel I threw on the floor to see what form it would reveal... suddenly I saw what to do. The peel had naturally fallen into the shape of the Orangina bottle! There it was, in the front of my eyes, all I had to do now was to add the metal capsule on the top. I worked hard, making many different models of the orange peel soft drink

CHAPTER 6

bottle, different angles, different lighting and different coloured backgrounds.

Maurice Chalhoub, my Armenian friend who I respected greatly for his taste and talent as a poster designer, excitedly said to me one early afternoon. "Paul Colin came in during the lunch hour, he stopped a long time to look at your poster and told me that he thought that your Orangina idea was excellent and that you were progressing rapidly! Isn't that good?" This was really nice to hear; it was the first time for many months that I felt recognized and appreciated by the Boss.

In my flat I had a large map of Paris on the wall. I generally loved maps and often looked at this one. I liked the graphics and the patterns made by its streets, squares and avenues. In my mind I connected to the Hippodrome, thinking creatively about Le Grand Prix de Paris and projected horses running wildly, weightless jockeys with their bottoms up in the air high over their tiny saddles, imagining them as if they were made of colourful ribbons... with the Eiffel tower somewhere in the background. But I wasn't satisfied - this type of image was not original enough.

One late afternoon after an intense day's work at the studios, resting on the settee at home, hands behind my head, I was blankly gazing at the map of Paris. Unexpectedly the poster was staring at me! There it was, coming from the map itself, the concept for the horse race poster. The river Seine, meandering through the city, produced the perfect profile of a horse's head and neck, with the oval racecourse at Longchamp as the horse's eye. Every Parisian had in their mind the map of their city. The Seine would be in blue, the shape of the city in white on a red background.

I developed the ideas and designed my posters. Paul Colin came around and complimented me, and by so doing, restored our communication. On that visit he told me that I should try to sell the poster to Orangina, but first I should register the two posters so that they could not be copied. Photos were taken of them, the necessary papers filled, the four thousand francs paid and the two posters were officially registered.

391

I presented the Orangina poster to the director of the advertisement section of the well-known firm. He liked it very much and begged me to leave it there with them, promising they would shortly get back to me. I felt chuffed with myself, and thought that I would wait for this one to be accepted, before presenting the other to the Grand Prix of Paris organisation.

Two weeks later, nothing had come back. I was advised to wait another two weeks. Then I phoned and with great difficulty got through to someone who vaguely said, "Yes, I think we're still studying it. Ring us back in a month." I refrained from phoning again. Finally, three months later I went back to Orangina and after half an hour of waiting, I saw an elegantly dressed secretary walking towards me with my portfolio under her arm. "Sorry, Mr Armand (the boss) says they're not interested and thanks you very much." I left the firm feeling hurt and unfairly treated. Why had they kept it so long? "This Monsieur Armand is so rude sending his secretary to return it to me." I was disappointed as I walked out of the wealthy Orangina offices.

A month later, on the walls of Paris was an Orangina poster: an orange peel in the shape of a parasol with the handle as a thick black line stuck into a sandy beach. The poster was signed by a famous artist of the time called 'Villemot'. The trouble I had taken to register my design had at least protected it from a direct copy. I was told later that one should never leave one's work behind, and so I learnt my first lesson in dealing with the commercial art world. (Note: some 60 years later, when the patenting protection elapsed, Orangina used my original idea of the peel in the shape of their round glass bottle).

Paul Collins often asked his students to help him with his large projects. There was much talent in our small design school and the Master had a good palette of students to choose from. I was chosen twice. The first time was to decorate the great Hall of the George V Hotel on the Champs Elysees. Nicole, Maurice and I were given the job of decorating the 20 colossal columns that supported the ceiling of the immense hall. The Boss gave us a simple sketch, rapidly executed in front of us on a piece of cheap brown paper. It was of a column with a vine motive winding its way up and around it, and he said, "Colours to be yellow, red and black, follow this grapevine design all the way up. You'll do it here in our studios, on rolls of paper that I will provide. The columns will be 10 m tall, you will carefully stick the design round each one of them."

After a few days we were halfway through, when he came to see what we had done so far and corrected us by demonstrating, with brush in hand, how we should paint more freely, with rhythm and accuracy. We could not help but admire his dextrous ability. A week later we took them to the renowned hotel and worked all night to fix them onto the columns.

The other job was for the Casino in Cannes and Maurice, Nicole, Florence and I were chosen. On a small strip of paper he rapidly drew a series of 10 female dancers, their long hair flowing behind in some imaginary wind. Maurice, leaning discreetly towards me, his mouth practically in my ear, shared his thoughts in a low voice, "Rather a sloppy drawing isn't it?" I did not answer as our Master started giving his instructions with authority, "Square them up and draw them up to double life-size on the heavy cardboard that I will provide. Once drawn, you will cut them out, paint them on both sides, five in pink, five in white! The materials will all be ready for you to start on Monday. I will be away in Cannes the whole week. Have them finished by my return." And he abruptly left the room without another word.

Our little team worked hard on the project. Friday lunchtime we had almost finished when Paul Colin entered. The cut outs of female dancers rested all round the walls ready for inspection. His eyes rapidly shifted from one cut out to another. We could read by the tortured expression of his mouth that he was not satisfied. "No! That won't do, this is not good enough... the cardboard has absorbed the paint and it all looks blotchy!" We stood in silence, distraught by his negative reaction to our work. Not one bit of recognition for our achievements. After all, we had done what he had told us to do, and we thought that they looked pretty effective. "You must work through the weekend so as to be ready by Monday morning. Here, François and Maurice, go and buy 20 rolls of aluminium foil paper, you will then carefully wrap it round the figures and stick it down with flour paste. They must all be covered and the finish completely smooth." He spoke loudly and pulled out a large banknote from his well-loaded, sharkskin wallet. Certainly he was not an easy man, and conversations with him were only one way. None of us dared to oppose him and we set back to work. Nicole and Florence bought flour to prepare the homemade glue by heating it on the gas stove until it thickened and became a translucent adhesive paste. We grumbled about the Boss's selfish behaviour.

By Sunday lunchtime, we had covered all the cut out figures and they were now again resting upright around the room. Exhausted but satisfied to have finished our tedious job, the four of us were sitting on the floor eating the sandwiches that Nicole had bought at the Brasserie. "I think they look terrible, I preferred them as they were before." Maurice muttered, his words getting mixed up with his mouthful of bread. "Yes, I do agree, they look all the same now." Florence added with her musical voice.

Nicole questioned, "What shall we do? I'm tired, I want to go home." I suggested, "I think some of us ought to stay on to make sure that the Boss is satisfied." In that instant, the door burst open and the Master walked in, his eyes watery, his floppy cheeks and big nose flushed pink due to the probably delicious lunch and wine he must have had in some renowned restaurant.

"So, how are you getting on? Oh! Oh! It looks as if you have finished, good that's splendid, I prefer them like this! I'll have them fetched Monday morning."

His meal seemed to have put him into a good mood. We felt relieved and looked at each other sharing our satisfaction with discreet smiles. The Boss added before leaving, "By the way, I will not be able to pay you now, only next week, on my return from Cannes."

CHAPTER 6

Was it due to my innocence, brought up in the country with plants, animals and insects, that I felt at times that life was forcing experiences down my throat quicker than I could digest them? One afternoon, after eating a quick sandwich at the Brasserie, I came back early to finish the poster I was working on. Entering the dark hallway I heard steps coming down the narrow staircase. It was Jean Paul, his deep blue eyes lit with excitement, his mouth revealing joyful anticipation. "Hey, François, come I'll show you what I have just discovered in the Boss's studio. Don't worry, he is away in Nancy to see his mother."

I had only been twice previously in the large attic studio, once with my mother's friend Line Viala, the other when the Boss asked me to help him to take down a large painting.

As I came up the steep staircase, the wall opposite was covered with an impressive collection of African ethnic wooden statues and masks of all sizes. They seemed to have been selected either for their aggressive appearance, or for their powerful male and female sexual parts. I stopped on the landing and turned to the west wall where large black/grey charcoal portraits of young females hung. To the right, white cushions were displayed on a large double bed dressed in a deep red quilt. Behind the bed rose a tall smoked glass window extending to the ceiling, providing the main source of light of the atelier.

Stacks of canvases rested against the walls and two enormous oak easels stood in the middle of the studio, one of them with an unfinished portrait of a dark haired girl. Three rickety old tables were crowded with tubes of oil and gouache paints, one of them used as a palette, making colourful hills of dried medium. Ceramic pots filled with brushes of all sizes stood on the few clear spaces left. The smell of turpentine and pipe tobacco was potent. To the right of the bed was a large desk littered with pencils of all colours, letters and bills; another pot was filled with old pipes, next to two bronze heads on square wooden bases: one of himself, the other probably of his daughter as a young child. To the extreme right there was a sink and a minuscule kitchen. Three Caucasian rugs covered part of the pine polished floor.

The room felt different without Paul Colin present. I had not properly looked at it before and forgot that Jean-Paul, who had been completely silent, was still in the room. "François come and see this!" He said in a high jubilant voice. The wide top drawer of the Master's desk was fully open, and my friend stood by it triumphantly, "Look! What the dirty old man is up to!"

I had already seen many sexual organs, male and female, of all shapes, sizes and colours on the Island or of the models in the art classroom, but these black and white explicit photos Jean-Paul was showing me were taken with the intention to provoke and arouse sexual feelings, I had not seen such pictures in my innocent 16 years of life. Jean Paul, impatient to share the importance of discovering this sexual trove, chose the most provocative ones and waved them under my nose, while sprinkling out a short broken laugh, "How about this one, hey?" I could not say a word; my only expression was a vague smile at the corner of my mouth. Probably slightly irritated by my non-communicative state, Jean Paul pulled out his trump card, "Okay then, what do you say about this one?" 'This one' was really too much for me; what he was showing me now was way beyond what I could have possibly imagined possible. I felt as if murky waters were polluting my brain and couldn't help saying gravely, "Really disgusting! Look at the tortured expression on the face of that poor woman being fucked by a pig! Isn't that terrible, shocking?" The few photos I saw were too disturbing for me. Already I felt them sticking in my brain like a magnet to metal. To my relief we heard the sound of the office buzzer downstairs, "Quick, let's put them back, I do not want anyone to know about this, imagine the Boss's reaction if he knew!" We left the studio hurriedly. The five pornographic photographs I had seen remained, like the egg of a cuckoo bird, nested in a corner of my mind, and continued to bother me with their disturbing power. I decided not to look at porn photos from now on.

CHAPTER 6

The Party

The two years in Paris was intense and diverse. I was confronted with many challenges, not only in my work, but also in my relationships with a variety of very different types of people and situations. I began to learn how to swim in the currents of different waters; some freezing cold, some warm even a few quite hot! Although life was at times turbulent, I somehow seemed to land back on my feet.

I enjoyed my work and coped with its creative challenges. Where it was more difficult, was deep down in myself, where I felt a frequent need to be closer to the feminine presence. Why was I so attracted by women? It seemed as if an important part of myself required not only their attention but also physical closeness, not specifically sexual, I felt more complete and alive in the immediate presence of women. To satisfy part of that need, I found it soothing to draw or paint the female body with gouache or watercolours, finding joy in expressing the light that caressed the curves of the imaginary figures. This was one of my ways to keep quietly close and connected, if only virtually, to the female desires in me that took so much of my attention.

Now in Paris for over a year, I was still attracted to Laura, although I had not managed to get really close to her. It was not for lack of trying, but somehow I never managed to invite her to my flat. Was I too hesitant, too gentle? Not bold enough? While I reflected, a wonderful idea came to me, why not have a party in the small apartment and invite her? I might be able to entice her to stay the night… I rejoiced at the idea, how could I not have thought of it before?

Fixing a date for a Friday evening, I carefully selected who would be invited – not too many, to keep intimacy, but enough to create a good ambience. We should not be more than 10 or 12 at the most. Pierre, Maurice, Jean-Paul and Nicole were an obligation, being close friends. I would have also invited Eric, but the poor man had been called up by the army to join to go to fight in the Algerian war. Florence, Laurence, Maïté, Marie-Claude and, of course, Laura who

397

was obviously the kingpin and the inspiring source of the party. Jean-Claude and Ron, the big American, who would have never forgiven me had I not invited him. The invitations were discreetly passed round as I did not wish the whole school to descend at n°6 rue Cardinet, particularly Eberhardt for I was aware of his keenness for Laura.

I left Paul Collin's early that Friday afternoon to tidy up the flat, buying a bouquet of anemones from an old lady who sold them in the street, on my way. Three by three, I excitedly climbed the steps to the seventh floor, entered the flat and immediately started cleaning up. I displayed the flowers on the mantelpiece in front of the mirror. I had just finished up the kitchen when Pierre arrived with the 12 glasses his mother had lent us for the occasion. Then he took me on his Vespa to a cheap wine merchant, stopping on the way back to buy bread, saucissons, cheese and a kilo of red Canadian apples.

"See you later, 8.30? 9?" He queried while he revved up his Vespa, "Yes, that'll do, thanks for your help!" I shouted as I hurried back to the flat.

I created a dancing space by putting my centre table against the wall and displayed the fresh food on it. On the mahogany chest of drawers, I arranged the glasses, a corkscrew and the few bottles of red and white wine. I displayed haphazardly on the grey and white marble mantelpiece under the large gilt mirror the red apples. The place was looking good now; I brought in the bedside table for the gramophone, 'That will be perfect', I thought as I stacked the records in the space of the chamber pot. With the few logs left, I lit a fire to warm up the atmosphere and give the flat a cosy feeling.

To decompress a little I lay down on the bed and closed my eyes and soon noticed my body imperceptibly vibrating; it was like having stage fright. This awkward timidity in myself irritated me, why couldn't I just be normal? Just relax simply, as I am with my friends at work?

'It's because you're frightened of the outcome of the evening, frightened that something might turn out not as you expected. That's what it is! And the anticipation of how it will be with Laura,' I cruelly thought to myself.

'In Summerhill it wasn't like that!' The other me replied in defence. 'Oh yes it was! Remember the first time you offered to dance with a girl… you were not feeling so normal, were you?' The loud sound of the bell made me jump and interrupted my reflections. I walked to the door, "Hello Nicole, great you are here, I see you have a heavy bag, let me help you…" I gave her a welcoming kiss on her round and dimpled powdery cheeks. "Yes, I came early to give you a hand and to bring a few things and some records." I helped her to take off her coat and threw it on the bed. "Hey, it's nice your place, wow! Look at that fire!"

Nicole had a quietening effect on me; I was so relieved that she was the first one to arrive. Her good humour and motherly nature immediately helped to dissipate my anxiety. She took out the food she had brought and gracefully re-arranged the table in her own way. I took pleasure in watching her move. "Where shall I put these soft drinks?" I pointed to the chest of drawers.

"By the way, would you care for a drink? Red or white?" I asked. "Do you mind if I first eat a bit of bread and cheese? I've had no lunch and I'm starving, I'll have red, thank you."

The doorbell rang; "Hello, look who's there! Laurence, Marie Claude, Maurice, Jean-Claude, come in… make yourself at home, your coats in the bedroom, food and drinks are in here." I started to show my guests where the drinks were when the bell rang again.

"Hi Pierre, you've bought Jean-Paul with you on the Vespa, you both look frozen, come in!" They both knew the flat and I left them to settle down while choosing a 78 record I thought would be appropriate: Sydney Bechet's Blues in Paris.

Everybody was talking, helping themselves to food & drinks; I was feeling relieved to see that all was going well. So far, everyone had brought something and there was plenty to drink and eat. The strident bell rang again, probably it was wishful thinking, but as I came to the door I imagined Laura standing behind it. I pulled the door open and there she was, standing on the doormat, smiling timidly holding one red rose that she offered to me before allowing me to kiss her. "Oh! How nice, thank you. I said as I took the flower and kissed her on both cheeks, smelling her delicate scent. Maïté was standing right behind her, smiling with her large green eyes, and I repeated the French greeting ritual on her cold, freckled cheeks. As I let the girls into the flat I thought, this habit of greeting women with a kiss is wonderful, so much can happen in that fraction of a second; as you get close somehow you feel where the person is at and you know that the other feels. I popped into the kitchen to find a tall glass for the red rose, which I placed at the opposite end to the anemones on the mantelpiece where I also kept a few books.

The air was thickening with smoke and sound, everybody seemed to be in a good place. Pierre became the disc jockey. Looking around I realised that Ron and Florence had not yet arrived. I directed Maïté and Laura to the food and drink corner; I felt the closeness between them. With a glass of wine and some bread and cheese, I sat on the bed next to Nicole. We chatted as we ate and I occasionally glanced discreetly at Laura who was still engaged in deep conversation with Maïté.

I asked Nicole to dance, she smiled and in her eyes I read that she knew why I chose her for my first dance. Muggsy Spanier was now playing I wish I could shimmy like my sister Kate and we spun into a jive. Couples were dancing now, with Pierre conscientiously sitting by the gramophone providing a good variety of music. Muskrat Ramble, by Louis Armstrong poured out of my gramophone's cornucopia. I was fond of this piece, which I used to dance to in Summerhill. I finally offered my stretched out hands to Laura, who was still talking with Maïté and suggested joyfully, "Come?" My body was already dancing. She looked deep into my eyes, smiled as she stood up and let me take her into the powerful rhythms of Muskrat Ramble.

Not having danced with her before, I was feeling my way, but the gusto of the music inspired my body to move. I felt her hands attentive, searching for the slightest indication and responding to my not always clear leads. We went into a jive and the rhythm took over and we clicked into harmony. Although our bodies were moving fast, I observed stillness. Giving me the impression of being an albatross flying over a choppy sea.

This first dance with Laura was for me another step to coming closer to her and reassured me that I could continue this passionate but precarious journey. I say precarious because I did not feel she was in the same frame of mind, there was something distant, as if she was not entirely there. Breathing fast, her milky skin showing tiny pearls of sweat like the drops of dew on the petals of a white rose. She murmured in a smile, "I am too hot, I must take off my woolly cardigan!" As she threw the pink garment on the back of a chair, the scent from her body delighted my nostrils; I greedily but discreetly, filled my lungs to the brim.

Giving no time for respite, Pierre put another record, a slow one called Black and Blue. The languorous music brought our bodies closer together, and my attention shifted to our bodily contacts. Now it was the inside of our knees lightly brushing… then it was the tips of her breasts landing gently on my chest, my right hand round the waist, wanting to bring her even closer but not daring. I could feel the heat from her cheek close to mine. I liked her perfume and the smell of her hair. I was now completely captured by her charm, floating like a cloud in a dream, letting the music conduct the world of my senses.

I knew that in a few moments Black and Blue would come to an end. I would have liked it to never stop… "Ring, ring!" The cruel bell forced me out of my reveries, "I'll be back, I just go to see who's come." "Hello Florence, come in." I greeted her with a kiss as she offered me the bottle of champagne she was carrying.

"Hey! Who's there too, Ron, you've made it! Good." I said in English tapping affectionately on his large shoulders. "Sorry for being a bit late. I've bought Eberhardt with me." He excused himself as he entered the flat like a bull entering the arena. As he passed by, I smelt he had been drinking heavily. Feeling disturbed by the presence of the uninvited guest, I wondered… 'Eberhardt, why on earth Eberhardt? The last person I wanted here!'

My heart effectively sank, as the tall German stood there staring at me with his icy blue eyes, a vague smile bringing a little light to his usually sad, angular face. "Oh, hello… come in and make yourself at home." I managed to utter out of my tight throat. The small sitting room was now filled with guests, and I was happy to see that they all seemed to enjoy themselves. Eberhardt walked by Laura, ignoring her and going straight for the drinks corner. Ron had already helped himself to a full glass of red wine and came smiling towards me; his minuscule blue eyes behind his thick tortoiseshell glasses were full of drunken cheerfulness. He was still wearing his dark blue woollen winter coat, holding his glass high, he said, "Nifty little place you've got here, hey?" Then he leaned closer to my ear, lowered the tone of his voice and inquisitively said, "How are you getting on with Laura?" I did not react to his intruding curiosity, although it caused great irritation in my heart. Desperate to change the subject I replied, "Come on, you're too hot! Here, give me your coat, I'll put it in the bedroom!" I held his glass while he removed his coat, revealing an untidy Viyela shirt that partly hung out of his dark blue trousers.

Still standing motionless where I left her, Laura was observing the late arrivals. She looked at me raising her eyebrows slightly, then smiled as if to say: 'well, look who is here?' Then her expression changed again, "Come on, let's go on with the dance!" Her silent expressive invitation reignited my heart, I rushed through the dancers feeling reassured and took her back into the world of senses guided by the music.

Now, we were back fully into our world, there was nothing in my mind as I was ravenously enjoyed her close feminine presence. To see her face, to look into her eyes to maybe reach deeper into her being, I pulled my head slightly away from hers to adjust my focus. Feeling a slight tension in my body, she looked up and responded to my inquisitive look with a tender and frail availability that expressed

CHAPTER 6

no resistance.

I felt my heartbeat change and my awareness shifted to the pulse of my veins. It was my shyness that caused this and I resented it. A strong urge to delicately place my lips on hers flooded me, increasing the turbulence. Not quite knowing how to handle these powerful feelings I felt overwhelmed by them and looked away trying to free myself, to loose myself a little from the grip of my passions.

Jelly Roll Morton finished playing his Mournful Serenade, when an unexpectedly raucous laugh harshly pulled me out of my enamoured state. We loosened our hold on each other and looked in the direction of the brawl. Stupefied I saw that Eberhardt was gesticulating in all directions holding my passport open, pointing at the page where it gave my date of birth; with his strong German accent shouted, "Look! François is only 16! Ha, ha, ha, ha, just a little boy! Ach-Zo… Laura is flirting with a boy now? Ha, ha, ha, how funny!"

Of course it wasn't funny at all, I felt angry towards him for embarrassing Laura, and angry with myself for having left my passport on the mantelpiece. I purposely had not told anyone my age except Pierre, as I did not want to be treated condescendingly because of it. Eberhardt pointing his long, knobbly finger at me went on, "He, him, François is only 16, simply a boy, a boy!" That was too much. I walked up to him and tried to grab my passport; he held it higher out of my reach and increased his mocking laughter. Everyone's attention was directed at us as a tense silence filled the room.

"Come on, don't be stupid and give me my passport back!" I said quietly but firmly.

He waved it under my nose, just to tease me a little longer and I saw in his eyes the devilish flames of mockery dancing for the joy at having created the effect he wanted.

He made the gesture of giving it to me, I put my hand out but he briskly pulled it away giving another nervous irritating laugh and then threw it onto the mantelpiece. I did not want to pick it up and left it there and seeing that the fire was low, I placed a log carefully onto the red embers to give myself a little space.

Pierre, who was now quite tipsy with white wine, wanted a radical change to what had become an unpleasant atmosphere, and thought it right to put on one of Nicole's favourite records C'est Mon Homme by Edith Piaf. In the corner of my eye I saw Nicole looking discreetly at my passport; she came towards me, put her arm round my shoulders murmured compassionately, "I've never liked him, he is insesitive. It's because he likes Laura, he wants to distract her away from you. I would never have thought that you are only 16 though, it must be your Summerhill School that made you look that much older."

I looked around desperately for Laura. Eberhardt was talking to her in German and laughing while she seemed embarrassed, not knowing whether or not to join the laughter. She was looking at the oak floor, one elbow resting on the marble fireplace, a disturbed smile on her face. The dynamics of the room had completely turned to an atmosphere of flatness, of nothingness, as if the taps of life and creativity had been turned off. Edith Piaf's words had become cruelly inappropriate. I looked at my watch, it was well past midnight and my party friends were fetching their coats from the bedroom, getting ready to go home.

Laura came slowly towards me and looked distantly into my eyes, her deep red lips expressing uneasiness. I saw in the blue immensity of her world that her orbit had changed, taking her away to some other universe, and understood that we'd never construct a future together. I felt the delicate touch of her so desired lips brush my cheek furtively as if she'd forgotten something left behind that she was hurriedly taking back. I heard her distant voice say, "Thank you François, I really enjoyed the evening… goodbye…" An instant of hesitation came in her "goodbye". Was it something in her that did not want it to end just like that or was she feeling sorry for me? I smiled nervously, not knowing how to be or what to say. The corners of my mouth flickered nervously as I watched Laura and Maïté disappear down the oak staircase.

CHAPTER 6

Practically everybody had left except Ron who was still drinking and Pierre who was putting on his duffle coat. "Don't worry about the 12 glasses, I'll bring them to Colin's tomorrow. Will you be okay driving home on your Vespa?" I was trying to get away from the heavy feelings that invaded my heart. "Yes, I'll be fine, don't worry, thanks for the party, see you tomorrow." He answered as he closed the door behind him. I breathed deeply trying to get rid off the weight that stuck to my being and turned to Ron who was lying on the floor. Seeing his drunken condition I offered, "Would you like to stay the night here?" "Where is my coat? I want to go home, now!" He mumled irritably trying to pull himself up.

"But you can't walk home in that state!" I replied worried that he might end up in the gutter and hurt himself. "Oh yes I can!" he insisted… so I helped him rise, his large size making the task difficult. "You see? I can stand." Ron tumbled towards the bedroom to fetch his coat.

He lived in a small attic bedroom near the Porte Champeret. In ordinary circumstances it would take half an hour to walk there, but, in view of his drunkenness, I felt I should help him to get there. We managed to wobble down the seven floors and came out into the cold early-morning Parisian air. We walked extremely slowly down Rue de Courcelles, as Ron wanted to go in different directions, or stop at every shop window. "Come on Ron, we'll never get there!" "Did you fuck her?" He crudely asked as he stopped and looked at me with his unconscious glare. "Fuck who?" I replied sharply, knowing full well whom he was talking about. "You know who I mean… the German girl you were dancing with, what's her name? Oh yes, Laura?" He said with a naughty smile.

"No, I actually didn't." "No, she's not for you, you'd do better with a juicy little French girl." He giggled. "Come on! You'll never get to your flat!" I said with some exasperation.

Although I had been through a painful realisation, my party had some positive effect on my relationship with the other students at the art school. Now they all knew the truth about my age and showed me all the more respect for it. I did not have to pretend that I was older – I could just be who I was. I also felt relieved by Laura's reaction as it showed me that her feelings towards me were not as strong as I had made them out to be. It was extraordinary to suddenly feel so free, realising how my passionate love for her had tied me up and obscured the real picture of our relationship. I now concentrated on my work completely, without being distracted by the wanting to be closer to her.

We met in the corridor a few days later for an instant, searching each other's eyes and I gave her a light message of detachment making sure that it carried no passion. But briefly noticed in her pale blue space, the small flame of an insatiable feminine need to be desired, giving me an impression that she was still accessible. I gave her a beaming smile and walk on.

I received a letter from my grandmother in December 1955, telling me that she could no longer continue to help me if I stayed in Paris, as life was more expensive there than in England. But, if I decided to come to London to further my studies, she would be able to offer me another year.

Short visit to England

Christmas 1955 suddenly arrived and it was time to leave Paris. After two years of studies in the art of poster design, I was ready to face new challenges. I put together two large portfolios with all my drawings and posters and was ready to go to London to meet the new life that was waiting there.

GG had always been greatly interested in my creative work and I kept her well informed of my progress. I decided to accept her generous offer and travelled to London to visit art schools. My uncle Tony took me in their home in Carshalton during the short visit and suggested three London art schools: the Central School of Arts and Crafts, the Slade and St Martin's. After selecting some of my best work, I rang the headmaster of the art department of the Central

School of Arts and Crafts. His voice on the phone was kind and it was arranged that I would visit him the next day at 10 a.m.

The art school building was colossal, standing at the corner of Southampton Row and Theobald's Road in front of Red Lion Square. The entrance was to the left of a powerful round tower dominating the intersection. Precisely at 10 am I knocked at the door of Mr Castleman's office, the art director.

I liked him instantly. He was a tall handsome man with peppery-grey curly hair and intense and kind blue eyes that peered out from behind a small pair of perfectly circular glasses. He was not missing any of my movements, keenly interested in what the young French man was bringing him. We spent over an hour together looking at my art. He liked the direct and bold approach of my posters and also my nude and still life charcoal drawings. "It is not in our policy to take foreign students, but I'll make an exception... Can you start in January?" I was delighted by his offer and hurriedly nodded as a sign of acceptance. We then discussed the subjects I would study: life drawing was for me a must, graphics and what was called at the time basic design, lettering and layout for advertising, etching and lithographs as well as sculpture one morning a week. We then went together to the office and I registered with much satisfaction. Surprised and chuffed at being accepted what seemed to me to be so easily, I did not bother to go and visit the Slade or St Martin's. The truth was that I instantly felt at home at the Central School, and there was no need for me to search any further. Tony and GG were both impressed and delighted by the quick and apparently easy registration, and it was agreed that I would start the course in January 1956.

The girl with the pony tail

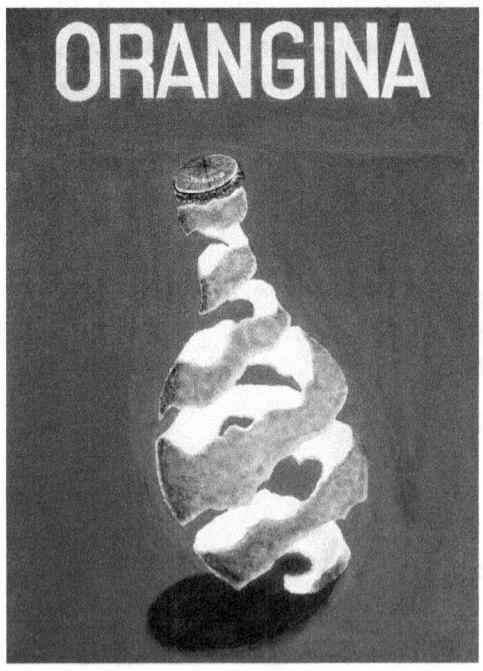
Orangina poster

CHAPTER 6

Sylvette and Toby, Vallauris April 1954

Myrette, Honor, Sylvette, Toby and Fonsou

Gany

409

Chapter 7

Student life in London 1956 to 1958

My first home in London was at 44 Harringtons Garden in South Kensington. The room was carpeted and spacious and had in one corner a small one ring stove set up for cooking, but it wasn't well furnished, with no table for either eating or drawing. I appreciated the use of a large bathroom, as in Paris I had had to go to the public baths. I knew that these digs were temporary as the price was beyond my means, but living there gave me time to look for a cheaper place.

Discovering cultural differences

The morning after my move, I started out early, well before 10 o'clock, for the Central School of Arts and Crafts, commonly called the Central. Bubbling with happiness I danced in the streets to the South Kensington underground station, feeling so fortunate to be in London, going to study at such an attractive academy.

My head teacher was Mr Cecil Collins who instructed me in what was called at the time Basic Design: the study of abstract forms with a view to applying it to graphic design. Hand lettering was considered old fashioned, so the students used 'Letraset', a transfer system of characters of all shapes and sizes printed on transparent sheets and transferred to paper by rubbing. The famous English typographer, Eric Gill, had designed most of the fonts.

Mr Collins introduced me to the teachers who helped me organise a timetable: Monday, publicity; Tuesday, composition (the relationship between form and space); Wednesday, typography using Letraset; Thursday, back to publicity and layout design; Friday, all day life drawing. Also I took evening classes in etching and lithography from 6-8 pm.

The atmosphere of this school was truly different from what I had known in the French capital. This art school was more like an art industry with many students, each with different thoughts in their minds. The many subjects offered gave the impression of it being a huge, artistic anthill. The cosy intimacy of the Paris studio became a memory, for the energies here were different, and I found them creatively stimulating.

It was fascinating to observe the radical differences in character and behaviour between the French and the English. The French, unconsciously holding on to their traditions with set manners, such as their looks, their food, (which I was already missing), their idea of beauty and style, somehow froze creative, spontaneous expression in their art. To them Paris was, and would always be, the capital of the Arts. They rested on their laurels gained through their rich history up until the early twentieth century. Of course there were always the exceptions here and there, when some highly gifted artist popped up. I was not conscious of this reality while I was studying at the Boulevard Péreire, but it became evident as soon as I became involved in the pulse of London's artistic activities.

The camaraderie, shaking hands, kissing the girls' cheeks, the jokes told in small groups and laughing together that I experienced at Paul Collins, was not present at the Central. Everyone kept to himself or herself, and I made friends individually by taking a special interest either in what they were doing or in who they were. One did not shake hands here but nodded giving a gentle smile instead; certainly you would not kiss girls when greeting them! In truth there was simply no physical contact with anyone. I felt I had to hold back my French impulses for hugging and kissing; here you did not touch another person except your girlfriend of course and certainly not in public!

People were more casually dressed, and in fact, it didn't seem to matter what you wore; no one took notice of you even if you wore a potato sack on your head. It was nice to feel that you were not judged by your appearance, but I soon found out that you were categorised by the way you expressed yourself – the way you spoke instantly placed you in a pigeonhole. I had not been aware that there existed such a class system in the UK when I was at Summerhill. Your level of education, and which part of society you came from, was instantly revealed by your accent and the way you spoke.

Although my French accent was not all that prominent, my origin was soon detected, "Oh, you're French are you?" Then came the usual comment, "I went to France on my holidays; couldn't get good tea but drank plenty of wine, ha, ha, ha!" The average Englishman had a stereotypical idea of the Frenchman: he would wear a beret, have a moustache, ride a bicycle and carry a baguette under his arm. I was surprised to find how little they knew about French culture, and there was very little space in our conversation for me to share any of the culture I loved. When I brought up anything about the French, my friends made such derogatory jokes that I soon learned it was better not to try to share my culture with them.

The layers of society did not really mix, except among art students who met in the pubs during lunchtime. I was pleasantly surprised to see that many of the teachers came to have a drink with their pupils, and deep conversations would start on inexhaustible artistic subjects, discovering new horizons, and searching for all the different means of expression. When the time came for the pub to close, some returned quite tipsy to the classroom, their minds blurred by the bubbles of the beer.

I rapidly found myself at home in my new surroundings. London was rich with different cultures and most inspiring to my inquisitive mind. The diversity of the subjects at the Central, its geographical location between the city and the artistic centre around Soho with many theatres and art galleries, combined to make this a fertile ground for creative activities. I could not compare it to Paris - it was a completely different situation. Here was a culture searching for its artistic identity, experimenting fully with all the ways provided by a freed imagination.

Coming into contact with a new awareness

Three months before I left Paris, during the summer holidays of 1955, I had met Bernard Kay, an English painter friend of Sylvette and Toby who had come down to Vallauris to stay for a few months. His intellectual knowledge of the arts and philosophy attracted me. We enjoyed his company greatly, although he had a distasteful tendency to dig into your personal life using a powerful language. I later discovered he was part of the Gurdjieff movement and practiced what was called 'The Work'. Our mother found him difficult and she felt he manipulated us with the intention of creating a separation in the family. There were very few people that my mother did not like, but Bernard was one of them.

"You see? You become different when he's around, and you behave strangely towards me," she remarked when she felt he monopolised us too much. It was true that when he was around, he had to be on top and have the last word. His tiny, sharp, brown eyes looked at you through his thick glasses while rolling an Old Holborn cigarette in his shaking fingers; with a short giggle emerging from behind his thin lips, he'd say, "Are you observing yourself, François? Watch it, hey!"

Bernard introduced us to The Tales of Beelzebub to his Grandson, more commonly known as All and Everything by George Ivanovitch Gurdjieff and also to one of his pupils called Ouspensky, who wrote In Search of the Miraculous. These books were certainly of great value to me as they brought to my attention how unaware I was of myself – how the "I' that I thought I was was always in flux. I realised that I had no permanent me. This newly discovered consciousness did not leave me, and these books became my bedside friends. Groups had developed in different parts of the western world following the Gurdieff and Ouspensky teachings, and from what I understood, Bernard had some connection with a group in London.

I am mentioning this because it was my first realisation that I did not really know who I was, or what went on inside my self. The Gurdieff work became the bait through which I became aware of my need for spiritual awareness. I mentioned earlier that my mother had never talked to us about spiritual matters; she had simply drawn a line across anything to do with the religions of the world. "You don't want to know about all that spiritual stuff. It's mostly lies and hypocrisy!" she once categorically said. I thanked her for this later; the way she brought us up gave us a virgin soil, where spiritual understanding could take seed and grow without any religious pre-conditioning.

Once I felt established at the Central School, I decided to give Bernard a ring, and we arranged that I would visit him in his flat in Cambridge Gardens near Westbourne Grove. Ladbroke Grove was then a poor area of London where the once white Edwardian rows of houses were now peeling and looked tatty. Broken cement steps led to the entrance of his flat. I entered into a spacious room, generously lit by two large north windows. Very worn antique rugs covered the floor; a dense smell of fried bacon and tobacco pervaded; I detected also turpentine and saw a large, unfinished painting of buildings on an oak easel. Bernard greeted me warmly, "Hello François. Come in. Would you like some tea?" The tastefully arranged interior revealed his interest in antiques; a worn seventeenth-century oak armchair attracted my attention, and so did other early oak English furniture.

Bernard asked me questions about the family, about Sylvette, about Toby, even about "your Mum", as he called her. He was talking to me while making tea in the tiny kitchen that overlooked an untidy garden leading to a railway line.

"Where are your digs? Are they okay?" It was the first time I had been alone with him. Previously Sylvette and Toby had always been present and now all Bernard's attention focused intensely on me. He came in holding two mugs of tea in his shaking hands, "That's correct isn't it? No sugar?" I took the mug, and thanked him.

"So, you don't like your flat, hey? I know an old lady in Westbourne Park Road who rents rooms. We can go and see her if you like. Her son was once a wrestler who became a world champion, and ended up in prison for stealing a pair of knickers from the local Woolworths! So, tell me, have you made any new friends at the Central?" He looked at me with attentiveness.

"Yes, I have made a friend called Kathleen. She is studying Fabric Design, speaks French and she is actually half Belgian." His expression changed slightly.

"A girl, hey?" He then changed the subject abruptly, "How are we doing with Ouspensky? Have you read any more?" I told him the book was fascinating and I was trying to apply some of the exercises on myself. Although I had been happy to see Bernard, I did feel a sense of relief and freedom as I came out into the street.

New digs and a girl friend

My lodgings in South Kensington were really not appropriate, so I decided to inspect 324 Westbourne Park Road. The little old lady greeted me kindly. Because of her hunched back she only came up to my hips, which made it difficult for me to see her face.

"Come, I'll first show you the room." Her voice was high-pitched and trembling. Opposite the entrance, the stairs led straight up to a half landing, and the bathroom with the hot water on a gas meter was behind a tinted glass door. Five steps further up to the right was the bedroom.

"The gas heater works on the meter over there and the water in the sink is cold, but I hope you'll like it!" I still had not seen her face. I followed her down the steps and she stopped by a brown door, "Please come in. I'll show you something." I was struck by her sitting room walls, covered in ancient, curled-cornered photographs and yellowed newspaper cuttings. With her long index finger and grey nail, she pointed to one of them and, turning her head at an angle, she looked up at me with witty, sunken blue eyes, "It's my son! World champion he was! My tenants had better behave themselves, or else!" A wry little smile appeared at the corner of her mouth as she finished her sentence and turned her head back to its original position, facing down towards the worn-out lino floor. The photo showed a young wrestler standing legs apart and stomach in, chest out, and on either side of his body, enormous biceps. His hair, well groomed with Bryl Cream, started just over his anxious inexpressive eyebrows.

"I will take the room." The fairness of the price incited me to take the room, even though it faced north.

Kathleen and I got on well with each other. We had many similar interests: education, music, cooking and the arts in general. Visiting the art galleries together was a mutual enjoyment. Kathleen had an elongated body, wide square shoulders, long elegant neck and auburn curls framing her attractive face. Her deep set pale autumn green eyes were expressive and as if continuously amused, her well-proportioned nose hung over her generous lips. Her smile displayed gleaming white teeth.

We enjoyed the days when we did not have evening classes, taking the underground to her minuscule flat behind High St Kensington. On the way, we stopped to buy fruit, vegetables, bread and cheese, and whatever we needed to prepare the evening meal. Like me, Kathleen had very little money, so we were selective in what we bought; wine and alcohol were too expensive to be present at our table. But that didn't matter, as our spirits were high with the excitement of discovering each other. Fresh food was a must, for we were both health conscious, and we discussed our menu and how to cook it as we walked towards her digs. Entering the flat, Kathleen went straight to find a jazz record, or a French singer like Charles Trenet or Georges Brassens. In my company she became very Francophile.

One evening sitting on her bed talking, since there was no armchair in the room, I looked into her eyes and suddenly felt a powerful amorous feeling.

"Hey, what's up?" She said smiling as she picked up my lively desires. I could not answer but gently guided her wide shoulders onto the bed. At first she gave a slight resistance, keeping her feet on the ground and protecting her chest with her forearms.

"Do you have a boyfriend?" I asked, thinking that might have been the cause of her tension. "No, I don't have a boyfriend!" Our faces were very close but I could feel her frail wrists making a barrier between our chests. I came closer and rubbed my nose lightly against hers. The feeling was good and my lips sought a soft place to land but she turned her head away. I kissed the cradle of her warm neck and smelt her hair. I could have gone on losing myself in the feminine, the strong desire was there, but felt that I was trespassing, as if walking onto virgin soil that was not ready to be shared.

I rested on my right elbow, while my left hand rested on her hip bone and looked into her eyes. "Sorry, but I don't believe in sex before marriage." There was a tone of embarrassment in her voice and she added, "I know if we carry on like this, we will end up having sex." I knew that this was correct, as it was my immediate desire, yet I had no intention of marriage in my head at that moment.

"Are you Catholic? Do you go to church?" I questioned while I raised myself back up into my original sitting position. "Yes I am, but I don't go to church. There's too much hypocrisy there!"

We sat on the bed for some time and talked about our feelings: she about her religion, I about the little I knew about the work of Gurdjieff and Ouspensky. She talked about her belief and faith. I understood the word 'believe', but didn't quite know what the word 'faith' meant, or what she meant when she used it. Looking up at the ceiling as if searching for a bright star, she finally said with some conviction, "It is to feel that everything will be all right, in fact, it is to trust that everything will be okay. Yes that's it! That's what I mean by faith." "You mean then, that when things are difficult in your life, you turn to your faith and they magically turn positive, making you feel better and more able to cope?" I was trying to understand what she meant… "Yes, something like that." She felt satisfied that my explanation had clarified it for her.

"You see I am too rational to believe. I like to know. The little I know, I know with some certainty. What I do not know, I leave until I come to understand it. So, I don't want to believe in God, or in Jesus, or in angels and all that stuff. But if one day I come to understand, through some kind of experience that makes sense to me, then I would not need to believe, I would simply know!" As I heard myself talk, it cleared my mind. It was as if I was explaining to myself some realities that up to then had been stored in a kind of fog.

"I don't agree with you. I think the world needs to believe, otherwise there is no hope, is there? If there is no Jesus, no angels, no God, what is there?" She insisted with some irritation. "It would make life pretty boring wouldn't it?"

I wanted her to understand my point, "But there is you…and there is me. And out there, everyone is 'I' with his or her own reality. So let's start from here, from the present. Surely you can only start to really understand the world from yourself, from where your own consciousness is? As soon as you believe, you must lose contact with your own reality? Or is your own reality a belief too?"

The subject absorbed me so much that all my amorous feelings dissipated and I became aware that she was upset. What I said, plus my earlier behaviour, disturbed her and she started crying. This time I only put one arm around her and she rested her head on my shoulder gently and sobbed quietly. We stayed like this for a long time. Then Kathleen looked at me with her now pink, watery eyes and said, as if she had suddenly woken up,

"I'm so sorry about all this, please forgive me. What's the time?" I looked at my watch and exclaimed, "Gosh, it's already one o'clock,

I'd better go!"

I stood up, took my jacket from the hook on the door and as I put it on, she came up and gave me a quick kiss on the lips. I tasted the salt of her tears.

I went on seeing Kathleen, but we spent less time together, mostly due to my young man's increasing need to be completely merged with the feminine.

Attracted to the Fine Arts

The early winter of 1956 was terribly harsh. One morning I woke up to find my moustache stuck to my top sheet; my breath had condensed and frozen on it during the night. I tried to turn my head but it was too painful as it pulled on my upper lip, so I covered it up with my warm hand while the ice slowly melted until my moustache was freed. As I moved my feet down to the bottom of the bed to stretch my legs, I felt a small warm furry thing wiggling. I lifted my head to see a little mouse jump out from under the sheets! I was unable to light the gas fire to warm up the room, for the gas itself was frozen, there was absolutely no pressure; the windows were covered in ice. I rapidly put on my frozen clothes and went out to find a warm cafe for breakfast.

Everything was silent and white with snow, truly arctic conditions! No cars or buses in sight. I reached the small workman's cafe Bernard and I called 'the greasy spoon', just behind Portobello Road. The warm atmosphere carried the smell of hot buttered toast, which immediately comforted me, and I ordered a cup of tea and a round of toast with chunky marmalade. Reading the Daily Mirror I picked up at the counter, I saw photographs of parts of the English Channel frozen, and huge blocks of icy sea stuck together in chaotic heaps. It was remarkable – some people had walked from Dover to Calais!

I stayed for some time in the cafe and wrote to my mother about the cold in London: how I bought a bottle of rum to make a grog with lemon, how the aluminium cap on the bottled milk was pushed up by a column of frozen creamy liquid. Jokingly I told her I had not been so cold in 18 years and was longing for their sunshine in Cannes. London came to a standstill for several days and many institutions were closed due to the lack of transport.

I had not met the tenants of number 324 Westbourne Grove yet. I left before they were up and often came back late, since my little room was not comfortable except for sleeping. This cold spell was the opportunity to meet the other tenants who lived in the semi-detached house. The top floor had two bedrooms and on my floor was another large room facing south. As far as I could gather, apart from my landlady, I was the only white person in the building. The other lodgers came from Nigeria and Ghana and brought with them their African way of life. They were extremely smiley, talkative and friendly, which pleased me as I found English people on the whole rather serious. I often had to squeeze by the other lodgers who sat on the worn wooden steps of the narrow staircase, chatting and laughing. Our communal space was full of the smell of their African cooking, which they shared as they shared everything else. My house-mates talked loudly so that they could hear each other throughout the building, or perhaps it was to override their loud music that continued late into the night? Silence rarely came before 2am. They did not get up in the morning like I did and soon I started to feel the need for more sleep, and decided to find other premises.

January, February and March of 1956 went quickly. The changes from Paris to London were stimulating and challenging, due to the variety of subjects I took at the Central, such as drawing with Hugh Stanton, who taught the craft in a complete different way from Paul Collin. I liked Mr Stanton very much for his natural discretion, his quiet manners, his soft persuasive voice and the logic of what he was showing me. He helped me discover a new approach to life drawing. He was not interested in the line itself, "There is no line, as form is continuous and everything is revealed by the relationship of the light to the shade." Taking my drawing board, he drew in the corner of the white sheet, "Look: where on the body does the light hit brightest? There on the shoulder, here on that bent knee. These will be your highest points of luminosity. From here all the tones of grey decrease down to the darkest, which is the furthest point away from the direct light. These changes reveal the form."

He then proceeded, with his light and precise touch, to reveal form on the paper. The line appeared magically, imperceptibly by itself just by the play of contrasts.

"But what about proportions?" "Do not search for proportions. Concentrating on the play of light on the body will teach you much more than measuring and looking for the right proportions. Do not worry François, proportion will come on its own through practice as your eye gets trained."

This was a completely new approach for me. Mr Stanton's fine explanatory drawings, together with his patient encouragement, opened my eyes to the ultimate importance of light and dark when expressing form in two dimensions. I never missed a drawing class, especially on Fridays, when they were held in daylight.

Attracted by the smell of turpentine and oil paints, I sometimes climbed up to the top floor to the fine art classes. I suppose that these odours projected me back to my youth on the island when I watched my mother paint. Looking at the fine art students' work in progress relaxed me in depth. I always knew that being a painter was more in my nature than advertising. In a strange way, my decision to do advertising was to please Mano, who implanted in my head that I must earn money first and paint later.

"There are sixty thousand painters in Paris! And only one will make it. Remember that!" His voice unexpectedly intruded on my mind each time I thought about taking up painting as a profession. Certainly the pull was there, as I often felt I was wasting my time doing advertising, and I knew that my mother or GG would have been delighted had I made that choice. But a visit from my uncle Ralph put me back on the money making track, and postponed the big step to come.

Tempted by fame and money

Uncle Ralph arrived at the Central unexpectedly during lunchtime one day. I was in the dining room and I saw him standing by the door looking for me. Moved by a surge of joy, I zigzagged my way around the dining tables and chairs and embraced him, kissing him three times on the cheeks. I felt my elegant and dignified uncle's sudden resistance – he became as rigid as a leafless tree in winter and turned bright red. I had publicly embarrassed him, completely forgetting that in England men never kiss, especially in public. Looking at the floor he said in an extremely soft voice, "Could I possibly treat you to a cup of coffee, somewhere outside the school?"

"Yes I would love it!" I was happy at the thought of spending some time just with him. We went round to the Italian coffee shop I knew, where the coffee was acceptable. At that time, London was not the place to find a good cup of strong coffee.

He explained his visit, "I came to the City on business and thought I'd call in to see you. We have decided at Ashton Brothers to try to increase our sales through advertising. Up to now it has not been necessary, but competition is high and if we don't, we might come up against some real problems." My uncle was the managing director of Ashton Brothers, a large cotton factory employing some three thousand people up in Manchester. My ears grew as he went on, "We are thinking of having a poster designed to help increase the sales of our Zorbit towels in the UK, and our board is looking for the right artist. I thought you might like to have a try, why not? We would of course ask others too, and choose the most appropriate design. How about it?" I was delighted to be offered this opportunity and agreed that within a month I would produce a candidate poster.

My brain immediately flared up with creative ideas. I had not designed a poster since I left Paris and the thought excited me. Lost in my thoughts, I faintly heard my uncle say, "Well, I'd better be going. I still have much to do in London before catching the six o'clock train home. Send me the poster as soon as you have it. We

CHAPTER 7

have a board meeting next month to decide which one to choose." He stood up, adjusted his grey felt hat, slipped the pigskin gloves on his immaculately manicured hands, smiled and his kind blue eyes looked into mine, "Take care, I'll be waiting to hear from you." And he disappeared into the crowded London streets.

This possible job for Ashton Brothers motivated me to move out of my digs, which were too cold, too small, and too dark. During the Easter holidays in Vallauris that year, I mentioned it to Toby who gave me the address of his friend Tristram Hull who was the editor of a small monthly art and literature journal called Nimbus. He lived in London, 5 minutes from where I was staying in Westbourne Grove, so I decided to ring Tristram, and we agreed that I would visit his large flat at 9 Powis Terrace, where he lived with his wife and baby daughter. Although the house was rather dilapidated, like most houses in that part of London, it had once been a house of some importance. The short stone staircase led up to a columned landing framing a nicely moulded front door. I rang the first floor doorbell and heard heavy footsteps coming down the stairs two by two. A thin, tall young man dressed in an oversized pale grey suit opened the door. Curly black hair came down over his right eye, and, looking straight at me with the other, he said kindly, "Come in; we are on the first floor." I did not have time to shake his hand nor to present myself, as he was already flying up the long stairway to their flat.

We entered the hallway and Tristram pointed to the door on the left, "In this room live two painters, Robert Colquhoun and Robert MacBryde." Without giving me time to ask any questions about the painters, he continued, "In this one lives a nurse from Ghana. She's rarely there and often works at night. Down the three steps, you'll find the toilets, the bathroom and to the right the kitchen where you can do your own cooking. Please keep it as tidy as you find it." Tristram did a half turn on his heels and now faced a door to the left, knocked gently twice and without waiting for an answer half opened it. I just managed to see a plump lady with short black hair in a large double bed, leaning on one elbow reading a book. "My wife; the child

423

is still asleep…" whispered Tristram as he closed the door behind him. There was one more to open. "Here you are! This one is yours. Let me know if you need anything. Here are the keys of the house. Now, I must rush to work."

The room was at least three times larger than where I lived. The ceiling was high with a big table under a wide sash window, looking onto a dark well and through which I could see the kitchen. A chair, an armchair, a narrow bed, bookshelves and a wall cupboard to hang my clothes, made this room relatively comfortable. By the evening I'd moved into my new habitat. The rent was reasonable for the comfort it gave me, although I would have less privacy, sharing the flat with six other people. Notting Hill Gate 20 minutes walk away, would be my underground station to the Central Line delivering me straight to Holborn. I often carried heavy folders and appreciated this direct line.

As I entered the flat carrying the last of my belongings, I met a strange, scruffy and stocky, unshaven man in the hallway. Looking amused behind puffy eyelids, I glimpsed his pale blue eyes; he removed an old cigarette from the brown corner of his lips, and, with a half smile, said in a broad Scottish accent, "You're the new French boy are you? Nice…" I immediately put down my briefcase and pulled out my free hand. "Yes! I am François, the new tenant, I'm just moving into this room." The man took my hand delicately and held it looking at me with absent eyes. "MacBryde, call me Rob for Robert. I live in there with Colquhoun, my mate, another Robert!"

He finally freed my hand and stood watching me going into my room. A disagreeable shiver ran down my spine, as I smelled a mix of whisky, tobacco and urine from his body. 'Never mind', I thought as I walked into my new space, "I'll make my room nice, but first I'll have a cup of tea." I opened the door just a little and, seeing that no one was in the hallway, I came out and went to the kitchen carrying a basket filled with tea, coffee and all my food bits and pieces. On my way, I popped my head into the long and narrow bathroom with a cast iron bath, a mirror and washbasin – 'one step up from the one

CHAPTER 7

in Westbourne Grove' I said to myself.

The pale blue kitchen was spacious, the floor covered by white lino, and there was a large kitchen table with a worn pine top. A long stripped pine dresser with cupboards underneath covered the wall and had a set of blue-rimmed tea mugs hang from it. I put the aluminium kettle on the old-fashioned cast-iron gas stove and inspected the room. A sudden ray of sunshine drew my attention to the large window, which looked across to my bedroom window. The kettle whistled and, while the tea brewed, I arranged my food in a corner of the dresser cupboard.

Walking back to the bedroom with a mug of hot tea, I saw Rob's door wide open, the evening sun pouring in from the bright, west lit room. As I came up the three steps to the landing, a foul smell came to my nostrils. The floor creaked when I stepped on it and a voice from the bedroom called, "Come on in, don't be shy!" I stood on the threshold of the open door holding my tea and saw an easel with an unfinished sepia drawing of a nude male, earthenware pots full of brushes on a table that was used as a palette, and half opened oil tubes littering the rest of its surface.

The studio was rather chaotic; drawings were pinned haphazardly on the walls, dirty clothes, unwashed socks and worn-out shoes lay about the filthy floor; there were mugs, bottles, brushes and books everywhere. A pile of blank canvases leaned against one wall, and several heaps of unopened boxes of oil paints rested beside them on the floor. Two worn-out leather armchairs faced a gas fire and on the mantle were small clay figurines made of wire. A bouquet of dried red roses stood precariously on the edge of a chest with open drawers next to a large untidy double bed in the corner of the room. On the bed were the two Scottish painters, looking quite drunk. Rob was sitting on his feet tucked up in the corner, his back to the wall, holding a book in his right hand and a shaking glass of whisky in his left. His skinny, tall friend was sitting on the edge of the bed, his long greasy brown hair drawn back from his elongated forehead. He glanced at me furtively with his deep-set, brown eyes and showed an irregular set of grey teeth. They were both looking at me grinning. Rob mumbled, "By the way, may I introduce Robert Colquhoun, and this is François, the French boy I told you about." "Hello."

"Hi!" grunted the other Robert in a deep voice. "Here! Listen to this smashing piece of poetry."

I sipped my tea and observed them as Rob read on his chosen poem. They both looked frighteningly miserable and I wanted to rush out, but I could not, as Rob was reading, with great emotional gusto, verses about some lost loved one. Colquhoun was staring absently at the floor; the long fingers of his artistic hands gripping an empty glass and squeezing a lit cigarette; his elbows rested on his knees causing his neck to sink into his shoulders. MacBryde, completely absorbed by the poem, did not notice me silently walking backwards and slipping away unseen.

Relieved to be out of their sight, I rushed across the hallway into my room and closed the door behind me. It took me some time to free myself from this scene and I lay on the bed looking at the ceiling, trying to get back into my own space. Finally, I decided to start working on the Zorbit towel poster project, the best way to clear my mind.

Certainly this flat was unusual: the gay painters, the invisible Ghanaian night nurse, Tristram who was rarely there, and his wife who spent most of her time in bed reading while her baby daughter trotted about the flat. And not forgetting me 'the French boy'; we made an incongruous collection of mixed personalities. I had a lot of work and decided to ignore the other lodgers as much as possible and concentrate on my work.

When observing posters on the walls in London and in the Underground, I found them old-fashioned, boring, lacking punch and directness. I asked myself... "what would distract the Londoners enough to make their head turn? At that time in the UK sex and nakedness were of the underworld and still taboo... A provocative idea came to my mind: How about showing the backside of a bright pink, naked man? That would make Londoners' heads turn, wouldn't it?" In my poster the bright pink, naked man would be seen from the back, with a yellow flower sticking out of his mouth to give it a humorous touch. He would be drying his back with a Zorbit towel! 'Zorbit Towels' would be written in large, white letters across the top of the poster, outlined by a thick black line and my little man would be holding the pale blue towel, one hand up, one hand down drying his back. I would make sure that his tight round bottom would be visible and this scene would be on a vivid, purple background.

In the fortnight that followed I stayed up late every evening, designing the poster. When my sketch gave me full satisfaction, I stretched cartridge paper onto a large drawing board, squared it up and proceeded to paint the poster. When I finally felt happy with the completed work, I carefully rolled it up into a thick cardboard tube and sent it off to my uncle in Manchester. I felt relieved although I did not know whether it would be accepted; but I knew I had done a provocative poster. I left it to fate to decide the outcome.

Life in London was busy on all fronts. Besides the interesting work I was doing at the Central, I saw my grandmother and my uncles, and friends like Bernard Kay, Ivor Cutler, or my old friend John Burningham, who I ran into accidentally one day on Waterloo Bridge.

"John! What are you doing here?" I was surprised to see him. "I could ask you the same question! What are you doing here? Should you not be in France?"

"Well, after two years of studying advertising in Paris, I decided to come and study here in London, at the Central School of Arts and Crafts. It's a great place; I've been there since January studying graphics."

Soon after that meeting on the bridge, John came to study book illustration at the Central and later published many illustrated children's books.

New awareness of the feminine

Most of my spare time was now spent with my new girlfriend

Sandy. I had noticed her once during lunchtimes at the canteen, often sitting alone. She did not seem to belong to the art school with her fair hair always neatly arranged and her makeup accurately painted on. I felt intrigued and attracted by her almost bourgeois presence. So, one day I plucked up my courage and approached her table with my hot lunch tray. "Would you mind if I join you for lunch?" I smiled, and she looked straight at me with her walnut brown eyes.

"No, not at all, do sit down!" From her accent I heard she was not English. 'She sounds American' I thought to myself as I sat down. That first lunch hour spent together evaporated in no time. The invisible magnetic force that drew us together activated our curiosity about each other, where we came from, and what we were studying.

Her father was a South African diplomat and her mother was Mexican. Sandy, the only daughter, was brought up in these two countries and spoke both languages fluently. Her parents were now retired in Johannesburg and she studied interior design. As I listened to her musical voice, my attention absorbed her feminine nature. She was petite, her well-proportioned and lively body was neatly dressed in a blouse with a round white collar and a light red cashmere jersey the same colour as her immaculate lipstick. She wore a tight sand-coloured skirt that emphasised her hips, and fine, red high-heeled shoes completed her stylish look. My inquisitive sense of smell detected a fine French perfume mixed with the recognisable scent that women, often unknowingly, have at the time of their periods. This mixture of fragrance added to my impatience to want to be with her again. We decided to meet the next day at the same time.

Each day for a week we found the time to be together and, when Friday evening came, she invited me to have supper at her place near South Kensington tube station. We travelled on the packed underground during rush hour. I carried a large portfolio with my drawings and poster projects that I planned to work on during the weekend. The crowds forced our bodies together, and Sandy, being too short to hold the ceiling rails, rested her body against mine, with my portfolio protecting her from the pressures of the commuters.

CHAPTER 7

For the first time our bodies were close and I could not help but simply enjoy this first contact while looking at the decorative patterns of her Hermès headscarf. Being too tall and too squashed to bend my knees to read the names of the stations through the window, I could not see which stations we passed, but it did not matter as I was quite content to let this moment of closeness last.

I was brought back to reality by a nudge into my ribs. Sandy's dark brown eyes were looking up at me saying, "Next station!" Most of the travellers were getting off at South Kensington and we were lifted out by the crowd as if by a tsunami and were quickly out of the tube station. A few minutes later Sandy stopped by an elegant row of houses on Onslow Square, and searched in her red leather handbag for the key. A few steps took us up to a porch supported by two large stone columns.

"Keep your voice down. I don't want my landlady to know that I have brought a man into my bedsit." She murmured this with a vague smile as we walked noiselessly up the thick pale green carpet to the first floor. Her bedroom was small and tidy, with a tall sash window giving on to the balcony over the entrance. The delicate smell of her cosmetics pervaded the room. In the far right corner a flowered, bright pink bedspread covered the single bed and over it was a shelf filled with art books. Immediately to the right was a large clothes cupboard next to a small table and chair, on the left a washbasin and near the window, a tiny electric cooking stove. "Cup of tea?" she offered, smiling broadly, as she took off her black raincoat and placed it in the cupboard. "Yes thank you Sandy, but no sugar."

I felt like a world traveller about to go on a journey to discover the southern continents of America and Africa. It was exciting and fascinating to think what I would experience in these faraway lands. I asked many questions about her childhood in Mexico City where her father had been an important diplomat. She told me how she used to go and visit the Inca and Mayan sites with her mum and dad, who were actually both of Spanish origin. Sandy attended an American International School and this explained where her accent came from. Was it my early childhood spent on the Ile du Levant that triggered my fascination for Africa, looking south at the horizon and imagining the world beyond the distant, pale grey-blue haze? I asked her many questions, since what I knew about Africa was through the Tarzan comics devoured during my pre-teen years in Dieulefit.

Through her answers I quickly realised that the Africa she was telling me about was not the same Africa I dreamt of. She told me about her large house, her black nannies, their Dalmatian bitch, the tall wall round their property with orange, lemon and grapefruit trees. The Afrikaners, with their secluded way of life, were completely separated from the black Africans. Sandy had an appealing ability to describe the beauty of the African landscape, wildlife and vegetation that she adored. She was equally keen to know all about my background, about France, the Cote d'Azur and Paris. I shared the rosier parts of my youth and some of my experiences at the Paul Colin arts school. Then she asked me inquisitively, "Please, could I look through your portfolio?"

I showed her my latest drawings and gouaches done on the London docks the previous week, engravings and the aquatints of my uncle asleep in his armchair, and also the sketches for the Zorbit poster. I could see she greatly enjoyed seeing my work and discovering who I was, and it pleased me that she appreciated my creativity. Sandy pointed to a quickly drawn sketch of a reclining nude she particularly liked. "It's yours, have it!" I instantly offered.

"You must be hungry… it's getting late. Like some supper? Do you like fried tomatoes?" I nodded in appreciation and noticed how her accent drew out the 'a' in the way she pronounced tomato. Sitting at the foot of her bed, she started to prepare the meal while I looked in the small food cupboard for the plates and cutlery. "Where shall I lay the table?" "We'll eat on our knees; it's simpler that way. You can sit on the chair if you like. I'll sit on the bed." I sat close and watched her attending to our tomatoes. After some time she turned her head, her gentle eyes giving me an affectionate look, her mouth slightly tight as if to say, "Just wait a little, I am cooking!"

CHAPTER 7

Pushed by the hunger of my passionate feelings, my hand round her waist, I bought her close and kissed her lips that immediately loosened agreeably. Vibrating like a bumblebee looking for the sweet pollen of a delicate flower, my lips were now venturing down her tender neck. To my surprise, this had the effect of sending a ripple of appreciation down her spine. Interested by this unexpected reaction, I repeated the delicate action and found that Sandy reacted in the same way, adding this time a little grunting sound of delight. I came back to her cheek and when I opened my eyes saw hers still closed and the wooden spoon in her right hand waving warningly.

'Oh! Yes! The tomatoes are frying in the pan!' I thought, as I let go of my affectionate grip. "You're making me burn the supper!" She exclaimed while desperately trying to detach them from the pan.

By the time we had finished our supper, it was time for me to leave so I could catch the last tube home. She accompanied me to the door and said, as she looped my scarf round my neck, "Hey, you're forgetting this!" With my arms wrapped round her waist, filled by an overwhelming joy, I lifted her off the ground, did three complete turns and kissed her again.

As I walked to the tube station I realized these few hours spent with Sandy had changed something in our relationship. A door to a new venture had been opened. When I saw her the following Monday at the Central, I was very tempted to kiss her on both cheeks, but held back my desires knowing that this would embarrass her. I resorted to simply smiling broadly.

Not able to see me on the following Friday evening, Sandy offered with suppressed excitement in her voice, "Come Saturday instead, at around seven, I'll have supper ready for you."

That Friday evening was turbulent at number 9 Powis Terrace, as Colquhoun and MacBryde were drinking heavily again; I heard them shouting and fighting in the kitchen. As they were violent, I did not want to go to in to make my supper, so I went out to a small restaurant in Notting Hill Gate. When I entered the flat some time later, I could hear the shouting still going on and slipped unnoticed into my bedroom. I did not sleep well that night as the row went on until the early hours of the morning.

I rose later than usual the next day and found Tristram tidying up the mess in the kitchen while preparing the breakfast for his wife and child.

"I'm sorry about last night, my two rowdy lodgers got rather drunk I'm afraid!"

Tristram said apologetically. "Yes I know, my bedroom window is opposite the kitchen and they were extremely violent. It was only after they retired to their bedroom that I could find some sleep!" I made the point that I was the one who had to hear most of it. "I've asked them to go, but they say they can't find anywhere else. I know they have been looking." He gave me the impression that he wasn't able to get them to move out. In the back of my mind I decided to find another place. Certainly I knew I would not go back there after the summer holidays.

Saturday morning was a beautiful late spring day and after a quick bath, I needed to get away from the unhealthy atmosphere of the house, to clear my feelings and my thoughts, I decided to tackle the long walk to South Kensington. I joined the Bayswater Road by the backstreets, took my time through Hyde Park, and watched the swans and the ducks paddling in the Serpentine Lake. Attracted by the songs of an inspired blackbird, I paused for a while to listen to its refreshing sounds. The cleaning and creative powers of Spring cleared my feelings, and filled me with a profound happiness and thankfulness for being present in the peaceful green beauty that surrounded me.

I stopped at the Natural History Museum, for prehistory had always fascinated me. Seeing and prodding the colossal skeletons of the prehistoric beasts, transported me into a different time dimension, where I willingly dwindled the 'I' of my person into non-existence. I enjoyed this timeless visit into prehistory immensely, but realised suddenly that it was now late afternoon and that the day had slipped away unnoticed. Walking by South Kensington tube station, I stopped to buy some cherries, strawberries and a pot of fresh cream. Across Cromwell Place was a good wine merchant, located beside a car showroom filled with Rolls-Royces, Bugattis and Aston Martins. I stopped a while, admiring their refined designs that expressed comfort, power, wealth and all the things the very rich go for. Then I walked into the wine merchant to select a red Burgundy that I thought would go nicely with our meal. My arms filled with the bags of goodies, I stretched out a hand to ring the bell of number 19 Onslow Square.

The shiny blue door opened wide, Sandy was standing there, smiling broadly in her pleated white skirt, a white blouse, a plain Nile green apron and a pair of bright red ballerina shoes. I followed her, closing the door behind me with my elbows. She talked as we climbed the stairs, her voice openly showing her excitement. "I hope that you will like my cooking, I've done cauliflower, Brussels sprouts in a tomato sauce and lamb chops as well... and by the way, my landlady has gone away for the weekend. She'll be back sometime on Sunday."

As we happily chatted in the small bedsit, all the problems of my world disappeared. It was as if we were thrown magically into a new orbit, pulled together by an irresistible force, invisibly paving our way to a distant galaxy. Sitting on the fitted carpet, chatting and laughing while eating her delicious meal and drinking the Beaujolais, we finally came to the dessert. I looked at her and thought how attractive she was while she was eating the strawberries and cream. The wine was contributing, creating a playful atmosphere and giggling was now part of our feast.

In Provence, cherries were an important part of our gastronomy and I was keen to show her how I could tie a knot in a cherry stalk using only my tongue. It was not easy by any means, and demanded concentration. Our laughing made the task more difficult, but she managed to tie the knot in the cherry stalk first and presented it to me triumphantly!

We were now both keen to discover where this irresistible and powerful creative natural process would take us. I completely relaxed into the instant, following step by step the interplay of our feelings and bodies. I felt that Sandy was equally taken, and willingly surrendered to the situation without resistance, responsive to the pulse of our passions. We were now lying on the bed; night had fallen for quite some time, and the room's only light came from the lamps of Onslow square. Our eyes were closed, both following our instincts, immersed in our feelings…

We were travelling together on the path of the senses, with such closeness that we became one. Under no pressure from 'ought and should', we let the journey take place naturally… All parts of our beings were now alive. I was far away from my ego as there was no 'I' present in this reality. It felt as if our essence was flying over hills covered in blossoming trees, bursting with fragrance. Our heavenly journey took us into a narrow gorge at the end of which was a tall slender arched door. For some time it resisted the gentle rhythmic push of our celestial vessel. And after some time its resistance brought me back to a more earthly reality, I murmured quietly into Sandy's ear,

"Is it okay, shall we?" "Yes, go on." She whispered back, as the powerful pulling force increased. We were both taken by surprise when finally the stubborn flexible membrane gave way, leading us into a wide virgin space where irresistible divine currents took us over embracing us up into a whirlwind of powerful blissful feelings. Tossed about by the extreme beauty, we were lifted out of our male and female identities and placed into a sphere of infinite oneness. The world of pure consciousness we experienced was light years away from the world of imagined, physical and crude emotions. Our most refined feelings were now permeating all corners of a universe neither of us had known before. The serene peaceful vibration carried us gently into a space no words can describe…

I woke up early the following morning to find us intricately folded into each other's arms. With great care, so as not to wake up my finer-feeling travelling partner, I extracted myself from her arms and slipped out of the bed.

As I quietly put on my clothes, I heard Sandy's sleepy voice, "Are you going already?"

"Yes, I'd better go in case your landlady comes back early. I also have to go and see my grandmother in Epsom later on this morning." Leaning over the bed to kiss her goodbye, I was strongly pulled by the desire to discover more unknown places with her. But I could not miss my appointment with GG and after kissing gently her forehead, I left the room. From that day on we spent more time with each other, at lunch times and after the study hours at the Central.

Darker sides of life

I came home late one night, after having spent the evening with Sandy, and as I entered the hallway I heard shouting down in the kitchen. 'Colquhoun and MacBryde are at it again,' I thought, as I walked into my bedroom to fetch my towel and toothbrush. As I popped into the bathroom, I noticed with great relief that the kitchen door was closed. I cleaned myself quickly and slid back into my room. I did not put on the light to let them know I was back, but stood by my window and looked discreetly into the kitchen. They were arguing fiercely, sitting opposite each other surrounded by an array of half empty bottles. MacBryde was waving a long kitchen knife seemingly out of control. I did not want to witness this violence. I pulled the thin linen curtain over the window, in the hope that this would lessen the noise, and went to bed. Of course I could not sleep, and after trying for an hour, I got up to look through a gap in the curtains. Separated by the large table, Colquhoun was throwing plates at his friend and holding in his left hand the neck of a broken bottle, while MacBryde was menacing him with the kitchen knife. Feeling exasperated and angry, I put on a pair of Levi's and rushed down to the closed kitchen door. I knocked loudly and shouted, "Shut up in there! It's late, I want to sleep!"

For a few seconds there was dead silence… then suddenly I heard

MacBryde's voice grunt loudly, "It's the juicy French boy! Where is the bastard? I'm going to bugger him!"

You can imagine how fast I ran when he opened the door to catch me. Thanks to the high level of alcohol in his blood and whatever else he had taken, he could not run straight. I dived into my bedroom, rapidly locking the door behind me, and stood just beside the entrance, holding a little axe I had recently found on a rubbish heap.

Hitting my door repeatedly with the long bladed knife, he shouted the most horrific things, grossly expressing his homosexuality and threatening to kill me if I did not open the door. Every time he hit the door, an aggressive wave of emotions penetrated my chest, increasing my heartbeat. I could see the point of the blade coming through the wooden panel! The effort to free the knife each time it was planted in the door, made him grunt like a wild beast.

In case the door finally gave in, I decided to hit him with the flat part of the axe, as I did not want to be responsible for a dead man. After 15 minutes he stopped, and giving a final raging yell, MacBryde left my door alone. A heavy silence followed. Trembling like a leaf, I thanked the carpenter who had 100 years earlier made that door so tough, slipped into my bed, keeping on my jeans, and placed the axe under my pillow. Then I waited for my emotions to calm down, and for sleep to arrive.

The following morning, I was the first to get up as usual. I decided not to go near the kitchen. As I opened my door to go to the bathroom I realised how lacerated it was, reminding me of the early morning drama. The hallway, lit by a long window, revealed that the parquet floor had wet shiny marks leading to Tristram's bedroom. I bent down to inspect them… to my horror I saw they were the tiny footprints of the owner's two year old daughter who had recently walked in some bright red liquid. On closer inspection, I realized it was not ink but blood! I followed the footmarks down the three steps thinking that the child might have hurt herself, and found the bathroom door half open. The light was on, and as I pushed it fully open, I found a most horrific scene: Colquhoun, white as the enamel bath he lay in, his eyes closed, his right wrist hanging over the edge dripping with blood, lay in vermillion waters, completely naked. His left wrist showed a deep cut, and his hand cupped his genitals. Avoiding the child's footprints, I rushed up the 3 stairs to find myself nose to nose with the Ghanaian nurse who was arriving from her night duty. Pointing to the blood on the floor I asked her to ring immediately the nearest hospital. She was a professional, and in no time an ambulance arrived to remove the unconscious man. Later that day Tristram told me that Robert had been saved in extremis and that he was now resting in a nearby hospital.

It took some time for these powerful images to dissipate from my heart and mind and, as I share these experiences with you, I see that they are still filed in the depth of my being; thankfully not only the gruesome ones but also the more happy ones. After this incident I made it clear to my landlord that I would not return after the summer, and he understood my decision.

A welcome holiday

Although I would miss Sandy's close presence very much, the anticipation of going to France for the summer holidays was soothing. I needed a break from London's darker sides. Knowing I would not return to 9 Powis Terrace, accelerated my search for another place before I left, for my return in early September 1956. I found a fair sized room in a small semi-detached house at 22 Alexander Road. It was not great by any means; the bedroom had no electricity and was lit by a central, noisy, bluish gaslight that hung rigidly down from the ceiling. It was probably the reason the old lady proprietor made the rent so reasonable, and allowed me to leave behind a few of my belongings in a space under the staircase.

The journey was straightforward on one of the first through-Paris trains direct to Cannes. Arriving was always a wonderful moment after a long night of noisy travel. Emerging noisily out of the dark tunnel into the station, the London-Nice train entered the glass and metal framed station and came to a standstill. The air was warm… the sky was blue… and I was revived by the gentle sea breeze that smelt of seaweed. Toby came to fetch me on his Vespa, and we drove back to Vallauris along the colourful coastline road.

We lived now in a recently rented house in the Quartier du Devens. A chalky track off the main road took us some 500 metres along to a large olive tree under which we parked the scooter. The tiny property stood just below the road. Six steps led us to a concrete terrace covered by a rusty metal trellis loaded with a grapevine. To the right an eight-foot deep-water tank was alive with many large orange and white goldfish.

"By the way, the loo is just a few steps down from the terrace, but I warn you, you have to bend in half and walk in backwards, it's so small!" Toby announced.

Entering the tiny kitchen through the grey, glass paned narrow double doors gave me the impression of coming into a Lilliputian's home…

"No! You are here at last! I can't believe it!" exclaimed my mother before hugging and kissing me affectionately. "It's really nice here, away from the village," I remarked while immersed in mother's affection. I stood there for a few instants and looked round at the low concrete sink opposite, it was surrounded by large terracotta tiles with a single brass tap. To the right protruded the hood of the small chimney over a gas stove, and against the right wall was the kitchen table covered with a red chequered oilcloth.

Maman warmed up the coffee, got out the bread, butter and home-made jam and we all sat tightly around the table for breakfast. As usual, I did most of the talking, sharing the latest events of the term, but not my time with Sandy. Sylvette, Toby and Maman showed me round the house. I would sleep in the smallest room just behind the partition wall by the kitchen table. The single bed was the size of the space! A window at its foot gave onto the terrace. To the left of the kitchen was a minuscule lobby and a staircase up to my mother's and Fonsou's bedroom. Two windows, one facing West overlooking the goldfish tank and the other facing north towards the Alps... and this was the entire house! Toby must have read my mind when I wondered where they were sleeping, "Come I'll show you where we are!"

East of the house, he had transformed an old lean-to shed into a fair sized, attractive bedroom. Toby was a handy man with a great sense of design. Although the house was small, it was charming. The steep terraced land surrounding the north and west sides were planted with lemon and orange trees and had a magnificent view of pine forest hills with the snowy mountains beyond.

The summer went by smoothly. The acquisition of a second-hand Lambretta brought a pleasant change in my life – independence and freedom of movement, something I had not had before. I was able to freely go where I fancied without having to borrow my mother's Sulky, a strange cross between a scooter and motorbike.

Toby's small business was thriving for he had a lot of work; while on holiday I often gave him a hand. Sylvette, a creative person, was writing poetry, painting watercolours and decorating pottery. Our lunches were taken in Golf-Juan on the open seaside of the long jetty of the fishing harbour. Colossal rocks protected the jetty from the waves and were a perfect platform to dive and swim from. The water was deep and clear and Toby had become a keen harpoon gun apprentice, who enjoyed going off with me on long fishing expeditions. We would leave Sylvette alone sunbathing on the rocks away from the crowds.

My sister did not realise how attractive and beautiful she was, and avoided displaying her body on the crowded beaches. Picasso knew that and had no choice but to paint her fully dressed, except for one painting where he imagined her topless holding an ear of corn! One day Sylvette and I went down to Golf-Juan on my newly acquired Lambretta, while Toby stayed behind in his workshop to finish an urgent order. As usual, before having our picnic lunch, I went out fishing with my goggles, snorkel, flippers and harpoon gun. Carried by the warm salted seawater, I chased a large silver bass flashing its wide body in the blue depths. My idea was to force it back towards the jetty, corner it and get close enough to adjust my aim. After filling my lung with as much air as possible, I dived down, making sure my chosen fish was between the coast and myself. So far the plan had succeeded and my appetising friend started to swim nonchalantly towards the jetty. I surfaced again to breathe and glanced in the direction of where I'd left my sister.

I immediately saw that she was having difficulties for, high above her on the jetty, stood a photographer taking pictures of her in her bathing costume. Moved by a profound instinct for family preservation and totally forgetting my bass, I swam at high speed towards the rocks. I came out of the water silently, secured my swimming and fishing gear on a flat rock and leapt from one boulder to the other to reach them. The professional photographer, excited by my sister's angry protest, was now taking photos of my arrival onto the scene!

"François, this horrible man will not leave me alone! I told him I do not want him to take photos of me like this! But he won't listen!" In my most authoritative tone of voice, I said to the intruder, "You have no right to take photos without my sister's permission! Give me your film!"

The man was framing his final shot of me and obviously took no notice of what I'd said. Climbing onto the quay I moved in to block his escape. He was of middle height, with a plump face, frizzy black hair and glasses. His vest was full of pockets and his wide belt carrying numerous bags indicated that he was a professional. The gentle purr from his expensive Hasselblad indicated that he had pressed the automatic rewind button. I forcibly grabbed the precious instrument from his pudgy hands and ran some distance away from the now angry man, giving myself enough distance to remove the film.

"Hey! Give it back to me, you have no right to do that. I'll call the police!" I walked back to him slowly holding out his Hasselblad with one hand, keeping the film in the other, and smiling broadly, gave him back his camera, "Next time, ask permission first before photographing people. I jumped back down onto the lower rocks where my sister, who looked quite relieved, was hiding her body under her large swimming towel. We developed the photos some time later and found them all very amusing... my sister with angry expressions and me looking menacing. We never did find out which newspaper or magazine this man worked for.

It was during these summer holidays that I really started to paint in oils. I was fascinated by the richness of the medium; applying colours on a freshly primed, taut canvas was a most sensuous experience. Toby had started to paint in oils too and we would paint together in the open air, inspired by the diversity and beauty of the shapes, forms and colours of the landscape. It was in the summer of 1956 that I first experienced the deep peace that establishes itself in the silence that concentration brings while observing nature. Communion is the closest word to express what happens between the subject and the painter; the feeling of oneness with the subject, whether a flower, an olive tree or a distant hill, creates an inner vacuum combined with a profound feeling of well-being. The canvas responded to my hand holding the brush and slowly revealed my new creation. While painting there was no thinking, only quietness and concentration that became unity with the subject. It was only when I stopped painting and stepped back to look at what I had done, that I saw that my mind did not always manage to choose the right colour or trace a harmonious line, or achieve a balanced composition. I then studied what I had done, turning the canvas upside down to see only the rhythms of the abstraction. After deciding what to alter or add, I went back to the surface, scrutinised again what I was painting, and let the creative process carry on until I could go no further. I rarely felt satisfied with what I had painted, but seeing the need for improvement always gave me the incentive to start another canvas. During these moments, I often felt close to the Impressionist painters that I revered, Cézanne especially, for his work spoke to me most at that time. The more I painted, the more I realised what a great master he was.

Mano used to tell us a story to illustrate the difference between one's own sensitivity to an art expression and what is recognised at a certain époque as Art. One late afternoon, his father was returning to Camaret sur Aygues from Aix-en Provence where he had been on business. Some kilometres outside the city by the side of the road he saw an elderly painter standing by his easel completely absorbed by the view he was painting. His curiosity and interest in the arts made him pull on the reins of his horse, park his cart alongside the road and walk eagerly towards the artist. He was himself keen on painting, having dabbled with watercolours, and he could not wait to see what this painter was up to.

The man was short, dressed in a dusty, crumpled black suit, and wore a black felt hat on his balding head. His piercing brown eyes looked at the new arrival, his long hooked nose hung over a generous mouth that was surrounded by a well-trimmed short grey beard. My sister's grandfather asked permission to look at the two freshly painted canvases. The artist agreed, pleased to see that someone was interested in his work. They talked about the paintings and art in general and Mano's father returned to Camaret with the two paintings, feeling full of joy at the thought of hanging them in his sitting room. He had bought them for five centimes each!

When his wife Mamiche saw the paintings the next morning, she exclaimed, "What on earth have you been up to? Are these the paintings that you paid five centimes each for? Have you gone crazy? Do you see how badly painted they are?" Mano's father stood there embarrassed, listening to his wife's reaction and then tried to convince her of his decision: "These paintings are actually a revolution in art, it is a completely new way to look at a landscape, it could be described as… Cubist painting? To me, this painter, called Cézanne, is absolutely unique and well ahead of his time. One day I'm sure he'll be famous!"

The newly acquired landscapes were stubbornly hung in the sitting room but his life became impossible, for his wife continuously complained about the paintings, wishing that he would take them down. Finally some weeks later, exasperated by the problems they were causing, he regrettably put them in an auction in Avignon, recuperated some of his centimes and tried to forget about the whole event. Grandfather David, through his sensitive artistic eye had recognised a genius.

The holidays had come and gone like a flash. With the fullness of the artistic life in the summer in Vallauris and the scooter rides along the Côte d'Azur, there had not been a day without an interesting event. In September the time came to return to England to continue my studies. I felt my home was now really in myself and I did not feel sad to leave the Côte d'Azur. My place was in the instant of wherever I was, and the house in Vallauris was my mother's and Fonsou's, Sylvette's and Toby's. Living for three years on my own detached me from the umbilical chord of the family and set me free into my own orbit. I felt self-confident and capable of taking my life into my own hands.

It was time for me to return to London. I was eager to know whether my poster had been accepted and I had other advertising jobs to attend to. I also missed Sandy and was looking forward to seeing her again. My mother wanted to see me off at Cannes Station and we followed each other, she on her Vespa, me on my Lambretta.

The train arrived in a cloud of white steam and charcoal-grey smoke. While my mother looked after my possessions, I rolled the scooter to the goods wagon at the back of the train. The railway officer instructed me to collect it at Victoria Station on arrival in London. I walked back to Maman waiting in front of the carriage, held her narrow shoulders and looked into the depth of her pale blue eyes. I saw there amidst great tenderness, a vulnerability I had not seen before. She was anxious, not about me but about her own future. She gave me a faint smile, "You remind me of my father. Every time we parted, he would hold me just like you do and look straight into my eyes." Her eyes were moist with emotion and she put her hand around the back of my neck and brought me gently close to kiss my cheeks.

The stationmaster's strident whistle vibrated through the station. Giving my mother a last hug, I hopped onto the high steps of the carriage and looked at her as the train moved off. As she diminished in the distance she stood on her tiptoes, waving a frantic goodbye. Floods of tears blurred my vision. I waved for the last time before the tunnel forced me to withdraw into the carriage. I pushed my luggage down the corridor with one foot until I found the compartment and my seat. The train was now going full steam emitting a mix of fast moving sounds.

Changes in my love life

Living in London was quite different. With a scooter, no more waiting for trains or buses and easy parking, I could carry my large portfolios around much more easily. Although Alexander Road was by no means adequate for my needs, it was quite a relief to be out of 9 Powis Terrace. But once more, I decided to find larger and lighter rooms, and if necessary, to share with someone – maybe with John Burningham who was now studying at the Central.

On that first Monday at the art school, I looked for Sandy during the tea break and found her sitting at a table in her usual corner. She saw me with my cup of tea and smiled. As I saw her face, I could instantly see there was a change in her feelings towards me. The smile was not clear but hesitant; her eyes did not look straight into mine as they used to do, but quickly looked down to her cup of tea that she stroked methodically with her index finger. I sat down and questioned her, "Did you stay in London for the summer holidays?" She nodded. Sensing that she was finding it difficult to express her feelings, I went straight to the point, "There is a weight on your heart…are you with somebody else?" She nodded, found the strength to look at me with the deep brown eyes that had so attracted me, and answered with a grain of apology, "Yes I am… I'm sorry…" A sudden turmoil came over me as I realised I had been abandoned for someone else. Her embarrassment showed me she suffered too

CHAPTER 7

and I didn't want to make it worse for her. "Do you love him very much? Is he a student in the Central?" I was stoic and while she replied, I understood I had lost her for her feelings had shifted to another man.

"Yes, he is…" "What's his name?" "Tom, he works in the industrial design department."

Her voice was suddenly lighter and positive. Although my ego had just taken a bashing, deep down I felt remarkably happy and free, almost relieved by the unexpected new reality. I was ready to let her float away with her new lover, without jealousy in my heart. I did not feel I had lost her, for in the time we were together we had pulled each other out of the teenage years into becoming adults. Our fine heavenly feelings of intimacy gave me a glimpse of a different dimension into an experience of consciousness not known before, and it increased my need to find out more about my spiritual world. And so we parted good friends.

Going to the pub after school was part of English culture, and there I discovered I had much more affinity with the students from the painting department. I became friendly with a Jewish man called John Epstein, whose parents were relatively wealthy from the clothing trade. They lived in Princess Gate in a spacious second-floor flat looking over Hyde Park. We spent much time together visiting galleries and talking about art and venturing out in his new, bubble shaped Austin Seven.

The dim gaslight of my room on Alexander Road, made it very difficult for me to work in the evenings, and on top of that, the room was cold and the bathroom very old-fashioned! I spent more time out of that house than in.

One day as I came down the stairs into the hallway, I found my landlady looking at me furiously, her arms crossed and legs apart, "Oh! Here you are, I've been waiting for you all day! You know the police came looking for you? I want you out of this house - you must leave by the end of the week!" First thing the next morning I went to Notting Hill Gate police station and effectively they were looking for me. Apparently I had not registered my scooter properly and this was an infraction that needed sorting out immediately. I managed to find the scooter's import documents and took them back to the police station where they promptly stamped them.

The following day, standing by the big billboard at the great entrance hall of the Central searching for 'Rooms to Let', I heard a soft male voice behind me, "You're looking for some digs are you?" I turned round and found a tall, fair-headed man with laughing blue eyes smiling while stroking his elegant moustache. "Yes I am! In fact it's pretty urgent." "Well, I'm looking for someone to share a flat with… how about it? It's in Belsize Park Avenue, near Hampstead Heath."

John Lawrence was in his mid-20s and studied book illustration. We decided to meet after work and off we went together on the Lambretta to see the flat. I liked John instantly and felt sharing a flat with him would be no problem, although I had not shared my living space with anyone before. We stopped at number 22, by a large elegant house with white painted sash-windows on the peaceful wooded avenue. The first floor flat was spacious enough for the two of us and faced north. A comfortable bathroom, toilet and a small kitchen completed the available space so we rapidly concluded the deal. Leaving the awful room at Alexander Road and moving into Belsize Park was a delightful change. Not only was my rent slightly lower, the comfort was heightened by central heating, fitted carpets and the light flooding in through the large windows. The entrance hall and the large staircase, leading to the different level flats, gave me a feeling of prosperity.

I found John very easy to share the flat with, and his extreme politeness and English ways amused and delighted me. The big locks of curly hair, neatly parted to one side, made him look like a full-grown public schoolboy. He was a practising Catholic with strong beliefs. My way of going about life was totally different from his. To me the idea of having a spiritual belief was like losing my own freedom of thought, as I based my understanding on factual life experiences. Tying my experiences to a belief that somewhere out there was a power outside myself would have made me feel very insecure. John and I had interesting long discussions on the subject, which I found stimulating because they helped me understand better the platform on which I stood.

He'd served as an officer in the British Army and some of his time had been spent in West Africa. When he drank a little too much Bass Bitter ale, a drink that he was most fond of, he would tell me the stories of what a young British officer in Africa got up to in his spare time... When John was tipsy, the conversation turned to sex related stories. He often came back very late from his London nightlife and I'd hear his key searching for the lock and, as he entered the room without putting on the light, he would say in a low voice, "I am awfully sorry, I am a bit late. I've done the rounds of the pubs again I am afraid!" He then popped into the kitchen, and I'd hear him lift the lid from the saucepan and exclaim, "Heavens above! That soup smells jolly good!" "Please have some, help yourself." I'd grunt, turn round and fall back to sleep.

I rose earlier in the morning and this gave a different rhythm to our lives, so we did not see each other as often as one would have expected. Our many lively conversations about our contrasted education intrigued us – from me he heard all about A.S. Neill, Summerhill and its education without punishment. He, on the other hand, attended a boys' Catholic public school and was exposed to rigid, imposed discipline. He argued that it was important to respect teachers and the only way was to do that was through punishment after all wasn't discipline in the Army based on this technique? This kind of statement would ignite an infinite appetite in me to argue that there were ways to impose discipline and respect other than through fear of punishment. I found it difficult to come to terms with the idea that a nice man, who I liked as if he was my own brother, could talk with what seemed to me so little intelligence or understanding about simple child psychology. His arguments regarding education were stereotypes, but how could he think otherwise never having known any other type of education? Yet with all our differences, we loved each other and never raised our voices to make our point. John was such a kind man, I was sure that when he'd have his own children, he would change his mind about authority in child education.

There is in my nature a tendency to tease and John was a perfect target to exercise this part of my nature. One evening I went to a party, that was not particularly enjoyable, and left around midnight grabbing on my way out a two foot long sausage-shape pink balloon. My roommate was not back in the flat when I returned. Resting the pink balloon on the mantelpiece by the lamp, I lit the gas fire below to warm-up the room. Then took off my clothes except my long johns to prepare myself for bed when I heard a floor creaking on the landing. John was coming back.

I quickly took the 2-foot balloon and pushed it down my long johns with the top part peering-up against my chest. With one elbow on the mantelpiece, my left hand hanging over the edge and the right one holding a book, I stood there resting my body weight on my right leg. John entered the room, his face expressing merriment. Although he immediately saw the enormous bulge rising out of my underwear, his extreme English politeness made him ignore it completely.

"Oh! Hello, you're still up? Did you have a nice evening?" He said as he flopped into the comfortable armchair opposite the fireplace. He was so intrigued by what he saw, that his eyes constantly returned to the raised pink shape rising above my long johns. Although it was terribly funny, I kept dead serious and replied, "No, my party was rather boring, so I came back… and how was your evening?" This situation was becoming too much for John and he did not answer my question. Stroking his moustache (something he did in emotional moments), he said in a trembling voice, "Heavens above! Forgive me for saying so François, but I have seen some pretty big ones while in Africa, but NEVER one as enormous as yours!" Now that he broke the silence of his curiosity, he leaned forward, pushed by the irresistible desire to see the pink shiny expansion up close.

"Oh, you mean my erection? Sorry about that, please forgive me," I replied nonchalantly as if it was an incident of no importance, pushing my pelvis forward and looking down thus making the sausage rise even more, his eyes and mouth were now wide with amazement, I went on, "Well these things do happen, don't they? We are not always in control of it, are we?" On saying this, I suddenly pricked the balloon with the sharp pin I held discreetly in my left hand and it exploded with a loud bang!

John was thrown back into the armchair completely shocked and then he burst-out laughing. "François! You are terrible, I really thought that it was the biggest I'd ever seen!"

A new direction

Not being with Sandy any more, I spent my spare time on other activities, like being with my male friends, attending parties and subscribing to more evening classes in etchings, aquatints and lithography, as well as sculpture one morning a week. These activities gave me more creative satisfaction for I was not fully satisfied with only studying graphic design. It was too monotonous and doing page after page of advertising layouts bored me. I watched my motivation slowly grinding down into a tedious rhythm. I was keener to work on the out-of-school jobs I acquired, including another poster through my Uncle Ralph to make a billboard for Ashton Bros to boost the sales of their sheets and pillow cases. I still had not heard anything about the Zorbit towels poster, had they finally silk-screened it? (A process of printing that was commonly used in the 1950s). It was already mid-October and the poster was submitted before the summer. Why this silence?

Coming up the spiral staircase of the Art School one day, I passed John Epstein who greeted me with a wide smile, "Is that your poster all over the London underground? I think I saw your signature on it. Are you going to become famous?" I could not believe it and turned round flying down the steps two by two and shouting up into the echoing stairwell, "Thanks for letting me know, I'll go and check!"

I ran through the crowded Southampton Row to Holborn tube station, but glancing through the station did not bring any good news. I searched my wallet for an underground ticket, went through the automatic gates and took the escalator down to the nearest platforms. I was stunned! There it was, obviously quite real - the little pink man drying his back with the Zorbit towel, a flower in his mouth, was in all the display windows down the long staircase of the tube station. As the stairs took me down I looked at each one carefully thinking, 'yes! They've got the colour right and they've done a good job!'

I rushed along the platform to see if the poster of my work was there in a larger size, but I could not see any. A little disappointed, I walked back following the crowd to the exit and hopped on to the escalator watching the little pink man drying his back all the way up. A middle-aged lady on the next step up from me was looking at the poster but her face gave me no clue about how she felt. What went on in her head as she looked at this naked, pink man with a round bottom? Would her subconscious push her towards Zorbit towels next time she was in a supermarket? It was an interesting question that I could not answer.

I could not resist taking the tube the following morning at Belsize Park station. There was no mechanical staircase in this station as the underground was too far below the city, and I squeezed into the overcrowded lift, just before the gates closed. I found myself right beside a Chinese girl jammed against the side of the lift. So as not to get completely squashed, she kept off the pressure of the crowd with her arched back, resisting in a determined manner, her hands resting on either side of the poster of the little pink man. Her nose was practically on the Plexiglas that protected it. I found it a rather amusing situation and looked discreetly at her and could not help smiling at the scene. She must have felt me watching her for she turned her head and behind her thick glasses her enlarged almond shaped eyes looked towards the ceiling as if to say, 'it is not funny!'

CHAPTER 7

I was not prepared for what was to come now that my work was displayed on the staircase walls and lifts in the London underground. It was as if I was advertising myself to the millions of people taking the tube every day and as a consequence, my diary began to get rather crammed with appointments. I was invited out for meals with directors of advertising agencies to discuss possible work. Toby's father, Paul Jellinek, owned a brush factory and asked me to do a page on his ' Tip, Top, Shine,' brushes. The Ambassador Magazine director, Elizabeth Juda, asked me to take on the design of the cover of the British export magazine. A Mr Brown from an advertising agency, asked me to make a proposal for a poster for soft drinks... and so on. There was so much to think about and much to do. What worried me though was that I had not yet been paid for the little pink man. I knew my uncle Ralph was a very busy man, but I decided to take some of his precious time and rang him up.

"Uncle Ralph? It's François, just to let you know, I am working on designs for the Zorbit sheets and pillowcases poster and I'm getting there! By the way, when is Ashton Bros going to pay me for the little pink man poster?" It was difficult for me to talk about finance to an important businessman such as my uncle. He answered in his slow kind voice, "Glad to hear you're getting on with the sheets and pillow cases poster. For the Zorbit towel poster payment, I'll see that you get paid. The board has decided to pay you £120, which should be sufficient for a budding young artist like you."

Feeling offended by the small amount offered I protested, "But that's only one 10th of what I should get for a poster that is on all the walls of the London tube!"

"You should think yourself a lucky young man to have your poster in the underground, but at the age of 18, you can't expect for any more, really... Incidentally, do you know that for the last months the sales of the Zorbit towels have increased considerably? It must be the effect of your poster in this new advertising campaign we launched isn't that encouraging?"

He said all this in what I felt was a condescending tone, but

451

I decided to leave the matter for it was not worth going on with this discussion. The cheque for £120 arrived the following week. The classes of graphic design now bored me and I welcomed all this new outside work. I spent much of my spare time in the flat at Belsize Park Avenue designing and making proposals to all my new clients.

One sunny autumn morning driving the Lambretta to the Central, I stopped at a red light at the bottom end of New Oxford Street. The pavements were crowded with busy pedestrians rushing in all directions on their way to work. I looked up and saw high up on a brick building, a large blank advertising space. I projected in my mind an image of the skyline of London at night, a large bright yellow crescent moon against a dark blue sky. In the cradle of the crescent was a happy smiling man wearing striped pyjamas, his eyes closed, snoozing with his head resting on a large white pillow, his body delicately covered by a white sheet.

'That's it! I've got it! That would make a splendid poster for Ashton Bros Sheets and Pillowcases. All these busy people would have to look up at the poster while they waited to cross at the red light!' The traffic lights turned green and I accelerated off, feeling exhilarated and satisfied by my new idea, but I heard a voice coming from the depth of my being, 'What right have you got to bother these good citizens with your posters advertising products that you haven't even tried yourself?'

Driving down the street, my mind elaborated the pros and cons of advertising. It was true... all the billboards that covered London were distracting and on the whole pretty ugly. I never thought of it before, but upon examination, most advertising tended to be devious, promoting the cleverness of its images and slogans and inciting people to purchase things whether the quality was good or not. 'Do I really want to belong to this world of manipulators, just to become a wealthy man?' I questioned myself.

The answer in reality was that I did not want to be part of this gigantic con - I wanted to be a painter. How could I be a painter if I spend my time making money designing for the advertising market?

CHAPTER 7

By the time I arrived at the Central, I had decided to stop all advertising work, and to spend the rest of my studies on painting full-time. I went straight to Mr Castleman, the headmaster of the art department, and informed him of this important decision.

"You want to be a painter but you're studying advertising. That does not feel right, I agree... let's see now... you can start next week in Hans Tisdall painting class and, if you like, we can increase your life drawing class to one full day a week with Hugh Stanton. How about that?" I was delighted although I did not know who Hans Tisdall was, but the thought of spending the whole day with Hugh Stanton for whom I had great respect and admiration, pleased me. I spent the next day purchasing painting materials in the fascinating, old-fashioned art shop called Cornelissen & Sons.

I produced quite a lot of work for my advertising clients, including the 'Tip-Top -Shine' design that was presented in many magazines, and a few of my poster designs were proposed to advertising agencies. The cover for the Ambassador magazine was designed and accepted. I found myself in a difficult situation and bravely met with all the clients who had entrusted me to create designs for them. Courage in hand, I explained I would not be continuing the projects and they would have to find another designer. I wrote to some, and phoned others. Most clients reacted angrily and expressed great disappointment in me. Mrs Judas's voice showed she had difficulty controlling her emotions, "This is incredible! I can't believe it! We give you, a very young man, an amazing opportunity and you throw it out of the window after only a few months!" I could only reply with shame, "I do understand, and I am truly sorry."

I felt bad having let all these people down; I had embarrassed them in front of their boards of directors when they'd defended my designs and obtained their approval to proceed. But what was I to do? Follow their needs, wants and my engagements to them? Or follow what I felt was a message from my soul asking me to take up full-time painting? It took quite some time for that feeling of guilt to dissipate. I honoured two jobs that were almost finished, and threw myself

100% into what I felt my soul was demanding.

Becoming a full-time fine art student completely changed my inner rhythm of life. It gave me a much wider space in my thoughts and creativity, and I knew that everything I did in the art classes contributed to developing the talent I always felt was the closest in myself: painting. My eyes began to look at things in a different way; in advertising everything was related to achieving a punchy and pertinent end result. The need to attract attention, which is the prime role of publicity, was no longer necessary and this gave me a new space to pay full attention to developing my talent. This change was by no means easy. I realised I knew nothing about painting as soon as I started. Day after day going back to a canvas that rarely reflected what I had in mind originally, continuously showed me I knew nothing about the art of painting. I did not fill my mind with thoughts on how to handle the next job, but became more of an observer. I started to be fascinated by the details in people's faces - the curve of an eye, the shape of an ear, the delicate contour of a lip. The living rhythm of a line dancing on the white surface of the canvas and the tones and colours I discovered in the world around me, was mirrored in my consciousness and fuelled my inspiration. At the beginning being de-stabilised in my feelings, sometimes even depressed, made me realise how much I had to learn in order to express what I wanted. I was overwhelmed with information and choices… why was this one preferably to that one? And what about the subject? And what about composition? Like a cork on the ocean, floating aimlessly, changing direction at the slightest breeze or current was the feeling.

My first art teachers were Hans Tisdall and Keith Vaughan, who added to my confusion because I did not understand where I was within myself vis-à-vis my creativity. They pushed their own concepts of art, as if they wanted to imprint their way of thinking into this fragile and influenceable new student. One afternoon, while painting a view of the Antibes harbour from a sketch done in the summer, and lost in the attractive silence of concentration…

CHAPTER 7

I suddenly heard Hans Tisdall's low authoritative voice behind me say, "Why do a blue sky? All artists have painted blue skies! Do it in pink, be modern! Be different!"

'I've never seen a pink sky in Antibes, why does he tell me to do a pink sky? I don't want to do a pink sky... that's his idea, not mine!' I protested angrily in myself. Hans Tisdall did not wait for my reaction, but moved on to give his observations to the girl painting next to me and exclaimed, "Ah! That's better, you see? But watch your composition, this line must not be so strong." The girl nodded silently and his voice faded away for I did not want to hear any more of his remarks, and felt that I would not be able to work with this teacher for long.

The other teacher I worked with was Keith Vaughan. Apparently I should have been very proud to attend his classes for he was a famous UK painter at the time. He was in his early 50s, a good looking man with ice-cold, blue eyes. He greeted me with a metallic feminine voice, "Grab yourself an easel and find yourself a place," is all he said. His class was very crammed and everyone was absorbed, working in complete silence. For several days Keith Vaughan did not come near me, but read his newspaper and smoked cigarettes on a high stool by the window. On rare occasions he bothered to stand by a student to discuss their work. From my summer holiday sketchbook I picked a lively drawing of the muscular backs of two men fighting on a sandy beach, which I thought would make an interesting painting. I white-primed a square board, the cheapest material on which to paint at that time, and started enthusiastically painting the sunburnt bodies in movement on the yellow sand, with the blue sea, the pale horizon and faded sky. I was quite pleased with parts of the painting, the struggle of the wrestlers, one on the back of the other gripping him tightly trying to pull him down, the other resisting and trying to throw him off, bulging legs and arms intertwined. I had done the sketch sitting on the beach looking up at the wrestlers which gave me an under view angle of the scene. I did not understand why the teacher hadn't come round yet, but absorbed in my painting I continued undisturbed. Maybe it was a new way of teaching, just being there and not giving his point of view, but still I expected some guidance - there were many points I needed technical help with. Finally, one day just before lunchtime when my painting was almost finished, the teacher came up beside me when I was about to complete the final touch.

Turning towards him, I saw anger on his deep red swollen face, as if about to burst… and which indeed it did! "Disgusting! How dare you paint this kind of rude scene? It is vulgar and indecent! Is it some kind of porn?"

His whole body shook and his musical voice snapped like the strings of a bow, his face was distorted by some hidden torment. Looking at him I didn't know what to do, but realising that nothing positive could come out of the situation I started washing my brushes and packing up my art materials I thought, 'My subject matter must have touched a deep down buried guilt to do with his homosexuality, he must think that my wrestlers are having a love affair and that it is too explicit!' A friend told me later that his speciality was to paint naked men. In France, all the students would have gathered around us, but here every one in the class froze silently behind their easels as they witnessed this strange happening. Keith Vaughan finished his tantrum by saying, "And don't paint subjects like this in my class again!" Well, I had no intention of working with such an emotionally unpredictable teacher in future and through the lunch hour I sat at a table by myself pondering what to do next.

Mr Castleman kindly signed me up in another painting class with an up and coming artist called William Turnbull, and I went to his lesson that same afternoon planning to decide whether to continue with this set of teachers or share my problem with the headmaster of the arts department. Similar to Mr Vaughan's classes, Mr Turnbull's 'Action Painting' sessions were packed with students. I did not know anything about Action Painting, I knew the work of Jackson Pollock, just to stay in the forefront of the arts movements, but I did not like his work, and his approach did not interest me. The

CHAPTER 7

Tachisme movement had started in Paris with the German painter Hans Hartung after World War II, but never drew my interest. The top floor studio was already filled with students squeezing themselves around three sides of a large white canvas pinned to the floor. I stood at the corner end of the canvas. The grey, heavy swinging doors burst open and a tall, thin, agitated Scotsman flew in, dressed in black from head to toe. Greasy shoulder length dark hair surrounded William Turnbull's large forehead, he had a prominent nose and a tortured sensuous mouth. His movements were jerky, punctuated by long silences while we waited for action to burst out. Large open industrial tins of bright oil paint, their lids off and each with its own brush, were in waiting for the master's impulses.

He first stood in the middle of the immaculate white space and gave a short introduction to what he was about to do. The man seemed to be in a hurry, he talked rapidly with much seriousness in a broad Scottish accent - there was no space or time for a smile. As if stung by a wasp, he unexpectedly leapt into action grabbing a black oil brush in his left hand, then a yellow in his right and went into a strange dance reminding me of the curlew bird looking for food on a wet marshland. After three rapid short steps, he stopped and using his whole body, swooped down making the dribbling paintbrushes scatter their heavy drops onto the white canvas. Certainly it was an entertaining show, everyone quietly observing the artist at work. I remember thinking... 'this is the kind of thing I did with Maman when I was two or three. I used to love throwing paint onto the white paper and seeing all the different patterns it produced.'

Unnoticed, I slipped out of the studio feeling dazed and in great need to share my dilemma. I did not want to continue with these classes and decided to take on full-time painting, but not to be told how to paint like this or like that but to learn the basic techniques, composition, colours, how to mix them and their effects on each other, how to transfer to my canvas the colours I saw out there.... to learn about the complexities of tone values, receding colours, and so on.

It was still early in the afternoon, so I went to see Mr Castleman again. He signed me in when I knocked on the glass pane door.

"So you're not satisfied with the teachers I recommended, but they're good English artists you know." He tried to reassure me with a slight feeling of sadness in his voice. He was obviously disappointed that I had not approved of his choice. "I do not deny that they are good artists in their own right, but what I'm interested to learn, is the academic basis of painting and drawing." He listened to my requirements with great attention, "Sorry, I misunderstood what you wanted, I have just the man you're looking for and his name is Leslie Cole. He is a member of the Royal Academy and a very fine painter indeed. I will talk to him…come back and see me tomorrow morning."

Next morning he introduced me to Leslie Cole, and I immediately felt at ease. In a few words Mr Castleman explained what I was looking for and departed. Leslie Cole was a short man with thick reddish brown hair combed back, a square face with a greying goatee, peaceful lively green eyes and thick tortoiseshell glasses.

Every day in Mr Cole's class we painted a nude model in the studio, well lit by northwest windows, located on the top floor, like all other studios of the fine art department. The eight to ten students were painting a dignified looking elderly lady with extremely white skin. She held her generous bulbous body erect, sitting on a crumpled white sheet directly on the floor. Behind her was a dark green velvet curtain; a large terracotta pot holding a few bulrushes completed the scene. Not wasting a minute, I went straight into action on the large primed board I'd prepared. This first nude oil painting was challenging and inspiring and I started to sketch with a piece of charcoal from the Paris days. Bringing in colours was exhilarating, I didn't stop even to light a cigarette, and so intense was my struggle with the subject that two hours passed without my noticing…

"Just pull back a little, give yourself a rest and let's see what you've done" Mr Cole said kindly as he came up behind me, "well, you do get on with it, don't you? Now, you see, you don't have to draw with charcoal; you can go straight into it with your brushes, thinning the colour with a little turpentine. Ah! I see you don't have an alizarin pink. Never mind – take this deep carmine instead, but take note: alizarin pink is a good colour when painting flesh."

He squeezed half an inch of the deep red onto the square board I used as a palette, dipped his flat, thin bristled brush in the turpentine, wiggled the rich colour out into a thin ink and proceeded to correct my first effort. The Master's brushstroke was accurate and steady, the movement slow, his observation of the model intense and in a few lines he achieved the correct proportions.

"You see this is painting, not drawing... drawing is fine, in fact it is excellent to train the eye, but here we paint. You will discover the line as you bring the colour of the flesh against the colour of the background. You only need a few lines to establish your composition and set your model in place." I felt so happy listening to what to me was sound advice. What he said and his approach was just what I was looking for and he opened my eyes to a world I longed to discover.

"Now... the colour of flesh changes all the time depending on whether it comes forward or whether it recedes. For instance, to make that knee really come forward, just add a speck of yellow ochre on this highlight. And then on that thigh... you see how it recedes into the background? Just add a touch of cerulean blue to your flesh colour and you will see how it recedes."

Inspiration took over, the master forgot that he was teaching and rejoiced at each stroke he added to my board. "Hey! I am getting too involved here... You've got it? Good..."

Happily storing all this appropriate information, I replied delighted, "Yes, thank you very much, it's clear."

I was off, moving into a new sphere where I could throw myself into what I loved doing most. Being with my palette, colours and brushes in front of a canvas every day made me feel I was in the right place. Leslie Cole's structured approach suited my character and working under him gave me great pleasure. I was usually the first in the studio in the mornings, taking time to put up my easel, arrange my palette and brushes to be ready for action when the model took their pose.

Jean

It is intriguing how large invisible currents of life, moved by energies that come from unknown places, can push one's destiny in a direction that one does not at all expect. This unexpected moment came in late September of 1956 when I entered the studio a little later than usual and gave a rapid glance towards the new model already in her pose. I felt startled by her unusual, wild beauty.

She was sitting with her straight back almost defiantly, yet with great dignity, on a tall stool draped in a white sheet. The corner of my eye told me discreetly she had noticed my arrival. Not wanting to miss one second of her resplendent grace and shaking with impatience to start working, I prepared my palette and brushes. There were only a few students that day, so I was able to choose where to set my easel, just to the right of where the model sat. I selected a large primed board, secured it on the easel, took a deep breath and, forcing my breathing to slow down into a more regular rhythm, looked at the inspiring subject.

Silky and dense jet-black hair fell on either side of her long Etruscan face, separating her forehead evenly and partly covering her alert, pale green eyes that seemed to be scrutinising the infinite space of her world. Her straight nose had well-defined small nostrils, her sensitive dark lips were slightly parted and a faint smile revealed a small gap between her front teeth. The fine curve of her chin harmonised her entire face, which rested on her elongated neck delicately swooping to her round shoulders. Firm and perfectly shaped breasts stood high on her short rib cage and her small waistline accentuated the curve of her generous hips. Her long legs led my eyes down to the heels of her narrow feet, one resting on the stool rail and the other on the ground. Artistic, practical hands were splayed out on her thighs. Impressed and moved by the arrival of this unknown nymph in our studio, I struggled to decide how to tackle the composition. Should I just go for a portrait? Or for a bust or perhaps just paint her attractive hands? I finally decided to paint the whole model.

Deep in silence and concentration everyone was now in their painting space. Using my brush as a measure and thumb as a marker I traced the sitting figure on the primed surface, closing one eye to avoid double vision like one does when shooting a gun. Dark burgundy velvet curtains fell to the ground in generous folds providing the backdrop to the scene.

Whether in Paris, or in my life classes here in London, I saw all sorts of models and, after a few minutes of posing, I was accustomed to seeing them enrobed in a state of sleepiness. Some times they even closed their eyes or fell asleep and lost their balance in the process! But this model surprised me by her awareness. Not only her pale green eyes, her face and body seemed to be awake, but she gave the impression of being in a state of acute consciousness. Her full presence reminded me of the relatively short time I had practiced the Gurdjieff exercises, to try to become conscious of my whole being, without the interference and relentless attempts of my thoughts to fill my mind. It was a difficult exercise and I could only hold it for a few seconds. I often tried during the day to keep that kind permanent attention in myself. Was our model doing something like this or something else I did not know about?

The marvellous English invention of the tea break came up when we heard Leslie Cole say in a monotonous voice, "Time's up." During our daily half hour rest, from 11 to half past, we usually went down to the dining room to have tea and biscuits. Our inspiring subject stretched as she moved off the chair and went behind the screen. Cleaning my brushes, I looked at my morning's work and felt okay about what I had done so far. While queuing to pick up my elevenses, I searched round the noisy dining room to see where I would sit. In the far right corner against the wall sat our striking model, looking sad with her head down holding a mug of tea in both hands.

"Do you mind if I join you?"

"No, not at all." She replied with a touch of indifference in her soft voice. It was the first time I heard her gentle voice and I found it delightfully soothing. I was closer to her than I had been before and noticed that she did not look happy. Her skin around those lovely green eyes was rather red, perhaps irritated by some unknown infection.

"May I ask you a question?" I said inquisitively as our eyes met directly for the first time. She looked at me in the same way a goat looks at a passers-by; the silent kind stare observed me without judgement.

"Well, tell me, what do you do inside yourself while posing?" I said with wonder and looking straight at me she answered, "Nothing!" I felt as if I had just walked into a private garden.

"I mean, most models tend to fall asleep when they pose, you seem to be awake, active in your mind?" This time a slight smile revealed her lovely teeth, "Do I?" She briefly replied not leading me on. "Yes you do! Are you doing some kind of exercise?"

Touched by the question, her expression became serious, she looked down at her still full mug of tea and timidly murmured, "Yes." Not wanting to stop my enquiry at this stage, I was too excited to know what kind of exercises they were, "Are they self remembering exercises? What do you actually do?"

Her face lit up, she looked radiant as our eyes met again and felt I was connecting to some profound reality. We were establishing a link of common understanding deep down in our inner feelings.

"Yes, they are… in my head, I count from 0 to a 100, while at the same time from 100 to 0… well I try! At the same time, I become aware of all the parts of my body right down to the tip of my toes." Now she laughed and her beauty exploded like a firework display. I continued, knowing that we were on the same key, "So you know about Gurdjieff and Ouspensky?"

She was posing as a model to make a little pocket money as she was actually working benevolently in a Gurdjieff centre called

Coombe Springs run by a Mr Bennett. She volunteered in the kitchen and the garden in return for lodging and food. Suddenly Jean exclaimed, "Oh dear! What time is it? The sitting - quick! I must go," and we both rushed back to the art room.

My three close friends at the Central, amusingly enough, were all called John. John Burningham and I were in Summerhill together, but even though he studied at the art school, we did not see much of each other. He was busy with his illustration studies in the day and with his girlfriend in the night.

John Lawrence and I shared a flat but the John I saw more frequently at that time was John Epstein. He also studied painting under different teachers and we became good friends spending much time together talking at length about art and women. He was not very sexually oriented at that time, more in his mind than in his body, and said to me once, "You've got sex on your mind! I don't see women in that way at all." One day he said to me with his usual seriousness, "You must meet this very attractive and interesting girlfriend of mine, you'll see she's very nice."

I was surprised to learn he had a girlfriend, as I had not seen him with one yet. After class we met in the great Hall and to my amazement, there stood with my friend the model that had been inspiring me so much. Smiling up to his ears, John mumbled as he made the presentation. "Err…Let me introduce Jean… and this is my friend François."

Neither Jean nor I mentioned that we already were acquaintance, and all three went out into the streets of the busy city.

Sitting with our pints of bitter ale, we listened to John who was doing most of the talking. John liked to be nice. It was important to him that his friends were happy and felt good. "Jean is a potter and worked for Harry Davies in Cornwall… and has met Bernard Leach. Tell François about your visit to Michael Cardew's workshop and how much you liked him…"

Jean was shy, and when she was put on the spot, she became self-conscious and the words tended to come out of the left side of her mouth. I felt for her, and changed the conversation by telling them I was applying for the Llewellyn-Smith Scholarship on Mr Castleman's suggestion.

"Would you mind Jean, if I exhibited for the prize, one of the two paintings I did of you? You know, the one of you lying down, showing your wonderful back, and holding the Apple in your right hand?"

"No, not at all, in fact I feel honoured." She replied with a feeling of lightness in her voice.

When I was in the company of attractive women I did not know well, I tended to be on my guard, and only displayed what I thought was the most appealing sides of myself. I was not as relaxed as when I was in my ordinary self. But on this first outing with Jean, I felt very comfortable and totally at ease in her presence.

A week later, on a Friday afternoon, John Epstein burst into the studio where I was painting. Seemingly under pressure and confused, he came up to me, looked into my eyes with great seriousness and said, "I've made a terrible mistake. I told Jean I would go out with her tonight and completely forgot that it is the Sabbath today! My mother will kill me if I don't turn up. I have to be with my parents this evening yet I can't cancel my appointment with Jean, she is somewhere on the train on her way to meet me. Could you possibly take care of her tonight? She's coming from New Malden to London specially and will be downstairs at 6 pm?" I had no other arrangements and the idea of being alone with Jean felt nice. While mixing my colours on the palette I showed no excitement and accepted, "Of course John, I will look after Jean tonight for you, that'll be fine, I'll be there at six and explain to her why you can't make it, don't worry!"

And with my brush still loaded with the mixed colour, I returned to my work – the foggy atmosphere of the houses of Notting Hill against a sombre sky.

It was already half past five and, as was often the case, I had to make an effort to pull myself away from my creative world. But I suddenly remembered Jean and rushed through my ritual clean up:

brushes, palette and washing my hands with the green disinfectant soap. I walked down the five levels of the spiral staircase and came round the last flight of stairs when Jean arrived in the great Hall. She was wearing a short, white, raglan raincoat; her jet-black hair dripping with rain intensified its colour. She was looking around for John and came up to me as I reached the ground floor. Her voice was anxious for it was already 6:10. "You haven't seen John by any chance? We planned to meet here at six, but the train was late!" I explained the change of plans and Jean said understandingly,

"Oh yes, his parents observe the Jewish traditions, he always forgets about the Sabbath! Oh, poor John!"

"He's asked me to take over…I mean to be with you this evening, since he doesn't want you to be alone. Do you mind?" To my surprise Jean did not seem to be bothered by this idea at all. In fact she seemed rather happy with the prospect and responded positively, "Okay then! What shall we do?"

It was cold and wet, so I thought it would be nice simply to go to the flat, as I knew John Lawrence wasn't there for the weekend. I invited her for a meal. She agreed and we set off on the Lambretta under the misty rain. First, we stopped opposite Belsize Park underground station at the grocer and bought a fresh lettuce, a pineapple, a few apples and some eggs. At the baker we picked up a nice wholemeal bread and finally at the wine shop, a bottle of red Burgundy. As I opened the door to the apartment an unusual feeling came over me: being here with Jean seemed completely natural, no special excitement, almost as if it was an every day matter. With other women my state would have been different, more hyper, keen to show what a nice man I was, keen to please; but always in the back of my mind, the longing to achieve oneness with the feminine.

With Jean, the currents between us were quite different. It was as if we had always known each other – in some other life maybe? I wanted to know all about her from the time she was born to the present and to tell her of my journey. The gas heater was lit, as we were cold and our sopping wet clothes needed drying. She appreciated the comfortable flat and looked around while I prepared Lapsang-Souchong tea and looked for the McVitie black chocolate digestive biscuits. I had many questions brewing up: Who were her parents? Did she have brothers and sisters and what were her interests? But especially, what she knew of the Gurdjieff Work and details of her life at Coombe Springs.

As we sat on the carpeted floor sipping our tea, warmed by the blue flames of the gas-fire, she told me about herself. Her mouth became more relaxed and she no longer talked from one side. Her voice soothed my ears; her body smelled to me like a rose garden; my eyes delighted in her harmonious face and the curves of her body. When listening to her stories, it was clear that she had suffered, mostly from a lack of parental affection and recognition. This brought in her a fear of not being loved, pushing away her self-confidence. Tears lay just under her apparently resilient surface yet together with this fragility, she had a great feminine, earthly strength. Verbal expression, in her family, was mostly used to communicate essential practical issues demanded by the house or the garden. Certainly, words were not for expressing emotions, nor for attending to the inquisitive minds of growing children.

Jean was the youngest and had two brothers, Pip and John. She adored Pip who was 10 years older and he gave her much caring attention. He was the artist in the family and liked poetry, drawing and playing the recorder. John seemed to her to always be studying. In the summer of 1941, Pip was called up to join a tank division in the Libyan Desert and it was not long before a letter came from a close friend announcing his death. His tank was destroyed and there were no survivors...

Jean was 10 at the time and her mother was not able to tell her, but instead gave her the letter to read. She received no consolation, no hug nor comforting and it was Jean who told her father this difficult news when he arrived later that night. She had dealt with this traumatic event completely by herself. From that day on, Jean's mother slept alone in her lost son's bed and never returned to sleep with her husband. A few days later Mrs Orton left on her daughter's pillow, a short letter telling her that she ought not worry, as they would all meet in Heaven one day! Jean rebelled and invented any excuse to be away from home.

The time had passed unnoticed; I offered Jean something to eat,

"Omelette, rice and salad for supper?" She smiled, followed me into the small kitchen and leaning on the doorframe, watched me cook. Chopping onions, frying them with a little thyme and spices, adding the Basmati rice, hot water and a lid; I reduced the gas and proceeded to beat the eggs. She enjoyed watching me preparing the food and it felt good having her there chatting. She offered, "Can I help? May I lay the table?" "Yes great! But there is no free table… we'll eat on the floor by the gas fire, how about that? There is a small table cloth in that drawer." I cut up some of the pineapple into little squares, added them to the omelette just before it fully took, flipped the sides over onto the fruit, sprinkled it with black pepper and carried it to our picnic table. Our plates were now filled with the garlicky salad, the spicy rice and the yellow omelette creating a harmony of colours and smells that sharpened our appetites. We looked at each other, smiled, lifted our glasses with Burgundy, and made a toast, "May this meal be the first of many together to come, bon appétit!"

Completely charmed by her smile and laugh, I did not like to see sadness descend on her face, so I clowned or said something funny just to bring her back into her full beauty. Jean was enjoying the meal and expressed her appreciation, "Hey! I did not expect this pineapple in the omelette to be so delicious! I have never eaten pineapple with omelette before…"

We both took time that evening to give us the space to get to know each other. The instinctive male/female attraction did not seem our priority in this new relationship, but inevitably, it followed that we also discovered and tasted, at first with some hesitancy, the fruits of our hidden passions. What followed felt completely natural and harmonious, as if it had always been. We then both rested into a place of union, silence and peace.

It was now too late for Jean to catch the underground and the train connections back to Malden, and the element of time came back with gruesome reality, but she kept it light by saying, "Never mind, I'll catch the early morning train." She had to go back to Coombe Springs to cook for the weekend when many activities were planned up to Sunday evening.

John Epstein met me at lunch the following Monday. "So, how did it go with Jean?" He asked me with some curiosity. "Well, it went fine, she is a nice person. I cooked her a pineapple omelette." I could not hide a slight smile.

"You will not mess her about I hope… will you?" He said indignantly. "Of course not! We both had a great evening together!" I was trying to reassure him. When I queried Jean about her relationship with John, she told me plainly that they had not slept together. "Jean is a very fine girl, you will take care of her won't you?" For some time John had been taking her under his wings and he felt that something had changed.

From then on Jean became my companion and although our worlds were at that time very different, we met at every available opportunity, but mostly in the evenings. I often drove to Coombe Springs and spent the night with her, then drove back to the flat in the early hours of the morning.

When I say Jean became my companion, this was of course in my view. Her reality was different, for her feelings were more confused than mine. She had had many short relationships with men whom she did not trust. Something in her could not believe that deep down in my heart I carried no one but her. She was always surprised by my interest in her and my fidelity, and I was surprised that she was surprised. As she felt more confident with our relationship, she wanted to share her close friends with me: Peter and Jenny Gibbs, Tom and Jen Pope, the Sullivans. I became very fond of them myself, especially Peter Gibbs, who I admired for his humour and his talent as an architect.

CHAPTER 7

It was difficult for me to hear about her previous boyfriends, yet I wanted to know all about them. Why had she been with them? Considering what seemed to me to be a great number, I had asked her why so many? She did not really know, but talking about it, we decided the reason was that she did not want to feel rejected - saying yes was easier than saying no. In addition, the sudden death of her beloved brother Pip created a large vacant space for male affection that she unconsciously tried to fill by not rejecting male affection when it presented itself.

We talked about the Gurdjieff Work. She told me in detail about the movement classes that she found so awakening and about her master, Mr J.G. Bennett, who called me 'her fly by night'. Mr Bennett established Coombe Springs in the 1940s to further the development of man's consciousness using techniques that he learned from Gurdjieff in Fontainebleau, near Paris. The large white Victorian house at Coombe Springs was set on a few hectares of wooded land not far from Kingston on Thames. Imposing wrought iron gates stood at the entrance, and on the left was the lodge where Mr Bennett, Elizabeth and their two children lived. There were several outbuildings where the people engaged in The Work' stayed. A large fruit and vegetable garden provided some of the food for the busy kitchens where Jean worked almost full time. The Work pupils I met there on brief occasions did not impress me. Most seemed overly serious and self concerned, and gave me the impression they had problems with feeling superior and wanting secrecy. Some of the men saw me as a challenge to their masculinity, taking all the attention of their so desired and beautiful Jean.

The dense atmosphere of Coombe Springs did not make me want to join them, although I enjoyed her architect friends. I was working hard on my paintings, preparing for an exhibition at the Central, where the Llewellyn-Smith scholarship was going to be given to the best student. It was an exciting time for me, spending all my energies with my creativity. Feeling settled in my heart about Jean, I did not need to look elsewhere and concentrated fully on my art.

Changes in the pulses of our individual lives

The Llewellyn-Smith exhibition was held in the first and second week of December 1956, on the ground floor behind the Central main hallway, in the well of the large square building. Fifteen students, each with three paintings, were chosen for the exhibition. To my immense surprise and joy, I received the first prize! Greatly honoured and chuffed, I would now be able to further my studies into 1957. GG's money for my studies had practically run out, so the news of my success delighted her.

I did not go to Vallauris that Christmas, but stayed in London by myself. I spent the early part of Christmas Eve with a few other lonely characters in a half empty pub in Swiss Cottage. I did not feel sad and I never minded being alone. I treated myself to a large plate of smoked salmon and pickles, and a pint of Bitter Bass beer. Later I went to see my Indian friend Mahmoud who was also alone and for whom Christmas was not a tradition. I enjoyed Mahmoud's presence greatly for he was kind and gentle. His thin frail body was topped by long, thick, black hair and his fine-featured face appeared through a bristling shiny beard, each hair carefully groomed. His almond shaped, brown eyes were witty and intelligent. We talked at length about religions, about living and being. He told me about his life in India, how he used to go to the beaches of Calcutta to develop his muscles and, upon seeing my surprised expression, he pulled from his wallet a yellowing photograph of himself bulging with impressive muscles on a sandy beach. He explained that body-building was his only way to impress the local girls.

Mahmoud was a meticulous painter, specially gifted in portrait painting and achieving photographic resemblance. He obviously lived on very little money. I never saw any food in his tiny attic bedroom except white Mothers' Pride bread that he carefully toasted and spread with New Zealand butter, which he served me together with a cup of strong black Indian tea. He was also a fine but shy Indian classical sitar player, and I considered myself lucky when he played his instrument. He played only twice in my presence, his small hands and long narrow fingers knowing exactly how to create the most exquisite sounds. He gave me an appreciation of Indian music and invited me once to the India Club, in an imposing 19th-century building off the Strand, near Charing Cross. The Club was in the basement down a steep staircase to a doorway, where a tall Indian made sure that only club members entered. In Hindi, Mahmoud negotiated my entry and finally the man looked at me… then smiled and said raising his index finger, "Okay, but only for this time! I tell you."

We entered into a small antechamber adjacent to a cloakroom, where we left our coats and scarves, and continued through thick richly embroidered red velvet curtains into a dimly lit room. The floor was covered haphazardly with colourful Indian rugs and already quite a few Indians were sitting on the carpets facing another curtain, in front of which was an empty space centred by a large red cushion, obviously for the musician. A rich array of new smells was instantly noticeable. There was no smell of tobacco, unusual for a public place, but instead several incense sticks burning somewhere in a corner. There was another distinctive scent this time more motherly and suave, probably due to the richly scented oils worn by the women in the room. As we sat on the floor Mahmoud whispered, "You are very lucky to be here, you know. Normally the club is exclusively reserved for Indians."

I was the only westerner in the room and found myself sitting beside a young woman dressed in a glittering gold and green sari, her exquisite profile looked to the stage. Although my temptation was to examine her beauty, I resisted firmly, not wanting to intrude on her space. Mahmoud touched my arm gently and said in my ear, "The young musician you are going to hear tonight has just come directly from India. You'll see he's very good! His name is Ravi Shankar…"

A thin, feline bodied young man of medium height appeared silently from behind the curtain with his instrument. Massive curly black hair neatly trimmed to his ear lobes framed his square powerful face. Gentle, large, dark eyes glanced at the audience as he sat down majestically and carefully positioned his sitar. The crowded room fell into a deep silence as he said a few words in Hindi and proceeded to play. Mahmoud's playing his sitar had charmed me, but this young man was taking me somewhere else. The sounds of his instrument elevated my consciousness to a nebulous place of peace where the magical sounds seemed to reverberate far away into an unknown universe. Closing my eyes I let each cascade of notes resonate deeply in my body, digesting fully this wonderful music. Each silence between the notes was as important as the bouquets of sounds creating in me moments of wonder never knowing the outcome of the next sound.

Ravi Shankar must have played for two hours. The whole room was in complete harmony with the artist and through his talent he took us to places not known before. After bowing in appreciation and a full applause from the audience, he disappeared behind the curtain as discreetly as he had entered.

Jean invited me to spend Christmas Day with her at Coombe Springs. On a bright sunny morning I arrived on my Lambretta a little late and went straight to Jean's room. She had saved us some roast turkey from the kitchen, stuffing and roasted potatoes, parsnips, onion sauce and chestnuts. I uncorked a bottle of white Chablis while she arranged our tiny dining table. Being next to her again was as if I had come home – I felt so at ease in her presence. As we chatted, she told me what she had done before arriving at Coombe Springs, "I rebelled against my bourgeois upbringing and all I wanted really was to find out who I was. I could not do that by staying at home, so I set off to work in different potteries, the first in Ambleside in the Lake District…"

As I listened to her, it became clear that her life had not been easy. The difficult circumstances she had been through had contributed to giving her the determination to find out more about herself. After Ambleside she worked for 3 years at Harry Davies, in the Crowan pottery in Cornwall. At weekends she hitched to St Ives where she met up with the wild artistic life in the small harbour. In those days girls did not usually hitchhike and on noticing concern on my face, she explained, "You see, I had fallen in love with a gay sculptor called John, he was kind to me, and introduced me to many artists who worked there at the time. I was naive, my sexuality was all over the place and I did not know how to handle it."

For me it was important to listen to her experiences although I did not particularly enjoy what I was hearing about her previous boyfriends. She needed to share everything of importance that had happened in her life up to now and I appreciated her direct honesty. Sometimes I could not hear any more and changed the subject to something more immediate. I did not 'love' Jean in the ordinary passionate meaning of the word. When thinking about her, or meeting her again after a few days apart, my heart was not invaded by a swelling passionate sensation, as I might have had with other women. On the contrary, being with her had a soothing effect, calming me as if I was reunited with the other part of myself.

We spent the Boxing Day with my grandmother in Epsom. It was the first time I had introduced my girlfriend to her and she seemed delighted. They hit it off right way and my beloved GG was reassured by Jean's unsophisticated and natural presence. Secretly I think she was happy I was with an English girl.

On my return to London on the 29th of December, I received a disagreeable letter from her Majesty's Customs and Excise ordering me to export my Lambretta out of the country by the 31 December or it would be impounded! A feeling of nausea overtook me as I read the dreadful letter that gave me neither time nor alternatives. I immediately went to the nearest phone box on Belsize Park Avenue and searched through the Yellow Pages for a shipping company that would export my scooter back to France. Because of the Christmas and the New Year holidays it was no easy matter. Finally, I found a small firm, way down in the London docks, willing to export the Lambretta.

Jean's birthday was on the 3rd of January and now that my scooter was out of the country, my visits to Coombe Springs became rare; we arranged to meet at Charing Cross station. She smiled broadly, happy to see me again, and as we hugged each other I brought her close said quietly in her ear a tender… "Happy birthday."

The crowds of the busy London at rush hour pushed us along the platform and into the streets. We were not in a hurry like the crowd around us and had the whole day in front of us just to be together. "Shall we find a café and have a nice breakfast?" I suggested.

It was bitter cold and we quickly crossed the Strand to a small Italian café at the corner with William IVth Street. The smell of Danish pastries and milky coffee filled our nostrils as we entered the warm cosy atmosphere. At that time in London, the only place to have a good cup of coffee was in one of the few Italian owned places and this was one of them. We asked the little round man behind the counter for a Danish pastry, a croissant, a large white coffee and a large black espresso and found ourselves a table. "So, it's your birthday! Where and when were you born?" I asked with some curiosity realising I did not know her age. "I was born in Beckenham, South London. My parents lived in a semidetached house. They were not very well off at the time, in 1931."

"So, let's see… That makes you 26? Is that right?" I was surprised to learn there was seven years difference between us. It did not feel like that - there seemed to be no age difference at all between us. It was as if our ages were set back from the time we met in the Central School refectory.

"You know, it's a very strange feeling not to have my scooter in London, I do miss it terribly. I have to think in a different way to travel now and to spend more shillings in fares too… I'll have to do more walking again." I shared my latest news about the trip to the docks and parting with the Lambretta.

Jean seemed to have very few clothes, so I offered to buy her a skirt for her birthday. She was excited at the thought, and so we set off to browse the London shops. Shopping was something that I practically never did, but when travelling on my Lambretta, I had seen that there were a lot of clothes shops in and around Oxford Street. It was the first time we'd shopped together and although she loved the idea, Jean was a little nervous and had great difficulty making decisions, especially when it concerned her. She searched silently through rows and rows of clothes and the more she looked at the vast choice, the more confused she became. "How about this one? You like it? I think it looks great!" Enthusiastically I held the skirt round my waist and pointed my right foot forward and slightly to the side, pretending I was a fashion model. She laughed for an instant and turning serious again mumbled, "I don't know, sorry…I'm not sure. Sorry to be so indecisive!"

After going in and out of many shops, we still had not found her present. As we walked in a side street off the famous Selfridge's, there was an attractive window display of all kinds of pretty skirts called 'Miss Selfridge'.

"Let's go in here! I feel we might find something." We walked arm in arm through the tall glass doors towards the skirts. Surrounded by clothes of all kinds, my hand flicking through one after the other, I looked up and saw that Jean was tired of looking at too many skirts of all shapes and colours. She stood there feeling lost about to cry. At the same moment my right hand fell on an extremely soft fabric, so exquisite that my hand pulled out the hanger and displayed the skirt on the stand. It was made of pure mohair with a plain design of large, loosely woven squares in different blues like a blown up tartan in a pale sky blue to a deep indigo. It was lined with a pale blue satin and the shiny soft mohair gave the whole an attractive fuzzy appearance. I took it to her, opened her white raincoat and I applied the skirt round her warm body, "How about that? It looks super on!" Jean gave me a hesitant smile, all mixed up with her tears now flowing, and I turned her round towards a tall mirror and held the skirt in place from behind while she looked… rested my chin on her shoulder and grinned. "Yes, I do like it, but it must be awfully expensive? Are you sure?" She murmured with a feeling of guilt in her voice.

"Of course I'm sure! If you're happy, I am happy too, as I like it very much. If it fits, it's yours! Try it on." I encouraged her, glad that we had found something that she liked. She disappeared behind the curtain of the change room to reappear a short time later looking radiant, holding out one side of her skirt, "How is it?" The tone of her voice was now positive. I'd never seen anyone in a mohair skirt before; it did look rather splendid and certainly was most attractive. "Brilliant. It's your birthday present, we'll take it!"

As we walked light and happy out into Oxford Street with our large bag from Selfridge's, we found a cheap restaurant, where we sat at a small round table and ordered a salad. I was intrigued by her difficulty in choosing something for herself. "Is it always so difficult for you to decide what to buy for yourself?" She explained, "When we went shopping with my mother, she never let me have what I liked but always said that what I chose was awful. Then she bought what she thought look right for me and I always felt dreadful in the clothes she chose. Not once did she approve of what I chose."

How fortunate I had been to be brought up by a mother who always let me choose, or would give me the time and space to make up my mind without pressure. It was clear now why Jean had a problem buying clothes and I realised this was probably why she had so few. She adored the skirt and every so often throughout the day we'd opened the bag to look at it and stroke it's softness. To complete the birthday, we went to the cinema in Leicester Square to see the latest James Dean film and afterwards, we went back to Charing Cross station so she could get back to Coombe Springs in time.

I had no doubt now about making our life together, though I knew that it was not the same for her. She loved me very much, but could not believe it was possible that I would stay with her, since too many men had previously let her down. She'd become part of me and I could not visualise living without her, so it was not even a question in my mind. I was happiest when I was close to her and always made it a priority to be with her, rather than with other friends or family.

I reorganised my life without the Lambretta and went back to my student routine at the Central. Working hard at painting and drawing, the more I learned about the techniques of the art, the more there was to learn. The language of colour relationships was fascinating. There were infinite variations possible just from the basic colours like, i.e. lemon yellow, red lacquer and cadmiums, burnt Siena, cobalt blue, ultramarine. I did not use ivory black but tended to make very dark colours by mixing Windsor green with alizarin red or ultramarine with Van Dyck brown - the combination was endless depending on what kind of dark colour I wanted. Using pure black made the colours look dirty and lifeless. In fact white and black are not colours in themselves, yet there are many different tones of them. Zinc white was wonderful to soften colours and silver white offered a transparency that I preferred for flesh tones. Colour was a world of its own: a delight to experiment with, to discover and to apply to my canvas. The more I observed, the more I became aware of the infinite subtleties when it came to colour relationships. What fascinated me was the musicality of colour that comes from light. Light itself is nothing but colour so objects became alive when their pigments mirrored the colours that were in the light. I could go on and on elaborating about painting, but I won't, as I am just sharing with you a little bit of my passion for painting.

Having a small cushion of cash from the 1rst prize money in my Lloyds bank account, and the desire to look smart, I set off to look for a pair of trousers. After looked in several shops, I found that all the trousers I liked belonged to suits I could not afford. At the bottom of Oxford Street, a pair of charcoal grey trousers in a tailor's narrow shop window attracted my attention. Their narrow cut, nice waistline, and angled pockets easily accessible for the hands, pleased my practical and aesthetic senses. Having never been into a tailor's shop before and driven by curiosity, I pushed the door open and activated the sound of a little bell.

Although the shop window was small, the inside was more spacious and the worn slippery oak floor gave a peculiar smell mixed together with the woollen fabrics piled everywhere. On the wide wooden counter the bolts of navy blue wool were spread out and, on top of one, was a gigantic pair of scissors. Behind the counter the oak shelves reaching up to the ceiling held a diversity of fabrics. A shy young man with neatly combed hair greeted me with a frail high-pitched voice, "Good afternoon Sir... you're looking for something specific Sir?"

"Yes, the trousers in the window, how much are they?" "Oh! But they're not for sale Sir, they're only there as a model, but we can make them for you to fit your size." He seemed surprised by my question. "How much would it cost then, if I had a pair made?" "But Sir, it depends on the material you choose!" He tried to hide his amusement at my naivety.

A small, bald Jewish gentleman burst in through the door of a large workshop where several elderly men were sitting in front of their sewing machines. He must have been the head tailor, for the collar of his old navy blue suit was covered in pins and needles, some still carrying bits of thread. His thick glasses were so dirty I wondered how he could see through them. He wore grey felt slippers, and a long fabric tape measure hung around his neck. "And what can we do for the young man?"

He looked up at me from over the dirty glasses. I explained how I fancied the trousers in the window, their cut, their colour and the fabric. Hardly I'd finished my sentence, when the sprightly old man flicked aside my jacket flap, pressed the tape on my hip and ran it down to my ankles."Breaking on the shoes, Sir?" I nodded, presuming that he meant that the material would just break resting on the top of my shoe. Now, taking me completely by surprise, the flat of his hand shot up the inside of my right leg up to my crotch and, looking up at me from down below, said, "Which side do you dress, Sir?" I had no idea what he meant. 'Both sides', I thought,' or does he mean where do I keep things in my pockets? My handkerchief is always kept in my left one'...."What do you mean?" I queried intrigued, "Your testicles Sir!" He replied bluntly as he looked at his tape to read the measurement of the inner leg. While I was trying to work out on which side my sex organs normally hung, the tailor said abruptly, "Left side I just discovered. Thank you Sir."

He then measured my waistline and with a well-used lead pencil, took note of all the dimensions in a little squared paper notebook. I glanced at the young man with his arm crossed watching the passers-by through the door window, a slight smile on his hackneyed face. I left a deposit of £3.50 and was to return in two days to collect the trousers.

Two days later I returned and tried the new trousers, while the tailor checked that they fitted to his satisfaction. Both now delighted, I paid the remaining £4.00, and wore the trousers out of the shop feeling like a new person.

These new trousers made me feel one with myself, not quite the same guy walking past Bloomsbury Square. I felt more erect and taller and I looked at passers-by with more ease. I was pleased to be out of my older deformed trousers, gone so thin at the knees that one could almost see through the weave. There was a François with the old pair and a new François with the new ones!

As Jean was no longer modelling at Central, it was more difficult for us to see each other, especially without the scooter. Mr Bennett asked her not to be a model any more, as he wanted her full-time at the Centre. 'Did he want to keep her away from me?' I wondered. 'Was my influence on Jean too distracting for her?' I felt I might lose her if we could not be together before too long. We arranged to see each other regularly at weekends at Coombe Springs or at her friends the Gibbs. Peter had brought a dilapidated old oast house, called Chillies Oast, on the edge of the Crowborough forest. He was now in the process of transforming it into a comfortable living space. When we visited, he came to fetch us at the tiny Eridge railway station in his ancient Austin Seven car. His large body filled the tiny seat and the steering wheel was so small in his big hands it was as if he was driving a bumper car. Jean and I both loved Peter and Jennifer very much and were immensely happy to spend the weekend with them. Peter had many stories to tell, laughed a lot and took pleasure in talking about his renovation projects. He drove fast, throwing the little car round corners, its thin wheels swaying and creaking on the small, winding East Sussex roads. My heart was filled with happiness being with Jean again, reuniting her presence with mine. Sitting at the back I looked at her lovely profile, enjoyed the smell of her hair that flickered in my face through the turbulence of the wind, and listened to Peter's explanation about his latest acquisition.

"You'll see, it's a large building with two enormous circular Oast Houses, linked together by a clinker built oak boarded barn, which I suppose was the place where they kept the hay… My God there is lots of work to do there!"

He talked at the top of his voice to over-ride the noisy engine of the old car, and, without reducing his speed, abruptly turned into a little dirt country road leading up to the property.

The Oasts were massive indeed and, as I stretched my arms and legs from the cramped sitting position, I looked at the buildings and silently appreciated its proportions and colour. Let me explain that in England, an Oast House is a round building in which the hops were dried. Its conical roof usually leads to a cowl through which the smoke from a fire escapes. In the fifties, many were converted into attractive living spaces. The old pink bricks harmonised well with the tarred, clinker boards that joined the two circular buildings. Cement and plaster covered boards, ladders and props, leaned against one of the Oast. It was obvious this was a building site, and the land around the property was rough and uncared for. Peter took us round the first oast, which had been restored.

Peter was telling Jean the family's latest news, while my attention was more on the attractive property. He opened a small white paned glass door and we entered into the circular kitchen. My nostrils were immediately filled with the appetising but heavy odours of Brussels sprouts, potatoes and probably a steak and kidney pie. An electric flex came down from the high ceiling, its global Chinese paper shade floated over a well-scrubbed white sycamore kitchen table, which reminded me of the ones I had breakfast on when I stayed in

CHAPTER 7

Summerhill. Opposite the entrance was a large stripped pine dresser loaded with rows of hanging pale blue and white mugs, and behind them rows of matching breakfast plates. Colourful tea cloths were drying on the warm handrail of the dark green Aga cooker. Immediately to my left was an opening leading into a small cosy sitting room. Jennifer, dressed in pastel blue, wearing a pale orange apron and a printed headscarf, came to greet us smiling, "Sorry, I am a bit late with my schedule this morning; the cooking will soon be ready. I apologise about the smell, it's the Brussels sprouts, I am afraid! Hello Jean, hello François... How do you like the Oast House?"

The question was addressed to me and I replied that I was most impressed by the project and that I found her kitchen truly delightful.

Two fair-headed young children, who I had not met before, stood in the doorway of the sitting room and looked up at us silently. In one large scoop their father picked them both up in his powerful arms and presented them to me, "This is Frances, our eldest and Pippin, her little sister." The children shyly studied me with their innocent clear blue eyes, fair curls surrounded their round healthy faces and their slightly raised shoulders expressed their timidity. Frances sucked her thumb and smiled imperceptibly.

"This is François, a Frenchman, he is Jean's boyfriend." Peter explained giving his body a slight jerk to readjust the heavy children in his arms. He showed us the rest of the house while Jennifer prepared tea in the blue and white teapot that matched the mugs. The small sitting room had a chimney in the corner that was the closest to the Oast, on the opposite wall were pine bookshelves filled with architecture and esoteric books. A window on the left looked onto an untended garden backed by a row of tall dark conifers. We came into an unfinished hallway covered with dust and builders materials. Still carrying his two young ones, Dad puffed his way up a wooden staircase leading up to a landing covered with coconut matting. One door led to a well-equipped toilet and bathroom, another to a bedroom with double bed, an oak table and chair. Just in time, I saw a large low beam under which I had to bend to enter the room.

"By the way, watch your head on that oak beam François! I've bumped my head many times on it! That room will be yours and Jean's when you come to visit us." Peter led us into their impressive circular bedroom over the kitchen. A large double bed covered in a colourful quilt stood opposite a chest of drawers with a big mahogany swing mirror. On either side were two Victorian chairs and two large sash windows. Jennifer must have been the interior design artist, for the good-looking heavy curtains and pastel cushions and Persian carpets contributed greatly to the general warmth of the room. Besides being a meticulous housewife, Jennifer was always extremely busy, often sitting at her sewing machine making cushions and curtains. I was impressed by her many talents as a cook, an interior decorator and above all a sculptor. Before she met Peter, she had studied sculpture at the Epsom art school where she met Jean. Some of her bronze sculptures, displayed around the house, showed her work to be full of life and joy. "Tea is ready!" She shouted from the bottom of the staircase, eager to share our company and to hear our comments.

The children were now running about between our legs and around us, feeling more confident with the newcomers. In fact they were rather attracted by the Frenchman and started to play with me as though they had always known me. "François, are you coming for your tea? It's getting cold!" I heard Jennifer's call coming from the kitchen and I raised myself slowly from the carpet, smiling at the children who were still so absorbed, that they did not see me leave the room.

The day went by quickly listening to the many stories Peter enjoyed sharing with us. At times, Jennifer stopped her sewing, or repairing some pullover or sock, adding some precision to make sure that we understood all the finesses in the story. He was good at expressing his feelings, often with a lot of humour, or telling us the funniest anecdotes that happened when attending to his clients. The log fire was burning and the cold and damp outside heightened the cosiness of the room. We had talked about education and they were interested to hear about my time in Summerhill School.

Education is a subject always close to my heart, so I never mind talking about my experiences at Summerhill. We exchanged views about the negative effects punishment has on educating children, how it represses while taking away the responsibility of the child for his own doings. Yet, following the flow of the child's actions without judgement helps the child to learn and see what is right or wrong for himself. But you know by now my point of view on education, so I will not go on further with the subject.

Peter brought us into fits of laughter when he talked about his time at public school. He had attended one called Christ's Hospital. He described how they had to dress in a long black cassock school uniform, as if they were wearing some sombre priest's outfit, and bright yellow socks were obligatory. In the evenings, before going to bed, after they had washed and brushed their teeth, the boys went through a strange ritual of standing in a row one by one offering their index finger to the matron. With great seriousness she held out a large tin of Vaseline and solemnly asked each boy to come forward and dip his finger into the Vaseline tub, "To this day, I still don't know what this ritual was about? Actually, what's so funny was the guy behind me who would always lean over my shoulder and ask in a quiet voice, "bags your Vaseline!" I would then willingly turn round and wipe the transparent grease onto his finger, as I never knew what on earth I should do with it!" Peter mimicked the young lad with his finger out and was hardly able to finish his sentence from laughing so much!

We talked about Mr Bennett and his approach to the Gurdjieff work. I had crossed his path a few times when I walked by the main house on my way to Jean's room. His pupils had a lot of respect for their master, with maybe a slight fear of his judgement, and I also noticed how his presence took a large place in their lives. I have no doubt JG Bennett was the equivalent of a European style Guru. What he said or advised was usually not discussed, but followed scrupulously with obedience.

Peter often mimicked Mr Bennett in action, to make us laugh, but it was another matter when he was in front of him - like the other followers, he would go into alignment. Like a guru, I suppose he was considered to be the one who knew the way, and certainly he was very knowledgeable in many fields, especially on how to obtain spiritual understanding. He chose to teach his followers his adaptation of the Gurdjieff Work. I was too independent to join anything officially or to subscribe myself to any religious or spiritual organisations. I felt at times as an outsider with my new friends, yet I was very close to them, although they belonged to what looked to me like a kind of a club.

Jean got off the train at Clapham Junction to return to Coombe Springs and I continued to Charring Cross station. We both felt good after the delightful long weekend at Chillie's Oast. Sitting peacefully in the empty swaying carriage that took me into the heart of the city, I felt her presence next to me, as part of myself, as if my awareness now including her in my being. I felt tired, relaxed and whole. We had not slept much during the nights we were there, our bodies discovering each other at every opportunity. Once in bed Jean liked talking about the day's events or whatever bothered her or came through her mind. I was learning to be patient when it came to expressing my physical instinct freely. No doubt the space would come… and when it did, I was surprised by the powerful energies that emanated from our union and by the spiritual tranquillity that followed…

CHAPTER 7

My dear reader...

I feel that I have to thank you for having stayed with me all the way through 'Walnuts and Goat Cheese'. I've come now to the age of 19, and in a few months will have finished my art studies at the Central School of Arts & Crafts, and will then leave England to do my military service in the French Army.

Meeting Jean brought me a new dimension and purpose in life. In her presence I felt closer to my whole. The spiritual path we came to follow soon afterwards completely changed our perception of what life seemed to be about, and made us travel to places in our consciousness that we were not aware existed before.

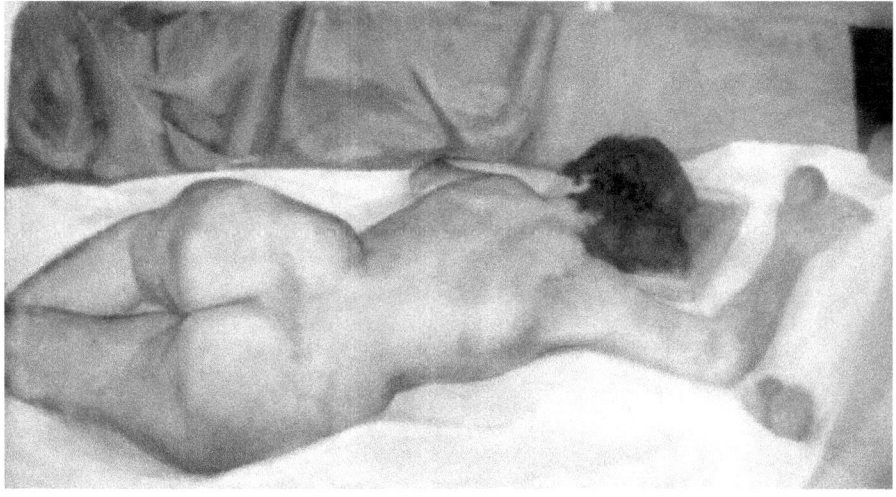

First prize painting of Jean holding an apple

WALNUTS & GOAT CHEESE

Sylvette and François taken by intruder photographer Golf-Juan

Jean in Golf-Juan 1958

Zorbit towels poster

CHAPTER 7

Jean, François, Maman, Toby and Sylvette
at Quartier du Devens

François and Jean in the Gibbs kitchen 1956

Epilogue

Discovering a large leather case in the attic

Dear reader, it might interest you to hear about an unexpected discovery that has clarified a few unresolved points relating to Marcel Lassalle:

As I was preparing the final layout of Walnuts and Goat Cheese, I realised that I did not have enough photos for the early parts of the book. I searched in my attic to see if there might be a suitcase of some belongings of my mother, who had died in 1992. I did find a large square hard leather case that revealed such interesting truths that I must share them with you.

Many of the photos I discovered showed new realities about my family, and there was a bundle of letters from my papa to my mother which I never knew existed; they were dated from late October 1942 to mid-February 1943 just before he died, and shone a new light on the family history.

Our mother had only told us what she wanted us to know, probably for safety reasons... the truth must have been hidden because of the dangerous wartime conditions. Dieulefit was quite an exception in Maréchal Petain's occupied France; it had become a hideout for communists, Jews, maquisards and foreigners.

I had always wondered how it was that I had loved my papa so deeply, when I must have been a toddler when he left the island. My mother had told me that he'd gone to Germany with the first STO (Service Travail Obligatoire,) well before we left. After reading his letters, I found that actually the truth was that he'd left three months after us, when I was well into my sixth year of existence. I now understand the question of how our belongings arrived at Les Tilleuls, when we'd only travelled with one large suitcase. It was our papa who'd sent them, including mother's paints, canvases, a few art books plus her 78rpm records. The photos show a very loving father to Sylvette and me, who carried me on his shoulders, introduced me to the salty sea and held me during my first steps. As I read on further truths were revealed, that she'd never mentioned: He was obviously very much in love with her and always asked about Sylvette and me, saying how much he missed the children. The first letter shows a very distressed Marcel, who regrets that they separated on a disagreement. 'Why had he lost his temper? And why did they have to argue while they were together, when they loved each other so much?' Having no work on the island due to the war, he sold cheaply all his tools and his lorry, and left for Germany in January 1943, of his own free will, hoping to earn a good living there, as he found it advertised in the local French papers. He would then be able to send us some francs to help us along. He seems to have sent us all the money he had, and travelled north with the little he had left, that he kept preciously for stamps; it took him over a month to reach Nuremberg. His last letters carry on the backs of the envelopes the German censorship stamp: a red and black eagle over the swastika. They give very little information, except that he missed us and loved us very much.

On February the 21st he died in the country that he hoped would have fed his family. None of his letters ever mentioned politics or the war. His last letter to our Mother says, "You had better find yourself another man as I do not know how the future will turn out."

How could our mum have told us that her husband went to work in Germany of his own free will, when Jews, communists and Gaullists surrounded her?

489

Glossary

Bise	North wind from the Alps
Butte	Mound
Bergerie	Sheepfold
Boulevard périférique	Parisian ring road
Étranger	Foreigner
Gendarmerie	Army police that deals with civilians
Les Halles	Parisian wholefood market
Île	Island
La Croix	The Cross
Lance	Spear
Lavoir	Washhouse
Maquis	Thicket
Maquisard	Underground resistance movement
Minimum	Sex-cover used on the island
Mistral	North wind of the Rhône valley
Pain d'épices	Type of Gingerbread
Palangrotte	Fishing-line
Pastis	Strong drink made from Star anise
Pension	Small family hotel
Percheron	Large workhorse
Piste	Ski run
Sablière	Hard sand hill
Saucisson	Dry sausage
Savon de Marseille	Traditional soap made of olive oil and potassium
Télégramme	Telegram
Voilà	Expression: here we go, here we are

About the author

François Xavier Lassalle (now known as Léonard Lassalle) was born on the 7th of December 1937 in Nice, France, to an English mother and a French father; both were painters. For his first six years he lived with his mother and older sister Sylvette on a wild island off the Var coast called the Ile du Levant. In the autumn of1942, in the midst of World War II, the family moved to a village called Dieulefit in the Drôme, where the children attended school. Then, keen on AS Neill's progressive method of education, his mother sent Sylvette and François to Neill's renowned Summerhill School.

By the age of 15, François was studying drawing and advertising in Paris, at the Paul Colin Art School. Then in September 1955, he began studying fine art, mostly oil painting, at the Central School of Arts and Crafts in London, where he met Jean Orton, the model who later became his wife, and with whom he had seven children.

In 1957 Jean and François began to follow the spiritual training of Subud, which they still practice today. They moved to Vallauris on the Côte d'Azur, married in August 1959 in Cowden, Kent, and in 1960 settled in Paris where their first three children were born.

François, now called Léonard, temporarily stopped painting from 1962, in order to provide a better living for his growing family. By1967 he had developed a successful antiques and interior designer's business in Royal Tunbridge Wells in the South of England.

He now lives permanently in Provence, France, with his wife, where they each enjoy developing their individual artistic talents: pottery, painting and writing.

Léonard has written another book called "Source of Life", where he tells many stories directly linked to his spiritual practice.

WALNUTS & GOAT CHEESE